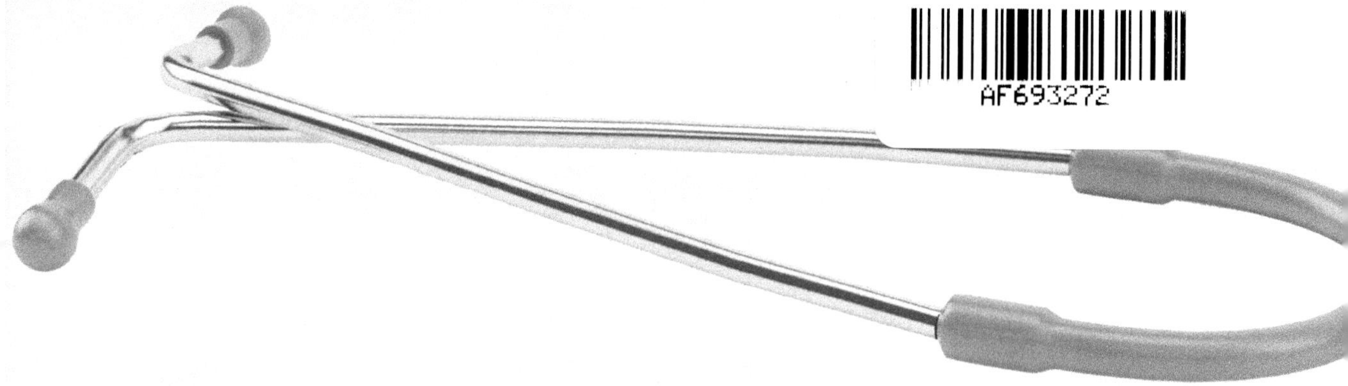

Applications in Health Communication

■ Edited by Michael H. Eaves

EMERGING TRENDS

Kendall Hunt
publishing company

Kendall Hunt
publishing company
www.kendallhunt.com
Send all inquiries to:
4050 Westmark Drive
Dubuque, IA 52004-1840

ISBN 978-1-4652-3787-3

Printed in the United States of America
10 9 8 7 6 5 4 3 2 1

CONTENTS

Unit One: Health and Disease Prevention

Unit Two: Medical Tourism and Culture in Medicine

Unit Three: Health in Later Life

Unit Four: Research in Health

Unit Five: Alternative Perspectives in Health

INTRODUCTION

This textbook, *Applications in Health Communication: Emerging Trends*, is a valuable resource for the health communication scholar. This publication represents a wide array of essays, from a variety of methodological approaches. Authors are a cross section of national and international professorships, and each chapter represents significant work in the field of health communication.

There are five units in the text with multiple chapters in each unit. Unit one begins by examining issues of health disease and prevention. In this unit, students will explore the world of cancer in two chapters. One focuses on the media in Singapore and how cancer is communicated in an international context. The other is a case study that examines a skin cancer clinic and how communication strategies are employed in that venue, particularly the use of nonverbal styles of communication between physician and patient. A third chapter in this unit closely looks at how HIV treatment is perceived in the media. Last, one chapter is devoted to incorporating a new perspective on disclosure, stigma, and its impact in the mental health arena.

The second unit examines the cultural implications of health communication. One chapter addresses college student binge drinking prevention. The other two chapters examine the impact of specific cultural contexts upon the practice of medicine and health communication concerns.

The third unit concerns health in later stages of life. Two chapters look at aging and the role of the communication scholar in that process. This might include family, spouse, friends, or others who assist in that care. One chapter in this unit looks at the near death or death experience from a communication experience, who is involved in that process and to what end we can help frame the last stage of one's life.

The fourth unit addresses research in health. Various case studies are examined here including corporations that frame how they market and label new health foods for human consumption, and how families are exposed to health information with their patients in the health venue. Other chapters are concerned with the role of social media in health communication, a close examination of ocular health and vision, and the role of empathy used in a variety of health communication circles.

The final unit looks at alternative perspectives in health. Such perspectives include the issue of eating disorders and how family and friends can provide the needed support, reframing sexuality and how we perceive issues of sexuality, and the community of running with others to stay healthy. The final two chapters address the need to prevent elder abuse, and a modern perspective on sex education.

Chapter 1:

Communicating cancer: Media agenda building for health promotion in Singapore

Angela Ka Ying Mak
Monash University

Augustine Pang
Nanyang Technological University

INTRODUCTION

The World Health Organization (WHO, 2010) anticipates cancer deaths to reach nine million in 2015. Singapore, with a population of 5.08 million (Singapore Department of Statistics, 2010), is one of the Asian countries where cancer rates are on the rise (Koh & Lee, 2007). Ranked sixth out of 191 countries on overall health system performance in WHO's World Health Report (Singapore Ministry of Health, 2007), Singapore has been devoting much resources to promoting cancer prevention, cure, and primary care in the past decades.

Health promotion activities are strongly connected with the social context (Cline, 2003; Thompson et al., 2008) and mass media is a powerful companion in health promotion actions (Aarva & Tampere, 2006). The media, with its broad outreach, has an important role to educate and interest the public on issues (Black, 2011). An important but often neglected area of health promotion is the role of the source, i.e., the health communicators, in crafting news content and the journalists. Viswanath et al. (2007) argued that health journalists and health communicators are "each relying on the other with the ultimate aim of making the information public from their point of view" (p. 281). Studies have shown that sources like health communicators influence about 44–80% of news content (Curtin, 1999; Sallot & Johnson, 2006). This highlights the co-creational potential of the health communicators' role (Botan & Taylor, 2004; Cameron et al., 1997; Qi & Cameron, 2008; Shin & Cameron, 2005; Taylor & Kent, 2007).

The study thus explores the roles of health communicators and journalists in Singapore in influencing media content, specifically relating to promoting cancer education, by adapting Qi and Cameron's (2008) media agenda building model to assess the extent to which health communicators and journalists in Singapore were consistent in their perceptions about cancer issues and news values.

Media agenda building model

The concept of media agenda building focuses on the role of communicators in setting the agenda for the media in the hope of influencing the media agenda and public opinion (Curtin, 1999; Kiousis et al., 2006). In studying the relationship between health journalists and communicators, Qi and Cameron (2008) proposed a model of agenda building which encompasses three key elements—health communicators and their materials of source agenda, journalists and their filtering function, and the use of source materials in the media content. The model suggested that journalists play a mediating role in the media agenda building process, and the effectiveness of public relations' agenda building efforts is subject to the extent to which journalists agree with health communicators on the importance and news values of an issue (Qi & Cameron, 2008).

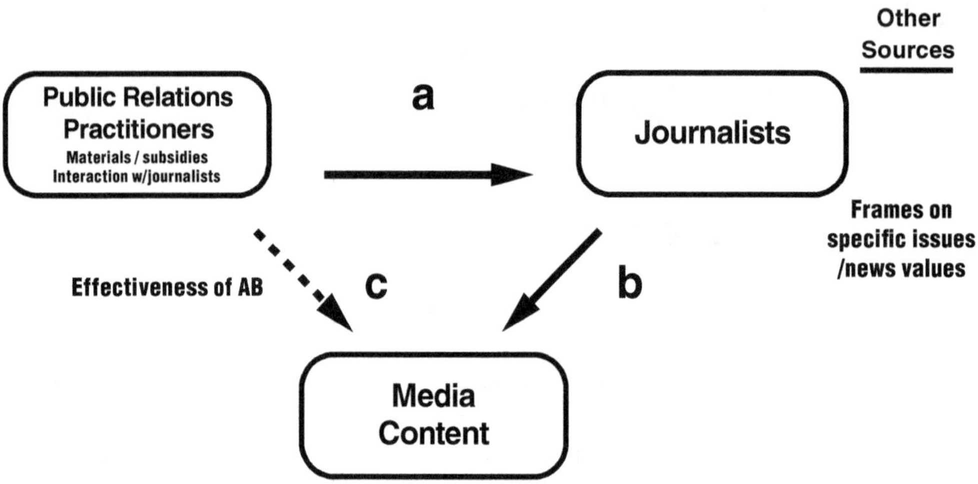

Figure 1.1 *The model of agenda building (Qi and Cameron, 2008)*

Health communicators provide journalists with subsidized information as part of their agenda building efforts, and collaborate with them to 'pitch' their stories. (Refer to arrow *a*). News journalists make their editorial decisions based on a range of influences besides the interactions with health communicators, such as news values, professional judgment, news frames, journalistic routines, media institutions, and social norms (Cameron & Blount, 1997; Pang, 2010). Culturally identified journalistic rules are also present in the media relations context that affect how health promotion materials should or should not be used (Len-Rios et al., 2009).

Certainly, health communicators can use blogs and other online tools such as Facebook and twitter to communicate directly with stakeholders, or even newsletters. These tools, by virtue of their unique features and interactivity, have been recognized as useful tools to reach out to target audiences, and to receive feedback. DiStaso, McCorkindale, and Wright (2011) argued that practitioners who use online media are more empowered. However, despite expectation for online media to enhance organization-stakeholder interactions and two-way communication, findings showed organizations were not exploiting the potential of these media (Shin, Pang, & Kim, 2013).

In essence, the model suggested that journalists have a greater power in the selection and use of subsidized information (arrow *b*) as compared to health communicators. Media content is a 'manifestation of reporters' filtering function' (p.11) as indicated by arrow *b*. Meanwhile, the link between health communicators and media content (arrow *c*) is depicted as an indirect link (dotted arrow) indicating the autonomy of journalists in their decision on how and how much the information subsidy will be used, depending on their perception of the importance of the subject matter and how they agree with the source interpretation.

Singapore's healthcare system and media landscape

This present study is situated in Singapore which has developed an efficient healthcare system through a unique combination of free market principles and careful government control (Lim, 1998). Healthcare policies are centrally planned and disseminated. Two national cancer centers are fully dedicated to cancer care specialization, complementing the treatment services provided by seven public hospitals and 12 private hospitals. A government statutory board, Health Promotion Board, provides complementary efforts in promoting cancer prevention, while voluntary organizations, some government-aided, provide aftercare support to cancer survivors.

In recent years, Singapore has witnessed an increased interest in the dynamics of health information seeking behavior, particularly in the context of cancer (Brashers et al., 2002; Johnson, 1997; Niederdeppe et al., 2008). Although Singapore is well-connected with the world, the local media still serves as the key mode of dissemination for public policies and educational campaigns (ST, 2011), including cancer. In Singapore, cultivating effective media relations with mainstream media still remains a paramount task (Pang, Chiong, & Nasrath, 2012). Top management often used successful and positive media coverage as a key indicator to assess effectiveness (Pang & Yeo, 2009). Qi and Cameron's (2008) model thus applies to Singapore.

The local media's role in serving national agenda and constant self-regulation enhances its perceived credibility as a trusted news source (Bokhorst-Heng, 2002), heightening its role in the promotion of important health-related issues.

Research questions

Based on Qi and Cameron's (2008) agenda building model, this study examines:

- RQ1: Where do the media obtain their sources of information in the reportage of cancer news?
- RQ2: What are the common cancer issues held by health communicators and journalists?
- RQ3: How do health communicators disseminate information about cancer and to what extent are these adopted by health journalists?
- RQ4: Where do health journalists and communicators agree on the issues and where do they diverge?

METHOD

A mixed approach combining content analysis and in-depth face-to-face interviews with the local media and health communicators was used to triangulate the findings.

Data collection for content analysis

Two prestigious, mainstream English newspapers were used. *The Straits Times* is the newspaper of record (Turnbull, 1995) with a circulation of about 400,000 (ST, 2011) and catering to a wide readership of 1.4 million. *The Business Times*, with a circulation of about 36,000 (SPH, 2010), caters to a high end, niche audience comprising businessmen, managers and executives.

The sample of cancer news stories was taken from the LexisNexis Academic database. A keyword search of "cancer and Singapore" from January 2008 to December 2009 was used. Of the total of 1,848 stories generated for analysis, the articles were further screened down to 585 articles. These stories that were chosen related specifically to cancer in Singapore and Singaporeans. Stories that were omitted included cancer stories about new treatment drugs from wire agencies, or editorials by columnists who wrote about a range of topics, including using traditional medicine to treat cancer.

The coding variables were adapted from Qi and Cameron's study (2008) to the context of cancer communication (see Appendix 1). All coding was done by two coders who were familiar with the method. Holsti inter-coder reliability tests were .80 and .87, which are within acceptable range.

In-depth interviews

A total of 10 face-to-face interviews were conducted with four senior news correspondents and one radio producer/presenter specialized in health/cancer stories from the local media and five health communicators from major government-linked and nonprofit cancer organizations. Interviewees were recruited between February and March 2010. Due to the media landscape, a small, purposeful, non-random sampling was employed, where representatives with a direct impact on the agenda building process were drawn.

Two sets of questions, one for health communicators and the other for journalists, were pre-designed and used as semi-structured guides to the interviews. Data were collected via face-to-face, supplemented by audio recording. The interviews were conducted in English and each lasted about 1.5 hours. Interviews were then transcribed and coded for recurrent themes according to the research questions.

RESULTS

Cancer media coverage and news sources

News coverage. Of the total of 585 newspaper articles reviewed, 87.7% (n = 513) were from *The Straits Times* (ST) and 12.3% (n = 72) were from *The Business Times* (BT). Based on the coding criteria, validity of articles was 87.7% and 100% respectively. The two most reported cancer topics were research (15.4%, n = 90) and survivorship (14.2%, n = 83).

Table 1.1 Breakdown of news coverage by topic

Cancer topics	Percentage	n=
Research	15.4%	90
Survivorship	14.2	83
Treatment	11.3	66
Funding and charity	10.9	64
Palliative care and cancer deaths	10.8	63
Others	10.1	59
Detection and screening	9.4	55
Causes	6.5	38
Prevention	4.8	28
Diagnosis	3.4	20
Healthcare industry	3.2	19

News sources and values. The majority of the articles adopted a neutral and balanced tone of reporting (62.9%, n =368), as compared to positive (26.0%, n = 152) and negative ones (11.1%, n = 65). More than half of the articles (58.6%, n = 343) used only a single source of information for their story, as compared to 30.8% (n = 180) for two sources, 7.2% (n = 42) for three sources, and 3.4% (n = 20) for four or more sources of information. Overall, the top five most commonly cited sources of information were on patients and ordinary people (29.6%, n = 173), government health agencies (20.9%, n = 122), universities and research institutes (20.7%, n = 121), public hospitals (20.2%, n = 118), and others (17.3%, n = 101) such as non-profit organizations and pharmaceuticals.

Common perceptions of cancer issues

Communicators' perceived cancer issues. Health communicators were generally aligned in what they perceived as important cancer issues. Cancer detection and screening was seen as the most important issue. Other issues commonly identified included cost of cancer treatment and healthcare, healthcare literacy and awareness on cancer. Specifically, respondents from hospital and non-profit sector saw the need to debunk certain myths about cancer and overcome fears which pose psychological barriers toward getting help early.

Journalists' perceived cancer issues. All respondents shared common perceptions of cancer issues. Urgent need for new cancer facilities, cost of treatment, education on cancer as well as prevention and early detection are top cancer issues in Singapore. While they seem to acknowledge the importance of screening and detection of cancer, health literacy and cancer education appear more critical. Most of them also saw the high prevalence of cancer as another emerging concern.

On issue perception, the media seemed more focused on their audiences' concerns. All of them saw the need to raise public cancer literacy. While most of the journalists agreed that early screening and detection of cancer remains an important issue, they would only carry the news if supported by fresh news hooks on which to carry the message.

Promotion versus adoption of health messages

Central messages promoted by communicators. The need for promoting more cancer education and building health literacy was identified as the key message. Early screening and detection of cancer were viewed as important prerogatives. Most of the interviewees noted the public concern on rising healthcare costs, in particular the high costs of cancer treatments, and expressed the importance of communicating and helping the public understand that higher healthcare cost is associated with improving quality of healthcare available in Singapore, even at public hospitals. To tackle the issue, Interviewee D highlighted the need to build awareness on the importance of medical insurance coverage[1].

In addition, interviewees pointed to some communication challenges in dealing with individual perceptions, emotions and attitudes toward cancer preparedness and social stigma, which become barriers to positive individual health management. These challenges are drivers for them to keep repeating the campaign messages year after year.

Media channels used by communicators. Respondents used a variety of methods to get their promoted messages to the media, ranging from news releases, advisories, organizing news briefings and conferences to verbal pitching of news stories or news angles. Most of the respondents would supplement the issuance of a news release with phone calls to pitch the news.

Footnote

1. Medisave is a national medical savings scheme which helps individuals put aside part of their income into their accounts to meet their future personal or immediate family's medical needs. Typically, every employee contributes 6.5–9% of one's monthly salary to one's Medisave account. The money can be withdrawn to pay for one's hospital bills or that of immediate family members. MediShield is a catastrophic illness insurance scheme to help people meet medical expenses from major illnesses, which could not be sufficiently covered by their Medisave balance. MediShield operates on a co-payment. Medifund is an endowment fund set up by the Government to help needy Singaporeans who are unable to pay for their medical expenses even after Medisave and MediShield coverage (www.moh.gov.sg/mohcorp/hcfinancing).

While most would prefer to pitch stories to *The Straits Times* because of its extensive reach, respondents sometimes found it difficult to get their news reported in it. Whether a story gets covered sometimes depends on the workload of the media, which has nothing to do with the ability to build agenda. Some cancer organizations have started to explore other channels of communication such as blog sites and community newsletters to facilitate direct engagement with their target audience.

Adoption of health promotion sources by journalists. All respondents used information provided by health communicators to varying degree and they were more likely to draw extensively from information subsidies provided by health authorities. They determined the extent of information subsidies to be used on the newsworthiness, timeliness, salience and clarity of information as well as relevance to readers/audiences.

Credibility of the information formed a key criterion. Most of the interviewees felt that materials offered by the government bodies, local hospitals and cancer centers are generally credible. Some of them expressed apprehension in using contents offered by public relations agencies as they would be representing pharmaceuticals "to peddle their drugs," said Interviewee I.

At times, health journalist respondents tended toward accommodation, agreeing to consider using a piece of news to maintain "goodwill" with supportive health communicators who have been helpful with information at other times.

Journalists' perception of news values. News values (proximity, currency, timeliness, conflict, and impact) were often the criteria used by journalists to determine the credibility and worth of information, the way they wrote the news—facts, stories or opinions and the tonality of the articles (Qi & Cameron, 2008). Mainstream media and vernaculars had dissimilar views on newsworthiness. For instance, the mainstream daily newspapers in Singapore would consider news value in terms of credibility of the information, accuracy of facts, objectivity and impact on society. For vernaculars, the relevance to their respective communities was an overriding factor.

News values attached to cancer education were largely congruent between health journalists and health communicator respondents. However, they diverge when "things that go wrong and patient care is compromised, then we (health journalists) are working in opposite ends," said Interviewer F.

Evaluations of agenda building effectiveness

Alignment on issue perceptions. Qi and Cameron's (2008) study suggested that the more health communicators and journalists agree on the most important issue in cancer, the more effective the agenda building efforts will be. Results indicated that they shared similar views on the top cancer issues (e.g. cancer education and awareness and quality of healthcare and cost) with slightly different priorities. Specifically, health communicators ranked early screening and detection of cancer as a top priority whereas health journalists believed larger socio-political issues were more imperative such as treatment and facilities, as well as literacy and education.

Despite some alignment on issue perceptions among the health communicators and journalists, this did not translate into media coverage. Findings from the content analysis indicated that detection and screening only accounted for 9.4%. However, cancer research (15.4%) and treatment (11.3%) had a better coverage, which corresponded to the views expressed by the journalist interviewees that new development in treatment, facilities, and medication was a key focus area of cancer news.

Alignment on news values. Qi and Cameron (2008) suggested that the more health communicators and journalists agreed on news values in covering cancer issues (use of sources, writing skill/style and localized news), the more effective the agenda building efforts would be. Four out of five health communicators used in-house medical research or expert opinions as primary sources to build their media agenda. Their sources were in line with those sought by most health journalists, except that the media would venture further to also consult overseas experts. In this study, most of the health communicators came from government or government-linked organizations which would draw policy directions from the Ministry of Health (MOH).

Content analysis findings corroborated such observation that health journalists preferred local authoritative sources of information: government health agencies, 20.9%; universities and research institutes, 20.7%; public hospitals, 20.2% versus overseas governmental health agencies, 3.4%. Journalists interviewed strongly felt that health communicators offering information subsidies should identify the news angle or be able to *localize* the news.

DISCUSSION

Findings suggested that media agenda building on communicating cancer is somewhat effective in Singapore. Specifically, journalists and health communicators shared similar views on cancer issues perceptions and news values. Findings revealed that media coverage is influenced largely by the prevailing issue perception held by health journalists. In addition, this study demonstrated the general applicability of the media agenda building model (Qi & Cameron, 2008), albeit with some modifications. In the Singapore study, it seems to suggest that the directional arrow a is more likely to be *bi-directional.* While health communicators mentioned calling the media to pitch their stories, they also acknowledged frequent enquiries received from the media, suggesting the relatively proactive role of the Singapore media in initiating the media agenda vis-à-vis health communicators.

However, the local media's effectiveness in agenda building is dependent on the comprehensiveness of information provided by the health communicators. It is also dependent on how willing and open the communicators are in supplying them with the needed information, showing a strong *interdependence* between them in the process of building the media agenda. Findings showed that sources from local health authorities are mostly cited and regarded highly credible. Hence, a bi-directional arrow *a* might be more representative of the agenda building process.

A unique observation in the local study is the hegemony of the Singapore government. Both the local media and health communicators seem to draw direction from government policies in their cancer education efforts, where the media saw their role as 'complementing' the health communicators' rather than being conflicting (Shin & Cameron, 2005). This can be explained by Singapore's developmental press system which means supporting the government's efforts to communicate policies to the public (Cenite et al., 2008, Heng, 2002).

Thus, in the modified model that applies to Singapore, we propose depicting the government as a *common source*, influencing the agenda building process. The content analysis results indicated the influential role of the government as an information source accounting for 41.1% of total sources mentioned.

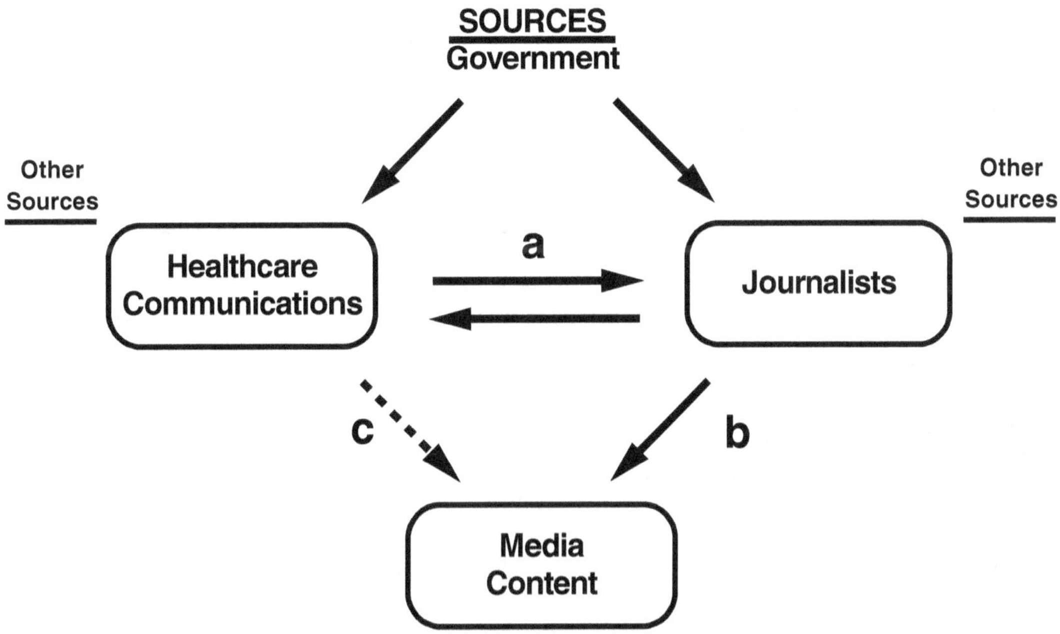

Figure 1.2 *Modified Agenda Building Model applicable to the Singapore context*

While most of the health communicators in this study have specific organizational goals on promoting screening and detection, health literacy is perceived to hold a higher degree of importance compared to screening and detection among the health journalists. To enhance effectiveness, health communicators could exploit the different news types by tailoring specific stories that suit the local media's preference, with strategic communication themes and messaging. From each perspective, the thematic messages would serve as different news points for the media. As a collective effort, the media agenda building process between health communicators and journalists will contribute to positive social change and advancement on cancer literacy and society will stand to benefit from a fuller understanding of how to cope, manage, and survive with cancer.

This study is limited to the Singapore context and the use of mainstream media. Future studies can explore how vernacular media and new media can be used complementarily to maximize health promotion to stakeholders. In conclusion, the current study has shown rigor of the model in the Singapore context, with the addition of the government as a unique element. Health communicators should leverage on the accommodating stance of the local media and use the model to proactively build effective media agenda for the benefit of the community.

ACKNOWLEDGMENT

We would like to thank Cheng Lee Ching, Lu Ting Ting, Adelin Toh and Terence Yeow for conducting the interviews and analyzing the news articles in the study.

REFERENCES

Aarva, P., & Tampere, M. P. (2006). Studying the striving and opposing forces in newspaper journalism: the actantial model of health promotion. *Health Promotion International, 21*, 160–168.

Black, N. (2001). Evidence based policy: proceed with care. *British Medical Journal, 323*, 275–279.

Bokhorst-Heng, W. (2002). Newspapers in Singapore: A mass ceremony in the imagining of the nation. *Media, Culture & Society, 24*, 559–569.

Botan, C., & Taylor, M. (2004). Public Relations: State of the field. *Journal of Communication, 54*, 645–661.

Brashers, D. E., Goldsmith, D. J., & Hsieh, E. (2002). Information seeking and avoiding in health contexts. *Human Communication Research, 28*, 258–272.

Cameron, G. T., & Blount, D. (1997). VNRs and air checks: A content analysis of on-air use of video news releases. *Journalism and Mass Communication Quarterly, 73*, 890–904.

Cameron, G. T., Sallot, L. M., & Curtin, P. A. (1997). Public relations and the production of news: A critical review and a theoretical framework. In B. R. Burleson (Ed.), *Communication Yearbook, 20* (pp. 111–155). Thousand Oaks, NY: Sage.

Cenite, M., Chong, S. Y., Han, T. J., Lim, L. Q., & Tan X. L. (2008). Perpetual development journalism? Balance and framing in the 2006 Singapore election coverage. *Asian Journal of Communication, 18*, 280–295.

Cline, R. J. W. (2003). Everyday interpersonal communication and health. In T. L. Thompson, A. M. Dorsey, K. I. Miller, & R. Parrott (Eds.), *Handbook of health* communication (pp. 285–313). Mahwah, NJ: Lawrence Erlbaum Associates.

Curtin, P.A. (1999). Re-evaluating public relations information subsidies: Market driven journalism and agenda-building theory and practice. *Journal of Public Relations Research, 11*, 53–90.

DiStaso, M.W., McCorkindale, T., & Wright, D.K. (2011). How public relations executives perceive and measure the impact of social media in their organizations. *Public Relations Review, 37*, 325–328.

Heng, R. H. K. (2002). *Media fortunes, changing times: ASEAN states in transition*, Institute of Southeast Asian Studies, Singapore.

Johnson, J. D. (1997). *Cancer-related information seeking.* Hampton Press, Cresskill, NJ.

Kiousis, S., Mitrook, M., Xu, W., & Seltzer, T. (2006). First- and second-level agenda-building and agenda-setting effects: exploring the linkages among candidate news releases, media coverage, and public opinion during the 2002 Florida Gubernatorial election. *Journal of Public Relations Research, 18*, 265–285.

Koh, W. and Lee, H. (2007). Postmenopausal gynecological cancers: the Singapore perspective and its general applicability. *Menopausal Medicine, 15*, 1–5.

Len-Ríos, M., Hinnant, A., & Park, S. (2009). Understanding how health journalists judge public relations sources: A rules theory approach. *Public Relations Review, 35*, 56–65.

Lim, M. K. (1998). Health care systems in transition: An overview of health care systems in Singapore. *Journal of Public Health Medicine, 20*, 16–22.

Niederdeppe, J., Frosch, D., & Hornik, R. (2008). Cancer news coverage and information seeking. *Journal of Health Communication, 13*, 181–199.

Pang, A. (2010). Mediating the media: A journalist-centric model in managing the media by corporate communication practitioners. *Corporate Communications: An International Journal, 15*, 192–204.

Pang, A., Chiong, V., Nasrath, B. (2012). Towards effective media relations in a changing media landscape in Singapore: Testing the mediating the media model. Melbourne, Australia: World Public Relations Forum.

Pang, A., & Yeo, S. L. (2009). Winning respect: Transformation to professionalization of public relations in Singapore. *Media Asia, 36* (2), 96–103.

Qi, Q., & Cameron, G. T. (2008). *Communicating Health Disparities: Ways toward a Supportive Media Agenda.* VDM Verlag Dr Muller, Saarbrucken, Germany.

Sallot, L. M., & Johnson, E. A. (2006). Investigating relationships between journalists and public relations practitioners: working together to set, frame and build the public agenda, 1991–2004. *Public Relations Review, 32*, 151–159.

Shin, J. H., & Cameron, G. T. (2005). Different sides of the same coin: Mixed views of public relations practitioners and journalists for strategic conflict management. *Journalism and Mass Communication Quarterly, 82*, 95–110.

Shin, W., Pang, A., & Kim, H. (2013). Building relationships through integrated social media platforms: Analysis of Top 100 global brands. London, UK: International Communication Association.

Singapore Ministry of Health. (2007). *Healthcare financing—What others said of us.* Retrieved March 20, 2010, from http://www.moh.gov.sg/mohcorp/hcsystem.aspx?id=22966

Straits Times. (2011). *About us, 15 November.* Retrieved November 15, 2010, from http://www.straitstimes.com/About%2BUs/About%2BUs.html

Singapore Department of Statistics. (2010). *Press release: Census of Population 2010: Advance census release.* Retrieved March 20, 2010, from http://www.singstat.gov.sg/news/news/press31082010.pdf

Singapore Press Holdings. (2010). *Our products—Newspaper—The Business Times.* Retrieved March 20, 2010, from http://www.sph.com.sg/ourproducts_newspaper_bt.shtml

Taylor, M., & Kent, M. (2007). Resisting the temptation of protocol journalism: How public relations can build media capacity. Paper presented at International Communication Association annual conference, San Francisco, CA.

Thompson, T. L., Robinson, J. D., Anderson, D. J., & Federowicz, M. (2008). Health communication: Where have we been and where can we go? In K. B. Wright & S. Moore (Eds.), *Applied Health Communication* (pp. 3–33). Cresskill, NJ: Hampton Press.

Turnbull, C. M. (1995). Dateline Singapore, Singapore Press Holdings, Singapore.

Viswanath, K., Ramanadhan, S., & Kontos, E. Z. (2007). Mass Media. In S. Galea (Ed.), *Macro-social Determinants of Population Health* (pp. 275–294). New York, NY: Springer Publishing Company.

World Health Organization (2010) Switzerland. http://www.who.int/cancer/WHA_cancer_presentation_final.pdf (last accessed 20 March 2010).

APPENDIX 1: CODING VARIABLES

a. Type of story: News, features and others which include forum, events announcement or column (Slater et al., 2008);

b. Primary cancer: causes, prevention, detection/screening, diagnosis, treatment, survivorship (inclusive of psycho-social aspects), palliative care/death of a person (Cortney et al., 2008) as well as healthcare industry (inclusive of policies and insurance), research (such as new technology and latest treatment method), funding/charity, and others. To avoid any overlapping topics, coders read the first three paragraphs to determine which cancer topic was emphasized the most as the beginning of a typical media story usually acts as a strong organizing element for the story (Slater et al., 2008);

c. Communication of cancer: how were the stories reported, i.e., what was the news value, the emotional tone, i.e. negative, neutral/balanced or positive (Cortney et al., 2008); and

d. Primary sources cited: medical journal and studies, universities and research institutes, pharmaceutical companies, private hospitals, public hospitals, overseas hospitals, government health agencies, overseas government health agencies, medical associations, cancer-related non-profit organization (inclusive of NGOs), patients/ordinary people and others (Cortney et al., 2008; Qi and Cameron, 2008).

Chapter 2:

Designing a disclosure-focused stigma intervention for mental health research

Amanda Carpenter
Rutgers University

Kathryn Greene
Rutgers University

INTRODUCTION

Approximately 57.7 million Americans per year experience a mental health disorder including but not limited to schizophrenia, bipolar disorder, post-traumatic stress disorder, obsessive compulsive disorder, depression, and anxiety disorders (National Alliance on Mental Illness (NAMI), 2009; Watson & Corrigan, 2005; Yamaguchi, Mino, & Uddin, 2011). Several misconceptions about mental illness contribute to stigma, including ideas that mental illnesses are a result of abusive parenting or poor upbringing (NAMI, 2009). Several efforts have targeted reduction of stigma associated with mental health disorders (e.g., Corrigan & Gelb, 2006; Heijnders & Van Der Meij, 2006; Stuart, 2008; Watson & Corrigan, 2005). Unfortunately, these initiatives have not experienced the desired effects over time (Heijnders & Van Der Meij, 2006; Link & Phelan, 2001; Watson & Corrigan, 2005). Few mental illness interventions are grounded in communication theory, thus designing such an intervention has the potential to advance the field of health communication and contribute to public health.

There is evidence that campaigns or interventions that focus on encouraging people with mental illness to disclose their illness is an effective approach to reducing stigma and increasing interpersonal outcomes (Davidson et al., 1999; King et al., 2007). This chapter presents a disclosure-focused mental health stigma intervention centered on decisions to share mental health diagnoses to create social support and decrease stigma for people living with mental health issues. This intervention utilizes the disclosure decision-making model (DD-MM, Greene, 2009) as the theoretical framework and extends an existing brief disclosure intervention to this new context (Greene, Carpenter, Catona, & Magsamen-Conrad, 2013). Applying theory to an intervention addressing a significant health topic further advances the field and study of health communication.

In this chapter we first highlight the importance of mental illness as a health condition in the United States. Next, we discuss various definitions of stigma and how stigma relates specifically to mental illness. The chapter continues with a review and critique of existing interventions targeting mental illness and stigma. In the later portion of this chapter we discuss the importance of disclosing mental illness and present a disclosure-focused mental illness intervention to reduce stigma. We begin by describing mental illness.

Mental Illness

Mental illness is a serious problem that can emerge throughout the lifespan and it primarily affects individuals initially during adolescence and young adulthood (NAMI, 2009). Mental illnesses are defined as "medical conditions that disrupt a person's thinking, feeling, mood, ability to relate to others, and daily functioning" (NAMI, 2009). The *Healthy People 2020* objectives include a focus on mental health and mental disorders as an area of health that needs to be further addressed in the next decade (United States Department of Health and Human Services [USDHHS], 2011). About 6% of Americans live with a serious mental illness such as schizophrenia or bipolar disorder (NAMI, 2009). These illnesses can be difficult to treat because "stigma often prompts people to hide their symptoms and avoid psychiatric treatment" (NAMI, 2010). NAMI (2010) estimates that "only one in two people with a serious mental illness seeks psychiatric treatment" and many patients discontinue recommended treatment plans. Untreated mental illnesses can lead to "unnecessary disability, unemployment, substance abuse, suicide and wasted lives; the economic cost of untreated mental illness is more than 100 billion dollars each year in the United States" (NAMI, 2009). Four of the top ten causes of disability in the United States are mental health disorders (NAMI, 2009).

Because of the many gaps in both care and coverage in the United States healthcare system, people living with mental illness are overrepresented in homeless and incarcerated populations (NAMI, 2009). Mental illnesses also affect physical health as several chronic health conditions such as obesity and diabetes are likely to co-occur (Centers for Disease Control and Prevention [CDC], 2011). It is also estimated that mental illnesses shorten the lifespan as significantly as illnesses such as cancer or heart disease (NAMI, 2010). This review of mental illness emphasizes the importance of mental health disorders and why developing an effective intervention would be beneficial. The prevalence of mental illness combined with its implications for overall health and the consequences of not treating it contribute to the importance of addressing mental health issues. Stigma is central to addressing such issues, as discussed next.

Conceptualizing Stigma

Stigma affects the lives of people living with mental disorders in a number of ways. First, stigma affects the way people living with mental illness are perceived, approached, and treated. Second, stigma affects the way people with mental illness perceive themselves. Third, the shame associated with stigma discourages people living with mental illness from seeking psychiatric treatment, which results in hiding symptoms and avoiding treatment (NAMI, 2009). Finally, negative stereotypes about mental illness interferes with people living with mental illness achieving life goals (e.g., obtaining employment, living in a safe home, and having satisfying relationships with friends, family, and romantic partners).

There are several competing conceptualizations of stigma that can apply to mental health, and each perspective emphasizes a different component. Goffman (1963) is credited with early theorizing related to stigma and defined stigma as "an attribute that is deeply discrediting" (p. 3). Goffman (1963) suggested that the stigmatized deviated from "normality," providing a broad lens through which to consider stigma. Goffman's framework is the most widely utilized to conceptualize stigma, but it was not adapted specifically for health but can loosely apply to public perceptions of people with mental illness as "abnormal." More relevant to health communication research specifically, Leary and Schreindorfer (1998) suggested that stigma consisted of identifying traits or characteristics that led to avoidance or rejection from others. They identified four characteristics of stigma relevant to health research: perception that individuals a) threaten others' health and/or safety, b) diverge from group standards, c) fail to contribute to society, and d) create negative emotional reactions in others. Although all four components of Leary and Schreindorfer's framework can be applied to mental illness, perhaps the threat to others' health and safety is most prominent in public perceptions of people with mental illness.

Corrigan and Watson (2002) added multiple levels to their conceptualization of stigma including defining stigma from a public perspective and a self-perspective. Both public and self perspectives incorporate stereotype, prejudice, and discrimination. Public stigma stereotypes include believing that group members are "dangerous, incompetent, or have character weakness" (Corrigan & Watson, 2002, p. 16). Prejudice associated with public stigma includes the negative reaction toward a particular group. Discriminatory behavior associated with public stigma includes "avoidance and withholding employment, housing opportunities, and help" (Corrigan & Watson, 2002, p. 16). Self-stigma stereotypes include views about the self, more specifically people perceiving themselves as "incompetent and having character flaws" (Corrigan & Watson, 2002, p. 16). Negative emotional reactions associated with self-stigma include low self-worth. Discrimination associated with self-stigma includes "a behavioral response to prejudice" (Corrigan & Watson, 2002, p. 16), which includes the failure to pursue employment or housing. Corrigan and Watson's framework can be applied to mental illness as well and adds focus on how people living with mental illness perceive themselves, in addition to the more widely described public perceptions that are central in stigma.

Link and Phelan (2001) identified two unresolved challenges to the conceptualization of stigma, the people studying stigmatized conditions and an individualistic focus, which Leary and Schreindorfer (1998) also identified. Link and Phelan (2001) suggested that researchers studying stigmatized conditions did not always belong to the stigmatized group, therefore potentially misunderstanding the illness experience. Link and Phelan (2001) also added power to their definition to address the individual: "stigma exists when elements of labeling, stereotyping, separation, status loss, and discrimination occur together in a power situation that allows them" (p. 377). Link and Phelan's framework can also be applied to mental illness and highlights the interpersonal experience of the person living with mental illness.

All of these conceptualizations apply to mental illness, either broadly or more specific to health. Each of these definitions focuses on a different component, either from the public's perception or the interpersonal experience of the person living with mental illness. These definitions of stigma highlight a core feature where people living with mental illness struggle with many aspects of stigma.

Mental Illness and Stigma

Mental illness is one of the most stigmatized health conditions (NAMI, 2009; Stuart, 2008; Watson & Corrigan, 2005; Yamaguchi et al., 2011). West, Yanos, Smith, Roe, and Lysaker (2011) found that people living with severe mental illness experienced an elevated level of self-stigma, which is particularly troubling considering the implications for self-esteem, support, and treatment. Several misconceptions about mental illness contribute to stigma including ideas that "mental illnesses are a result of personal weakness, lack of character, or poor upbringing" (NAMI, 2009). These perceptions highlight the personal responsibility (Corrigan et al., 2002) or blame that people living with mental illness confront. Cases of untreated mental illness also contribute to the misconception that all people living with mental illness are dangerous and violent, and this "fear leads to avoidance" (Corrigan & Watson, 2002, p. 16).

Media content perpetrates and propagates beliefs that mental illness is associated with violence (Philo, 1994). Media, including news, movies, and television, often present an exaggerated depiction of people living with mental illness, portraying them as unstable, erratic, and unsafe, and these representations influence and shape our perceptions of mental illness (Thornicroft, 2006). Further, the preponderance of media depictions of mental illness is negative (Wahl, 1992). Media may also sensationalize negative events and emphasize the mental health components associated with violent behaviors, for example in national school tragedies, yet underrepresent success stories, such as people coping well with their condition.

Stigma and outcomes. Stigma affects the lives of people living with mental disorders in a number of ways. Stigma affects how people living with mental illness are perceived, approached, and treated (Link & Phelan, 2001). A study conducted by the CDC (2010) reported discrepancies between perceptions of the general public and people living with mental illness where 57% of the general population believed that people are caring toward people living with mental illness, while only 25% of people living with mental illness perceived people to be sympathetic toward people living with mental health disorders. Taylor and Dear (1981) specifically identified three stigmatizing attitudes people held toward mental illness: a) people with serious mental illness are to be feared and therefore do not deserve acceptance in communities with non-mentally ill people; b) people with serious mental illness are unable to make their own decisions; and c) people with serious mental illness lack maturity and require constant care. Additionally, the historic treatment of mental illness that included segregating mentally ill people and thus implicitly labeled them as "dangerous," and this pattern of separation may also contribute to the perception that people living with mental illness are unsafe. These negative attitudes and perceptions affect the way we behave toward and respond to people living with mental illness, additionally affecting the way this population perceives themselves.

Stigma affects the way people with mental illness perceive themselves. Public attitudes and beliefs about mental illness create negative beliefs about the self (Corrigan & Watson, 2002). These stigmatizing attitudes are internalized, creating negative self-worth and self-esteem, and eroding self-efficacy to live a productive life (Corrigan & Watson, 2002). With low self-esteem and self-worth, people living with mental illness have little confidence to engage in society, resulting in increased social isolation and decreased access to social support. These outcomes may further exacerbate the symptoms of mental illness, for example, leading to a spiral of depression.

Stigma prevents people living with mental illness from seeking psychiatric treatment by encouraging people to hide their symptoms and avoid treatment (NAMI, 2009). Contributing to this barrier are public beliefs that coercive treatment and segregated institutions are the best methods for treating mental illness (Corrigan & Watson, 2002). Stigma "erodes confidence that mental disorders are real, treatable health conditions" (NAMI, 2009). The World Health Organization (2010) reported that "between 35 and 50% of people with severe mental health conditions did not receive the necessary treatment for their condition" (p. 16). Mental health has high documented treatment effectiveness rates, with between 70 and 90% of those seeking treatment seeing improvements in symptoms and quality of life (NAMI, 2009). Without treatment, people living with mental illness have a greater chance of relapsing during the recovery process (NAMI, 2010).

Additionally, stigma often hinders people living with mental illness from achieving life goals. People living with mental illness have desires to live productive and fulfilling lives that include obtaining employment, living in a safe home, and having satisfying relationships with friends, family, and romantic partners. However, obtaining these goals is complicated by stigma. Stigmatizing behaviors include withholding help (e.g., refusing to lease safe housing) and social avoidance. Even people intending to help mental illness patients may smother, overwhelm, or be perceived as "taking over" (see unhelpful social support for people living with HIV/AIDS, Barbee, Derlega, Sherburne, & Grimshaw, 1998). Martin, Pescosolido, and Tuch (2000) reported that more than half of their survey respondents were opposed to a range of interactions with people living with mental illness including: a) socializing with a person living with mental illness, b) working with a person living with mental illness, and c) having a family member romantically involved with a person living with mental illness. Thus, people would rather avoid than interact with people living with mental illness.

This review highlights the barriers that stigma creates for people living with mental illness. Stigma affects how people living with mental illness perceive and value themselves, how the public perceives and approaches people living with mental illness, people living with mental illnesses' willingness to seek treatment, and how people living with mental illness are able to achieve life goals.

Existing Interventions Addressing Mental Illness

With all of the negative outcomes of mental illness stigma, it is not surprising that several initiatives to reduce mental illness stigma already exist. Each of these initiatives relies on different strategies to deliver the intervention. However, most of these anti-stigma initiatives have shortcomings that prevent long-term sustained effects and changing attitudes and behaviors (Heijnders & Van Der Meij, 2006; Link & Phelan, 2001; Stuart, 2008; Watson & Corrigan, 2005). Watson and Corrigan (2005) identified three different types of anti-stigma efforts: protest, education, and contact.

Protest. Protest, the first category of anti-stigma initiatives, relies on a moral demand to the public to stop stigmatizing people living with mental illness (Watson & Corrigan, 2005). Protest involves a "punishing consequence" (Watson & Corrigan, 2005, p. 283) such as shaming the public for its bad behavior or negative attitudes. An example of a protest initiative is the program StigmaBusters, launched by NAMI in 2000. StigmaBusters is a system run by mental illness advocates that alerts members when national media portrays people with mental illness in a stigmatizing manner (NAMI, n.d.). Members are then expected to report the negative representation to the offending organization and create pressure (NAMI, n.d.). This particular initiative has experienced some success, contributing to the cancellation of a television program (ABC's Wonderland, 2000) that depicted people living with mental illness as dangerous and violent (Watson & Corrigan, 2005).

Protest sends a strong message to combat stigma, and this strong message could be a benefit or a risk. This approach was effective in canceling Wonderland and shaming the major network and its sponsors (Watson & Corrigan, 2005). This may be an effective way to approach media to reduce stigmatizing portrayals of people living with mental illness. However, this approach has several inadequacies. Because protest sends such a strong message, psychological reactance may occur as "freedom of behavior is a pervasive and important aspect of human life" (Brehm, 1966, p. 7). Specifically the protest could backfire and increase negative attitudes toward mental illness and stereotyping. StigmaBusters has also had limited success, canceling only the one television show. This approach also does not take power into consideration, part of the stigma definition provided by Link and Phelan (2001). Media organizations could find ways to ignore advocacy groups' complaints. The protest approach may work best at a higher level, such as public policy, where organizations would face the risk of lost revenue should they continue perpetuating stigmatizing representations.

Education. The second anti-stigma initiative category was education. Education attempts to "replace stereotypes with factual information" (Watson & Corrigan, 2005, p. 283). This approach relies on several ways to disseminate information such as through public service announcements, flyers, or videos. A well-known effort utilizing this approach was the Elimination of Barriers initiative launched by the Substance Abuse and Mental Health Service Administration [SAMHSA] in 2004. Created using social marketing principles, Elimination of Barriers sought to educate the public and reward positive portrayals of people living with mental illness (Bell, Colangelo, & Pillen, 2005).

Education is useful for targeting and reaching large audiences (Corrigan & Gelb, 2006). This mass marketing approach requires fewer resources (unless the intervention requires purchased advertising time or space) and less planning time than the protest and contact processes. Previous research also suggests that education can create changes in attitudes (Corrigan & Gelb, 2006). However, this attitudinal change is often short-term and it is unclear how to best sustain change in attitudes and behaviors (Corrigan & Gelb, 2006). A specific problem with the Elimination of Barriers initiative is the broad scope of the project, and social marketing calls for more specific goals (Lee & Kotler, 2011). The mass approach may not be the most effective way to reduce stigma, in fact, targeting more specific audiences and tailoring messages to these audiences may be a more efficacious strategy (Heijnders & Van Der Meij, 2006).

Contact. Contact was the third anti-stigma intervention category, where people living with mental illness engage in interpersonal interaction with small groups of the public. For a contact initiative to work, four elements must be present: a) equal status between the groups, b) common goals, c) no competition, and d) sponsorship by an organization (Watson & Corrigan, 2005). Developed by NAMI, In Our Own Voice is an example of a contact initiative aimed at reducing stigma (Corrigan & Gelb, 2006). In Our Own Voice is a 90-minute program directed by people living with mental illness about their mental illness experience. The program utilizes peer discussion with small groups (e.g., a class of college students, police officers, or teachers) about mental illness (Corrigan & Gelb, 2006). The presenters must complete training before they can lead the program; as leaders, people with mental illness are seen as credible sources because they have undergone treatment for their mental illness and can discuss information pertinent to their illness (Corrigan & Gelb, 2006). This is similar to other intervention strategies where a cancer patient or person living with HIV/AIDS credibly speaks about prevention or screening.

Comparing intervention categories. This discussion of anti-stigma interventions reviews several existing initiatives and approaches, including the advantages and disadvantages of these types of interventions. There are no direct comparisons across these categories of mental illness stigma interventions. We first compare the interventions and then in the following section we outline an interpersonal disclosure intervention that falls into the contact category.

Previous research has indicated the best results for contact initiatives out of the three intervention categories (Corrigan & Gelb, 2006; Watson & Corrigan, 2005). Intergroup contact reduces prejudice and increases positive attitudes toward mental illness (Corrigan & Gelb, 2006). Contact initiatives are unable to address mass audiences, and these smaller and more interpersonal approaches may be better strategies for reducing stigma. There are also more resources required for contact initiatives (e.g., personnel, planning, time) than the protest or education initiatives. Although most of these anti-stigma efforts have not sustained long-term effects (Heijnders, & Van Der Meij, 2006; Link & Phelan, 2001; Watson & Corrigan, 2005; Yamaguchi et al., 2011), important insights from these efforts can be used to improve future interventions and campaigns.

Several features of existing initiatives are worth noting. First, the literature suggests that the most successful feature of earlier anti-stigma initiatives was interpersonal interaction with a person living with mental illness (Corrigan & Gelb, 2006; Read, Haslam, Sayce, & Davies, 2006; Watson

& Corrigan, 2005; Yamaguchi et al., 2011). Hearing firsthand from a person living with mental illness increased positive attitudes toward mental illness and reduced negative stereotypes about mental illness (Watson & Corrigan, 2005; Yamaguchi et al., 2011). This "mere exposure" could reduce uncertainty and increase positive attitudes toward mental illness. Positive expectancy violation is another explanation for the effect, where the audience was expecting a negative or strange interaction but ended up enjoying the experience of learning about mental illness (Yamaguchi et al., 2011). Regardless of the reason why positive attitudes are increased through interpersonal interaction with people with mental illness, future initiatives should continue to include people living with mental illness because this personal interaction appears to resonate with the public. This inclusion of people living with mental illness in these initiatives also reduces the separation of people with mental illness from the general public. In the following section we outline the importance of disclosing a mental illness as one mechanism for increasing interpersonal interaction.

Disclosure and Mental Illness

Disclosure is a component of contact interventions and is defined as "an interaction between at least two individuals where one intends to deliberately divulge something personal to another" (Greene, Derlega, & Mathews, 2006, p. 411; also see Derlega, Metts, Petronio, & Margulis, 1993). Disclosure has been studied with many health issues such as HIV/AIDS, cancer, nonvisible illness, sexual abuse, heart conditions, and infertility. Some research on disclosure and health examines how patients share their diagnoses (when and with whom), for example, a patient with a heart condition may be selective about who knows the diagnosis particularly early in treatment. Other emerging research focuses on how patients share updates regarding their health condition, for example, a breast cancer patient may be selective about what is shared regarding treatment, recurrence, or side effects. Disclosure of both diagnosis and ongoing updates is relevant in the context of mental health issues.

Studying disclosure of a mental illness specifically is important for several reasons. First, disclosing a mental illness is associated with potential increased social support (Davidson et al., 1999) because people must be aware of the condition to be able to provide appropriate social support. This social support can be received from several sources including family, friends, peer support groups, and from healthcare providers (Davidson et al., 1999). Increasing social support may lead to important outcomes such as symptom improvement, social network enhancement, and increased quality of life (Davidson et al., 1999). Second, disclosing mental illness can reduce stigma by reducing negative stereotypes (King et al., 2007; SAMHSA, 2008). Third, disclosing a mental illness is often necessary to receive certain accommodations, for example, from work or school. For example, it is common for college students in the United States to receive testing accommodations such as additional time and a quieter setting if they document a disabling medical or mental health condition. Fourth, nondisclosure can negatively affect life satisfaction because secrecy and avoidance can lead to social ostracism (Rosenfield, 1997). Fifth, disclosing is a necessary step for contact interventions to be successful and reduce stigma (SAMHSA, 2008). Finally, more openness and disclosure is related to overcoming discrimination by creating a sense of self-empowerment and self-worth (SAMHSA, 2008).

People living with mental illness who are considering disclosing their diagnosis must weigh the risks and rewards of sharing this information. Because disclosure involves risks, people carefully calculate whether to reveal or conceal a diagnosis and whether to later share ongoing updates. Benefits of disclosing a mental illness include more openness and less secrecy and reducing the burden of nondisclosure or "holding it in." Disclosure can lead to identifying similar others and finding people who can provide assistance. Disclosure can also educate others, impact stigma, and allow people to "promote a personal sense of power and act as a living testimony against stigma and discrimination" (SAMHSA, 2008, p. 11). Risks of disclosing a mental illness include social rejection, discrimination, anxiety, and stress (SAMHSA, 2008). Further, people who share also lose control of the information because the recipient may further share the information (Venetis et al., 2012). Because the risks are high, people with mental illness may choose to be cautious in how they weigh decisions to share, opting for less openness to protect themselves.

SAMHSA (2008) identified several strategies that people used to disclose their mental illness including selecting a safe place in which to disclose, planning what to disclose, selective disclosure, and trusting the disclosure target. These strategies are similar to research on disclosing other stigmatized health conditions (e.g., Greene et al., 2013). These disclosure strategies often require a training or intervention to fully develop the skills necessary to disclose a mental illness. The following section outlines a mental illness disclosure intervention designed to reduce stigma and improve outcomes for patients.

Proposed Disclosure Intervention

This chapter presents a revision of an existing disclosure intervention to increase the disclosure efficacy of people living with mental illness. Focusing more on an interpersonal perspective, this intervention suggests that selectively disclosing a mental illness can yield positive outcomes such as increased social support and reduced stigma. This intervention uses the DD-MM (Greene, 2009) as the theoretical framework, described next.

DD-MM. The DD-MM suggests that several variables predict whether a person will disclose a health issue such as a mental health disorder (Greene, 2009). These variables include information assessment, receiver assessment, and disclosure efficacy. Information assessment includes stigma, prognosis, symptoms, preparation, and relevance to others and addresses *what* a person is considering disclosing. Receiver assessment includes relational quality and anticipated response, incorporating *who* is the potential disclosure recipient and how this person might respond to the information. Disclosure efficacy is the belief that sharing information will result in a positive outcome or *how*, encompassing confidence related to disclosure skills and message enactment. If information and receiver assessments are positive and disclosure efficacy is high, it is likely that people will choose to disclose. The DD-MM specifically identifies factors that people weigh in a disclosure decision that can be applied to sharing a mental health diagnosis.

The DD-MM has been applied to several health conditions including HIV/AIDS (Greene et al., 2013), heart disease (Checton & Greene, 2012), nonvisible illness (Checton, Greene,

Magsamen-Conrad, & Venetis, 2012), cancer (Venetis, Greene, Checton, & Magsamen-Conrad, under review; Venetis, Magsamen-Conrad, Checton, & Greene, in press), and infertility (Steuber & Solomon, 2011). Greene et al. (2013) used the DD-MM as the framework for a disclosure intervention to increase disclosure efficacy for people living with HIV/AIDS. Checton and Greene (2012) considered how illness uncertainty affected ongoing disclosure about the patient's heart condition to partner and focused on two sources of uncertainty, prognosis and symptom. Checton et al. (2012) examined different sources of uncertainty and illness interference, and how uncertainty and interference affected communication efficacy and health condition management. Two studies relating to cancer examined how cancer patients made decisions to engage in topic avoidance with their partners (Venetis et al., under review; Venetis et al., in press). Steuber and Solomon (2011) considered how disclosure of infertility to social network members related to perceived stigma and disclosure efficacy. These studies highlight the different contexts to which the DD-MM has been applied. The DD-MM serves as the theoretical framework for a brief disclosure intervention, described next.

Brief disclosure intervention (BDI). The Brief Disclosure Intervention (BDI) is guided by the DD-MM, and this intervention focuses on evaluating options for disclosing by increasing efficacy in ability to share a difficult piece of information. The original version of the BDI was developed and utilized with another highly stigmatized population, people living with HIV/AIDS (Greene et al., 2013). Results of the BDI implemented with people living with HIV/AIDS indicated, from pretest to posttest, that the intervention increased disclosure efficacy, and decreased anxiety and worry about disclosure (Greene et al., 2013). Thus, preliminary evidence indicates that the BDI is effective.

The BDI is grounded in brief motivational interviewing. Brief motivational interviews consist of engaging motivational discussion (Miller & Rollnick, 1991). Brief motivational interviewing affords a shortened version of an intervention where participants are encouraged to reflect on specific behaviors or decisions through a brief tailored conversation with an interviewer. The BDI asks participants to assess the risks and benefits of disclosure and incorporates the three main DD-MM assessments of information, receiver (relationship quality and anticipated response), and efficacy. The focus of the BDI is on options and methods for sharing sensitive information.

A trained interviewer delivers the intervention to participants in three phases. The first phase asks participants, "If you were telling someone else about how to share their HIV status, what would you recommend? What would you say works well?" The first question in this section asks participants to identify recommendations for sharing their HIV status and is less threatening than asking participants about sharing their own HIV status. In this phase, participants are also asked about specific disclosure strategies including planning, location, non-face-to-face, practice, gradual disclosure, and hinting. The second phase asks participants to identify additional strategies they would use to disclose their own HIV status. These disclosure strategies include third party disclosure, taking another person when disclosing, and testing reactions. The interviewer also asks participants to assess the risks and benefits of using each strategy. The third phase asks participants to think about several people who do not know about their HIV status but they might tell in the next six months. This third phase also asks participants to consider how they would disclose this information and how the person might respond.

BDI applied to mental health. This present mental illness application of the BDI is derived from the intervention tailored for HIV/AIDS. HIV/AIDS and mental illness are both highly stigmatized health issues, nonvisible (i.e., diagnoses must be shared), and share the misperception that the illness is not treatable. We propose that the BDI can also apply to mental illness and label this applied version the Brief Disclosure Intervention-Mental Illness (BDI-MI). This BDI-MI intervention is intended for participants living with a mental illness. This intervention is designed for people diagnosed with a mental illness who have undergone treatment rather than focusing on people in crisis or undiagnosed patients. For people who are in treatment, increasing social support through disclosure is also one way to maintain adherence to treatment, an added benefit.

The three phases in the original BDI are adapted for the BDI-MI. The goal of the BDI-MI is not necessarily for people to disclose but for patients to better anticipate outcomes, maximize productive social support, and decrease stigmatizing responses. In the first phase, participants are asked, "If you were telling someone else about how to share their mental illness, what would you recommend? What would you say works well?" In this phase participants are asked about the strategies identified in the original BDI: planning (e.g., having a script to follow), location (planning a specific place to disclose), non-face-to-face (writing a letter or email disclosing mental illness), practice (imagining the disclosure situation and possibly rehearsing dialogue), gradual disclosure (incremental disclosure where symptoms or medication are initially shared), and hinting (asking indirect questions about mental illness or saying you are not feeling well). The participants are asked to complete the risk/benefit assessment where they describe the risks and benefits of using each strategy for disclosure. For example, what is the upside of utilizing gradual disclosure? What is the downside of non-face-to-face disclosure? Follow-up questions and prompts ask about the benefits and costs or pros and cons of each specific strategy.

The second BDI-MI phase asks participants to identify any additional strategies they would use for disclosing their own mental illness. These strategies are in addition to the six aforementioned strategies in Phase I. These additional strategies include third party disclosure, for example, asking an immediate family member to tell a relative. Another additional strategy is taking another person when disclosing, for example, bringing a parent or sibling along when telling a friend about mental illness. The risk/benefit analysis continues in this phase when participants identify the benefits and drawbacks of using each of these additional strategies to disclose their own mental health issues.

The final BDI-MI phase asks participants to think about the people in their social network who do not know about the mental illness. The prompts ask how they would disclose this information to these people. Participants use the previous two phases to assist in developing this plan and weigh the risks and benefits of sharing the diagnosis. If participants disclose to someone in the near future, they should be better prepared for a productive interaction based on these strategies. Even if they choose not to share, participants should feel better equipped to disclose when they feel it is beneficial.

This modified BDI-MI intervention follows a very similar pattern to the original BDI because HIV/AIDS and mental illness have several similarities. It is likely that the BDI-MI will yield similar outcomes to the original BDI. HIV/AIDS and mental illness are similar, in part, because of the high levels of stigma associated with the disease. Results from the original BDI included increased disclosure efficacy, decreased anxiety about disclosure, and decreased worry about disclosure, which are also expected outcomes of the BDI-MI. The BDI-MI has the potential to decrease the stigma associated with mental illness by increasing social support, empowering people living with mental illness to share their story, and decreasing prejudice. By emphasizing the risk/benefit evaluation process, participants are better equipped to evaluate and likely avoid the most stigmatizing responses.

CONCLUSION

Anti-stigma interventions have not experienced the sustained effects that were expected (see Heijnders, & Van Der Meij, 2006; Link & Phelan, 2001; Stuart, 2008; Watson & Corrigan, 2005). The prevalence of mental illness makes the illness and the problems associated with it far too significant to ignore. Stigma is a central feature that contributes to the challenges of people living with mental illness, including low self-worth and self-esteem in people living with mental illness, avoidance of medical treatment of mental illness, and as a barrier to achieving life goals. Disclosure is one way to decrease stigma and increase social support for people living with mental illness. The present BDI-MI intervention takes a step to prepare participants to engage in one form of contact interventions. The intervention is theoretically grounded, incorporates prior disclosure research, and has been previously tested with a stigmatized group. The adaptation to mental illness is a significant step forward.

Any future interventions should include a contact or interpersonal component; these positive effects are promising for stigma reduction (Corrigan & Gelb, 2006; Read et al., 2006; Watson & Corrigan, 2005; Yamaguchi et al., 2011). The scope of the effort is another consideration, and a model such as the BDI-MI for reducing stigma could empower people with mental illness to share their story. These suggestions for future anti-stigma initiatives and research could increase the chances of sustained attitude change toward mental illness. Anti-stigma efforts should include the narratives disclosed from people living with mental illness as those strategies have yielded positive effects (Corrigan & Gelb, 2006; Read et al., 2006; Watson & Corrigan, 2005; Yamaguchi et al., 2011). Finally, empowering people with mental illness to be proactive in disclosing and reducing stigma is something else that future initiatives should focus on such as current contact interventions.

In this chapter we propose a disclosure intervention tailored for people diagnosed with mental illness. The BDI-MI tailors an existing intervention designed for people disclosing their HIV status. The goal of the BDI-MI is for people with mental illness to increase efficacy by anticipating the outcomes of disclosure and increasing the amount of received social support. The BDI-MI follows three phases and utilizes several strategies to increase participants' efficacy and anticipate the response of the disclosure target. This intervention provides a valuable tool for increasing options for sharing. It also increases the range of potential strategies for participants to disclose their mental illness. The BDI-MI intervention can also apply to updates in mental illness treatment, not just diagnosis. This chapter outlines an intervention that can be implemented with people diagnosed with mental illness. Future research should test this BDI-MI intervention and track participants' progress over time. Communication-focused interventions are significant approaches to public health issues, and we need additional theory-grounded, effective interpersonal communication interventions to improve health.

REFERENCES

Barbee, A. P., Derlega, V. J., Sherburne, S. P., & Grimshaw, A. (1998). Helpful and unhelpful forms of social support for HIV+ individuals. In V. J. Derlega & A. P. Barbee (Eds.), *HIV & social interaction* (pp. 83–105). Thousand Oaks, CA: Sage.

Bell, J., Colangelo, A., & Pillen, M. (2005). *Highlights of the final report of the evaluation of the Elimination of Barriers initiative.* Retrieved from http://www.promoteacceptance.samhsa.gov/archtelPDF/EBIReport_FINAL_Tagged.pdf

Brehm, J. W. (1966). *A theory of psychological reactance.* Waltham, MA: Academic Press.

Centers for Disease Control and Prevention. (2011). *CDC report: Mental illness surveillance among adults in the United States.* Retrieved from http://www.cdc.gov/mentalhealthsurveillance/fact_sheet.html

Centers for Disease Control and Prevention. (2010). Attitudes toward mental illness—35 states, District of Columbia, and Puerto Rico. *Morbidity and Mortality Weekly Report, 59,* 619–625.

Checton, M. G., & Greene, K. (2012). Beyond initial disclosure: The role of prognosis and symptom uncertainty in patterns of disclosure in relationships. *Health Communication, 27,* 145–157. doi: 10.1080/10410236.2011.571755

Checton, M. G., Greene, K., Magsamen-Conrad, K., & Venetis, M. K. (2012). Patients' and partners' perceptions of chronic illness and its management. *Families, Systems, & Health, 30,* 114–129. doi: 10.1037/a0028598

Corrigan, P., & Gelb, B. (2006). Three programs that use mass approaches to challenge the stigma of mental illness. *Psychiatric Services, 57,* 393–398.

Corrigan, P. W., Rowan, D., Green, A., Lundin, R., River, P., Uphoff-Wasowski, K., . . . Kubiak, M. A. (2002). Challenging two mental illness stigmas: Personal responsibility and dangerousness. *Schizophrenia Bulletin, 28,* 293–309.

Corrigan, P. W., & Watson, A. C. (2002). Understanding the impact of stigma on people with mental illness. *World Psychiatry, 1,* 16–20.

Davidson, L., Chinman, M., Kloos, B., Weingarten, R., Stayner, D., & Tebes, J. K. (1999). Peer support among individuals with severe mental illness: A review of the evidence. *Clinical Psychology: Science and Practice, 6*, 165–187. doi: 10.1093/clipsy.6.2.165

Derlega, V. J., Metts, S., Petronio, S., & Margulis, S. T. (1993). *Self-disclosure*. Newbury Park, CA: Sage.

Goffman, E. (1963). *Stigma: Notes on the management of spoiled identity*. Upper Saddle River, NJ: Prentice Hall.

Greene, K. (2009). An integrated model of health-disclosure decision making. In T. Afifi & W. Afifi (Eds.), *Uncertainty and information regulation in interpersonal contexts: Theories and applications* (pp. 226–253). New York, NY: Routledge.

Greene, K., Carpenter, A., Catona, D., & Magsamen-Conrad, K. (2013). The Brief Disclosure Intervention (BDI): Facilitating African Americans' disclosure of HIV. *Journal of Communication, 63*, 138–158. doi: 10.1111/jcom.12010

Greene, K., Derlega, V. J., & Mathews, A. (2006). Self-disclosure in personal relationships. In A. Vangelisti & D. Perlman (Eds.), *Cambridge handbook of personal relationships* (pp. 409–427). Cambridge, England: Cambridge University Press.

Heijnders, M., & Van Der Meij, S. (2006). The fight against stigma: An overview of stigma-reduction strategies and interventions. *Psychology, Health, & Medicine, 11*, 353–363.

King, M., Dinos, S., Shaw, J., Watson, R., Stevens, S., Passetti, F., . . . Serfaty, M. (2007). The stigma scale: Development of a standardized measure of the stigma of mental illness. *The British Journal of Psychiatry, 190*, 248–254. doi: 10.1192/bjp.bp.106.024638

Leary, M. R., & Schreindorfer, L. S. (1998). The stigmatization of HIV and AIDS: Rubbing salt in the wound. In V. J. Derlega & A. P. Barbee (Eds.), *HIV and social interaction* (pp. 12–29). Thousand Oaks, CA: Sage.

Lee, N. R., & Kotler, P. (2011). *Social marketing: Influencing behaviors for good* (4th ed.). Thousand Oaks, CA: Sage.

Link, B. G., & Phelan, J. C. (2001). Conceptualizing stigma. *Annual Review of Sociology, 27*, 363–385.

Martin, J. K., Pescosolido, B. A., & Tuch, S. A. (2000). Of fear and loathing: The role of 'disturbing behavior', labels, and causal attributions to shaping public attitudes toward people with mental illness. *Journal of Health and Social Behavior, 41*, 208–223.

Miller, W. R., & Rollnick, S. (1991). *Motivational interviewing: Preparing people to change addictive behavior*. New York, NY: Guilford Press.

National Alliance on Mental Illness (2010). Achieving the promise: Transforming mental health care in America. *President's New Freedom: Commission on Mental Health.* Retrieved from http://www.nami.org/Template.cfm?Section=New_Freedom_Commission&Template=/ContentManagement/ContentDisplay.cfm&ContentID=28340

National Alliance on Mental Illness (n.d.) *StigmaBusters-fight stigma.* Retrieved from http://www.nami.org/template.cfm?section=about_stigmabusters

National Alliance on Mental Illness (2009). *What is mental illness: Mental illness facts.* Retrieved from http://www.nami.org/Content/NavigationMenu/Inform_Yourself/About_Mental_Illness/About_Mental_Illness.htm

Philo, G., Secker, J., Platt, S., Henderson, L., McLaughlin, G., & Burnside, J. (1994). The impact of mass media on public images of mental illness: Media content and audience belief. *Health Education Journal, 53,* 271–281. doi: 10.1177/001789699405300305

Read, J., Haslam, N., Sayce, L., & Davies, E. (2006). Prejudice and schizophrenia: A review of the 'mental illness is an illness like any other' approach. *Acta Psychiatrica Scandinavica, 114,* 303–318. doi: 10.1111/j.1600-0447.2006.00824.x

Rosenfield, S. (1997). Labeling mental illness: The effects of services and perceived stigma on life satisfaction. *American Sociological Review, 62,* 660–672.

Steuber, K. R., & Solomon, D. H. (2011). Factors that predict married partners' disclosures about infertility to social network members. *Journal of Applied Communication Research, 39,* 250–270.

Stuart, H. (2008). Fighting the stigma caused by mental disorders: Past perspectives, present activities, and future directions. *World Psychiatry, 7,* 185–188.

Substance Abuse and Mental Health Services Administration. (2004). *Implementation Tips for Public Mental Health Authorities.* Retrieved from http://download.ncadi.samhsa.gov/ken/pdf/toolkits/family/10.FamPsy_Tips-Authority.pdf

Substance Abuse and Mental Health Services Administration. (2008). *Self-disclosure and its impact on individuals who receive mental health services.* Retrieved from http://store.samhsa.gov/product/Self-Disclosure-and-Its-Impact-on-Individuals-Who-Receive-Mental-Health-Services/SMA08-4337

Taylor, S. M., & Dear, M. J. (1981). Scaling community attitudes toward the mentally ill. *Schizophrenia Bulletin, 7,* 225–240.

Thornicroft, G. (2006). *Shunned: Discrimination against people with mental illness.* Oxford: Oxford University Press.

United States Department of Health and Human Services. (2011). *Healthy People 2020.* Atlanta, GA: CDC. Retrieved from http://www.healthypeople.gov/2020/default.aspx

Venetis, M. K., Greene, K., Checton, M. G., & Magsamen-Conrad, K. (under review). *Communication in the cancer-recovery continuum: Decision making in topic avoidance.*

Venetis, M. K., Greene, K., Magsamen-Conrad, K., Banerjee, S. C., Checton, M., & Bagdasarov, Z. (2012). "You can't tell anyone but ...": Exploring the use of privacy rules and revealing behaviors. *Communication Monographs, 79*, 344–365. doi:10.1080/03637751.2012.697628

Venetis, M. K., Magsamen-Conrad, K., Checton, M. G., & Greene, K. (in press). *Cancer communication and caregiver burden: An exploratory study.*

Wahl, O. F. (1992). Mass media images of mental illness: A review of the literature. *Journal of Community Psychology, 20*, 343–352. doi: 10.1002/1520-6629(199210)20:4<343::AID-JCOP2290200408>3.0.CO;2-2

Watson, A. C., & Corrigan, P. W. (2005). Challenging public stigma: A targeted approach. In P. W. Corrigan (Ed.), *On the stigma of mental illness: Practical strategies* (pp. 281–295). Washington, DC: American Psychological Association.

West, M. L., Yanos, P. T., Smith, S. M., Roe, D., & Lysaker, P. H. (2011). Prevalence of internalized stigma among persons with severe mental illness. *Stigma Research and Action, 1*, 3–10. doi: 10.5463/sra.vlil.9

World Health Organization. (2010). *Mental health and development: Targeting people with mental health conditions as a vulnerable group*. Retrieved from http://whqlibdoc.who.int/publications/2010/9789241563949_eng.pdf

Yamaguchi, S., Mino, Y., & Uddin, S. (2011). Strategies and future attempts to reduce stigmatization and increase awareness of mental health problems among young people: A narrative review of educational interventions. *Psychiatry and Clinical Neurosciences, 65*, 405–415. doi: 10.1111/j.1440-1819.2011.02239.x

Chapter 3:

"It happens to those people": Phenomenological study of HIV in the media

Malynnda A. Johnson
Carroll University

INTRODUCTION

Despite prevention and treatment advances made over the past 30 years, the HIV epidemic continues to thrive. Of those newly diagnosed, one in four will be between the ages of 13–24 (CDC, 2012). In addition, one estimate suggests that about 60% of all youth living with HIV do not know they are infected, are not getting treated, and can unknowingly pass the virus on to others (CDC, 2012). According to the American College Health Association (2012), when it comes to the use of preventative behaviors, fewer than 4% used a condom during the last oral encounter, 50% reported the use of condom during the last vaginal intercourse experience, and among those reporting anal sex, roughly 26% used a condom during the last occurrence. While many studies continue to find that young adults do have accurate knowledge about HIV and AIDS, this knowledge is not being translated into accurate estimates of risk (Ellen et al., 2002; Albert & Steinberg, 2011; Foster et al., 2011).

For many scholars it has become clear that many young adults have become complacent, not only in their behaviors, but also in their perceptions of risk (Cline & Johnson, 1992; Polacek et al., 2007; Vermund and Wilson, 2002). One possible explanation is that while prevention campaigns and safe sex education are provided worldwide, the manner through which HIV is framed in the media domestically may be undermining the education being offered by public health campaigns. Be it news reports of medical advances, the lack of HIV related deaths being reported, or the media's use of HIV narratives to create dramatic effect, it seems likely that consumers of modern day HIV frames will feel justified seeing HIV as less of a personal concern and more a concern for only a certain groups of people.

Given that that young adults more often than not learn about health issues through the observation of others (Dutta, 2004; Kaiser Family Foundation, 2006), health communication research should be looking not only at what perceptions of health issues are, but also look at where they might be coming from. One area scholars have begun looking at how health issues are presented using Entertainment Education (E-E) as a communication strategy to encourage behavioral and social change (Singhal & Rogers, 2004). Simply put, the goal of E-E is to increase awareness and knowledge, and it aims to positively influence attitudes and/or behaviors through the shows in which viewers are already invested (Kaiser Family Foundation, 2006; Singhal & Rogers, 1999; Singhal & Rogers, 2002). Over the years, there has been a number of studies of social and health issues in entertainment programming, and E-E has been found to significantly impact many health issues. One possible test might involve how young adults spend a great deal of time and educate themselves watching television, while applying theoretical frameworks such as Social Cognitive theory and Extended Elaboration Likelihood Model to the notion that television media's current frames HIV. Thus, the following chapter presents a mixed method approach examining and dissecting how HIV has been portrayed in prime time television shows and the impact these narratives have on viewers.

MEDIA AND ENTERTAINMENT EDUCATION

It has been said "television...now escorts children across the globe even before they have permission to cross the street" (Meyrowitz, 1985, p. 238). Applying decades of media effects research, scholars have found strong support for the use of media, specifically television media, as a mode for strategic communication. As a means of understanding where perceptions of illness could be stemming from, thorough examination of the frames used to talk about health topics in the media has been a common area of research. For instance, the means through which a health topic is framed has been found to hold the key in explaining why some messages have a greater impact on viewers. For example, media research has suggested that television viewers learn more from the media when they do not know much about the topic at hand (Dutta, 2004). Reese (2003) found that under heuristic conditions, viewers of health messages who have not personally experienced the topic at hand believe the myths provided by entertainment media as "secondhand reality" (p. 9). In other words, when it comes to a topic that one has not personally experienced, or known someone who has experienced, viewers are less likely to challenge the messages presented. As a result, passive learning can occur based on what is provided by television media. Additionally, research has postulated that viewers take more from shows in which they already like or watch on a regular basis (Sparks, 2010).

Given that research has found television media messages have a tremendous effect on both individuals and society as a whole, health promotion through the media has evolved into a thriving field for research and practice. In an attempt to capitalize on the potential impact mediated messages can have on viewers, numerous health messages have been created and strategically placed within television shows. Aiding in the examination of the use of television narratives as a means of disseminating health education, the following offers a brief overview of two significant theories used to examine media effects.

Social Cognitive Theory

To explain how behaviors are modified, one of the most commonly applied theories in the area of E-E has remained Bandura's (2001) social cognitive theory (SCT). Overall, the theory explains that cognitive factors, drawn from personal experiences, partly determine which environmental events will be observed as well as the meaning that individuals place upon them (Bandura, 2001). Ultimately these constructions serve as the motivations and rationalizations for final behavior outcomes.

By observing others who appear to be similar, viewers can learn vicariously by witnessing the interactions and consequences of those they observe (Bandura, 2001). Social models, such as those on television, are then thought to transmit "knowledge, values, cognitive skills, and new styles of behavior" to viewers (Bandura, 2004a, p. 78). Bandura argues that for the translation of health knowledge into effective preventative behaviors to occur, social and self-regulative skills and a sense of personal power to exercise control over sexual and drug activities must be present. As health topics continue to be present within meditated narratives, the promotion of behavioral change can be achieved by informing, enabling, motivating, and guiding the audience (Bandura, 2004b).

Extended Elaboration Likelihood Model

While it is common for SCT to be included in E-E studies, recent work on narrative persuasion in entertainment-education have also included the E-ELM (Slater, 2002b; Slater & Rouner, 2002). This model focuses its attention on the unique ability of E-E to influence beliefs, attitudes, and behavior by reducing viewers desire to argue with the messages presented (Slater & Rouner, 2002). Specifically, E-ELM posits that when viewers are engaged in a entertainment aspect of a television show they are less likely to be critical of the messages presented (Shrum, 2004). Moreover, the deeper the viewer is engaged in the medium the greater the influence these frames will have on beliefs, attitudes, and behaviors. One of the dominant components of this theory is the importance of one's identification with the characters.

Identification

Identification refers to the emotional and cognitive process of a viewer forgetting about his or her own reality and temporarily becoming the character, taking on the character's perspective (Cohen, 2001). During this process the viewer shares in the experience and imagines what it would be like to be the character. This imagining "replaces his or her personal identity and role as audience member with the identity and role of the character" (Cohen, 2001, p. 251). This process is thought to occur on four varying dimensions: empathic (shared feelings with the character), cognitive (sharing the character's perspective), motivational (internalizing the character's goals), and absorption (the loss of self-awareness during exposure) (Cohen, 2001).

Identification also occurs when an individual adopts the attitudes, values, or beliefs of another individual or group based on a "self-defining" relationship (Kelman, 1961). Thus, perceived similarities occur when an individual perceives that he or she is similar to a character. These similarities may refer to physical attributes, demographic variables, beliefs, personality, or values (Eyal & Rubin, 2003; Hoffner & Cantor, 1991). In effect, each of these areas of similarity aid in the connection a viewer may experience with a character, increasing the likelihood of a viewer to identify with and become involved with the show.

The study of identification as a process of social influence is essential given that people regularly identify with the characters they see on television and are often influenced by the messages with which they are presented (Hoffner & Buchanan, 2005). As such, identification can arguably be understood as a process of social change in which an individual who has established a relationship with a character on a show allows the character's attitudes, values, beliefs, and behavior to influence the viewer, resulting in the reinforcement of existing attitudes, values, beliefs, and behavior perceived to be similar to those of the persona or the adoption of new ones modeled by the character (Brown, 2011). Given that viewers regularly identify with at least one of the characters they see on television and that through observations many lessons about normative behavior are acquired, it becomes essential to examine how HIV is framed in popular media.

THE PRESENTATION OF HIV IN PRIME TIME

To understand how television media has framed HIV, one can began by critically watching any popular TV Show which incorporates HIV/AIDS Story lines. To do so this study began by looking at how HIV has been discussed in popular television shows. Based on Nielsen Ratings, ability to obtain episodes that focused on HIV, and a focus on HIV as drama and not as satire episodes of the following shows were included; *Brothers and Sisters, CSI-NY, Girlfriends, Grey's Anatomy, House, Law and Order SVU (Special Victims Unit), Private Practice, Nip/Tuck, Sex in the City*, and *Without a Trace*. By critically examining such narratives one can see how media is reflecting and shaping viewer's perceptions of HIV. The purpose of this narrative criticism should not to determine if the story was appropriately told, nor to simply count how often a topic is mentioned, but to examine the lessons presented and manner through which HIV is framed. By looking at the frames used within HIV narratives, we can begin to see how they function didactically, or serve as an educational texts. This initial phase of study specifically broke down each of the episodes by their basic narrative structures, including theme, character, and structure; the language within each narrative can be examined.

Theme

Often defined as recurring and unifying ideas or values within a message, themes can function as starting points for criticism. Presently two dominant themes can be found as frameworks for addressing HIV in prime time television. The first is the medicalization of HIV. Given that HIV is a health issue it is not difficult to for the viewer to accept lessons presented in shows such as *Grey's Anatomy*, or *Private Practice*. Such a narratives would seem commonplace; however the danger is in how HIV is discussed. For example, although the actors are only playing doctors, research has found that viewers often believe the information presented by actor/doctors in television shows (Treichler, 2006). Viewers see the behaviors these doctors engage and listen to the ways in which they talk about topics and as a result can form their perceptions based on these frames. Shows such as *Nip/Tuck*, *Grey's Anatomy*, *Private Practice*, and *House* all portray doctors casually sleeping with the other doctors. These sexual behaviors are rarely shown as being risky nor do the characters suffer any consequence for their actions.

An additional component to any medical show is the ability for medical professionals to be able to speak in accurate medical terms if they want to appear to be believable (Treichler, 2006). Further, doctors must also be mindful of how they trivialize the illnesses they discuss. For the majority of the medical shows examined, the manner in which the doctors discuss HIV provides a potential lesson that HIV is "not a big deal." In both *Grey's Anatomy* and *Nip/Tuck* a charter states, "HIV is the new diabetes," framing HIV as an illness that is inconsequential. These lines also frame HIV as a manageable illness, something you take a pill for and is "no big deal." Such representations risk obfuscating that HIV is a 100% preventable disease. None of the analyzed medical episodes, beyond the previously mentioned episode of *Grey's Anatomy*, included facts about HIV.

While testing for HIV should be a common practice for doctors given the CDC's 2006 call for testing, none of the medically focused episodes examined included a character being testing for HIV. When HIV testing was included, some level of medical influence, and therefore the possibility for facts about HIV to be discussed, was present. However, of the twelve shows only two included scenes where testing for HIV could be observed, those being *Brothers and Sisters* and *Sex in the City*. Both of these episodes spent time modeling the conversation medical staff would engage in by asking questions about behavior. In the case of *Brothers and Sisters*, the doctor specifically addressed common misperceptions such as knowing you do not have HIV by the lack of symptoms. The doctor explained, "If you're asking me if someone can be asymptomatic for decades, the answer is yes." Both *Brothers and Sisters* and *Sex in the City* included typical questions asked during the risk assessment portion of an HIV test, "How often are you using protection?," "How many partners have you had?," "Do you ever have unprotected sex?" These simple yet vital questions allow viewers to observe the types of questions they will face when choosing to test for HIV, and given the ease and sometimes humorous ways the characters answer these questions, a viewer may find the conversation less uncomfortable than originally anticipated.

The second theme for addressing HIV in the shows was the relational strategy. In these episodes the topic of HIV was a discussion between a character and a friend or partner. Here the viewer is allowed into the personal lives of the characters and given glimpses of the fears many might share when considering testing for HIV. For example, in *Sex in the City* and *Girlfriends* a current partner suggested the character take a test for HIV, and the episodes included detailed conversations about the when, why, and hows of HIV testing. In *Sex in the City* Samantha reports to her friends, "I just met this VERY hot guy and he won't sleep with me unless I have a test." Samantha follows her announcement by inquiring if any of her friends have taken such a test. Each of the women reported they have tested not once, but multiple times. However Samantha, the most promiscuous of the group, admits that she has never taken one for fear that she might have "it," referring to HIV. In response, her friends attempt to convince her that she doesn't have "it." The use of this theme is compounded with an additional theme of reassurance from friends. Stating that one "doesn't have it" was found in nearly every episode that focused on peers discussing the issue of testing for HIV. However, the question remains if this dialogue actually helps normalize HIV by helping the viewers overcome any of their own fears of testing.

Structure

To examine the structure of a narrative, one must look at how elements are working together to reveal the theme. Structure includes both the order and the unity of events or topics. At the most fundamental level, order can refer to having a clear beginning, middle, and end. However, in many dramatic shows these basic components are twisted and rearranged for dramatic effect. Most shows do tend to follow a week-to-week structural order allowing for new viewers to join in at any point. However, Sillar and Gronbeck (2001) argue that repeated formulaic order eliminates the potential for discovery. In other words, if the viewer is able to predict the ending, given the history with the show, then they may be less likely to completely engage and allow themselves to become involved. Therefore, if the structure used to present HIV is formulaic, it may eliminate the ability for audiences to make connections to their own lives.

One of the dominant structures found within the episodes centered on a redemptive structure. In the episodes of *Nip/Tuck*, *Girlfriends*, *Sex in the City* the main character is confronted with the need to test for HIV. This confrontation typically occurred when a past lover returned announcing that they have HIV. These secondary characters are frequently only included in one or two shows and used simply to offer localized complication and drama. As a result, the main character is overwhelmed with "what ifs" and a fear that HIV will be the punishment for past behaviors. One example of this is when the character Toni states, "I'm telling you Maya, getting the AIDS… it's going to be my punishment" (*Girlfriends*). Ultimately however, each of the charters are redeemed by a negative HIV test and order is returned. By utilizing such a structure, risky behavior is represented as inconsequential. As a result, the viewer, especially if identifying with the character and situations, may feel less vulnerable to such consequences and therefore may not feel the need for HIV testing.

This redemptive structure appeared in a number of shows all sharing a happily ending. Some shows, however, utilized a different structure. One show that offered a twist to the redemptive structure was *Brothers and Sisters*. In this show Saul, a beloved family friend, discovers on Facebook that a past partner is HIV positive. Filled with concern, he goes in for an HIV test and discovers he is HIV positive. Strikingly, this was the only show to included a homosexual man seeking testing, and in the end Saul is the only character to receive a positive test. While the plot shift may highlight potential consequences of risky sexual behavior, the risk is that audiences do not identify with Saul. Without character identification, Saul may function as representative of the sexually promiscuous homosexual man, reifying the punishment plot while obfuscating the risk of many young viewers.

Significantly tied to the evaluation of structure and order is the unity within a theme. Here one examines how well the artifact holds together so that the observer is able to understand the theme (Sillars & Gronbeck, 2001). For almost all of the shows, this is not a point for concern, given that most shows keep themes packaged neatly in one-episode bundles. However, connections between characters and the context of particular conversations interwoven between shows might impact a new viewer's understanding and connection with the theme.

Character

Although some may argue the structure is the most important (Benoit, 2000), many genre critics find the characters of a narrative play a vital role in the development of a connection between the audience and the theme. Speaking to this directly, Burke (1950) argues that often for persuasion to occur identification must also take place. Viewers are likely to be persuaded if they feel they share similar interests with a character. Therefore, if the goal is to teach the audience about their risk for HIV, the characters must be presented in a manner that encourages such identification. If this identification does not occur, Burke warns that distancing and division will be likely. In cases where identification does not occur, the persuasion or lesson may be lost, given the audience's desire to disconnect from the charters.

To increase the likelihood of connection between viewers and characters, each character should play a specific role and be both relatable and believable to the viewers. When examining the characters portrayed within a show discussing HIV, the character becomes increasingly important given the stigma and numerous stereotypes already attached to those living with HIV. In the past many shows portrayed HIV patients as being white homosexual males who would often be gaunt, sickly, and covered in lesions (an example of this representation can be seen in an episode of *House*). However, this type of representation is problematic because anyone can become infected with HIV, and someone may be infected with HIV but not have any apparent symptoms.

If television shows were to represent HIV using a variety of backgrounds and characteristics, viewers may be better able to see how HIV could affect them. Many stereotypes pervade portrayals of AIDS-positive characters: having used intravenous drugs, homosexuals, and a few who have had numerous partners or met people online for anonymous sex. Fortunately, a wide variety of bodies where used across the shows including men, women, heterosexuals, homosexuals, Caucasians, African Americans, young people, and people in their sixties. Further, a few specific characters have helped breakdown the misconception of who is a risk. *Grey's Anatomy*, *Private Practice*, and *Without a Trace* included young Caucasian heterosexual women, *Law and Order* as well as *Private Practice* focused attention on young heterosexuals, and *Girlfriends* included a married African-American woman. This wide range of backgrounds, races, and experiences could help the viewer to identify with the character while also learning that HIV is not something that affects only one group.

The physical appearance of sickness is also an important factor in representation of character. In fact, only one character portrayed as having the illness was shown gaunt and sick. In this case, the character on *House* was also suffering from additional illness. Beyond this episode of *House*, each of the remaining ten HIV positive characters appeared healthy looking. All were visibly upset by their conditions. However, given the contexts of how they were brought in each scene, it would be surprising for them not to be upset. Four of the characters were dealing with medical issues such as seeking abortions, being the only donor match for a sibling, pregnancy, as well as a mystery illness. Others were shown dealing with everyday issues such as helping friends understand the illness and how to handle the issue of having a friend with HIV. Other depictions included the typical situation of having to disclose to previous partners the need for testing, as well as the less common issue of a teen finding out for the first time that he has HIV or characters having to go to court to help prosecute someone for knowingly infecting others with HIV.

Although a diverse cast of characters is found in the present shows, significant holes also existed. Foremost is the lack of homosexual African American men and Latinos, regardless of sexual orientation. The absence of these populations not only inaccurately portrays the issue, but also neglects to offer a character for viewers to connection to while modeling of how these populations could approach topics of HIV. According to the CDC (2009), among men who had been diagnosed with HIV or AIDS who had become infected through male-to-male sexual contact, 44% were black/African American, 21% were Hispanic/Latino and 35% were white. Among women diagnosed with HIV or AIDS who had become infected through heterosexual contact, 64% were black/African American, 15% were Hispanic/Latina and 21% were white (CDC, 2009). By observing the characters shown on television viewers, may be misled to believe that Latinos and African American men have nothing to worry about. Yet, of even greater concern are the charters shown receiving a positive HIV test.

While many of these shows do a considerable job of highlighting the vast array of people living with the illness, they do the viewer a disservice by including only one person testing positive. Five characters implied or were shown being tested for HIV. A variety of ages, backgrounds, races, as well as economic standings were included, however only one tested positive. *Brothers and Sisters* was the only show to include a positive test. While the character did offer education that one can be asymptomatic for decades, the fact that the only character to receive a positive test was also a white homosexual could perpetuate the idea that in the end it is still a "gay disease."

THE DIDACTIC DICHOTOMY OF HIV NARRATIVES

Through the analysis of the episodes, it became apparent that HIV was represented within a very rigid dichotomy: normalized versus stigmatized. On one hand, narratives highlight various groups talking about the issue of HIV over coffee or with friends and family. Using phrases such as "It's normal," "Everyone should be tested," "I test all the time," and "It's like spring cleaning," frames the topic of testing for HIV as something everyone does. As a result viewers are able to witness that conversations about sexually related topics are not taboo or difficult to discuss.

Yet, based on the conventions represented within television shows, the normalcy of talking about testing is not as common for African American and Latino men (both straight or gay). Overwhelmingly these populations were left out of the discussion. Latino men may be modeled in telenovelas; however these were not included in the present analysis. These are two populations have been found as being at great risk for contracting HIV; however their absence on television shows may perpetuate the internalized discrimination felt and fear that they are not normal and have no voice.

Many of the medical shows also normalize the issue, stating that "HIV is the new diabetes," "It's better to have AIDS than die of kidney failure," and "We have medication now, HIV is not a big deal." Many similar frames were found in these shows, each focusing on the medial advancements of the treatment. This kind of framing may be helpful in breaking down the fear that HIV is a death sentence. However, this representation can also make people think that they don't need to be cautious, or worse, feel that given that HIV is insignificant and there is no need for testing.

On the other end of the chasm, HIV is discussed as a punishment for poor choices, an illness only some people get, and something to be feared; therefore stigmatizing those who have HIV. A number of characters who tested for HIV or talked about testing used language framing HIV as a punishment: "Maya I am really scared. I haven't always practiced safe sex. I haven't always walked with Jesus. I'm telling you Maya, getting the AIDS…it's going to be my punishment" (*Girlfriends*). For Christian in the show *Nip/Tuck*, the threat of punishment was not his own rumination, but one of the women who may have given it to him. In the scene, Gina tells Christian that she is positive, and given the number of partners he has had, she was certain his fate would be the same. Fearing HIV would be his punishment for poor choices, he takes a test.

While many characters, like Christian, took HIV tests in the end, only one individual found out that he was positive, whereas the others were offered a chance for redemption. Unfortunately, instead of presenting HIV as a non-discriminating illness, the fact that the only character to receive a positive outcome was gay may perpetuate the idea that only this population is affected. All the other characters, especially the young heterosexual individuals, were shown receiving a negative test result and, therefore, saved from the punishment they felt they had coming.

Given the way HIV is discussed, many viewers that do identify with the characters shown with the illness may be found to have an increased sense of internalized stigma, fearing that those around them will think they are positive or will be punished with it. Other viewers may also learn that HIV is a punishment for wrong doings, which may manifest in the continued stigmatization of certain lifestyles and those living with HIV. Finally, of most importance for the present study, the manner through which HIV has been presented may, in fact, teach young viewers that they do not have to be concerned about their own risk, given the ages, backgrounds, and sexual orientations of the characters shown impacted by HIV.

Overall, TV shows have chosen to be strategic in their inclusion of HIV information, working with outside organizations such as the Kaiser Family Foundation, to offer support to the idea that mediated narratives can be effective in disseminating prevention messages. However, many of the shows analyzed for this phase of study were not working with an outside organization and may not have considered the implications of including HIV plot line. Nonetheless, by examining these narratives, it becomes evident that regardless of intent, many lessons could be learned from these shows. While it is clear that HIV is presented in a manner that can enabled viewers to connect with the narratives, further research is need to determine if that connection is made.

SHIFTING FROM "FANTASY" TO PHENOMENON

To understand if the HIV lessons portrayed in these popular narratives are having an impact on perceptions of risk for HIV, this study conducted a secondary study by employing both qualitative and quantitative methods. Particularly this phase of study employed a phenomenological approach, which sought out the perceptions of young adults concerning their own risk for HIV as a means of offering both the perceptions of those interviewed as well as a wider understanding of college student's knowledge and general perceptions of HIV. Potter (1996) explains that by incorporating both qualitative and quantitative methods, researchers are able to strengthen their argument by building in various dimensions. This approach, commonly referred to as triangulation, is seen as a method of gaining greater understanding of phenomenon (Fontana & Frey, 2000). For the present study, quantitative methods were used to gain demographic information, knowledge of HIV, perceptions of ability and comfort in using preventative methods, such as condoms, as well as recall of seeing shows that included a theme of HIV. Based on overall knowledge of HIV and their reporting of having seen the shows examined in the first phase of study 25 participants we selected and interviewed. The following section highlights what was found through this interview process.

PERCEPTIONS OF HIV

With research maintaining that young adult populations do not personally connect with HIV, the first research question asked was what college students' perceptions are, in terms of risk for HIV. What was identified is that overwhelmingly participants felt HIV is not framed by the media as a problem in the United States, is a topic that is to taboo to discuss, and that while certain groups are at risk, college students do not consider their actions risky.

General Perceptions of Risk for HIV

The college students interviewed for this study shared an accurate understanding of what would put someone at risk for HIV. Therefore, it was not surprising that when asked to define risk for HIV, many participants focused on the transfer of fluids. For example Kayla stated "Anyone who is sexually active. Anyone who is a drug user and shares needles. Anyone who gets any kind of blood. Or a mother who doesn't know and has a child." Kathryn also focused on the fluid aspect of risk, "Any kind of fluid contact. Blood, semen, but not saliva." Going a bit further in depth, Heather noted "Any types of bodily fluid that you would come into contact from another person. I know you can't get it from saliva, but semen, vaginal fluids, blood, any contact or during other outbreaks of other STDS."

Many others found risk to be less technical, and felt risk for HIV was as simple as having unprotected sex, "Risk is anything unprotected. Not thinking before you act is a risk," Holly explained. Similarly, Heather indicated that one must also be smart about their behaviors, "I think you just have to be smart about what you are doing and who are you with." Although young adults knowledge scores have been found to be consistently high the theme of "needing to be smart" about HIV and particularly who you are with, remained a common theme when asked about what would put someone at risk for HIV. When asked who would be at risk for HIV, Conrad continued "People without knowledge to a point. Like any other disease, it's easy to pick up if you don't know how to protect yourself." The issue is however that based on their knowledge scores college students are "smart" in terms of knowing about HIV and should know better. Yet many remain unable to use put this knowledge into action.

Perceptions of Who is at Risk for HIV

In general, participants had two categories for who would be at risk for HIV. The first included stereotypes including drug users, homosexual men, and prostitutes. The second being the general perception that everyone is at risk.

Stereotypical perceptions. Given that young adults are noted for not being able to identify their own risk or HIV and STDs, participants were asked to describe who they considered being the most likely to contract HIV. While a number of types of people were mentioned, strikingly most perceptions focused on popular stereotypes. As Conrad identified "I think it is just because that is how it has been portrayed in the media. Early on it was always seen with homosexuals. I think it's not so much the case for younger generations but more so the older ones." Ashley also commented on how some groups, such as homosexuals, and others were at an increased risk:

> *I feel like gay people are the most at risk. I mean thinking about the epidemic it has greatly affected them. Therefore, that is one community that has really been affected. The other being Africa. So yeah those to groups need to worry.*

When Kayla was asked who was at risk for HIV she remarked, "Any homosexual dude, and pretty much all African Americans in general."

Finally, while Sophie did draw attention to another common group, drug users, she was the first and only participant to identify social economic status and education as determinants:

> *I guess that is a tough one. I do not want to say drug users. I guess anyone who has multiple partners. But like a group specific I would say low-income areas. Going back to the fact that maybe they do not have the money to buy new drug equipment. Or have the education, or the money, or funding to get birth control or condoms and stuff like that. They would be the most at risk.*

Statements such as these draw clear attention to the fact that HIV is not discussed in a manner that teaches viewers the facts about HIV. It may be understood that HIV does not pick and choose whom it infects, but for some of the participants the impression remains that only some groups are at risk.

Everyone, but me. The second population participants identified remained far broader; this being anyone, as well as anyone who has unprotected sex. While only mentioned by two participants, the idea that "everyone" is at risk was presented. Far more common however what the notion that anyone having unsafe sex would be at risk. Holly noted, "Risk is anything unprotected. So if you have unsafe sex you are at risk. It's pretty simple." Specifically taking note of what unsafe sex meant, Kathryn stated "Anyone who doesn't use condoms is having unsafe sex." Yet while many participants agreed that everyone engaging in unprotected sex could be at risk, the fact remained that many were unable, or unwilling, to see themselves as someone at risk.

When asked if they felt they were at risk only three felt they "might be." The remainder finding comfort in either being married, no longer having sex, or as Anna identified have a partner they "know and can trust." Feeling that they "know" their partners not only decreases the need to discuss topics such as STDs and HIV.

HIV is Too Taboo

Speaking to why HIV is not shown as a problem in the United States, Audrey major differences differences between the United States and her home country of Brazil. She explained that in her country sex messages are "everywhere "and talking about sex was always a natural thing, "Like we talk about safe sex like people talk here about getting a flu shot." Yet nearly all the other participants specifically noted that in the United States talking about safe sex has always been a "taboo" topic. Before HIV, and topics surrounding the idea of safe sex, can be health topics young people can actively think about, the frame surrounding them must be challenged.

Participants felt that, in general, talking about HIV or STDs, "makes people uncomfortable." Nearly all participants explained that the reason people and the media do not talk about HIV is because it's a taboo topic. Dorothy explained, "It's one of those taboo things." Similarly Sophie mentioned, "It's too taboo and will make people feel uncomfortable." Kristina added, "It's difficult. It is just not something you want to talk about. You do not want to talk about death or body issues. Dying. That is a taboo topic and HIV causes death." Sex has always been a topic that parents, teachers, and pastors alike have feared talking about. As a result this fear may be passed on to their children, who they believe are not engaging in the behaviors that are difficult to discuss.

Yet while many find that HIV is a taboo topic, many commented that other sexual topics are covered at great length. Ali explains "I think people are draw more to the teen pregnancy topics. So HIV just gets pushed to the way side." Furthering this idea Austin notes "I think it is just become a common thing," indicating that maybe HIV does not need to be discussed given that "everyone knows about it, so why focus on it." Although teen pregnancy is the result of unprotected sex, the "sexiness" of it has allowed for multiple shows and movies to attract a great deal of attention. However this has never been the case for HIV or STDs.

VIEWER IDENTIFICATION WITH CHARACTERS

Once an individual perceives similarities with HIV-positive individuals, he or she is increasingly more likely to personalize their own risk of HIV (Crowell & Emmers-Sommer, 2000). Therefore in order for viewers to learn from television narratives they must be able to connect with characters and see themselves within the shows. Unfortunately, for many of the participants the portrayal of HIV was either found to be unrealistic or appeared to only focus on stereotypical groups.

An Unrealistic Portrayal of HIV

As postulated by Cohen (2001), a viewer's identification to a character relies on both emotional and cognitive processes in which the viewer forgets about his or her own reality. However one problem noted by participants was that in general, fictional shows are seen as over dramatizations and therefore regardless of the topic may be perceived as being less realistic.

Ben states:

> *No (they are not realistic). TV never shows the consequences. They make light of it or use it to get your attention and then move on. You know, they show someone getting pregnant or contract something and it's a joke. They never tell the story of the person who didn't have safe sex and got something. It's always a joke or everything ends up working out. But that is not reality. So no, they do not express, portray, or show consequences in a realistic way.*

Another issue participants mentioned was the proliferation for sex to be used to sell, and that focusing on consequences would not be perceived as sexy enough to retain viewers. Ginger also addressed the concern that shows she has seen have neglected to show how HIV could actually impact one's life or who was at risk for HIV:

> *I think they need to cut out the fluff. Like really show you how terrible life can get or how it affects your life. Also if they that it was possible for anybody to get it if you're not having safe sex or using condoms or doing what you are supposed to be doing to prevent it. I feel like they just make it seem like only some people can get it. And it was a lot more like I feel I was more aware of it when it seemed like anyone could get it and not just these people. And I guess that it seems like it is only some people get it which I do not know.*

By showing young heterosexual adults engaged in risky behavior without consequences of STDs or HIV also perpetuates normative behavior. Young adults are often found to feel that they are not at risk for anything and if shows are going to offer the social model of the consequence of unsafe sexual behavior than greater attention will need to be pain to who is shown being subject to the consequence.

With this in mind, it should be noted that television has long been criticized for portraying unrealistic depictions of health-risk behaviors (Ward, 2002). As a result there is the potential for these depictions to be accepted as the norm, thus influencing viewers' perceptions and behaviors. Within the current study the majority of participants were only able to recall HIV positive characters who were drug users, homosexuals, or dying. Scott comments, "I feel like they need to do a better job of not just portraying some demographics. Not only showing gays but also straight people."

WHAT DOES THIS ALL MEAN?

The aim of this chapter is to supplement the current knowledge and understanding of how television narratives about HIV impede the ability for college students to accurately perceive their risk. In doing so, such studies extend the conversation of media effects by illuminating ways in which observational learning may be dependent upon a viewers' identification with the show's characters. Relying upon rhetorical analysis, this study not only identified how HIV was presented, but it also dissected the content, characters, and situations used to frame the topic of HIV. As a result, valuable dichotomies in which this illness is socially constructed were revealed.

Overall what this study found was that although the rhetorical analysis indicated two primary didactic narratives, normal and stigmatized, only the stigmatized narratives are reflected in the perceptions of college students. Results of this study indicate that identification with mediated HIV narratives impact viewers perceptions of risk and behavior. Unfortunately, for college students, the lesson learned from these narratives was that only certain groups are affected by HIV, and they are not one of those groups. Ultimately, while it is clear entertainment education can be an effective tool for educating viewers about health topics, a number of challenges for using television as a tool for modifying the perceptions of risk for HIV remain.

CHALLENGES TO ENTERTAINMENT EDUCATION

It can be argued that by using a narrative structure, like those in a television show, messages may be less likely challenged or resisted if the viewer is under the impression the goal is to entertain. In fact, research has shown that the less overtly persuasive a message is perceived to be, the more accepting receivers are to the influence (McGrane, Toth, & Alley, 1990; Weinstein, Grubb, & Vautier, 1986). With this in mind, E-E programing, when used strategically, can offer a mode through which informative and persuasive health messages can be hidden under the guise of entertainment and drama. The concern remains that when shows include health topics without strategically embedding accurate information, viewers may absorb inaccurate messages and lessons. As a result, shows incorporating health messages for the sake of drama risk unintentionally creating or reinforcing misperceptions, stereotypes, and stigma. For the present study this occurred by miseducating viewers about the consequences of risky behaviors and perpetuating stereotypes. Ultimately, these shows missed the opportunity to show HIV in a realistic and relatable manner as well as the chance to breakdown one of the biggest barriers to HIV prevention, the ability to talk opening about sexual health.

Shifting from Unrealistic fictions to reality TV

Many of the participants of this study felt that the only way to end the stigma related to HIV as well as the perception that only certain groups are at risk for HIV is for the discourse surround HIV and safe sex to become a normal part of society. They noted that often times the way HIV is presented in the shows is in medical dramas where the patient is sick and dying. However they know that this is not the case for all people who have HIV and many remarked that they wished television shows would do a better job of accurately depicting the everyday life of someone living with HIV. In doing so, the viewers would learn not only that someone living with HIV is just like them but also it could help breakdown the stigma that those with HIV are less than human.

One of the most interesting and consistent points drawn out by participants was that they nearly all agreed that one of the fastest ways to gain the attention of young adults is to included "real" people living with HIV into the shows they watched. Suggestions for characters on show like *Jersey Shore* or *Real World* to at the very least talk about testing for HIV or using condoms were specially noted. Participants argue that condoms would not have to be shown being used, but may be mentioned or shown on a table. By simply implying they would be used might help to increase the perception that this is a normal behavior. Additionally participants felt that if more real people, especially young people, were shown living with HIV then viewers would be better able to connect to the characters.

Sex is a Taboo Topic

Regardless of how realistic a show is, or how similar a viewer is to the character one fact remains, talking about HIV and STDs is perceived as a taboo topic. Scholars would agree that sex is a personally and socially sensitive topic (Ingold, 2010). A topic, Ingold argues, that society has established norms about what is appropriate and moral regarding sex. While television narratives have come a long way in terms of talking about sex, shifting from showing married couples sleeping in separate beds, to near strangers or coworkers finding the nearest coatroom for a "quickie," many of the participants pointed out talking about HIV or condoms remains a taboo topic. As a result, the goal of showing HIV as normative doesn't resonate with young populations. Until HIV and other sexually related topics are not seen as taboo and difficult topics to talk about with peers, partners, as well as doctors then it seems likely that no amount of HIV narratives within television shows will ever overcome the perception that sex is not discussed.

REFERENCES

Albert, D., & Steinberg, L. (2011). Judgment and decision making in adolescence. *Journal of Research on Adolescence, 21*, 211–224.

Baitz, J.R. (Writer), & Olin, K. (Director). (May 16th, 2010). On the road again. [Television series episode]. In G. Berlanti. (Producer), *Brothers and Sisters*. Network: ABC.

Bandura, A. (2001). Social cognitive theory of mass communication. *Media Psychology, 3*(3), 265–299.

Bandura, A. (2004a). Health promotion by social cognitive means. *Health Education & Behavior, 31*,143–164.

Bandura, A. (2004b). Social cognitive theory for personal and social change by enabling media. In A. Singhal, M.J. Cody, E.M. Rogers, & M. Sabido (Eds.), *Entertainment-education and social change: History, research, and practice* (pp. 75–96). Mahwah, NJ: Lawrence Erlbaum.

Brown, W.J., (2011). Assessing processes of relational involvement with media personas: Transportation, parasocial interaction, identification and worship. Paper presented to the National Communication Association, November 16–20, 2011, New Orleans.

Brown, J. D., L'Engle, K. L., Pardun, C. J., Guo, G., Kenneavy, K., & Jackson, C. (2006). Sexy media matter: Exposure to sexual content in music, movies, television, and magazines predicts black and white adolescents' sexual behavior. *Pediatrics, 117*(4), 1018–1027. doi: 10.1542/peds.2005–1406

Burke, K. (1950). *"The range of rhetoric." A rhetoric of motives.* U of California (pp. 3–46).

Centers for Disease Control and Prevention (2009). HIV/AIDS Surveillance Report 2007, (Vol. 19).

Centers for Disease Control and Prevention (2012). Diagnoses of HIV infection and AIDS in the United States and dependent areas, 2011 HIV in the United States: At a glance

Cline, R. W., & Johnson, S. J. (1992). Mosquitoes, doorknobs, and sneezing: Relationships between homophobia and AIDS mythology among college students. *Health Communication*, *4*, 273–289.

Cohen, J. (2001). Defining identification: A theoretical look at the identification of audiences with media characters. *Mass Communication & Society*, *2001*, 245–264.

Crowell, T. and Emmers-Somer, T. (2000). Examining condom use self-efficacy and coping in sexual situations. *Communication Research Reports*, *17*, 101–202.

Dutta-Bergman, M. J. (2004). Primary sources of health information: Comparisons in the domain of health attitudes, health cognitions, and health behaviors. *Health Communication*, *16*(3), 273–288.

Ellen JM, Adler NE, Gurvey JE, et al. (2002). Adolescent condom use and perceptions of risk for sexually transmitted diseases. *Journal of Students and Alcohol*, *29*: 756–62.

Eyal, K. (2010). The role of television characters in explaining audience sexuality. Conference Papers—International Communication Association, 1.

Eyal, K., & Rubin, A. M. (2003). Viewer aggression and homophily, identification, and parasocial relationships with television characters. *Journal of Broadcasting & Electronic Media*, *47*, 77–98.

Eyal, K., & Kunkel, D. (2008). The effects of television drama shows on emerging adults' sexual attitudes and moral judgments. *Journal of Broadcasting & Electronic Media*, *52*, 161–181.

Fisher, D. A., Hill, D. L., Grube, J. W., Bersamin, M. M., Walker, S., Gruber, E. L. (2009). Televised sexual content and parental mediation: Influences on adolescent sexuality. *Media Psychol. 12* (2), 121–147.

Foster, D. G., Higgins, J. A., Biggs, M. A., McCain, C., Holtby, S., & Brindis, C. D. (2011). Willingness to have unprotected sex. *Journal of Sex Research*, *49*, 61–68.

Hennessy, M., Bleakley, A., Fishbein, M., & Jordan, A. (2008). Validating an index of adolescent sexual behavior using psychosocial theory and social trait correlates. *AIDS and Behavior*, *12*, 321–331.

Hoffner, C., & Buchanan, M. (2005). Young adults wishful identification with television characters: The role of perceived similarity and character attributes. *Media Psychology*, *7*(4), 325–351.

Hoffner, C., & Cantor, J. (1991). Perceiving and responding to mass media characters. In J. Bryant & D. Zillmann (Eds.), *Responding to the screen: Reception and reaction processes* (pp. 63–101). Hillsdale, NJ: Lawrence Erlbaum.

Kaiser Family Foundation, Survey of Americans on HIV/AIDS, Conducted March 24–April 18 2006.

Kaiser Family Foundation, 2009 Survey of Americans on HIV/AIDS—Summary of Findings, Conducted April 2009.

Kopfman, J. E., & Smith, S. W. (1996). Understanding the audiences of a health communication campaign: A discriminant analysis of potential organ donors based on intent to donate. *Journal of Applied Communication*, *24*, 22–49.

Kunkel, D., Cope, K., & Colvin, C. (1996). *Sexual messages on family hour television: Content and context.* Menlo Park, CA: Kaiser Family Foundation.

Kunkel, D., Eyal, K., Finnerty, K., Biely, E., & Donnerstein, E. (2005). *Sex on TV4.* Menlo Park, CA: Kaiser Family Foundation.

Marburger, K. (Writer), & Garretson, K. (Director). (March 17th, 2003). The Pact. [Television series episode]. In D. Dugan. (Producer), *Girlfriends.* Network: CBS.

McGrane, W. L., Toth, F. J., & Alley, E. B. (1990). The use of interactive media for HIV/AIDS prevention in the military community. *Military Medicine*, *155*, 235–240.

Meyrowitz, J. (1985). *No sense of place.* New York, Oxford University Press.

Murphy, R. (Director), (June 22, 2004). Erica Noughton. [Television series episode]. In M. Robin. (Producer), *Nip/Tuck.* Network: FX.

Polacek, G., Hicks, J., & Oswalt, S. (2007). 20 years later and still at risk: college students' knowledge, attitudes, and behaviors about HIV/AIDS. *Journal of Hispanic Higher Education*, *6*, 73–88.

Reese, S. D. (2003). Framing public life: A bridging model for media research. In S. D. Reese, O. H. Gandy, & A. E. Grant (Eds.), *Framing public life* (pp. 7–32). Mahwah, NJ: Lawrence Erlbaum Associates, Inc.

Rhimes, S. (Writer), & Tinker, M. (Director), (May 1st, 2008). Piece of My Heart. [Television series episode]. In D. Dugan. (Producer), *Grey's Anatomy.* Network: ABC.

Rhimes, S. (Writer), & Tinker, M. (Director), (October 1st, 2008). A Family Thing. [Television series episode]. In D. Dugan. (Producer), *Private Practice.* Network: ABC.

Rhimes, S. (Writer), & Corn, R. (Director), (October 15th, 2009). Right Here, Right Now. [Television series episode]. In D. Dugan. (Producer), *Private Practice.* Network: ABC.

Rhimes, S. (Writer), & Corn, R. (Director), (February 18th, 2010). The Time Warp. [Television series episode]. In D. Dugan. (Producer), *Grey's Anatomy.* Network: ABC.

Rideout, V. (2008). Television as a health educator: A case study of Grey's Anatomy. Menlo Park, CA: Kaiser Family Foundation.

Shore, D. (Writer), & Muzio, G. (Director), (November 22nd, 2005). Hunting. [Television series episode]. In J. Bicks. (Producer), *House M.D.* Network: FOX.

Shrum, L. J. (Ed.). (2004). *The psychology of entertainment media: Blurring the lines between entertainment and persuasion*. Mahwah, NJ: Lawrence Erlbaum.

Sillar, M.O., & Gronbeck, B.E., (2001). *Communication criticism: Rhetoric, social codes, culture studies*. Prospect Heights, IL: Waveland Press.

Singhal, A., & Rogers. E. M. (1999). Entertainment-education: A communication strategy for social change. Mahwah, NJ: Lawrence Erlbaum Associates.

Singhal, A., & Rogers, E. M. (2002). A theoretical agenda for entertainment-education. *Communication Theory, 12*, 117–135.

Slater, M.D. & Rouner, D. (2002). Entertainment-education and elaboration likelihood: Understanding the processing of narrative persuasion. *Communication Theory, 12*, 173–191.

Sparks, G.G. (2009). *Media effects research: A basic overview.* (3rd Ed.) Belmont, CA: Wadsworth Publishing.

Treichler, P.A. (2006). *How to have theory in an epidemic: Cultural chronicles of AIDS*. London. Duke University Press.

Ward, L. M., & Rivadeneyra, R. (1999). Contributions of entertainment television to adolescents' sexual attitudes and expectations: The role of viewing amount versus viewer involvement. *Journal of Sex Research, 36*, 237–249.

Weinstein, N. D., Grubb, P. D., & Vautier, J. S. (1986). Increasing automobile seat belt use: An intervention emphasizing risk susceptibility. *Journal of Applied Psychology, 71*, 285–290.

Vermund, S.H., Wilson, C.M., (2002). Barriers to HIV testing—where next? Lancet, *360*, 1186–1187.

Chapter 4:

Styles and strategies: A case study of the Skin Cancer Specialty Clinic

Michael H. Eaves
Valdosta State University

The photos in this chapter appear in Dermatology Associates, a skin cancer medical office in Tallahassee, Florida. Dr. Armand B. Cognetta is the chief medical partner at that office. The author would like to thank Cognetta for his valuable interview and revision of an earlier draft of this chapter.

INTRODUCTION

One recent report suggests that skin cancer is the number one cancer in the United States, with about 700,000 cases per year (MSNBC, 2013). With skin cancer being at epidemic levels, health communication scholars should closely examine the strategies that physicians are using in this environment.

In this essay, I plan to examine communication strategies used in skin cancer management. As a theoretical overlay, I will use the taxonomy outlined in Leathers and Eaves (2008) when they state that the five major communication strategies used in the medical field between physician and patient include: 1) exchange of emotions, 2) meta-communication, 3) self-concept protection, 4) impression management, and 5) reassurance.

Exchange of Emotions

Skin cancer medical facilities have to delicately communicate strong emotions to their patients, especially when a skin cancer has to be treated or re-treated and involves additional surgery, or in the case of newly diagnosed malignant melanoma. Arguably, the exchange of emotions is one of, if not the most important of, communication functions between physicians and patients (Leathers & Eaves, 2008).

The exchange is never more important than when the physician must deliver bad news to the patient. Patients report a variety of emotions when dealt bad news about their cancer status. These emotions range from fright, shock, disbelief, acceptance, sadness, or outright indifference, with the predominant emotions being fright and shock (Lee, Back, Block, & Stewart, 2002). For melanoma in particular, the cancer may not be just at the location of the primary lesion, but may have metastasized and additional tests and surgery, chemotherapy or immune therapy may be necessary (Cognetta, 2013). This series of medical events require sensitive communication of care with the patient and/or family involved.

The ability of a physician or physician staff to effectively communicate bad news about cancer with their patients is noteworthy. A physician must be able to control his or her own emotional level in order to deliver these negative narratives to their patients (Berry, 2006; Kreps, 2003). The ability to encode and decode proper nonverbal messages with their patients is paramount for the communicative interaction to go well. Some scholars have referred to this process as nonverbal echo, or the ability of someone to mirror his or her nonverbal signals to better relate or strike a better rapport with the other (Leathers & Eaves, 2008). Apparently, most physicians do a rather positive job of relating bad news, but patients have reported that their needs are not always met in the discussion of bad news (Lee, Back, Block, & Stewart, 2002). Similarly, for ventilated patients in particular, they report that their medical needs are often not met and incomplete communication often leads to misunderstandings (Carroll, 2004).

One scenario for poor communication of emotions in the medical context appears to be patient-centeredness. Indeed, research suggests that the physician's ability to use a patient-centered strategy is more like to have favorable outcomes including patients following medical recommendations. In fact, one study found that a patient's quality of life is connected to the doctor's stress or anger levels (Ong, Visser, Lammes, & de Haes, 2000). For example, if the doctor was able to control his or her stress or anger levels, patients reported higher levels of satisfaction and quality of life.

Some of the more significant findings of the Ong et al. (2000) study were that patients responded more favorably to positive physician cues such as those communicating interest, engagement, friendliness, and warmth. Furthermore, an absence of the following physician negative emotions in care seemed to also help. Those negative behaviors were anger, irritation, anxiety, and nervousness. While every doctor is different, striking a balance between these two extreme polarized behaviors is important for rapport in maintaining and strengthening the physician-patient interaction.

While anecdotal, I can recall being treated recently for a yearly checkup. During that office visit, my attending physician exaggerated the positives and deemphasized the negatives, thus helping to ease my anxiety and stress in the interaction. As a result, he was calmer, and was able to communicate with me in a warm, yet professional manner.

Recognizing patients' emotions and facial displays of such cognitive states may be more daunting than appears on the surface. Repeatedly, coders have had difficulty recognizing the myriad of motions that appear on one's face. While recognizing universal emotions of happiness or sadness is not taxing, the ability of a decoder to decipher the list of up to 30 or more different facial emotions has consistently led to poor results. Thus, medical practitioners (particularly physicians and their staff) must be continually trained and updated in nonverbal behaviors of emotion in order to properly recognize and decode the correct or "true" facial display of emotion (Leathers & Eaves, 2008). A good example of this emotion is what experienced physicians call "a deer in the headlights" expression. Recognizing this as a sign of a lack of understanding or bewilderment allows the clinician to slowly and simply communicate the knowledge that a patient needs to make an informed decision (Cognetta, 2013).

Touch is a vital aspect of communication, in which emotions between physician and patient signal interest, engagement, and most notably care (Leathers & Eaves, 2008). This skill would be especially valuable for the nurses or other attending physician staff, especially when interacting with a skin cancer patient who has suffered facial or other bodily form of disfigurement. In rare cases, skin cancer patients must have repeated biopsies and procedures to diagnose and treat multiple skin cancers. As a result, the physician may refer them to receive plastic surgery for facial parts such as on the nose, ear, eyelid, cheek, chin, neck, or other anatomic areas to minimize scarring (Cognetta, 2013).

Now that I have addressed the exchange of emotions by physicians and patients, let us examine the meta-communication that surrounds this content.

Meta-Communication

Nonverbal communication fills in the gaps that verbal communication lacks, thus serving an important meta-communicative function in the medical clinic. With skin cancer clinics in particular, doctors and staff can use very technical language and not fill in missing gaps for patient understanding. As with any medical setting, a premium is placed on communication within the skin cancer clinic. Dealing with a potentially disfigurement or even terminal illness, skin cancer professionals must strive for a healthy balance between verbal communication and its accuracy with the delicate delivery and method of nonverbal codes and cues sent back and forth from physician to patient.

One seminal article on the meta-communicative aspects of health communication appeared over two decades ago. Sharf (1990) identified the nature of physician-patient communication as a medical narrative: a doctor's story and a patient's story. The ultimate goal of the physician is patient understanding and the ability to follow a medical plan and recommendations for treatment. Importantly, skin cancer specialty clinics place a premium on promoting necessary skin cancer prevention strategies. These strategies might include use of sun screen, hats, sun glasses, or other recommended forms of behavior during sun exposure.

The ability of the physician and physician staff to be sensitive to patients occurs primarily when they use their nonverbal behavior as meta-communication; filling in the medical gaps and incompleteness of verbal forms of communication. If a doctor is in a hurry, is distracted in the office, or is in a "mood," the patient may suffer from incomplete or fragmented communication. Thus, the meta-communicative nature of the medical narratives and other nonverbal codes fill in these gaps to help promote understanding and overall patient satisfaction.

The medical narrative serves two main functions: fidelity and coherence. Fidelity means the story appears to be believable; it resonates from a previous experience. For example, the physician might explain what happens when the melanoma is not controlled or spreads to other places in the body. Coherence means the story makes sense. The physician and physician staff must use language that is understandable and can be comprehended by the patient. The use of jargon, technical speak, or other complex terms serves to break down understanding and places a wedge between patient and physician (Sharf, 1990). Barriers between physician and patient in the skin cancer clinic only deteriorate communication efforts and hurt any relationship that has been established.

If the "style" of the story is told in different ways, this can harm the physician-patient relationship. The physician needs to use a medical narrative that engages the patient, to improve listening, active involvement, that leads to followed and recommended behavior. The use of power by the physician or a paternalistic strategy is often rejected and can harm the delicate nature of the relationship. The communication strategy must be transactional, and must have a "take home" message. That is, a story that can be repeated to medical colleagues for the physician, or a narrative that can be shared with family or friends by the patient (Sharf, 1990). Problems that result from incompatible stories can cause the patient to disclose less to the doctor, be uncomfortable during interaction, or be misunderstood throughout the exchange (Leathers & Eaves, 2008). Patient disclosure is vital in the skin cancer doctor's office in order for the patient to receive the best possible medical care he or she deserves.

Finally, one must remember that meta-communicative cues can communicate fluidity, calmness, or serenity. In their worst form, however, those cues can be an grimace, shifty eyes, or gestures that communicate levels of tension in the diagnosis. Thus, both parties in the physician-patient relationship should emphasize positive nonverbal cues, and reduce those meta-communicative cues that detract from the overall success of the medical interaction (Leathers & Eaves, 2008).

Now that I have discussed the meta-communicative functions of the skin cancer clinic, it's time for us to discuss self-concept protection.

Self-Concept Protection

Part of protection for patients involves reduction of anxiety. Comfort with one's self helps to define, maintain, and change one's self-concept. One study reported that patients seek information from physicians to gain control over the medical interview and reduce anxiety (Henman, Butow, Brown, Boyle, & Tattersall, 2002). As a result, the information serves a valuable role of protecting a patient's self-concept. In addition to seeking information from doctors, patients have faith in their medical experts to give them the peace of mind they need (Leydon, Boulton, Moynihan, Jones, Mossman, Boudioni, & McPherson, 2000).

Several nonverbal variables and cues play a fundamental role in helping a patient maintain his or her self-protection in the medical setting. Such cues include privacy needs, protection of the territorial self, gestures or eye behaviors from the physician that signal a partnership with the patient, and other positive displays of patient affection (Leathers & Eaves, 2008).

Since skin cancer represents a treatable and preventable form of cancer, the physician staff has to be careful to frame the medical narrative in a way to not damage the patient's ego or self-concept. Reminders about their behavior in the sun, types of sunscreen to use (how much and how often), and what tale-tell signs to look for in detecting melanomas or other skin abnormalities have to be handled with tact and decorum.

Impression Management

Impression management is a vital role for both the physician and the patient in the medical relationship. Typically, like most medical venues, the skin cancer specialty clinic is adorned with doctor's credentials-diplomas on the wall, special clinic tech certifications, etc. This atmosphere leaves the patients with a positive impression, especially if it is the first office visit. Moreover, patients who rate medical clinics as positive are more likely to form high credibility impressions about their visit to the physician's office.

Look at the photos of these diplomas at a regional skin cancer clinic in Tallahassee, Florida. What impression do you have when you see these plaques on the wall?

Or what about this picture?

Reassurance

The last area we need to discuss is reassurance, or the ability of the physician to help assure the patient that he or she will receive effective care with the most degree of sensitivity in a professional manner. Unlike other physical settings where nonverbal communication occurs, the medical arena may depend on communication professionals to use reassurance more so than in any other venue (Leathers & Eaves, 2008).

One study in particular found a number of nonverbal elements are used in the medical setting. Rapport, understanding, and reassurance were correlated with physician behaviors such as self-touch (adjusting tie, moving glasses, etc.), head gaze, head nods, or forward leans. In each of these nonverbal behaviors, patients felt reassured in the physician-patient relationship (Beck, Daughbridge, & Sloane, 2002).

Reassurance is a vital ingredient in the skin cancer specialty clinic and medical office. Physicians must communicate with confidence to the patients that their surgery was successful, that the clinic tests are accurate and reliable, and that no known carcinogens or malignancies are present in the infected area.

REFERENCES

Beck, R. S., Daughbridge, R., & Sloane, P. D. (2002). Physician-patient communication in the primary care office: A systematic review. *Journal of the American Board of Family Medicine, 15*(1), 25–38.

Berry, D. (2006). *Health communication: Theory and practice.* Buckingham, GBR: Open University Press.

Carroll, S. M. (2004). Nonvocal ventilated patients perceptions of being understood. *Western Journal of Nursing Research, 26*(1), 85–103.

Coelho, K. R. (2012). Bridging the divide for better health-harnessing the power of emotional intelligence to foster an enhanced clinician-patient relationship. *International Journal of Colclinicorative Research on Internal Medicine & Public Health, 4*(3), 181–188.

Coelho, K. R., & Galan, C. (2012). Physician cross-cultural nonverbal communication skills, patient satisfaction and health outcomes in the physician-patient relationship. *International Journal of Family Medicine, 2012,* 1–5.

Cognetta, A. B. (2013, July 1). Personal interview.

Cuneo, A. Z. (2007, February 26). Office space: Think outside the cubicle. *Advertising Age, 78,* 1–4.

Duffy, S. A., Ronis, D. L., Waltje, A. H., & Choi, S. H. (2013). Protocol of a randomized controlled trial of sun protection interventions for operating engineers. *BMC Public Health, 13,* 1–7.

Elfenbein, H. A., & Ambady, N. (2003). When familiarity breeds accuracy: Cultural exposure and facial emotion recognition. *Journal of Personality and Social Psychology, 85*(2), 276–290.

Fentiman, I. S. (2007). Communication with older breast cancer patients. *The Breast Journal, 13*(4), 406–409.

Given, B. A., & Northouse, L. (2011). Who cares for family caregivers of patients with cancer? *Clinical Journal of Oncology Nursing, 15*(5), 451–452.

Greener, I. (2007). The politics of gender in the NHS: Impression management and `getting things done.' Gender, Work and Organization, 14, 281–299.

Henman, M. J., Butow, P. N., Brown, R. F., Boyle, F., & Tattersall, M. H. N. (2002). Lay constructions of decision-making in cancer. *Psycho-Oncology, 11,* 295–306.

Heppner, P. P., & Pew, S. (1977). Effects of diplomas, awards, and counselor sex on perceived expertness. *Journal of Counseling Psychology, 24,* 147–149.

Jowett, S., & Ryan, T. (1985). Dermatology patients and their doctors. *Clinical and Experimental Dermatology, 10,* 246–254.

Kreps, G. L. (2003). The impact of communication on cancer risk, incidence, morbidity, mortality, and quality of life. *Health Communication, 15*(2), 161–169.

Leathers, D. G., & Eaves, M. H. (2008). *Successful nonverbal communication: Principles and applications*. Fourth edition. Boston: Pearson.

Lee, S. J., Back, A. L., Block, S. D., & Stewart, S. K. (2002). Enhancing physician-patient communication. *Hematology, 2002*, 464–483.

Leydon, G. M., Boulton, M., Moynihan, C., Jones, A., Mossman, J., Boudioni, M., & McPherson, K. (2000). Cancer patients' information needs and information seeking behavior: In depth interview study. *British Medical Journal, 320*, 909–913.

MSNBC news broadcast (2013, June).

Nasar, J. L., & Devlin, A. S. (2011). Impressions of psychotherapists' offices. *Journal of Counseling Psychology, 58*, 310–320.

Postrel, V. (2008, April). The art of healing. *The Atlantic Monthly*, 119–122.

Price-Haywood, E. G., Roth, K. G., Shelby, K., & Cooper, L. A. (2009). Cancer risk communication with low health literacy patients: A continuing medical education program. *Journal of General Internal Medicine, 25*, 126–129.

Sharf, B. F. (1990). Physician-patient communication as interpersonal rhetoric: A narrative approach. *Health Communication, 2*(4), 217–231.

Skiveren, J., Mortensen, E. L., & Haedersdal, M. (2010). Sun protective behavior in renal transplant recipients: A qualitative study on individual interviews and the Health Belief Model. *Journal of Dermatological Treatment, 21*, 331–336.

Song, L., Northouse, L. L., Zhang, L., Braun, T. M., Cimprich, B., Ronis, D. L., & Mood, D. W. (2012). Study of dyadic communication in couples managing prostate cancer: A longitudinal perspective. *Psycho-Oncology, 21*, 72–81.

Wanless, M. (2010). Can you help your patients through better communication? *Vital*, 23–26.

Zulman, D. M., Schafenacker, A., Barr, K. L. C., Moore, I. T., Fisher, J., McCurdy, K., Derry, H. A., Saunders, E. W., An, L. C., & Northouse, L. (2012). Adapting an in-person patient-caregiver communication intervention to a tailored web-based format. *Psycho-Oncology, 21*, 336–341.

Chapter 5:

Medical tourism: The role of communication regarding risks and benefits of obtaining medical services abroad

Kevin B. Wright
George Mason University

Alicia Mason
Pittsburg State University

The ever-increasing globalization of healthcare has led to a greater number of consumers using the World Wide Web for the purpose of accessing health information and medical services that transcends international borders (Kangas, 2010; Lunt, Mannion, & Exworthy, 2012; MacReady, 2007; Snyder, Crooks, Adams, Kingsbury, & Johnston, 2011). When faced with the high cost of health care or limited treatment options in the United States, more and more Americans are looking to developing countries to obtain a variety of health-related services, including cosmetic surgery, dentistry, diagnostic testing, fertility treatment, and major surgeries such as heart valve operations and organ transplants (Dalstrom, 2012; Snyder et al., 2011; Sono, Herlihy, & Bicker, 2011). The number of people buying health-related products and accessing health information and medical services in developing countries via the Internet is increasing (Lunt, Hardey, & Mannion, 2010).

According to Turner (2010), in the United States, popularization of medical tourism is related to social inequalities, loss of employer-provided health insurance, rising premiums for health insurance, limited public funding of health care, and lack of access to affordable health care. Turner (2010) also contends that the United States, due to its large and growing population of uninsured, underinsured, and people struggling to pay rising health insurance premiums, has become a leading target market for foreign medical facilities seeking international customers. In contrast to these motivators, patients from countries with less restricted health care, such as Canada and the United Kingdom, can choose to travel to foreign countries for immediate medical attention as an alternative to the long wait periods of nationalized health care systems (Boyle, 2008).

Bookman & Bookman (2007) note additional elements of this demand result from (1) *demographic factors*; we, as a human species are living longer; (2) *medical factors*; we are also experiencing increases in non-communicable disease development requiring the assistance of more medical specialists and/or elective procedures; and (3) *economic factors*; individuals with economic resources such as disposable income and/or portable health insurance are contributing to the growth rates of medical tourism; and *social factors* such that people know more about the world today, they are willing to travel, and can use the Internet to fulfill their health needs.

A key driver of medical tourism is consumer use of the Internet for gaining access to health-care information, including exposure to medical tourism advertising. Recently released data from Pew's 2013 Health Online poll found 72% of Internet users reported looking online for health information within the past year. 77% of those online health seekers say they began their last session at a search engine such as *Google*, *Bing*, or *Yahoo*. Another 13% say they began at a site that specializes in health information. The report found that the most commonly researched topics of online health information searches are specific diseases or conditions; treatments or procedures; and doctors or other health professionals (Fox & Duggan, 2013); all of which are germane to the medical tourism process.

Web-based health resources are often utilized not only as educational material, but also as a means of trading health-related products including accessing health services from a foreign country. The medical tourism marketplace consists of a growing number of countries competing for patients by offering these services as well as access to restricted procedures (e.g. stem cell surgery) or products (e.g. restricted pharmaceuticals) at prices that are often considerably lower than in the U.S (Snyder et al., 2011; Turner, 2011). These types of consumer activities have been labeled "medical tourism," and this phenomenon has attracted the attention of a number of researchers in recent years, including health communication scholars (Mason & Wright, 2011; Mason, Wright, & Bogard, 2011; Lunt et al., 2007).

Those who engage in the process are often called "medical tourists;" however, additional labels are used to distinguish medical tourists. When travelers engage because of a lack of health insurance or inability to access services in their country of origin they are referred to as *medical refugees* or *medical exiles*. Individuals are also identified based on the purpose of travel such that those engaging in the medical tourism process for the purposes of kidney or liver transplants are referred to as *transplant tourists*, those seeking stem cell injections are called *stem cell tourists*, those seeking reproductive technology such as in vitro fertilization, or commercial surrogacy are often called *reproductive tourists* (Turner, 2011).

Medical tourism is qualitatively different than other forms of international patient mobility. Temporary visitors abroad who receive emergency access to medical care as a result of an accident or sudden illness while on vacation are not considered medical tourists, as their travel did not begin with a goal-pursuit to secure medical services. However a significant amount of other consumers resulting from retirement migration, long-term residents of other countries, and outsourced patients from countries with nationalized health care programs may find themselves engaging in the medical tourism process (Lunt, Mannion, Exworthy, 2011).

While advertising certainly exposes potential consumers to medical tourism services and facilities, medical tourism tends to be driven by the consumer, especially in cases where medical tourism facilities offer cheaper or more convenient access to health-related products or services coupled with low cost travel incentives, including discounted airfare and lodging (all of which are typically included as a package by medical tourism facilities in different locations around the world). In some cases, health services are offered in conjunction with travel to major tourist attractions within the country offering the services, such as Buddhist temples in Asia and safaris in South Africa (Turner, 2010). Despite a growing interest in medical tourism among researchers, including communication scholars, relatively few studies to date have sufficiently medical tourism websites and the potential benefits and risks for patients who decide to participate in medical tourism.

The purpose of this chapter is to explore emerging research in the area of medical tourism from a communication perspective. Toward that end, the chapter is a call to strengthen our understanding of the role of communication in medical tourism through empirical research as well as integrating medical tourism research within a broader conceptual framework. Specifically, the chapter begins with an overview of medical tourism and the role of new communication technologies in promoting these services to a worldwide marketplace. In addition, the chapter explores framing theory as a conceptual framework for analyzing medical tourism websites, and it further discusses how the globalization of health, through medical tourism, impacts individuals, societies and cultures.

MEDICAL TOURISM AND MEDICAL TOURISM WEBSITES

Medical tourism is not a new concept. Throughout history, people have sought relief from physical ailments by travelling to many different sites known for therapeutic or healing powers (Connell, 2006). Some of the early accounts document Greek pilgrims who traveled from the Mediterranean Sea to Epidaurus, which was believed to be the sanctuary of Asclepius, known as the healing god (Ben Natan, Ben Sefer, & Ehrenfed, 2009). Pilgrims in Roman Britain traveled to the waters at Bath (Boyle, 2008). In the 18th and 19th centuries, Europeans and Americans flocked to health spas along the Nile and sanitariums for relief from conditions, such as tuberculosis, gout, bronchitis, or liver diseases. Our modern age finds a plethora of individuals worldwide are engaging in the medical tourism process for a variety of reasons.

In our contemporary era of high medical insurance costs and easy access to health information via the Internet, consumers often search for alternative medical options via medical tourism when services in their home country are unavailable, unaffordable, or waiting lists are too long. By obtaining medical services outside of their home country, patients are often able to avoid high out-of-pocket payments or lengthy periods of compromised quality of life due to the pain incurred while on a surgical waiting list. Turner (2010) contends that medical tourism offers a large population of individuals lacking health insurance, and with limited economic resources, access to treatment for medically necessary care (in many cases beyond purely cosmetic procedures). With more and more patients turning to the Internet to research healthcare options coupled with overseas medical centers that hope to attract foreign consumers, medical tourism is increasingly being viewed as a viable way to obtain medical care.

Bookman and Bookman (2007) argue that medical tourism has created a dual delivery health care system within these specialized regions around the world: one that caters to rich foreigners and one for poor locals. In a bulletin published by the World Health Organization (WHO) NaRanong & NaRanong (2011) confirmed this effect of medical tourism in Thailand. Hospitals and other health-related facilities around the world, particularly those located in low and middle income countries, often offer a more comprehensive range of surgical and diagnostic procedures a lower price than in higher income countries (such as the United States), and they are increasingly active in their efforts to attract international patients (Dalstrom, 2012; Snyder et al., 2011). Many countries outside of the United States are particularly active in the delivery of medical tourism services, including Brazil, Costa Rica, Dubai, Hong Kong, Hungary, India, Malaysia, Mexico, Poland, Singapore, South Africa, and Thailand. Each region tends to differ in terms of the services and products that are offered.

For example, heart valve operations and fertility treatments are common in Asia, stem cell therapies are often associated with Europe, and restricted pharmaceutical products are often easier to obtain in Mexico and Central America. Many U.S. consumers seek medical care abroad because they: face long waiting lists in their home systems; want to access procedures that are illegal or unavailable at home; are seeking procedures not covered by a public health care system in their home country; or are uninsured or underinsured and are looking for an affordable care option (Lunt et al., 2012; Milstein & Smith, 2006; Turner, 2011). In addition, in the United States, the denial of health insurance coverage on the basis of preexisting conditions means that people who can afford to purchase health insurance are often unable to gain access to coverage for the medical treatments they are most likely to need. In many cases, medical tourism facilities offer individuals who have had their insurance coverage denied due to preexisting conditions affordable access to health-related services. For individuals in the United States who cannot afford to travel to Southeast Asia or Europe, there are numerous medical tourism facilities in the bordering countries Canada and Mexico. However, in April 2011 President Obama reiterated his preference for Americans to avoid engaging in medical tourism process, specifying the countries of India and Mexico.

While it is difficult to assess the exact number of individuals who cross boarders for medical treatment due to the absence of an internationally agreed definition of what is considered to be medical tourism (Helble, 2011), anecdotal evidence suggests that the global medical tourism industry currently generates annual revenues up to $60 billion, with 20% annual growth (MacReady, 2007). This global trend has been integrated into India's National Health Policy which declares that treatment of foreign patients is legally an "export" and deemed "eligible for all fiscal incentives extended to export earnings" (n.p.) Both the Government and private sector estimates project that medical tourism in India could bring between $1 billion and $2 billion US into the country by 2012.

Websites are a particularly important marketing strategy for organizations promoting medical facilities abroad. The investors and administrators associated with medical tourism facilities have a significant financial interest in attracting new clients, and so they must be strategic in terms of crafting messages that will appear on their websites (Mason & Wright, 2011; Turner, 2011). In addition to providing a variety of appeals regarding medical facilities, staff, and services, medical tourism websites typically include other appeals, such as the opportunity to travel or the benefits of recuperating from medical procedures in a beautiful location (Lunt et al., 2012; Penny, Snyder, Crooks, & Johnston, 2011; Sobo et al., 2011).

Given this financial interest in attracting new global customers, many medical facilities around the world often employ medical tourism brokers to develop websites in other languages and to market them to specific countries. According to Penney et al. (2011), medical tourism brokers are agents who specialize in making international medical care arrangements for patients. In addition, since they are a key source of information for these patients, and they appear to play a key role in communicating the risks and benefits of undergoing surgery or other procedures abroad to their clientele. For example, medical tourism brokers (via websites) typically answer questions from prospective customers, help them make travel arrangements, and/or act as customer service liaisons between the consumer and the medical facility abroad (MacReady, 2007; Turner, 2011).

Furthermore, medical tourism brokers typically assist consumers by suggesting physicians and facilities abroad, booking surgeries, assisting in the transportation and translation of medical records, helping arrange for follow up care, and overseeing postoperative complications. Many medical tourism brokerages and international hospital chains are lobbying major U.S. health insurance companies to sell plans covering offshore health care (Turner, 2010). Some U.S. health insurance companies, such as Blue Cross and Blue Shield South Carolina, currently offer customers plans that include health services in hospitals/medical facilities in Costa Rica, Thailand, India, Singapore, and Turkey (Turner, 2010).

In addition, medical tourism broker websites typically present basic information about medical procedures and services offered by overseas medical facilities. Medical tourism patients are essentially consumers who purchase a variety of services, including travel arrangements, accommodations, medical procedures, and services related to postoperative care (e.g. nursing services, etc.). Most medical tourism brokers have a strong online presence, and their websites are an important tool for patients seeking information about possible treatments and destinations as well as financing and insurance information. These websites are often the first source of information patients encounter when considering seeking medical services abroad. Therefore, the information about the benefits and risks of engaging in medical tourism presented on these sites may have a strong impact on a consumer's decision to ultimately use medical services in a foreign country.

While the availability and cost of worldwide medical tourism services may provide various benefits for consumers, a number of researchers, providers, and government agencies have expressed concerns about the possible risks associated with medical tourism in recent years. These include the relatively high risk of infections during post-operative care, procedural risk, medical complications, and the lack of legal recourse if a patient wishes to pursue malpractice litigation (Hopkins,

Labonté, Runnels, & Packer, 2010). The Center for Disease Control (CDC) warns "The blood supply in some countries comes primarily from paid donors and may not be screened, which puts patients at risk of HIV and other infections spread through blood," (n.p.). Any surgery carries with it a certain degree of risk, and there is always the possibility of anesthesia complications, blood clots, uncontrolled bleeding and human error during surgery as well as delayed healing and infection after surgery (Hopkins et al., 2010).

Moreover, medical tourism carries additional risks, including language and cultural misunderstandings between providers and patients, risks associated with lengthy flights post-operatively, difficulties obtaining follow up care, and the danger of infectious disease transmission (Hopkins et al., 2010; Lunt et al., 2012). As medical tourism websites have become more common in recent years, the quality and range of information that they provide needs to be examined critically. Medical tourism brokers have become an indispensable component of the medical tourism industry, as they connect hospitals and physicians to patients across the world. Understanding the role and functioning of medical tourism brokers as mediators between patients and clinicians is crucial, particularly since what most patients know about the medical tourism services being offered are largely based on the content within medical tourism brokerage websites (or interaction with medical tourism brokers through these web portals).

A number of studies have found that medical tourism websites tend to present content that emphasizes benefits of health-related services while downplaying potential risks (Mason & Wright, 2011; Mason, Wright, & Bogard, 2011; Turner, 2011). Pachisa (2007) identified messages within medical tourism websites that appear to attract consumers to seeking medical services abroad. Pachisa (2007) found that lower cost of services expense is often the most attractive feature to consumers, and messages about reduced cost are prominent within medical tourism websites (Mason & Wright, 2011). In addition, Pachisa (2007) found that lack of wait time, quality of service, and travel opportunities are attractive to potential consumers.

However, there are a number of negative aspects of medical tourism, including the fact that government and basic medical insurance may not cover international medical procedures, requiring patients to pay in cash, and there is little postoperative care for potential negative side effects. Moreover, most countries that offer highly attractive medical procedures offer little malpractice recourse as well as the risk of potential exposure to viruses in postoperative care (Mason & Wright, 2011). Because the possibility of a negative treatment outcome is appealing neither to the physician nor the patient, there is a tendency to avoid direct discussion of risk in medical tourism contexts, which can lead to patients making decisions without having truly considered the risks involved. Information about the quality of care that is available abroad and the possible risks involved in a procedure is critical information that patients need to understand.

Several concerns have been raised regarding some of the business dimensions of medical tourism facilitation. For example, facilitators may neglect to inform patients of how their services are paid for, which could lead medical tourists to misunderstand their roles. Patients may travel abroad lacking proper informed consent for medical procedures or an understanding of how their facilitator chose the destination and providers being used. Moreover, lack of regulation within the industry may further impede patients' understanding of facilitators' roles along with other complex dimensions of medical tourism. While under normal circumstances patients may receive this information from their family doctor or from a nurse or surgeon at a hospital in their home country, medical tourists may need to rely on additional sources of information. As medical tourism involves travel to a foreign country that patients and their families may be unfamiliar with, this practice creates uncertainties not found in traditional treatment that may add additional risks.

FRAMING THEORY AS A CONCEPTUAL FRAMEWORK FOR STUDYING MEDICAL TOURISM WEBSITES

Framing theory appears to be a useful theoretical framework for identifying arguments and persuasive appeals used within medical tourism websites. Widely used in social sciences, "frame" has been regarded as the cognitive schemata of interpretation, the central organizing idea or story line to locate, identify, label and provide meaning to a specific issue (Gamson & Modigliani, 1989; Goffman, 1974). Framing theory has emerged as a dominant model in media effects research (Price & Tewksbury, 1997). These frames serve as cognitive filters that can vary audience members' perceptions of events within their social worlds and Kahneman and Tversky (1984) previously found that the framing of language variations created significant perceptual shifts of mediated reports.

Entman (1993) argues that framing means to "select some aspects of a perceived reality and make them more salient in a communicating text" (p. 52). An increase in salience can enhance the probability for receivers to perceive the information, discern meaning, process it, and store it in memory (Fiske & Taylor, 1991; Entman, 1993). Therefore, framing researchers pay attention to the salience of different media frames (Zhou & Moy, 2007).

Media, health, and advertising researchers are often interested framing effects because the manner in which information is presented has been shown to influence consumers' decisions and judgments toward products (for a review of framing research, see Levin & Gaeth, 1998). Framing research typically focuses on the way the presentation of information in gain- versus loss-frames scenarios affects an individuals' cognitions, intentions, and dispositions toward health-related behaviors or products (e.g., Block & Keller, 1995; Rothman, Martino, Bedell, Detweiler, & Salovey, 1999).

The effects of gain- and loss-framed messages are based on the tenants of a theory related to framing theory, Kahneman and Tversky's (1979) prospect theory, which posits that people's choices under uncertain situations depend largely on how its consequences are framed. More specifically, people tend to be risk-averse when the outcomes are framed as gains while they tend to be more willing to accept risks (risk-seeking) when the outcomes are framed as losses. The theory lends itself well to understand the effects of message framing on health-related persuasion as it explains how people perceive and make behavioral decisions under risk situations (Kahneman& Tversky, 1974).

Various studies point to the conclusion that loss-framed messages are effective when promoting detection health behaviors (e.g., Meyerowitz & Chaiken, 1987) while gain-framed messages are effective for conveying health prevention behaviors (e,g., Detweiler, Bedell, Salovey, Pronin, & Rothman, 1999). For example, Meyerowitz and Chaiken (1987) found that compliance towards breast self-examination advocacy message was higher when it was framed in terms of the losses (i.e., you can lose several potential health benefits by failing to spend only 5 minutes each month doing BSE. Do not fail to take advantage of this opportunity) compared to when framed in terms of gains (i.e., you can gain several potential health benefits by spending only 5 minutes each month doing BSE. Take advantage of this opportunity). On the contrary, Detweiler et al. (1999) found that gain-framed messages were more effective in persuading people to use sunscreen to prevent skin cancer than loss-framed messages.

However, more recent findings show results contradicting the premises of prospect theory. A recent meta-analysis of 53 studies found that the significance of the advantage of loss-framed messages over gain-framed messages for disease detection behaviors was quite small, and only statistically significant for breast cancer detection but not for any other specific detection behaviors (O'Keefe & Jensen, 2009). Still, Rothman, et al. (2006) propose that using gain-framed messages to promote prevention behaviors and loss-framed messages to promote detection behaviors is well-founded, with the recognition that the "predictive value of the distinction between prevention and detection behaviors rests on the assumptions regarding how people construe engaging in these two classes of behavior" (p. 208).

Medical tourism websites appear to differ from traditional health information web sites in the sense that their primary objective is to attract patients or potential patients (as consumers) into visiting and choosing their facility and medical services, opposed to simply providing information about various types of medical conditions and medical procedures. Therefore, the traditional premises of gain- and loss-messages frames for promotion versus detection behaviors may apply differently for medical tourism websites. Instead, it may very well be that gain-framed messages dominate for medical tourism websites because the brokers fear that providing any information illustrating the risks or malevolent outcomes from undergoing medical procedures at a foreign facility could potentially scare away patients (consumers). Indeed, previous research has found that medical tourism websites highlight the beneficial outcomes of the health-related services while downplaying any potential risks (Mason & Wright, 2011; Turner, 2011).

Two additional theoretical frames for possible further exploration may also provide heuristic understandings of consumer responses to the persuasive appeals utilized by brokers to attract consumer patients. Consumers respond differently to the various types of health-related messages. For instance, some consumers have a chronic psychological preference toward a promotion or prevention focus (Higgins, 1997). This frame duality is presented through regulatory focus theory (RFT, Higgins, 1997; 1998) which argues there are two fundamental self-regulatory systems: those dealing with positive outcome focus and those dealing with negative outcome focus. Regulatory focus research has been incorporated into a variety of contexts including social policy issues (Cesario et al, 2004), health behaviors (Cesario et al., 2004; Speigel, Grant-Pillow, & Higgins, 2004) commercial advertising (Lee & Aaker, 2004). Higgins and colleagues (1998) have demonstrated positive outcome focus and negative outcome focus can be primed to modify motivational orientation processes and actually induce individuals to seek certain types of information most suitable for a given orientation. Regulatory focus can be primed by the situation or messages, commonly presented to audiences through medical tourism websites.

Kees, Burton, & Tangari (2010) hold that some consumers are effective at self-regulating their health-related behaviors, whereas others struggle with the self-discipline it takes to maintain good health. Differences in how concerned individuals are with the longer-term potential future consequences of their behaviors, and the extent to which individuals let such potential consequences influence their decisions in the short term, may play a strong role in the decision process (Joireman, Strathman, and Balliet 2006; Strathman et al. 1994). Furthermore these preferences for certainty, or tolerance for uncertainty, tend to vary cross-culturally thus making it difficult to narrowly regulate medial tourism brokers, and web providers, as the content would be expected to have a differential impact on global audiences.

A consumer, or potential medical tourist, who is more promotion focused would center on the positive goals and desired end states and views the decision with eagerness (e.g., "I'm always willing to try something new"). They may be willing to take risks and consider substandard possibilities so as to enhance their chances of accomplishing their goals (Crowe & Higgins, 1997). In contrast, a consumer who is more prevention focused will center on guarding against risks and be more vigilant toward the decision so that they might limit the chances of making mistakes (e.g., "What are the risks involved with this new behavior?").

Framing theorists argue that the media not just set the public's agenda about what issues are important to think about, but also tell people how to think about an issue by selectively highlighting certain aspects (Peng & Tang, 2010). Communications research suggests that there are conventions that provide computer mediated messages and other mass communicators with the power to influence public opinion. Frames organize thoughts by arranging content in persuasive ways by presenting certain interpretations over others. These frames explicitly present what information is important and what information is irrelevant to audiences.

Opposed to other common framing dualities such as gain versus loss frames (Kahneman & Tversky, 2010), and the promotion versus prevention frames (Higgins, 1997) covered above, the framing effects generated from the episodic and thematic formats of presentation are of particular concern to health communicators (Major, 2011). Episodic frames are considered to be concrete illustrations, specific case studies, and issue-oriented, timely reports. In contrast, thematic frames refer to the wide-angle, or "big picture" snapshots of contexts and environments. As we begin to analyze the artifacts of medical tourism through news media, web sites, and economic reports this frame duality may offer new insight. Major (2011) found that episodic and thematic frames mitigated audiences emotional responses to media reports on key health issues such as obesity and lung cancer. Previous research utilized an episodic and thematic frame analysis to understand trends in media such as coverage to disease-specific health issues such as alzheimers (Kang, et al., 2010). This type of frame duality is particularly useful when examining how isomorphic patterns or trends develop over time, and cross-culturally.

GLOBAL PUBLIC HEALTH ISSUES

The rising rates of those engaging in medical tourism are of particular concern to biomedical applied health practitioners, ethics scholars, health communication researchers, and policy makers. While the benefits of the process are largely portrayed to be associated with the utopian allure of "tourism," the medical component of the process has serious social and cultural implications that require attention from a wide variety of scholars. Toward that end this section will focus the societal and cultural impacts of the specialized services provided through boutique clinics and niche medical facilities.

Transplant tourism is used to describe medical travel for the purpose of buying organs that are available in common markets such as Colombia, China, Pakistan, and the Phillipines. Transplant tourism is a subset of the broader marketing term "medical tourism," and Turner (2008) argues belongs in a family of misleading phrases such as "organ transplantation tourism" "reproductive tourism" and "stem cell tourism," opposed to acceptable phrases like "spa tourism," because "the procedures are [too] risky, invasive and consequential to be characterized as a form of tourism" (p.1377). Many acknowledge that the donors involved in transplant tourism often sell their organs as a way of maintaining life in impoverished conditions, thus perpetuating gaps in their own access to quality health care treatments.

Direct-to-consumer marketing of unproven stem cell therapies raises both ethical and policy concerns as well. Two recent studies examined website content of approximately 20 clinics and found "the claims made were optimistic and unsubstantiated by peer-reviewed literature" (Levine, 2007, p.27). Through examining the communicated contents of medical patients' illness blogs (Heilferty, 2009) found stem cell tourists blogged to keep friends and families updated on their progress, yet still relatively little is known as to how the process of illness blogging contributes to the recovery process with distant social support networks.

Beyond the role of technology to assist in a patients' convalescence period by providing a coping tool, additional developments are empowering the consumers with portable health information platforms, which subsequently raises additional concerns over patient-privacy and information security. If "health," in general, is to become a commodity for consumers to "buy" then the bi-product of this payment, or investment, are matters of important concern. The tangible receipt exchanged (e.g., medical records) face extreme security threats when transferred electronically. The arguments for the development of electronic health records are that the consumer, or patient, can play a more active role in his/her own healthcare experience, by taking responsibility for and control of their medical records. Yet, *electronic health records (EHRs)*, or *portable health records* (PHRs), have been a contested issue for some time, mainly resulting from privacy and information security concerns.

Almalga© was one of the first comprehensive health information systems [HIS] that provides an integrative platform for patients' critical information, including *registration*, *clinical systems*, *laboratory*, *radiology*, *pharmacy*, *allergies*, and *vital signs*, giving clinicians and administrators access to information within and across departments. Yet doctors and healthcare providers are reluctant to rely solely on information provided by the patient, especially when there are chronic or critical health problems. The Medical Tourism Association's global Health Congress has begun the phased roll out of a new service using Microsoft's HealthVault©, an online personal health application platform. By connecting HealthVault to its Microsoft Amalga hospital information system (HIS), Bumrungrad, Thailand will be the first to allow their patients' access to their Bumrungrad medical records online. This allows patients to maintain continuity with doctors in their home country. Once their information is stored in HealthVault, the patient can then provide it, as desired to other clinicians and caregivers, or use it with a wide range of personal health applications.

Aside from information security concerns, biosecurity risks resulting from the international travel component of the medical tourism process is a security threat with respect to humans acting as vessels for drug-resistance bacteria (Hill, 2011). As a result the medical tourism process amplifies potential societal-level public health risk factors. Falkow (2008) argues that "the greatest threat to U.S. security is not bio-terrorism but a global health crisis from a new or existing pathogen."

International travel and increased urbanization allow epidemics to spread more quickly. The medical tourism industry was recently stigmatized by such as a pathogen. Brought to light in August 2010 in the Lancet Infectious Disease journal, the discovery of the New Delhi Metallo-β-lactamese virus (NDM-1) is among the most recent superbugs to receive international attention and was directly linked to medical tourism facilities in India which sparked worldwide controversy (Mason & Wright, 2013). Antibiotic resistant bacterial infections are expected to rise as more medical tourists travel to international hospitals and receive treatments in international health-care settings. Therefore informed consent of these classifications of risk factors prior to purchase should be disclosed, but the latest research indicates it is rarely addressed in the medical brokers' web-based content.

DISCUSSION AND FUTURE DIRECTIONS

Medical tourism is a complex area of study. As this consumer-driven form of healthcare continues to exponentially rise, there are many opportunities provided for those interested in health communication through direct applied engagement and social science research. Accessible contemporary international communication systems coupled with skilled medical experts in state of the art facilities are catalysts for the growth of medical tourism worldwide. Both mass media and computer-mediated communication scholars have demonstrated interest in furthering the understanding of the role of technology in these medical encounters and environments. The globalization of "health" in the context of medical tourism motivates educators to expect more intercultural competence of future practitioners through intercultural health communication education; it also spurs additional interest in other computer mediated communication such as interactive telemedicine, video conferencing for moderating and facilitating long-distance physician-patient relationships, especially when post-operative care and follow-up is not immediately available in the tourists' home country.

While some positive outcomes can emerge, others maintain medical tourism is a process which commodifies public health services thus reinforcing gaps between those with economic resources to purchase reasonable and accessible health services and those who do not, both within and between societies. The benefits and risks for both the individual and collective public health is a large context where a significant amount of additional research is needed (Hall, 2011).

Although a number of government Web sites now exist to encourage Americans to make better lifestyle choices (e.g., nutrition.gov, smallsteps.gov, healthierus.gov, mypyramid.gov, 5aday.gov, healthierfeds.gov) one niche context in which strategic communication may play a particularly important role is that of medical tourism. The process of medical tourism poses several issues but also opportunities for regulatory and public health agencies to be proactive in creating and facilitating health literacy regarding the process.

Research is needed to identify additional motives for engaging in medical tourism. In addition, future research may explore how consumers process information from medical tourism websites as well as the decision-making processes individuals engage in when weighing the risks and benefits of seeking medical services abroad. The majority of medical tourism studies published to date have been content analyses of medical tourism websites. However, surveys and interviews of medical tourists are needed to uncover motives and decision-making processes. Moreover, future research in this area would benefit from studies of broker-consumer and provider-patient interactions within medical tourism facilities, particularly research on how these interactions influence the decision-making process to engage in risky health procedures. Finally, longitudinal studies are needed to assess key variables such as patient satisfaction with medical tourism at various points in the process of obtaining and recovering from medical services.

CONCLUSION

The rise medical tourism reflects the complexities of globalization and modern medical insurance issues. Since medical tourism appears to be a growing, health communication researchers can contribute to our understanding of this phenomenon by researching persuasive messages designed to attract consumers to medical tourism products and services. Prior work has relied on framing theory and similar conceptual frameworks in an effort to identify persuasive arguments within medical tourism websites as well as the portrayal of risks and benefits of engaging in medical tourism. While these frameworks have yielded (and will likely continue to yield) interesting descriptive data about medical tourism messages, more research is needed to understand the complexities how consumers process medical tourism messages and their decision-making processes when navigating the medical tourism landscape.

REFERENCES

Ben-Natan, M. Ben-Sefer, E. & Ehrenfeld, M. (2009). Medical tourism: A new role for nursing? *Online Journal of Issues in Nursing, 14*(3).

Boyle, K. (2008). A permanent vacation: Evaluating medical tourism's place in the united states healthcare system. *The Health Lawyer, 20*(5), 42.

Bookman, M.Z., & Bookman, K.R. (2007). Medical tourism in developing countries. New York: Palgrave Macmillian.

Center for Disease Control (CDC). (2013). Medical Tourism—Getting Medical Care in Another Country. Retrieved from: http://wwwnc.cdc.gov/travel/page/medical-tourism.

Cesario, J., Grant, H., & Higgins, E.T. (2004). Regulatory fit and persuasion: Transfer from "feeling right." *Journal of Personality and Social Psychology, 86*, 388–404.

Connell, J. (2006). Medical tourism: Sea, sun, sand and…surgery. *Tourism Management, 27*, 1093–110.

Crowe, E., & Higgins, E.T. (1997). Regulatory focus and strategic inclinations: Promotion and prevention in decision-making. *Organizational Behavior and Human Decision Processes, 69*, 117–132.

Dalstrom, M. (2013). Shadowing modernity: The art of providing Mexican healthcare for Americans. *Ethnos: Journal of Anthropology, 78*, 75–98.

Detweiler, J. B., Bedell, B. T., Salovery, P., Pronin, E., & Rothman, A. J. (1999). Message framing and sunscreen use: Gain-framed messages motivate beach-goers. Health Psychology, 18, 189–196.

Entman, R. M. (1993). Framing: Toward clarification of a fractured paradigm. *Journal of Communication*, *43*(4), 51–58.

Fiske, S. T., & Taylor, S. E. (1991). *Social cognition*. New York: McGraw-Hill.

Fox, S., & Duggan, M. (2013). *Health Online 2013*. Pew Internet.org. Retrieved from: http://www.pewInternet.org/~/media/Files/Reports/2013/Pew%20Internet%20Health%20Online%20report.pdf.

Gamson, W. A., & Modigliani, A. (1987) The Changing Culture of Affirmative Action. *Research in Political Sociology, 3*, 137–177.

Goffman, E. (1974). *Frame analysis: An essay on the organization of experience*. New York: Harper and Row.

Hall, C. M. (2011). Health and medical tourism: A kill or cure for global public health? Tourism Review of AIEST—*International Association of Scientific Experts in Tourism, 66*(1/2), 4.

Heilferty, C. M. (2009). Toward a theory of online communication in illness: Concept analysis of illness blogs. *Journal of Advanced Nursing, 65*(7), 1539.

Helble, M. (2011). The movement of patients across boarders: Challenges and opportunities for public health. *Bulletin of the World Health Organization, 89*, 68–72.

Higgins, E.T. (1997). Beyond pleasure and pain. *American Psychologist, 52*, 1280–1300.

Higgins, E.T. (1998). Promotion and prevention: Regulatory focus as a motivation principle. *Advances in Experimental Social Psychology, 30*, 1–46.

Hill, T. L. (2011). The spread of antibiotic-resistant bacteria through medical tourism and transmission prevention under the international health regulations. Chicago *Journal of International Law, 12*(1), 273.

Hopkins, L., Labonté, R., Runnels, V., & Packer, C. (2010). "Medical tourism today: What is the state of existing knowledge?" *Journal of Public Health Policy 31*, 185–198.

Joireman, J. A., Strathman, A., & Balliet, D. (2006). Considering future consequences: An integrative model. In L.J. Sanna & Chin-Ho Change (Eds.). *Judgments Over Time: The Interplay of Thoughts, Feelings, and Behaviors.* Oxford: Oxford University Press, 82–99.

Kahneman, D. & Tversky, A. (1979). Prospect theory: An analysis of decision under risk. *Econometrica, 47*, 263–291.

Kang.S., Gearhart, S., Bae, H.S. (2010), Coverage of Alzheimer's disease from 1984 to 2008 in television news and information talk shows in the United States: An analysis of news framing. *American Journal of Alzheimer's Disease and Other Dementias, 25*(8), 687–697. doi:10.1177/1533317510387583

Kangas, B. (2010). Travelling for medical care in a global world. *Medical Anthropology, 29*, 344–362.

Kees, J., Burton, S., & Tangari, A. H. (2010). The impact of regulatory focus, temporal orientation, and fit on consumer responses to health-related advertising. *Journal of Advertising, 39*(1), 19–34.

Keller, P. (2006). Regulatory focus and efficacy of health messages. *The Journal of Consumer Research, 33*(1), 109–114. doi:10.1086/504141

Lee, A.Y., & Aker, J.L. (2004). Bringing the frame into focus: The influence of regulatory fit on processing fluency and persuasion. *Journal of Personality and Social Psychology, 86*, 205–218.

Levin I.P, Schneider S.L, & Gaeth G.J. (1998). All frames are not created equal: A typology and critical analysis of framing effects. *Organizational Behavior and Human Decision Processes, 76*(2), 149–149. doi:10.1006/obhd.1998.2804

Levine, A.D., Ryan, K.A., Sanders, A.N., and Wang, D.D. (2010). Tracking the rise of stem cell tourism. *Regenerative Medicine, 5*(1), p.27.

Lunt, N. T., Hardey, M., & Mannion, R. (2010). Nip, tuck and click: Medical tourism and the emergence of web-based health information. *Open Medical Informatics Journal, 4*, 1–11. doi: 10.2174/1874431101004010001

Lunt, N. T., Mannion, R., & Exworthy, M. (2012). A framework for exploring the policy implications of medical tourism and international patient flows. *Social Policy & Administration* doi: 10.1111/j.1467-9515.2011.00833.x

MacReady, N. (2007). Developing countries court medical tourists. *Lancet, 369*, 1849–1859.

Major, L. H. (2011). The mediating role of emotions in the relationship between frames and attribution of responsibility for health problems.(author abstract). *Journalism & Mass Communication Quarterly, 88*(3), 502.

Mainil, T., Platenkamp, V., & Meulemans, H. (2011). The discourse of medical tourism in the media. Tourism Review of AIEST—*International Association of Scientific Experts in Tourism, 66*(1/2),31. doi:10.1108/16605371111127215

Mason, A.M., & Wright, K. B. (2011). Framing medical tourism: An examination of appeal, risk, convalescence, accreditation, and interactivity in medical tourism websites. *Journal of Health Communication, 16*, 163–177.

Mason, A.M., Wright, K. B., & Bogard, J. (2011). Assessing cultural representations of physician and patient imagery in medical tourism websites. *Journal of Intercultural Communication, 25*, 163–177.

Mason, A.M., & Wright, K.B. (2013). The liefecycle of a virus: The infectitous disease narrative of NDM-1. *Journal of Health Communication.*

Meyerowitz, B. E., & Chaiken, S. (1987). The effects of message framing on breast self-examination attitudes, intentions and behavior. *Journal of Personality and Social Psychology, 52*, 500–510.

McCombs, M., & Shaw, D. L. (1972). The agenda-setting function of mass media. *Public Opinion Quarterly, 36*, 176–187.

Milstein, A., & Smith, M. (2006). America's new refugees—seeking affordable surgery offshore. *New England Journal of Medicine, 355*, 1637–1640.

NaRanong & NaRanong (2011). The effects of medical tourism: Thailand's experience. Bulletin of the World Health Organization. Retrieved from: http://www.who.int/bulletin/volumes/89/5/09-072249/en/

O'Keefe, D.J., & Jensen, J.D. (2009). The relative persuasiveness of gain-framed and loss framed messages for encouraging disease prevention behaviors: A meta-analytic review. *Journal of Communication, 59*, 296–316.

Pachisa, M. (December, 2007). *Top 10 Reasons Why Medical Tourism is Popular.* Retreived March 19, 2009 from: http://www.associatedcontent.com/article/506179/top_10_reasons_why_medicaltou

Peng, W., & Tang, L. (2010). Health content in Chinese newspapers. *Journal of Health Communication, 15*, 695–711.

Penny, K., Snyder, J., Crooks, V. A., Johnston, R. (2011). Risk communication and informed consent in the medical tourism industry: A thematic content analysis of Canadian broker websites. *BMC Medical Ethics, 12* doi:10.1186/1472-6939-12-17.

Price, V. & Tewksbury, E.P. (1997). Switching trains of thought: The impact of news frames on readers' cognitive responses. *Communication Research, 24*(5), 481–506. doi:10.1177/009365097024005002

Rothman, A. J., Bartels, R. D., Wlaschin, J., & Salovey, P. (2006). The strategic use of gain-and loss-framed messages to promote healthy behavior: How theory can inform practice. *Journal of Communication, 56*, 202–220.

Snyder, J., Crooks, V. A., Adams, K., Kingsbury, P., & Johnston, R. (2011). The 'patient's physician one step removed': The evolving role of medical tourism facilitators. *Journal of Medical Ethics, 37*, 530–534.

Sobo, E. J., Herlihy, E., & Bicker, M. (2011). Selling medical travel to US patient-consumers: The cultural appeal of website marketing messages. *Anthropology & Medicine, 18*, 119–136.

Speigel, S., Grant-Pillow, H., & Higgins. T. (2004). How regulatory fit enhances motivational strength during goal pursuit. *European Journal of Social Psychology, 34*, 39–54.

Strathman, A., Gleicher, F., Boninger, D.S., & Edwards, S.C. (1994). The consideration of future consequences: Weighing immediate and distant outcomes of behavior. *Journal of Personality and Social Psychology, 66* (4), 742–752.

Turner, L. (2008). Let's wave goodbye to "transplant tourism". *British Medical Journal, 336*(7657), 1377–1377.

Turner, L. (2010). "Medical tourism" and the global health marketplace in health services: U.S. patients, international hospitals, and the search for affordable health care. *International Journal of Health Services, 40*, 443–467. doi: 10.2190/HS.40.3.d

Turner, L. (2011). Canadian medical tourism companies that have exited the marketplace: Content analysis of websites used to market transnational medical travel. *Globalization and Health, 7*, doi:10.1186/1744-8603-7-40.

Zhou, Y., & Moy, P. (2007). Parsing framing processes: the interplay between online public opinion and media coverage. *Journal of Communication, 57*, 79–98.

Chapter 6:

Traditional Chinese medicine as emerging domain for health communication study

Jim Schnell
Ohio Dominican University

INTRODUCTION

Traditional Chinese Medicine represents an emerging area for health communication study within China and around the world. This emergence can best be understood via emphasis on the historical context from which it has evolved. The People's Republic of China has been engaged in reforms that involve development of its economic, cultural, educational, and political processes. The need for reform was realized when China fell behind the development of the Western world in many areas. China closed its doors to the outside world in 1949 and it experienced limited interaction with the outside world until reform began in 1979.

The Cultural Revolution (1966–1976) was especially hard on development in China. During this period, political upheaval discouraged, and in some cases banned, technological developments. Since 1979, though, China has focused considerable emphasis on developing itself and promoting more interaction with the western world.

The 1980s was a period of significant modernization in China. This modernization occurred in a wide range of areas and resulted in a wide range of effects. Such modernization typically involved steps toward progress but what progress looks like, and how it is understood, is subject to redefinition. This report recognizes the 1980s as being primary, regarding modernization in China, and focuses on how this has occurred within the context of larger global concerns.

One of many areas that has been the focus of modernization is medicine and this medical modernization provides fertile ground for health communication study. Medical treatment in China is based on the practices of Traditional Chinese Medicine (TCM). Traditional Chinese Medicine has evolved during China's long history, which dates back over 5,000 years. "Throughout history, Chinese medicine has seen many transformations, most of them reflective of the times . . . . The Western world began ingesting bits of Chinese medicine over the last several decades; it has only just begun to digest them" (Garran, 2008, p. 2).

The effectiveness of TCM has not been questioned, but Chinese physicians have sought to better understand TCM by seeking interaction with Western physicians. The intended result is that both Chinese and Western medical practices can be enhanced through cross-cultural collaboration. Such cross-cultural collaboration has been enhanced via mass mediated venues.

In September 1981, the *Journal of Traditional Chinese Medicine* was founded by the All-China Association of Traditional Chinese Medicine and the Academy of Traditional Chinese Medicine. The journal was the first English periodical of Traditional Chinese Medicine published in China.

In the first issue Chui Yueli, President of the All-China Association of Traditional Chinese Medicine, stated, "Traditional Chinese Medicine is not a treasure belonging to the Chinese people alone, but it is an integral part of world civilization and a common benefit for all mankind. . . . All Chinese-Western collaboration has shown more satisfactory results than could have been expected with either Western or traditional Chinese medicine alone" (Yueli, 1981, p. v).

The creation of the *Journal of Traditional Chinese Medicine* has been instrumental in providing impetus and foundations for China-Western partnership formation. This, along with evolution of other English language journals based in China that periodically carry Traditional Chinese Medicine articles, has helped to convey a forum for dialog and inquiry. Similarly the increased number of professional conferences that include TCM presentations serves as framework for those who are engaged in this exchange.

Traditional Chinese Medicine has proven to be effective within the Chinese culture and some practices have been exported to Western nations. One such example is acupuncture. Although Chinese practitioners are confident in their methods, and they have little problem explaining "how" the procedures are to be performed, they have expressed difficulty explaining "why" the procedures are effective.

Interaction with Western physicians provides a climate whereby Western physicians can learn more about "how" and "why" the procedures are effective. Thus, through the merging of TCM and Western medicine, old ideas are being cross-culturally communicated through new perspectives. This report is concerned with how considerations affecting the merging have evolved since the open-door reforms were initiated by the People's Republic of China in 1979, how mass mediated venues have been part of that process and what this means as an area of health communication study.

Interaction between Chinese physicians and Western physicians has increased significantly since the opening of China. Dr. Kie Zhufan, head of Traditional Chinese Medicine at Beijing Medical College, lectured and did research on the integration of TCM and Western medical systems during a six month period in 1981 ("Dr. Kie Zhufan Invited...," 1981, p. 97). This is recognized as one of the seeds of the many exchanges which have occurred since.

A symposium sponsored by France's International Health Centre, held in April 1987, exemplifies the early medical exchanges that occurred during the 1980s. A Chinese delegation met with government officials from ten Western European nations during the three day symposium. "They had an in-depth exchange of views on Western and Chinese traditional medicine, their different viewpoints and methods, and their past development and present state. They also explored fresh channels for greater cooperation in the field" ("East-West Work," 1987).

Since that time the creation and evolution of Confucius Institutes in the West, as example, have provided forum for exchange, learning and development among Chinese and U.S. physicians, teachers and patients. The Confucius Institute concept, though based in China, has branches throughout the West. This kind of phenomena, within the larger context of information age technological connectivity, exemplifies the potential for even greater dialog and sharing.

Traditional Chinese Medicine is a legacy composed of centuries of experiences by the Chinese in dealing with disease. These experiences have evolved into a unique system of theories and beliefs. A discussion of medical exchange between China and the West must consider fundamental ideas about TCM which are foreign to Western medicine. The Yin and Yang and the five elements exemplify such ideas.

Yin and Yang holds that everything in the universe is composed of two opposite aspects which are constantly interdependent and in conflict. Water and fire symbolize basic properties of Yin and Yang. "That is to say, the basic properties of Yin stimulate those of water, including coldness, downward direction, dimness, etc., while the basic properties of Yang are like those of fire, including heat, upward direction, brightness, etc." ("Lectures on Essentials...," 1981, p. 73).

The theory of the five elements maintains that wood, fire, earth, metal, and water are the basic materials which comprise the physical world. A relationship of interdependence and inter-restraint exists among these elements. A fundamental premise of Traditional Chinese Medicine is to "classify natural phenomena, tissues and organs of the human body and human emotions, into different categories and to interpret the relationship between human physiology and pathology and the natural environment with the law of the inter-promoting, interacting, overacting, and counteracting of the five elements" ("Lectures on Essentials...," 1981, p. 77). This premise is central to their medical practice.

The emphasis on Qi is another primary concept in Traditional Chinese Medicine. "Qi is the fundamental substance constituting the universe. Everything is different manifestations of this energy force called Qi. All vital activities of the human body are explained by changes and movement of Qi" (Cuellar, 2006, p. 57). Western medicine does not have such a phenomenon that serves as a driving force the way Qi does in Traditional Chinese Medicine so the convergence of it with Western medicine has posed challenges.

The merging of TCM with Western medicine has occurred effectively in a variety of areas. They have used combined Chinese and Western medical means to treat acute abdomens, bone fracture, arthritis, soft tissue trauma, coronary heart disease. . . . All have shown more satisfactory results than could have been expected with either Western or Traditional Chinese Medicine alone. At the same time a deeper insight has been gained into the nature of certain diseases and the mechanisms for recovery. (Yueli, 1981, p. v)

The practice of acupuncture, the 3,000 year old Chinese process of using needles to treat a wide range of illnesses, by Western physicians has received much attention in the past 30 years. Acupuncture is now taught in the West. The Hwa To Acupuncture Centre, in the Netherlands, was the first school in the West to grant full Chinese diplomas for acupuncture study. "The object of the whole exercise is to come to a synthesis of Western medicine and Traditional Chinese Medicine in the hope it benefits patients" says Henk Termeulen, director of the Centre ("Chance Meeting Spawns...," 1987).

The combining of Traditional Chinese Medicine and Western medicine has also been used for patients with orthopedic problems. Wang Congshu, president of Baoding Orthopedics Rehabilitation Hospital, cures orthopedic illnesses "by using qigong, or Chinese traditional breathing exercises, combined with other Chinese traditional and Western methods" ("Old and New Combine...," 1987). Benefits of combining approaches have also been realized in the radiation treatment of cancer ("China Leads in...," 1987) and the removal of gallstones ("Shock Waves Remove...," 1987).

The 1980s were pivotal with the initiation of such innovative alignments. Since then, the aforementioned Confucius Institutes have helped to perpetuate meaningful exchange among Chinese-Western individuals and organizations. The Confucius Institutes exemplify what can happen from the foundation of intention and technological innovation. Necessity and desire are often the mother of invention and innovation as various constituencies seek to reach out to others in the medical community.

Concern with the connection between mental well-being and physical well-being has received increased emphasis in the U.S. in the past 40 years. A similar emphasis has occurred in China. The Sino-Japan Friendship Hospital, founded in 1984, bases its approaches on Western perspectives and TCM. Cheng Lirong, a nurse at the hospital, reports, "One characteristic of nursing is emotion nursing, similar to psychological nursing in the West" (Jianhua, 1987). It is believed that seven emotional factors (joy, anger, melancholy, brooding, sorrow, fear, and shock) can cause disease.

The merging of TCM with Western medicine has produced many benefits but there have been problems which have hindered the process. "Differences in historical backgrounds and language barriers still place some limits on international academic exchange concerning Traditional Chinese Medicine and integrated Chinese and Western medicine. This is particularly so in the West where many medical workers are unfamiliar with Traditional Chinese Medicine" (Yueli, 1981, p. v).

"Traditional Chinese Medicine products are highly complex, being composed of many herbal contents. . . . there is a need to develop a method to monitor the total quality of Traditional Chinese Medicine products in an efficient way" (Ching, 2007, p. 185). Development of such quality control measures can be especially difficult due to the cross-cultural contexts that provide backdrop for such evolutionary processes.

Cultural norms can be one category of obstacles that exists regarding the exchange of medical practices. Blood transfusions have become more common in China "but it is still difficult to find enough donors because of a traditional Chinese fear of losing blood," reports Xing Lixiang, a senior official of the Beijing Blood Centre (Tingting, 1987). Greater emphasis on science in China, and the scientific method, has helped to reduce the fears embedded in these cultural norms.

Yu Fangouing, director of the maternity ward at Beijing Hospital for Gynecology and Obstetrics, points out that many women are reluctant to use new practices based on scientific approaches. "They stick to the old-fashioned teachings of their mothers or in-laws and make a list of taboos after delivery—abstaining from taking a bath, cleaning their teeth, eating fruits and getting out of bed within one month of delivery. Babies are completely bound up for one month" (Manhong, 1987). Such practices can be deeply embedded within cultures and subcultures.

It is helpful to acknowledge three primary realizations that have occurred in relation to Traditional Chinese Medicine as a result of interaction with foreign medical orientations: "1) First, there would no such term as Traditional Chinese Medicine if Western medicine had not been introduced in China; . . . 2) Second, the introduction of Western medicine into China brought much basic scientific knowledge of biology to Traditional Chinese Medicine; . . . 3) Third . . . the introduction of Western medicine into China, to some extent, had the effect of promoting the development of Traditional Chinese Medicine (China Intercontinental, 2011, pp. 13–15)

The merging of TCM with Western medicine in China exemplifies a situation where old ideas are cross-culturally communicated through new perspectives via mass mediated venues. That is, Chinese medical approaches are explained through western perspectives. As such, more doors have opened for possibilities regarding health communication study. This kind of health communication study is particularly relevant because it involves reporting about Traditional Chinese Medicine and this, in turn, impacts what Traditional Chinese Medicine will become.

The Confucius Institute system provides a forum for exchange, learning and growth in relation to enhancement of TCM, Western medicine and medical conceptions based on this merging. With this increased sharing has come the potential for even more sharing. Such interaction is breeding ground for more interaction and innovation.

Though there are obstacles within this process, the benefits have been viewed as being well worth the costs (obstacles which have been encountered). This report is concerned with the benefits of such interaction, and some of the problems which have arisen, in hopes of better understanding a process which can continue to improve health care practices around the world. It is clearly evident that mass mediated venues will play a significant role in the conveyance of information within this process and this, in turn, will enhance health communication inquiries.

REFERENCES

Chance meeting spawns acupuncture Centre. (April 22, 1987). *China Daily*, p. 1.

China Intercontinental. *Traditional Chinese medicine.* (2011). New York: Cambridge University Press.

China leads in cancer treatment. (April 28, 1987). China Daily p. 3.

Ching, F. (ed.). (2007). *Chinese herbal drug research trends.* New York: Nova Scotia Publishers.

Cuellar, N. (2006). *Conversations in complementary and alternative medicine.* Sudbury, MA: Jones & Bartlett Publishers.

Dr. Kie Zhufan invited to lecture in USA. (December 1981). *Journal of Traditional Chinese Medicine* (Vol. 1, No. 2), p. 97.

East-West Work Urged in Medicine. (April 6, 1987). *China Daily* p. 4.

Garran, T. (2008). *Western herbs according to traditional Chinese medicine.* Rochester, VT: Healing Arts Press.

Guanfeng, C. (March 31, 1987). Top expert warns of shortage of doctors, *China Daily*, p. 1.

Jianhua, A. (April 6, 1987). Nurse tailors her care. *China Daily* p. 6.

Lectures on essentials of traditional Chinese medicine. (September 1981). *Journal of Traditional Chinese Medicine* (Vol. 1, No. 1), p. 73.

Manhong, S. (April 16, 1987). Teaching science of nurture. *China Daily* p. 5.

Meizhong, Y. (September, 1981). To my colleagues. *Journal of Traditional Chinese Medicine* (Vol. 1, No. 1), p. i.

Old and new combine to heal. (May 14, 1987), *China Daily* p. 6.

Shock waves remove gallstones. (April 8, 1987). *China Daily* p. 5.

Tingting, Z. (April 20, 1987). Blood donors get new incentives. *China Daily* p. 3.

Yueli, C. (September, 1981). A welcome event in international academic exchange on traditional

Chinese medicine. *Journal of Traditional Chinese Medicine* (Vol. 1, No. 1). , p. v.

Chapter 7:

Cultural considerations in health care practices

Nan Yu
North Dakota State University

Charles Okigbo
North Dakota State University

INTRODUCTION

Good health is the most valuable asset to the individual because without it all other resources of people, their organizations, and communities will be suboptimal. Not surprisingly, every human community places a high premium on health and wellness through designs that help avoid illness and improve wellbeing. Good health is not only the absence of disease but more importantly the presence of wellbeing for, as the World Health Organization (WHO) has asserted, health is "a state of complete physical, mental, and social well-being and not merely the absence of disease or infirmity" (WHO, 1948, p.1).

Human culture, which is the sum total of people's learned values, beliefs, customs, and behaviors, is intrinsically implicated in health and wellbeing. Many cultural practices such as birth rituals, perceptions of diseases, nutrition and diet, and rites of transition to adulthood have serious health implications for both natives and immigrants. With ever increasing globalization and immigration, cultural considerations of health and wellbeing are taking center stage and deserving more attention. Our goal in this chapter is to show why it is imperative to adopt a multicultural approach in the delivery of health care services and also to provide a strategic framework for culture-based health communication intervention in the present environment of cultural diversity, especially with regard to immigrant communities in the U.S. To achieve these, we describe the increasing cultural diversity which ramifies into important subcultures—each of which has implications for health, and also note the challenges of health disparities and the need for building cultural competency skills in society. In view of the increasing inflow of new immigrants into the U.S., we show why acculturation is a vital aspect of contemporary cultural diversity and the strategic framework for health communication.

A More Diverse Nation

One of the most characteristic features of the United States of America is the astounding variety of people who call it home. These include the Native Americans, who were the original inhabitants before the waves of colonizers from Europe, new arrivals from Africa, and immigrants from Asia and Latin America. The history of the United States is the history of incessant waves of immigrants from virtually every country and continent, and this is still continuing up to the present day. Indeed in recent years the U.S. has been "absorbing a tide of immigrants from Latin America and Asia that rivals the great tide of immigrants from eastern and southern Europe that arrived at the beginning of the twentieth century" (Faragher, Buhle, Czitrom, & Armitage, 2000, p. xliv). The immigrants from Europe constitute the majority of the population and have always been the dominant culture, accounting for 73.3% of the total population in 1996, 71.8% in 2000, and 63.0% in 2012 (U.S. Census Bureau, 2012). The tide is turning regarding majority-minority representation of the races such that by the middle of the 21st century, white people may not constitute more than half the population of the country.

According to the U.S. Census Bureau (2012) the minority population in the U.S. is expected to comprise more than 57% of the overall population by 2060. The minority population is comprised of ethnic groups that are "differentiated from the dominant group on the basis of cultural differences such as language, attitudes towards marriage and parenting, and food habits (Schaefer, 2000, p. 9). Ethnic groups are identifiably different from each other because of their unique national origins and distinct cultures. These have implications for health beliefs and practices. It is in this respect that public health professionals and scholars are increasingly concerned about how to successfully address the health needs of these ethnic groups. The ethnic groups often share different cultural values, ethnic customs, and world views. Some may have low English proficiency (Flores, 2005), some may have unique health beliefs, and some may have their own health-related customs (Ayala, Baquero, & Klinger, 2008; Fadiman, 2012; Lee-Lin, Menon, Nail, & Lutz, 2012). These cultural differences can prevent them from receiving quality health care services, delaying their participation in early screening or preventive health care, or create barriers for them to engage in effective communication with their health care providers (Arcia, Skinner, Bailey, & Correa, 2001; Flores, 2005; Shpilko, 2006; Zunker, Rutt, and Meza, 2005; Lee, 2000; Lim, 2010).

By 2012, the overall minority population accounted for 37% of the total population and this number is projected to be 57% by 2060 (U.S. Census Bureau, 2012). As of 2012, Latin America remained the largest minority group (17%), followed by African America (13%), Asian (5.1%), multi-racial (2.4%), American Indian and Alaska Native (1.2%), and Native Hawaiian and other Pacific Islander (0.2%).

Among the newborns, minorities babies under age one made up 50.4% of births in a 12-month period from July 2010 to July 2011. This was the first time that most of the U.S. babies were from minority and ethnic groups in U.S. history (Morello & Mellnik, 2012). As of 2011, 12 states and the District of Columbia had white population below 50% among children under age 5. These states are Hawaii, California, New Mexico, Texas, Arizona, Nevada, Florida, Maryland, Georgia,

New Jersey, New York, and Mississippi ("Majority of U.S.," 2011). The Hispanic and Asian population is estimated to be double by 2060. It is projected that, by 2043, the non-Hispanic white population will still remain the largest single group, but no group will make up a majority (U.S. Census Bureau, 2012). This presents a challenging scenario which will require adjustments to the prevailing methods and practices of health communication campaigns targeting the mass society because effective interventions must be related to the cultures of the recipient groups. Heath communication interventions that are not culturally appropriate are doomed to be unsuccessful, and for this, it is imperative to appreciate the vital role of culture.

What is Culture?

As the country becomes more culturally diverse, it is important to consider the role of culture in promoting or inhibiting the reception of quality health care. In general, *culture* is defined as a group of people who share a set of beliefs, values, and attitudes that guide their behavior (Gudykunst, Ting-Toomy, & Chua, 1988). Another way of explaining culture is with recourse to the approach that focuses on the full range of learned activities and behaviors of the people to underline the fact that culture includes knowledge, morals, customs, and any capabilities and habits which are acquired by people as functioning members of their communities. Culture is a powerful tool for communication in a society because it provides the context for people to decode messages and make sense of the information received.

It is possible to have a smaller group within a cultural group, and thus have a subculture with its shared traits that set the members apart from the rest of their society. Examples of subcultures in the United States include ethnic groups such as Jamaican Americans, Mexican Americans, Indian Americans, and Hmong Americans. Each of these subcultures shares a common identity, food tradition, health beliefs and behaviors, and language. Subcultures are easily identifiable among recent immigrants. However, with the passage of time and successful acculturation and assimilation, the children and grandchildren of immigrants gradually lose some of the characteristics of their subculture making the subculture less distinctive in some respects.

Whereas the cultural differences between members of some subcultures and the dominant national culture in the U.S. may blur, they hardly disappear completely. Today, there are still identifiable communities of German, Irish, and Jewish immigrants, just as African American and Asian communities are easily identifiable. Therefore, it is important to recognize the nexus between immigrant cultures and heath beliefs. Individuals immigrating to the U.S. often share different understandings of health or illness because of the prevailing health cultures in their countries or regions of origin.

For example, Asians and Pacific Islanders perceive mind and body as interlinked and the curing of the physical illness requires the healing of the mindset first. Many Asian cultures consider the mention of the word "death" in conversations as extremely inappropriate because it can signal a wretched fortune or a curse. During interpersonal communications, Asians are usually reluctant to raise questions voluntarily especially to people with authority (e.g. physicians) because question-asking can be seen as a challenge to the speaker. Because patients from Asian cultures may be passive during their interactions with physicians, health care providers need to purposely encourage them to participate in the health decision-making process (DuPre, 2010, "Reducing health disparities," 2005).

In Hispanic cultures, the cause of an illness can be attributed to shocking or frightening experience in some cases. The family or the patient may be reluctant to share those horrifying stories with their doctor (Willies-Jacobo, 2007). Patients from Hispanic cultures also value warm interpersonal relationships and often have high respect for senior individuals or those in power. Therefore, during their interactions with physicians, they tend to avoid conflict and prefer an establishment of a trustworthy relationship before they can be open to their health care providers (Añez, Silva, Paris, & Bedregal, 2008, DuPre, 2010).

The above examples signify the importance of considering the impact of culture in health interactions. Neglecting the cultural uniqueness of ethnic groups can cause harmful consequences including missing necessary screening for early prevention of illness, failing to follow proper medication, and suffering from diagnosis errors due to ineffective communication (Brach & Fraserirector, 2000; Flores, 2003).

Many public health organizations and programs have started to put enormous efforts in understanding and addressing the cultural needs of ethnic groups. The National Institute on Minority Health and Health Disparities, for example, is an organization aiming at promoting training of a diverse workforce, translating research information, evaluating minority health and health disparities research and activities, and increasing the visibility of minority health disparities. The Office of Minority Health with the U.S. Department of Health and Human Services, which was established in 1986, offers various funds and recourses to improve the health of racial and ethnic minority populations and to decrease and ultimately eliminate health disparities. For example, one of the shared goals of *Healthy People 2010* and *Healthy People 2020* is eliminating health disparities and improving health equity. The establishment of these organizations and initiatives signifies the increasing attention from the administrative level in addressing the cultural needs in health care practices.

Health Disparities in the U.S.

Health disparities describes the variations in accessibility to health care services, health outcomes, risks pertaining to certain diseases, and quality of health care which exist across racial and ethnic groups (Brach & Fraserirector, 2000, Betancourt, Green, Carrillo, & Ananeh-Firempong, 2003). Starting from 1946, the U.S. Centers for Diseases Control and Prevention (CDC) started to monitor the gaps on "illness, injury, risk behaviors, use of preventive health services, exposure to environmental hazards, and premature death" and to identify the least and most vulnerable groups associated with certain health risks in the nation (CDC, 2011, p1). In this part, we include some basic facts about health disparities existing among different racial and ethnic groups in the United States.

American Indians/Alaska Natives (AI/AN)

American Indians and Alaska Natives population comprises 1.7% of the U.S. total population (U.S. Census, 2012). AI/ANs often maintain tribal affiliations or community attachment. More than half of AI/ANs do not permanently live on a reservation. The leading causes of death for AI/ANs include heart disease, cancer, unintentional injuries, diabetes, and chronic liver disease and cirrhosis (CDC, 2012a). Below are some examples of health disparities for AI/ANs (CDC, 2011; CDC, 2012a; CDC, 2012d):

- In 2007, the suicide rate among AI/ANs was the highest among all racial and ethnic populations.
- In 2009, the prevalence of smoking for AI/AN youth (aged 12–17) and AI/AN adults remained the highest among all racial and ethnic populations.
- In 2009, AI/AN adults had highest prevalence of binge drinking among all racial and ethnic populations.
- In 2008, the percentage of AI/AN adults living in poverty ranked the top compared with other racial/ethnic groups. Compared with white adults, 12% more AI/AN adults lived below the federal poverty level.
- In 2006, the AI/AN infant death rate was second to the rate among African American mothers and 48.4% greater than the rate of white mothers.
- In 2007, AI/ANs had the highest rate of motor vehicle-related deaths compared to all other racial and ethnic populations.
- In 2001, the prevalence of syphilis among AI/ANs was six times higher than among non-Hispanic whites, the Chlamydia rate was 5.5 times higher, the gonorrhea rate was four times higher, and the AIDS rate was 1.5 times higher.

Asian

As of 2012, the Asian population, including Chinese, Asian Indians, Filipinos, Vietnamese, Koreans, and Japanese, accounts for 5.1% of the U.S. population (U.S. Census, 2012). California and New York host the largest Asian population whereas Hawaii had the biggest concentration (57%) of Asian population (CDC; 2012b). Some of the primary health disparities for Asians who live in the U.S. include (CDC, 2011, CDC, 2012b; CDC, 2012d):

- Asian American women's rate of having a pap test (68%) was slightly lower compared with women from other ethnic groups: non-Hispanic white (72.8%), non-Hispanic black (77.4%), Hispanic (73.6%), and AI/AN (73.4%).
- Asian American women have the longest life expectancy (85.8 years) compared with all other racial and ethnic groups.
- In 2008, Asian Americans had a slightly higher age-adjusted prevalence of diabetes (8.2%) compared to whites.

- From 2006 to 2008, the percentage of Asian Americans and Hispanics who lived in counties whose air quality did not meet Environmental Protection Agency (EPA) standards was higher compared with other racial and ethnic populations.
- From 1988–1992, Vietnamese American women had the highest age-adjusted prevalence of cervical cancer (43 per 100,000); nearly five times higher than non-Hispanic white women.
- Asian Americans and Pacific Islanders had the highest rate of tuberculosis (TB) (33 per 100,000) in 2001 among all racial and ethnic groups.

Hispanics

Hispanics form the largest ethnic minority in the U.S., representing 17% of the overall population. Individuals from Mexico, Puerto Rico, Cuba, Salvador, and Dominica, make up over 80% of this minority group (U.S. Census, 2012, CDC, 2012e). California hosts the largest Hispanic population in the country whereas New Mexico has the highest concentration (46.7%) of this group. The top five leading causes of death for Hispanics in 2009 were cancer, heart disease, unintentional injuries, stroke, and diabetes (CDC, 2012e). Some other facts about health disparities of Hispanic population include (CDC, 2011; CDC, 2012d; CDC, 2012e):

- Compared to Asian Americans and non-Hispanic whites, the uninsured rate among Hispanics (42.7% in 2004, and 22.6% in 2008) was significantly higher.
- During the flu season of 2009-2010, the influenza vaccination coverage rate among Hispanics aged six or above was lower compared with non-Hispanic whites.
- Hispanic males aged 2–19 had a higher prevalence of obesity than non-Hispanic whites or African Americans. Among males aged 40 or above, racial/ethnic differences were not found.
- From 1993–1995, the asthma death rate was 34 per million among Hispanics in the northeast U.S.; more than twice the rate for non-Hispanic whites.

African Americans

African Americans were the second largest minority group as of 2012, accounting for approximately 13% of the overall population (U.S. Census, 2012). About 55% of African Americans lived in the southern states of the U.S. The highest concentration of this group appears in District of Columbia (57%), Mississippi (37%), Louisiana (32%), Georgia (31%), Maryland (30%), South Carolina (28%), and Alabama (27%). The leading causes of death for African Americans include heart disease, cancer, stroke, diabetes, and unintentional injuries (CDC, 2012c). The following are some highlights about health disparities among African Americans (CDC, 2011; CDC, 2012d; CDC, 2012c):

- The average life expectancy for African American was 74.5 years, which was lower than the national average of 78.5 years.

- African American women aged 20–39 had the highest prevalence of obesity compared to other groups of African Americans.
- In 2007, African Americans had the highest death rate of homicide compared with all other racial and ethnic groups.
- Similar to AI/ANs, the percentage of African American adults living in poverty was higher than other racial and ethnic groups.
- African Americans accounted for more than 50% of all new HIV infections reported in 2011.
- The age-adjusted death rate of heart disease was 30% higher for African Americans than for non-Hispanic whites in 2011.

Many factors can cause health disparities between different racial and ethnic groups. Low socioeconomic status, such as inadequate education, poverty, and unemployment, directly link to insufficient access to health care services or worse health outcomes (Brach & Fraserirector, 2000; Lillie-Blanton & Laveist, 1996). However, in some cases, minority groups had different health care experiences even when they shared similar socioeconomic status and insurance coverage. Some scholars conclude that part of health disparities may be caused by the different health customs and beliefs, community features, personal behaviors, cultural and linguistic barriers, and inadequate consideration of cultural needs of racial and ethnic minorities (Betancourt et al., 2003; Brach & Fraserirector, 2000).

Understanding health disparities is so critical to the generalized health care services in today's society that closing the gaps is at the root of many new strategies for "Health for All" at local, national, and global levels. At the national level, it has provided impetus for Obamacare, which is designed to ensure that no patient will go untreated or uninsured. At the global level, it has provided the energy for such egalitarian policies as the Health Millennium Development Goals. Whereas two decades ago, many critics called attempts at addressing health disparities "socialized medicine," today it is becoming increasingly more fashionable to accept that our society is in danger if some sections do not have ready access to the medical treatment they need. Closing the gaps in health care services cannot be achieved by waving a magic wand as there are many obstacles, many of which are cultural and indeed often start with language, which is one of the most important cultural artifacts.

Language

Language is the basic tool that makes interpersonal communication possible. In the realm of health communication, it is the medium for exchanging information in verbal or non-verbal contexts. Here is an illustration of the critical value of language in health:

> *Kim experienced severe lower abdomen pains after a quick lunch followed by an hour of gym exercise. The pains didn't go away even up to midnight and he also had a fever. He finally decided to go the emergency*

room. After he was tested and evaluated, he was diagnosed with appendicitis. Wayne, however, had never heard of this word before because English is his second language. He had to call his friend and ask him to search the meaning of the word on the Internet so he can know what was wrong with him.

Medical conversations can sound like a foreign language even to people who speak English fluently. So imagine if a healthcare professional wants to discuss the risks and benefits of a surgery or a medication to individuals who speak only Spanish, Chinese, or Greek.

Over 57 million Americans (20% of the total population five years old or over) speak a non-English language at home. The top five home foreign languages are Spanish, Chinese, Tagalog, French, and Vietnamese (U.S. Census Bureau, 2009a). The use of foreign languages at home is especially high in some states including California (43.1%), New Mexico (35.8%), Texas (34.2%), New York (29.0%), and New Jersey (28.5%) (U.S. Census Bureau, 2009b). The frequent use of foreign languages often accompanies inadequate English proficiency. By 2010, individuals with limited English proficiency (LEP) reached 25.2 million, accounting for approximately 9% of the U.S. population over age five. This number grew by 80% from 1990 to 2010. The six traditional immigrant-destination states—California, Texas, New York, Florida, Illinois, and New Jersey—had the highest numbers of LEP population by 2010 (Pandya, Batalova, & McHugh, 2011).

As the U.S. population becomes more diverse each year, the demand for medical interpreters is also growing. The use of competent medical interpreters is effective and useful to improve communication between physicians and patients, reduce the likelihood of misunderstanding of diagnoses and medication errors, and increase compliance with medical advices and patient satisfaction (Flores, 2005). Physicians nowadays are encouraged to learn how to work effectively with trained medical interpreters (Hart, Bowen, DeJesus, Maldonado, & Jiwa, 2010).

However, the availability or the quality of medical interpreters is limited. Instead, ad hoc interpreters, such as family members, friends, strangers in the waiting rooms, are commonly seen in medical encounters. Baker et al. (1996) surveyed 467 native Spanish-speaking and 63 English-speaking Latino patients with non-urgent medical problems in an emergency department. The researchers found that professional interpreters were not used 34% of the time when patients had limited proficiency in both English and Spanish and 87% of the patients felt the need for a medical interpreter was not met. When interpreters were used, some most-often-made errors during medical interpretation included omitting instructions on the proper use of medication or necessary inquiries of drug allergies (Flores, et al. 2003). Additionally, clinicians often received inadequate training in working with medical interpreters (Flores, 2005).

The communicative challenges during medical encounters caused by language barriers can have serious consequencies. Patients with LEP may require additional meeting time with their doctors (Kravitz, Helms, Azari, Antonius, & Melnikow, 2000). They are less likely to receive quality health care or preventive service or be incorrectly diagnosed due to linguistic barriers (Flores, 2005). In one case, an 18-year-old Spanish boy was mistakenly treated for 36 hours before the patient was reevaluated and offered proper treatment due to a language misunderstanding. This case cost the hospital $71 million for malpractice settlement (Flores et al., 2003; Flores, 2005).

The accessibility to language assistance in medical settings has been gradually improving. California became the first state to pass a law in 2003 that requires commercial health insurance providers to offer translating and interpreting services (at least by telephone) to their subscribers with LEP (Chen, Youdelman, & Brooks, 2007; Kravitz, 2000). By 2006, at least 43 states in the U.S. had enacted at least one law addressing language access in healthcare settings (Chen et al., 2007). Most of these laws, however, focused on patient education (e.g. mandating multi-lingual educational pamphlets for certain diseases) rather than concentrating on providing real-time interpretation during medical visits (Chen et al., 2007). The competency of medical interpreters still remains an issue in many places because the interpreters must have competency in at least two languages, the medical terminology, as well as an understanding of the ethics issues (i.e. privacy). As important as language is, it is only part of the entire portfolio of cultural needs that must be purposively addressed in the context of cultural considerations of health care practices.

Cultural Needs in Health Practices

As members of subcultures or cultures, individuals in society must learn to navigate the challenges that confront them as patients or clients needing health care services. Even when they have successfully overcome the language barriers, they still have to beat the other obstacles that are results of performing in multicultural environments. The following case study illustrates cultural needs in health practices:

> *Gine was in labor for 12 hours before she successfully delivered a baby boy. The first thing she wanted when she woke up after the exhausted "journey" was to have a glass of warm water. She found that the nurse had kindly put some water with ice in the room and she decided to wait for the ice to melt before she could take a sip. Helen fell asleep during this waiting because she was too tired. When she woke up again, she found that the nurse had replaced the old water with fresh icy water again. This time, she decided to tell the nurse directly that, in the Asian culture that Helen belonged to, cold water is not recommended for new moms. They can only drink water that is warm or hot.*

Each culture has its uniqueness in preferences, beliefs, and needs in health care practices. Some of these differences can become obstacles for minority groups to receive quality health care. Some of the cultural variations may create unusual expectations for patient-doctor communication. The following discussion highlights some examples regarding cultural differences and needs in health care practices.

Russian immigrant families prefer doctors to share the news of a severe diagnosis with the patients' families first before the patient is informed. These families believe that they are obligated to take the burden of telling the truth to their beloved family member. This culture is completely different from the common health practices in the U.S., where patients' autonomy, privacy, and independence are highly valued (Shpilko, 2006). There is also a tendency in Russian immigrant communities for participation in regular cancer-screening tests to be initiated by their physicians and if the health care providers do not provide routine reminders, they are less likely to voluntarily engage in such preventive tests (Ivanov & Buck, 2002). Many Russian immigrants prefer to use the medications that are imported from their home country because they are cheaper or because they know more about how to use the medications in their own languages (Ivanov & Buck, 2002). Alternative treatment, such as herbal medications, spiritual healing, and hydrotherapy, are still preferred by many Russian-speaking immigrants (Shpilko, 2006).

Chun, Chesla, and Kwan (2011) examined how Chinese immigrant couples performed daily diabetes management. They discovered a high level of stress and anxiety among these patients and their families because they struggled with communicating with their health care providers, scheduling medical appointments, or buying necessary over-the-counter diabetes care products using a second language. The stress was eased when they received instructional or emotional support from medical staff (e.g. nurses) who offered them medical advice in both English and Chinese. Surprisingly, some patients felt that they were reluctant to ask diabetes care questions when they met with Chinese American physicians because they appeared to be less courteous, patient, and attentive than European American physicians. This interesting phenomenon occurred because the interaction with Chinese American physicians reinforced the patients about the Chinese cultural norm of hierarchical doctor-patient relationship, whereas such norm was not expected when communicating with a European American physician. The scholars also noted that some patients were unsatisfied with the translation services, but they highly praised the professional standards of American physicians (Chun et al., 2011).

Hispanic women reported a feeling of social isolation and lack of social support after moving to the United States (Sanchez-Birkhead, Kennedy, Callister, & Miyamoto, 2011). They were accustomed to the tradition that people who were ill were first taken care of at home by their immediate families. When they seek health care providers, family or friends would serve as trustworthy sources. After moving to the U.S., Hispanics still rely on their mothers or relatives as direct health information sources because they have learned most of their knowledge in their families. When necessary, they would even make international phone calls to seek for health advice rather than looking for more geographically convenient sources. Family ties also influence Hispanics to engage in regular preventive screening or tests because parents, especially mothers, often remind them to get their bodies checked routinely. The combined use of home remedies or western medicines is very common among Hispanic population. They believe the natural or herbal remedies can naturalize some of the strong and harmful effects caused by the western medications. However, most of the Hispanics prefer a utilization of western techniques when it comes to surgical treatment. Many Hispanics still feel stressful during clinical visits after years of living in the U.S. because they often feel they were differently treated during medical encounters (Sanchez-Birkhead et al., 2011).

Gregg, Nguyen-Truong, Wang, and Kobus (2011) revealed that Vietnamese immigrants closely follow their beliefs about health and illness. They believe that illness is "a result of internal imbalance from mental or physical stress or external processes such as food, drink, or infection" (p.1086). They strongly believe that individuals' life routines and habits largely determine whether a person is ill or healthy. Therefore, they commonly prioritize good personal hygiene habits in preventing illness rather than relying on regular protective tests or screening (Gregg et al., 2011).

The influence of culture on health beliefs and practices cannot be gainsaid. Language and cultural needs are necessary to building an effective communication, which is necessary for improved health. As Beers and Jones note (2004), "an effective communication with doctors and other health care practitioners improves health. Understanding how to communicate effectively and how to go about it are not so simple. As the old expression goes, 'The devil is in the details' (p. 78)." The details are inherent in the various expressions of culture including language, cultural needs, and other aspects of learned conduct and behavior. Proper conduct in any particular culture requires proper development of cultural competency skills through acculturation.

Cultural Competency Building and Acculturation

Effective health communication between a patient and a service provider should reflect a two-way symmetrical exchange based on mutual trust and respect and requiring that both parties have reasonable expectations of each other. The onus is more on the health care service provider to exercise cultural competency in dealing with multicultural (particularly ethnic minority) patients or clients. Scholars and practitioners agree that a situational approach is best in dealing with cross-cultural audiences because a "one-size-fits-all" health care approach cannot meet the different cultural needs of the diverse populations in the United States.

Cultural competency refers to the behaviors, attitudes, and policies in a congruent system that enable professionals to work effectively in cross-cultural situations (Betancourt et al., 2003; Brach & Fraserirector, 2000). Public health scholars and practitioners have proposed several necessary means to increase cultural competency in health care practices with a goal of reducing racial and ethnic health disparities. Specifically, the suggestions made to increase cultural competency include the following seven steps:

1. Developing programs to support the provision of interpreters (e.g. professional interpreters, ad hoc interpreters, or simultaneous remote interpreters) for patients who speak a different language.
2. Recruiting or retaining medical staff from minority group members in the health care systems.
3. Including cultural competency training in undergraduate or graduate medical or other professional school education, an orientation process for new staff or network members, or part of in-service training programs.

4. Coordinating with the traditional healers or medications that patients use while they are seeking for biomedical care. This requires an acknowledgement of different cultural beliefs and an education of new health knowledge.
5. Including community health workers or family members to help promote cultural-orientated health care because minority groups tend to rely on personal circles for health care directions.
6. Improving health promotion efforts by including culturally adapted messages and language-appropriate health educational materials.
7. Improving administrative and organizational accommodations to increase the accessibility of health care service (Betancourt et al., 2003; Brach & Fraserirector, 2000):

On face value these procedures appear easy to implement but the many incidents of failed intercultural health communication testify to the difficulty experienced by health care professionals in developing cultural competency. The test of cultural competency is seen in the level of acculturation success.

Acculturation

Acculturation is a term that describes the process of cultural adjustment that follows intercultural contact (Berry, 2003). It involves selective adoption and rejection of aspects of the new culture by the immigrant resulting in one of four possible outcomes: integration or biculturalism, assimilation, separation, or marginalization (Berry, 1986). The amount and quality of first-hand contact and interaction that new immigrants have with members of their host communities affects acculturation outcomes (Dumka & Roosa, 1997). The most evident results and outcomes are the behavioral and attitudinal changes that immigrants display in adjusting to the new culture (Christenson, Zabriskie, Eggett, & Freeman, 2006). The cultural changes during the acculturation process may include psychological changes to adjust individuals' attitude toward acculturation process, individuals' cultural identities, and their social behaviors (Berry, Phinney, Sam, & Vedder, 2006).

Acculturation is a complex phenomenon that can affect how individuals handle their daily health practices and medical encounters. Whereas health care providers are expected to exhibit a high degree of cultural competency when they operate in multi-cultural health contexts, members of ethnic minorities, especially the immigrants among them should endeavor to embrace positive acculturation by adapting to the desirable health-related values, attitudes, and behaviors prescribed by health professionals.

Ayala, Baquero, and Klinger (2008) examined numerous studies of immigrants from Mexico and Puerto Rico and found that Hispanics who are less acculturated into the U.S. culture consume more whole milk and use more fat in food preparation. The more acculturated Hispanic, however, consume more fast food and snacks. Less acculturated Hispanic individuals also consume more fruit, rice, and beans, than those who are more acculturated ones. The consumption of sugar-sweetened drinks is higher among more acculturated Hispanics. The authors concluded that the acculturation can be undesirable because the dietary habits of Hispanics deteriorated during the acculturation process.

Acculturation can work in a desirable way, too. Latinos living in California who are more acculturated are three to four times more likely to engage in colorectal cancer screening than those that are less acculturated (Johnson-Kozlow, 2010). Korean women, a group that is often associated with low calcium intake and relative high rate of fractures, consume more milk to increase calcium intake after being acculturated into American lifestyle (Irvin, et al., 2013). A study of Bosnian refugees indicated that more acculturated individuals are more likely to perceive smoking as a risky behavior than those who are less acculturated (Helweg-Larsen & Stancioff, 2008).

In an action research study of African refugee and immigrant women in the Fargo-Moorhead Area to determine how well they were adjusting to their new social realities of living as minority group members, Okigbo, Reierson, & Stowman (2009) reported the prevalence of dialectical tensions, acculturation challenges, mental health issues, and depression among the study participants many of whom complained about racism and language difficulties. The results showed that the common aspirations of the women "involved adjusting successfully enough to operate like fully-integrated members of the societies while still retaining important aspects of their African culture" (p. 135). Successful acculturation implies positive adjustment that allows for the mixing and matching of aspects of original and new cultures without wholesale assimilation or separation. The African women recognized the need for mutual respect and support services and reported "they would like better appreciation of their African values and culture and more support from social service agencies" (p. 136). Building cultural competency and promoting positive acculturation present serious challenges in culturally sensitive health care practices, hence the great need for a strategic framework for health communication interventions.

Strategic Framework: Five Elements

With the minority population continuously on the increase and many members of immigrant communities facing serious challenges of cultural competency and acculturation, it is imperative that more serious attention be paid to developing strategies for successful management of intercultural communication in health care practices to avoid the deleterious consequences of communication failure. Many of the new immigrants differ significantly from the immigrants of yore in that they (the former) are not integrating as successfully as the latter in their new communities because of what Huntington (2004) characterized as declining assimilationist demands and a rise in multiculturalism and group rights. Add to this The Third Generation Principle that proposes more strident promotion and propagation of some cultures of emigration countries. A strategic framework must start with the recognition of the value of *strategic planning* as the first step in devising culturally sensitive health care practices that leave nothing to chance or serendipity. The other four elements are *audience, tactics, participation*, and *mutual respect*.

Whereas many health care professionals recognize the importance of cultural competency and acculturation in their work, their daily practices are often more correctly characterized as trial and error than reflective of strategic planning. A strategic planning approach will provide effective and cyclical training for all health care professionals who interact with multi-cultural patients, accompanyied with a systematic monitoring of performance, a provision of obvious and significant rewards and punishments, and periodic audits by independent external experts. Part of the strategic planning process includes a clear delineation of target audiences of health care practices so that adequate provisions would be made for meeting the needs of multi-cultural audiences.

Audience delineation goes with an accurate profiling to identify vital segments such as opinion leaders, influencers, and decision makers among them. As our society continues to fragment further into smaller units such as LGBT (i.e. lesbian, gay, bisexual, and transgender community) within ethnic minority groups, it is important to respect any new significant subcultures that may warrant special communication interventions, especially with regard to message encoding and the tactics of delivery.

The third element of the framework is tactics, which means the specific recommended actions, ways, and means of achieving the objectives of communication and health care practice. As specific actions, tactics can also be said to be the message packaged in such a way to maximize impact on a target audience in a specific situation. It is also a channel, since every message needs a medium for transmission. Thus we can conceive of tactics as "a channel with a message" (Guth & Marsh, 2006, p. 270). The three broad categories of channels are special events or occasions, controlled media, and uncontrolled media. With respect to multicultural publics, community events and small group meetings are vital channels and tactics because they engender audience participation.

Strategic planning, audience profiling, and tactical channels will yield only limited results if minority group members do not get the sense that they are fully appreciated, respected, and engaged within their own rights. Thus it is desirable to actively involve minority individuals and their groups and let them participate in making decisions on health care practices, to the extent possible. Participation of the minority groups is vital. Many organizations pay lip service to participation and engagement without true empowerment of members of minority groups. In seeking their active involvement, due recognition must be accorded to cultural practices relating to how some immigrant communities conduct public discussions and mixed gender seating arrangements. Some individuals are easily offended by trying to engage in ways that show ignorance of or disrespect for their cultural values and practices.

The fifth element of the framework is the cultivation and propagation of an environment that shows mutual respect. Many minority groups complain about outright or disguised discrimination at the hands of health care service providers some of whom on their part feel disrespected by some immigrants' sense of time. Being culturally competent should make both parties more empathic and appreciative of the other's cultural influences.

CONCLUSION

As the demographic profile of the United States changes with increasing diversity, it is imperative that we seek new strategies for optimizing the inevitable intercultural currents in managing health care among majority and minority ethnic groups. Such strategies must build on the notions of cultural competency and successful acculturation as the foundation for a strategic framework that will incorporate strategic planning, audience profiling, tactics as a channel with a message, active participation of individuals and their groups, and the nurturing of an environment of mutual respect. The costs of failed inter-cultural communication in health care practices are much too expensive to be condoned and the prospects for effective communication are too attractive to ignore. The final picture fills one with hope if the partners are willing to adopt empathy and eschew self-pride built on ignorance.

REFERENCES

Añez, L. M., Silva, M. A., Paris Jr., M., & Bedregal, L. E. (2008). Engaging Latinos through the integration of cultural values and motivational interviewing principles. *Professional Psychology: Research and Practice, 39*(2), 153–159.

Arcia, E., Skinner, M., Bailey, D., & Correa, V. (2001). *Models of acculturation and health behaviors among Latino immigrants to the U.S. Social Science & Medicine, 53*(1), 41–53.

Ayoko, O. B., Härtel, C. E., & Callan, V. J. (2002). Resolving the puzzle of productive and destructive conflict in culturally heterogeneous workgroups: A communication accommodation theory approach. *International Journal of Conflict Management, 13*(2), 165–195.

Baker, D. W., Parker, R. M., Williams, M. V., Coates, W. C., & Pitkin, K. (1996). Use and effectiveness of interpreters in an emergency department. *JAMA: The Journal of the American Medical Association, 275*(10), 783–788. doi: 10.1001/jama.275.10.783

Beers, M. H., & Jones, T. V. (Eds.), *The Merck manual of health and aging.* Whitehouse Station, NJ: Merck Research Laboratories.

Betancourt, J. R., Green, A. R., Carrillo, J. E., & Ananeh-Firempong, O. (2003). Defining cultural competence: A practical framework for addressing racial/ethnic disparities in health and health care. *Public Health Reports, 118*(4), 293–302.

Berry, J. W., Phinney, J. S., Sam, D. L., & Vedder, P. (2006). Immigrant youth: Acculturation, identity, and adaptation. *Applied Psychology: An International Review, 55*, 303–332.

Berry, J. W. (2003). Conceptual approaches to acculturation. In K. M. Chun, P. B. Organista, & G. Marin (Eds.), *Acculturation: Advances in Theory, Measurement, and Applied Research*, pp. 17–37. Washington, DC: APA Press.

Berry, J. W. (1986). The acculturation process and refugee behavior. In C. J. Williams & J. Westermeyer (Eds), *Refugee mental health in resettlement countries*. New York: Hemisphere.

Brach, C., & Fraserirector, I. (2000). Can cultural competency reduce racial and ethnic health disparities? A review and conceptual model. *Medical Care Research and Review*, *57*(4), 181–217. doi: 10.1177/1077558700574009

Centers for Disease Control and Prevention (CDC). (2011). CDC health disparities and inequalities report—United States, 2011. Retrieved from www.cdc.gov/mmwr/pdf/other/su6001.pdf

Centers for Disease Control and Prevention (CDC). (2012a). Minority health: American Indian & Alaska Native populations. Retrieved from http://www.cdc.gov/minorityhealth/populations/REMP/aian.html

Centers for Disease Control and Prevention (CDC). (2012b). Minority health: Asian American population: Examples of important health disparities. Retrieved from http://www.cdc.gov/minorityhealth/populations/REMP/asian.html

Centers for Disease Control and Prevention (CDC). (2012c). Minority health: Black or African American populations: Retrieved from http://www.cdc.gov/minorityhealth/populations/REMP/black.html

Centers for Disease Control and Prevention (CDC). (2012d). Minority health: Brochures. Retrieved from http://www.cdc.gov/minorityhealth/brochures.html

Centers for Disease Control and Prevention (CDC). (2012e). Minority health: Hispanic or Latino populations: Retrieved from http://www.cdc.gov/minorityhealth/populations/REMP/hispanic.html

Chen, A., H., Youdelman, M. K., & Brooks, J. (2007). The legal framework for language access in healthcare settings: Title VI and beyond. *Journal of General Internal Medicine*, *22*(2), 362–367.

Chun, K. M., Chesla, C. A., & Kwan, C. M. (2011). "So we adapt step by step": Acculturation experiences affecting diabetes management and perceived health for Chinese American immigrants. *Social Science & Medicine*, *72*(2), 256–264. doi: 10.1016/j.socscimed.2010.11.010

Christensen, O., Zabriskie, R., Eggett, D., & Freeman, P. (2006). Family acculturation, family leisure involvement, and family functioning among Mexican-American. *Journal of Leisure Research*, *38*(4), 475–495.

Dumka, L. R., & Roose, M. W. (1997). Risk, conflict, mother's parenting, and adjustment in low-income Mexican immigrant, and Mexican American families. *Journal of Marriage and Family*, *59*(2), 309–323.

DuPré, A. (2010). *Communicating about health: Current issues and perspectives*. New York: Oxford University Press.

Fadiman, A. (2012). *The spirit catches you and you fall down: A Hmong child, her American doctors, and the collision of two cultures.* New York: Farrar, Straus and Giroux.

Flores, G. (2005). The impact of medical interpreter services on the quality of health care: A systematic review. *Medical Care Research and Review, 62*(3), 255–299. doi: 10.1177/1077558705275416

Flores, G., Laws, M. B., Mayo, S. J., Zuckerman, B., Abreu, M., Medina, L., & Hardt, E. J. (2003). Errors in medical interpretation and their potential clinical consequences in pediatric encounters. *Pediatrics, 111*(1), 6–14.

Faragher, J. M., Buhle, M. J., Czitrom, D., & Armitage, S. H. (2000). *Out of many: A history of the American people* (3rd ed.). Upper Saddle River, NJ: Prentice Hall.

Gregg, J., Nguyen-Truong, C. K., Wang, P. R., & Kobus, A. (2011). Prioritizing prevention: Culture, context, and cervical cancer screening among Vietnamese American women. *Journal of Immigrant and Minority Health, 13*(6), 1084–1089.

Gudykunst, W. B., Ting-Toomey, S., & Chua, E. (1988). *Culture and Interpersonal communication.* Newbury Park, CA: Sage publications.

Guth, D. W. & Marsh, C. (2006). *Public relations: A value-driven approach.* Boston: Allyn and Bacon.

Hart, D., Bowen, J., DeJesus, R., Maldonado, A., & Jiwa, F. (2010). Using medical interpreters. *Minnesota Medicine, 93*(4), 42–44.

Helweg-Larsen, M., & Stancioff, L. M. (2008). Acculturation matters: Risk perceptions of smoking among Bosnian refugees living in the United States. *Journal of Immigrant and Minority Health, 10*(5), 423–428.

Huntington, S. P. (2004). *Who are we? The challenges of America's national identity.* New York: Simon & Schuster.

Ivanov, L. L., & Buck, K. (2002). Health care utilization patterns of Russian-speaking immigrant women across age groups. *Journal of Immigrant Health, 4*(1), 17–27.

Irvin, V. L., Nichols, J. F., Hofstetter, C. R., Ojeda, V. D., Song, Y. J., Kang, S., & Hovell, M. F. (2013). Osteoporosis and milk intake among Korean women in California: Relationship with acculturation to U.S. lifestyle. *Journal of Immigrant and Minority Health*, 1–6.

Johnson-Kozlow, M. (2010). Colorectal cancer screening of Californian adults of Mexican origin as a function of acculturation. *Journal of Immigrant and Minority Health, 12*(4), 454–461.

Kravitz, R. L., Helms, L. J., Azari, R., Antonius, D., & Melnikow, J. (2000). Comparing the use of physician time and health care resources among patients speaking English, Spanish, and Russian. *Medical Care, 38*(7), 728–738.

Kritz, F. L. (2010, December 27). Medical interpreters are a patient's right. *Los Angeles Times.* Retrieved from http://articles.latimes.com/2010/dec/27/health/la-he-medical-interpreters-20101227

Lee, M. C. (2000). Knowledge, barriers, and motivators related to cervical cancer screening among Korean-American women: A focus group approach. *Cancer Nursing, 23*(3), 168–175.

Lee-Lin, F., Menon, U., Nail, L., & Lutz, K. F. (2012). Findings from focus groups indicating what Chinese American immigrant women think about breast cancer and breast cancer screening. *Journal of Obstetric, Gynecologic, & Neonatal Nursing, 41*(5), 627–637.

Lim, J. W. (2010). Linguistic and ethnic disparities in breast and cervical cancer screening and health risk behaviors among Latina and Asian American women. *Journal of Women's Health, 19*(6), 1097–1107.

Lillie-Blanton, M., & Laveist, T. (1996). Race/ethnicity, the social environment, and health. *Social Science & Medicine, 43*(1), 83–91.

Majority of U.S. babies are non-White for first time, census finds. (2011, June 13) *Associated Press.* Retrieved from http://www.huffingtonpost.com/2011/06/23/census-whites-now-make-up-minority-of-babies_n_883082.html

Morello, C., & Mellnik, T. (2012, May 16). Census: Minority babies are now majority in United States. *The Washington Post.* Retrieved from http://www.washingtonpost.com/local/census-minority-babies-are-now-majority-in-united-states/2012/05/16/gIQA1WY8UU_story.html?hpid=z1

Okigbo, C., Reierson, J., & Stowman, S. (2009). Leveraging acculturation through action research. *Action Research, 7*(2), 125–140.

Pandya, C., Batalova, J., McHugh, M. (2011). *Limited English proficient individuals in the United States: Number, share, growth, and linguistic diversity.* Washington, DC: Migration Policy Institute. Retrieved from http://www.migrationinformation.org/integration/LEPdatabrief.pdf

Reducing health disparities in Asian American and Pacific Island populations. (2005). Management Sciences of Health. Office of Minority Health and Bureau of Primary Health Care. Retrieved from http://erc.msh.org/aapi/ca6.html

Sanchez-Birkhead, A. C., Kennedy, H. P., Callister, L. C., & Miyamoto, T. P. (2011). Navigating a new health culture: Experiences of immigrant Hispanic women. *Journal of Immigrant and Minority Health, 13*(6), 1168–1174.

Schaefer, R. T. (2000). *Racial and ethnic groups.* Upper Saddle River, NJ: Prentice-Hall.

Shpilko, I. (2006). Russian-American health care: Bridging the communication gap between physicians and patients. *Patient Education and Counseling, 64*(1–3), 331–341.

U.S. Census Bureau (2009a). Language spoken at home: 2009. Retrieved from http://www.census.gov/compendia/statab/cats/population/ancestry_language_spoken_at_home.html

U.S. Census Bureau (2009b). Language spoken at home by state: 2009. Retrieved from http://www.census.gov/compendia/statab/cats/population/ancestry_language_spoken_at_home.html

U.S. Census Bureau (2010). The foreign-born population in the United States: 2010. Retrieved from http://www.census.gov/prod/2012pubs/acs-19.pdf

U.S. Census Bureau (2012). U.S. Census Bureau projections show a slower growing, older, more diverse nation a half century from now. Retrieved from http://www.census.gov/newsroom/releases/archives/population/cb12-243.html

Willies-Jacobo, L. (2007, August). Susto: Acknowledging patient's beliefs about illness. *Virtual Mentor, 9*(8), 532–536.

World Health Organization (WHO). (1948). Preamble to the constitution of the World Health Organization. Official records of the World Health Organization, no. 2, p.100. Retrieved May 25, 2013 from http://www.who.int/about/definition/en/print.html

Zunker, C., Rutt, C., & Meza, G. (2005). Perceived health needs of elderly Mexicans living on the U.S.-Mexico border. *Journal of Transcultural Nursing, 16*(1), 50–56.

Chapter 8:

Health communication in the context of aging: The development of an intergenerational communication intervention to reduce biases and discrimination

Kate Magsamen-Conrad
Bowling Green State University

Lisa Hanasono
Bowling Green State University

China Billotte-Verhoff
Bowling Green State University

INTRODUCTION

According to the U.S. Census Bureau (2011), there are over 40 million people living in the United States who are 65 years and older. With an average life expectancy of 78.7 years (Hoyert & Xu, 2012), the proportion of elderly people is growing faster than all other age groups in the United States (U.S. Department of Health and Human Services, 2011). In fact, the National Institute on Aging (2006) projects that nearly one out of five Americans will be 65 years or older by the year 2030.

Although medical advances, scientific discoveries, and lifestyle changes have facilitated the longevity of adults in the United States, the increasing number of elderly people has resulted in new challenges in the context of public health and health communication. From rising health care and Medicaid costs to the need to treat greater numbers of people with chronic illnesses like Alzheimer's disease, cardiovascular disease, and diabetes, it is imperative to promote and investigate ways to facilitate more effective health communication with older adults (Wiener & Tilly, 2002).

New technologies have resulted in major changes, advances, and challenges in health communication. For example, patients can email health-related questions to their physicians, and healthcare providers can send text messages to remind patients to monitor their blood sugar levels or take medications. Patients can use new mobile health applications to manage chronic illnesses, and the general public can access a wide spectrum of health-related information by logging onto the Internet with their smart phones, tablets, and laptop computers.

New communication technologies have the potential to affect health and health communication in both positive and negative ways (Neuhauser & Kreps, 2003), especially in the context of health and aging. Older adults are a segment of the population in which the potential positive effects of new communication technologies on health may be underutilized. For example, in terms of access to health-related information on the Internet, older adults are an underserved population (Rice, 2001). In response, the National Institutes of Health (NIH) have made health literacy and e-health literacy among older adults a priority. For example, NIH launched *NIHSeniorHealth.gov* in 2003 and funded a curriculum developed by the National Institutes of Aging that teaches seniors how to search for health information (Xie, 2012).

Technological advances provide a variety of sources of information and networked tools for monitoring health, however, for some individuals, especially older adults, utilizing this technology is similar to learning a new language (Logan, 2000). Many older adults need training in how to use new technologies, and although some efforts have been made, these efforts are do not sufficiently address the diverse needs of this rapidly growing demographic. For example, an organization called SeniorNet works to provide computer access and training to older adults in senior centers. Although SeniorNet (2013) has more than 50 learning centers located in 25 different states, this is insufficient to meet the needs of this population, as it still leaves a large number of older adults who do not have access to this type of program (see also Kreps & Sparks, 2008; Mo, Malik, & Coulson, 2009; Sparks & Nussbaum, 2008; Stalberg, Yeh, Delbridge, & Delbridge, 2008). One cost effective solution to this challenge is to partner university students with seniors and community centers for the purpose of technology training as part of a service-learning course. This partnership has the potential to benefit both groups, as well as create a sustainable source of needed training resources.

In the upcoming years, younger adults will become increasingly important in the promotion of older adults' health and well-being. Loved ones will provide medical assistance, offer social and informational support, and engage in end-of-life conversations with aging family members. Health professionals will be responsible for providing care to elderly patients. Working professionals will contribute financial support to the United States' public healthcare system, and health communication experts and community leaders will develop interventions and programs to promote our aging population's well-being. Therefore, it is imperative for younger and older adults to work together on health issues and communicate effectively.

Despite the need for effective intergenerational communication, researchers have documented a series of age-related outgroup biases that can hinder effective communication and collaborative relationships between younger and older adults (e.g., Hehman, Corpuz, & Bugental, 2012; Kane

& Kane, 2005). Drawing from the framework of Intergroup Contact Theory (Allport, 1954; Pettigrew, 1998; Pettigrew & Tropp, 2000), we contend that a series of systematic and supportive interactions between younger and older adults enrolled in an intergenerational communication intervention (ICI) program will reduce negative attitudes and facilitate the development of positive interpersonal relationships while older adults gain necessary technology skills. Although both students and seniors will benefit from this partnership, this paper focuses on the potential benefits of an Intergenerational Communication Intervention for college students participating in task-based (e.g., teaching technology) interactions with seniors in their community. By engaging in intergroup interactions, ICI participants' should decrease levels of outgroup anxiety and elevate levels of self-efficacy. These attitude shifts may, in turn, affect broader attitudes about civic engagement and communication skills, such as political awareness, leadership skills, social justice attitudes, and interpersonal and problem-solving skills (see Figure 8.1).

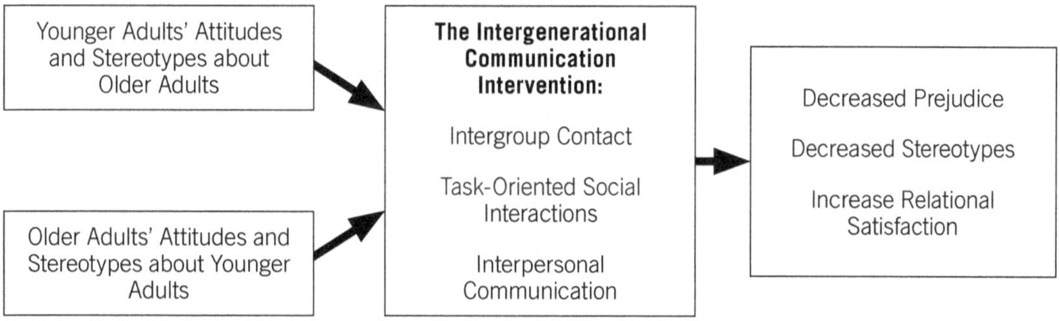

Figure 8.1 *Conceptual Framework for Reducing Intergroup Prejudice and Discrimination using Intergroup Contact Theory and the Intergenerational Communication Intervention*

LITERATURE REVIEW

Ageism and Health Outcomes

As younger adults move into the workforce, they will prove crucial to educating and assisting older adults both medically and technologically. Unfortunately, negative attitudes about the elderly often harm communication and strain relations between younger and older adults. Ageism and prejudice against older adults are widespread in the U.S. (Barnes et al., 2008). Nussbaum, Pitts, Huber, Krieger, and Ohs (2005) describe ageism as "a social phenomenon [that] manifests in prejudice against elders in the form of negative and positive stereotypes" (p. 288). They explain that many Americans wrongly stereotype the elderly as frail, senile, lonely, and unproductive. Researchers have found that ageist attitudes can promote discriminatory communicative behaviors toward older persons, such as patronizing, disrespectful, and controlling speech (Giles & Gasiorek, 2011; Hehman, Corpuz, & Bugental, 2012).

Ageist attitudes can negatively affect older persons' well-being. For example, Lagacé and colleagues (2012) found that the exposure to ageist attitudes was linked to reduced levels of quality of life among the elderly. In the medical community, researchers found that a growing number of physicians are limiting the number of elderly patients (Damiano, Momany, Willard, & Jorgerst, 1997). Older patients tend to receive less medical information from their healthcare providers than do younger patients (Street, 1991). Patients aged 65 years and older are often denied certain treatment options. While some medical treatment decisions are made in an effort to protect the elderly, decisions may be partly motivated by ageist attitudes and incorrect stereotypes of older people (Curtis, 2006; Kane & Kane, 2005). Grant (1996) reported that ageist attitudes led some physicians to dismiss older persons' symptoms as part of the aging process.

Beyond the medical community, ageist attitudes can negatively affect the well-being of older adults. Older adults are discriminated against in the workplace (e.g., being assumed less effective than younger workers, Dennis & Thomas, 2007, see also Cuddy, Norton, & Fiske, 2005; or being denied employment, Roscigno, Mong, Byron, & Tester, 2007), despite policy changes, such as the Age Discrimination in Employment Act (Rothenberg & Gardner, 2011). As a result of ageism, older adults are more likely to experience social exclusion (Blugental & Hehman, 2007), poor social exchange outcomes, elder abuse (Pillemer, 1985), and ambivalent responses from family in the context of sharing health problems (Kurzban & Leary, 2001). Older adults may internalize the negative stereotypes and according to Stereotype Embodiment Theory, begin to believe themselves to be dependent, incompetent, useless, and frail (Levy, 1996; Levy, Hausdorff, Hencke, & Wei, 2000; Levy, Slade, & Kasl, 2002; Wurm, Tesch-Romer, Tomasik, 2007). One way to reduce ageist attitudes among younger adults is to facilitate positive exposure to and productive social interactions with older adults.

Intergroup Contact Affects Apprehension and Attitudes

Intergroup Contact Theory (Allport, 1954; Pettigrew, 1998; Pettigrew & Tropp, 2000) may provide a framework to explicate how planned, supported, systematic interactions between college students and older adults may facilitate a change in students' attitudes and perceptions, both about the elderly and about themselves. Intergroup Contact Theory contends that social interaction between groups can serve as a viable means to reduce prejudice and discrimination (see Figure 1). Researchers have found that intergroup contact can humanize and personalize outgroup members, thus reducing biases related to key identity markers like race, gender, and age (Dovidio, Gaertner, & Kawakami, 2003; Pettigrew & Tropp, 2006). Specifically, intergroup contact can diminish prejudice by (a) reducing anxiety about communicating with outgroup members, (b) increasing individuals' knowledge about outgroups, and (c) enhancing levels of empathy between group members (Pettigrew & Tropp, 2008).

Communication apprehension. Communication apprehension is an anxiety that develops as individuals determine whether or not to communicate in a scenario (e.g., with older adults as individuals or in groups), during which perceived benefits from the interaction are often outweighed by the anxiety experienced (Auter, 2008; Burgon, 1976; Phillips, 1968). Intergroup contact between older adults and college students may reduce apprehension related to communicating with older adults in addition to decreasing ageism. Both positive and negative stereotypes of older adults can contribute to inter-generational communication avoidance (Hummert, Garstka, Shaner, & Strahm, 1994; McCann, Dailey, Giles, & Ota, 2005).

There is evidence of communication apprehension between older and younger adults. Harwood (1998) discovered that many younger adults experienced high levels of discomfort and anxiety when interacting with those significantly older than themselves. Analyses of statements describing younger adults' past interactions with older adults revealed that age was central to their communication apprehension (Harwood, 1998). Age-difference communication apprehension is caused by various factors ranging from concerns regarding conversational topics (e.g. "It was difficult finding something to talk about") to pressures to be overly polite to older adults that result in feelings of relief at the end of interactions (e.g. "I was relieved it was over") (Harwood, 1998).

Experiences of outgroup-related communication apprehension have the potential to be affected by systematic intergroup contact. Harwood and Williams (1998) found that younger adults who had a stronger sense of age identity, or the tendency to route their sense of identity in their conceptualization of belonging to a particular age group (e.g. young, middle-aged, elderly, etc.) experienced more outgroup-related apprehension (both positively and negatively). This hyper awareness of age differences can be partially responsible for outgroup-related communication apprehension, such as the previously mentioned example where concern is expressed on finding something "in common" that both the young adult and older adult can talk about. In this scenario, systematic, guided, task-based intergroup contact may more strongly facilitate reduction in outgroup-related apprehension. Further, young adults who hold negative attitudes and stereotypes of older adults also experience more communication apprehension and anxiety and expect to feel more compassion or pity towards older adults (Harwood & Williams, 1998).

Self-efficacy. Self-efficacy is, broadly, an individual's confidence in his or her ability to complete tasks and attain goals, or the belief in her or her ability to succeed in specific situations (Bandura, 1977). Self-efficacy commands a central role in Social Cognitive Theory (Bandura, 1977), and helps explain the connection between observational learning and social experience. Some research suggests that the link between intergroup contact and related attitudes is mediated by self-efficacy (Mazziotta, Mummendey, Wright, 2011). In addition, the concept of self-efficacy is also consistently related to service-learning experiences, such that some service-learning experiences (e.g., training older adults to use technology) positively affect self-efficacy (Knapp, Fisher, & Levesque-Bristol, 2010). Other research indicates that self-efficacy, then, affects civic engagement (Flanagan & Bundick, 2011). That is, the service learning experience builds self-efficacy, which then positively affects civic engagement (see Figure 1). One explanation for how community engagement can empower young adults and increase self-efficacy uses social empathy as a framework (Wagaman, 2011).

Social empathy. Social empathy is a theoretical construct that may explain how intergroup contact can affect ageism, communication apprehension, and self-efficacy. Social empathy exists when empathy is combined with a contextual understanding and social responsibility (Segal,

2011). Young adults may cultivate empathy through intergroup contact with outgroup members, which, according to the social empathy model (Segal, 2011) is the proximate mechanism for directed altruism (see also, de Waal, 2009). Social empathy fosters civic attitudes and skills, such as social responsibility (Paner & Pratt, 1999) and social justice (Hoffman, 2000; Morrell, 2010; Rifkin, 2009). The social empathy model also contends that limited contextual experience with outgroup members can result in ingroup members who are more prone to stereotyping, prejudice, and scapegoating (Glick, 2002, 2005, 2008).

Intergroup Contact and Civic Attitudes and Skills

Systematic, guided, task-based intergroup contact between college students and older adults may influence a number of positive outcomes. In addition to the knowledge gained by older adults about a particular task (e.g., technology training), students may experience a positive shift in their attitudes about older adults, which may then affect their civic attitudes and skills. Reduction in ageist attitudes may also positively affect college students' potential career opportunities.

Students who participate in service-learning or community engagement (e.g., partnering with older adults to teach tablet skills) develop higher levels of interpersonal problem solving skills, leadership skills, develop positive social justice attitudes, and report higher levels of academic learning (Moely, Mercer, Ilustre, Miron, & McFarland, 2002) than students who do not. Community engagement with older adults provides an established forum for both providing students with a method of developing skills necessary for the work-force as well as changing attitudes towards aging. Indeed, intergroup contact between college students and older adults working together on a project (e.g., technology instruction) may affect college students' civic attitudes and skills including: civic action, interpersonal and problem-solving skills, political awareness, leadership skills, social justice attitudes, and diversity attitudes.

Reducing ageist attitudes in college students may facilitate career opportunities. Cummings and Galambos (2002) revealed a strong link between the intention to work with older adults or in geriatrics and attitudes towards aging and that negative stereotypical beliefs often drive students away from working with the elderly. Fighting stereotypical attitudes is a challenge even for those who intend to work with older adults, and intergenerational interactions have the potential to humanize older adults for the youth of today through intergroup contact. For example, previous research involving medical students found that students who engaged in intergenerational community engagement experienced positive interactions and that their contact allowed them to view the older adults in a more humanistic manner rather than simply viewing interactions with older adults as clinical (Kodadek, Bettendorf, Uihlein, Derse, 2010). Additionally, research has shown that students who have more experience in interacting with older adults have more confidence in dealing with aging-persons and express more positive attitudes towards older adults (Gutheil, Chernesky, & Sherratt, 2006).

Ageism, aging stereotypes, communication apprehension, aging anxiety. and intergroup contact all affect student perceptions and future interactions with older adults. Collectively, these factors (ageism, knowledge about aging, communication apprehension, and self-efficacy) can be mediated through intergroup contact. This research proposes an intergenerational communication intervention (ICI) to positively develop students' attitudes toward older adults and aging and provide older adults with technological skills to access online social support and health information. As an initial step in the ICI development, we are interested in the link between ageism, communication apprehension, self-efficacy, and civic attitudes and skills. Based on the previous review our central hypothesis is that:

> H1: Ageism (stereotypes, separation, and affective attitude), knowledge about aging, communication apprehension, and self-efficacy predict civic attitudes and skills (civic action, interpersonal and problem-solving skills, political awareness, leadership skills, social justice attitudes, and diversity attitudes).

METHOD

Participants

Participants were recruited from undergraduate communication courses at a mid-sized Midwestern university from social science (e.g., communication, psychology) and health care administration programs. The final sample included 98 male (n = 45, 46%) and female (n = 53, 54%) undergraduate students. Most participants were seniors (49%) and juniors (37%). The age of our student participants ranged from 18 to 50 years (*M* = 21.83 years, *SD* = 3.88). Participants were predominately Caucasian (69.5%); others were Black (20.4%), Hispanic/Latino/Mexican (6.1%), Asian (2%), and Biracial (2%).

Procedure

After providing their informed consent, participants provided self-report data on a confidential paper survey about their self-efficacy, communication apprehension, ageism, knowledge about aging, and civic attitudes and skills. Students were awarded a small portion of extra credit for their participation.

Measures

Variables measured include general self-efficacy, communication apprehension, ageism (i.e., stereotypes, separation, and affective attitudes), knowledge about aging, and civic attitudes and skills (i.e., civic action, interpersonal problem solving, political awareness, leadership skills, social justice attitudes, diversity attitudes).

General self-efficacy. We measured participants' general self-efficacy with the GSESH (General Self Efficacy—Sherer, modified by Bosscher & Smith, 1998; originally developed by Sherer and colleagues, 1982). The scale measures three dimensions: initiative, effort, and persistence with 12 Likert-type items with responses ranging from 1 (*strongly disagree*) to 5 (*strongly agree*) (assessed in prior research as a single composite). A CFA revealed that ten of the items loaded onto one latent construct, $\chi^2(35) = 54.87$, *relative* $\chi^2 = 1.57$, $p = .02$, $CFI = .91$, $RMSEA = .08$. One sample item included "If I can't do a job the first time, I keep trying until I can." The items had good reliability ($\alpha = .83$, $M = 3.27$, $SD = .45$) and were averaged to form a scale with a higher score indicating more general self-efficacy.

Communication apprehension. We measured participants' communication apprehension with 12 Likert-type items from McCroskey's (1978) PRCA (Personal Report of Communication Apprehension) adapted to specifically reflect communication apprehension with older adults with responses ranging from 1 (*strongly disagree*) to 5 (*strongly disagree*). We conducted a second order CFA because we assessed two subfactors of the PRCA, CA in groups and CA with individuals. First the CFA was arranged so items were assigned to their relative subfactors; subfactors were assigned to the latent Communication Apprehension. Six items were assigned to CA with Older Adults in Groups and six to CA with Older Adults in Conversation (individuals). The initial model did not fit ($\chi^2(53) = 234.71$, *relative* $\chi^2 = 4.43$, $p < .001$, $CFI = .85$, $RMSEA = .19$). The model fit after removing three items from each subscale ($\chi^2(8) = 11.26$, *relative* $\chi^2 = 1.41$, $p = .19$, $CFI = .99$, $RMSEA = .07$). One sample item from the *communication apprehension with older individuals in groups* subscale included "Engaging in group discussions with older adults makes me tense and nervous." The items had good reliability ($\chi = .93$, $M = 2.12$, $SD = .81$) and were averaged to form a scale with a higher score indicating more communication apprehension with older adults in groups. One sample item from the *communication apprehension older individuals* included "Ordinarily I am very tense and nervous in conversation with an older adult." The items had good reliability ($\alpha = .86$, $M = 2.06$, $SD = .75$) and were averaged to form a scale with a higher score indicating more communication apprehension with an older adult in conversation.

Ageism. We measured ageism with 17 Likert-type items selected from The Ageism Scale based on factor loadings (Rupp, Vodanovich, & Credé, 2005, see also Fraboni, Saltstone, & Hughes, 1990) with responses ranging from 1 (*strongly disagree*) to 5 (*strongly agree*). We conducted a second order CFA arranged so, first, the items were assigned to their relative subfactors, then subfactors were assigned to the latent Ageism. Eight items were assigned to Stereotypes, five to Separation, and four to Affective Attitude. The initial model did not fit ($\chi^2(116) = 188.51$, *relative* $\chi^2 = 1.63$, $p < .001$, $CFI = .87$, $RMSEA = .08$). The model fit after correlating two items on the stereotypes subscale ($\chi^2(115) = 169.24$, *relative* $\chi^2 = 1.47$, $p = .001$, $CFI = .90$, $RMSEA = .07$). One sample item from the *stereotypes* subscale item included "Older people complain more than other people do." The items had good reliability ($\alpha = .80$, $M = 2.48$, $SD = .61$). One sample item from the *separation* subscale included "I sometimes avoid eye contact with older people when I see them." The items had good reliability ($\alpha = .80$, $M = 1.80$, $SD = .64$). One sample item from the subscale *affective attitudes* included "The company of most older people is quite enjoyable (R)." The items had good reliability ($\alpha = .75$, $M = 2.02$, $SD = .56$). All items were averaged within their respective composites to form subscales with a higher score indicating more presence of ageist attitudes.

Knowledge about aging. We measured participants' knowledge about aging the revised 25 item Facts on Aging Quiz (Harris & Changas, 1994; see also Palmore, 1980, 1981, 1988, 1992). This is a multiple choice measure where participants select what they believe to be the correct answer in each multiple choice prompt. One sample prompt included "The rate of poverty among the elderly:" followed by four options of which only one, "is lower than among those under 65" was correct. We calculated the number of correct items and gave students a score out of 100 (M = 46.0, SD = 9.10) where a higher number of correct answers indicated more knowledge about aging.

Civic attitudes and skills. We measured civic attitudes and skills with thirty-two items from The Civic Attitudes and Skills Questionnaire (CASQ) (Moley et. al, 2002) selected based on factor loadings in prior research with responses ranging from 1 (*strongly disagree*) to 5 (*strongly agree*). We also modified the original item stems adding a time orientation of "this year" to the questions about civic action (n = 5 of 7) based on behavioral intention and change research. We conducted a second order CFA by assigning items to their relative subfactors, then assigning subfactors to the latent Civic Attitudes and Skills. Seven items were assigned to Civic Action, seven to Interpersonal and Problem Solving Skills, six to Political Awareness, four to Leadership Skills, four to Social Justice Attitudes, and four to Diversity Attitudes. The initial model did not fit ($\chi^2(458)$ = 626.18, *relative* χ^2 = 1.37, p < .001, CFI = .88, $RMSEA$ = .06). The model fit after correlating two items on the civic action subscale ($\chi^2(457)$ = 588.40, *relative* χ^2 = 1.29, p < .001, CFI = .91, $RMSEA$ = .05). One sample item from the *civic action* subscale included "I plan to do some volunteer work this year." The items had good reliability (α = .87, M = 3.65, SD = .72). Items were averaged to form a scale with a higher score indicating more intent to engage in civic action in the next year (outside of the purview of service-learning as part of a class). One sample item from the *interpersonal and problem solving skills* subfactor included "I can work cooperatively in a group of people." The items had good reliability (α = .89, M = 4.41, SD = .47) and were averaged to form a scale with a high score indicating more perceived interpersonal and problem solving skills. One sample item from the *political awareness* subscale included "I am aware of the events happening in my local community." The items had good reliability (α = .80, M = 3.49, SD = .60) and were averaged to form a scale with a higher score indicating more political awareness, especially in the local community. One sample item from the *leadership skills* subscale included "I am a better follower than a leader" (R). The items had good reliability (α = .88, M = 3.74, SD = .73) and were averaged to form a scale with a higher score indicating perceptions of more leadership skills. One sample item from the fifth factor was *social justice attitudes* included "People are poor because they choose to be poor" (R). The items had good reliability (α = .82, M = 3.50, SD = .83) and were averaged to form a scale with a higher score indicating a stronger level of commitment to social justice. One sample item from the final subscale, *diversity attitudes*, included "I prefer the company of people who are similar to me in background and expressions." The items had acceptable reliability (α = .63, M = 3.72, SD = .63) and were averaged to form a scale with a higher score indicating more positive attitudes toward diversity.

RESULTS

Table 8.1 Bivariate Zero Order Correlation Matrix for All Variables

1	1.00											
2	.28**	1.00										
3	.24*	.19	1.00									
4	.12	.55**	.05	1.00								
5	.01	.19	–.024	.01	1.00							
6	.17	.49**	.14	.39**	.23*	1.00						
7	.28**	.45**	.29**	.39**	.05**	.31**	1.00					
8	.02	–.17	–.30**	.07	–.32**	–.18**	–.05	1.00				
9	–.05	–.43**	–.27**	–.24*	–.23*	–.37**	–.28**	.38**	1.00			
10	–.25*	–.45**	–.27**	–.31**	–.10	–.34**	–.28**	.28**	.54**	1.00		
11	–.02	–.34**	–.33**	–.28**	–.14	–.45**	–.39**	.34**	.54**	.46**	1.00	
12	.03	–.33**	–.38**	–.34**	–.03	–.31**	–.33**	.28**	.49**	.44**	.87**	1.00

1–Civic Action; 2–Interpersonal Problem Solving; 3–Political Awareness; 4–Leadership Skills; 5–Social Justice; 6–Diversity Attitudes; 7–General Self-efficacy; 8–Ageism: Stereotypes; 9 Ageism: Separation; 10–Ageism: Affective Attitudes; 11–Communication Apprehension: Older Adults in Groups; 12–Communication Apprehension: Older Individuals;

* $p < .05$; ** $p < .01$; two-tailed

This section describes analyses and results of the predicted associations. Table 1 presents the zero-order correlation matrix for all variables. We conducted CFAs on multi-item scales to ensure that items met the criteria of face validity, internal consistency, and parallelism (Hunter & Gerbing, 1982). Three goodness-of-fit indices estimated the fit of the models. The χ^2/df adjusts the χ^2 statistic for sample size (Kline, 1998). The comparative fitness index (CFI) calculates the ratio of the noncentrality parameter estimate of the hypothesized model to the noncentrality parameter estimate of a baseline model (Bentler, 1990). The root meal square error of approximation (RMSEA) accounts for errors of approximation in the population (Browne & Cudeck, 1993). We determined that the model fit the data if χ^2/df was less than 3, CFI was greater than .90, and RMSEA was less than .10 (Browne & Cudeck, 1993; Kline, 1998). We estimated reliability using Cronbach's alphas. Data were analyzed by stepwise regressions, the alpha level was set at $p < .05$ for all analyses. Results are presented next by civic attitude and skill subscale.

Intergenerational Communication Intervention

The primary goal of this paper was to explore how attitudes and perceptions that have the potential to be changed through the ICI (see Figure 1) would affect civic attitudes and skills. The central hypothesis seeks to understand how attitudes and skills related to community engagement, are affected by ageism, knowledge about aging, communication apprehension, and self-efficacy. We explored this question with series of regression analyses to examine the combination of predictors. For each regression, ageism (stereotypes, separation, affective attitudes), knowledge about aging, outgroup-related communication apprehension (in one-on-one encounters and in groups) and self-efficacy were the predictors with civic attitudes and skills (intended civic action within the next year, interpersonal and problem solving skills, political awareness, leadership skills, social justice attitudes, and diversity attitudes) as the criteria.

Civic action. We conducted a *stepwise regression* analysis with civic action as the criterion and knowledge about aging, ageism (stereotypes, separation, affective attitudes), communication apprehension with older individuals, communication apprehension with older adults in groups, and general self-efficacy as the predictors. In the final model (Adj. $R^2 = .08$, $F(1,94) = 9.35$, $p < .01$; $\beta = .30$, $t = 3.06$, $p < .001$), general self-efficacy positively predicted 8% of the variance in intentions to engage in civic action within the next year.

Interpersonal and problem solving skills. We conducted a *stepwise regression* analysis with interpersonal problem solving as the criterion and knowledge about aging, ageism (stereotypes, separation, affective attitudes), communication apprehension with older individuals, communication apprehension with older adults in groups, and general self-efficacy as the predictors. The first step was significant (Adj. $R^2 = .21$, $F(1,93) = 26.20$, $p < .001$), ageism: separation negatively ($\beta = -.47$, $t = -5.12$, $p < .001$) predicted interpersonal and problem solving skills. The second step produced significant change, $\Delta R^2=.08$, $F(2,92)= 19.86$, $p < .001$, with ageism: separation negatively ($\beta = -.39$, $t = -4.26$, $p < .001$) and general self-efficacy positively ($\chi = .30$, $t = 3.28$, $p < .001$) predicting interpersonal and problem solving skills. The final step produced significant change, $\Delta R^2 = .03$, $F(3,91) = 15.28$, $p < .001$, with ageism: separation negatively ($\beta = -.26$, $t = -2.50$, $p < .01$), general self-efficacy positively ($\beta = .27$, $t = 3.04$, $p < .01$), and ageism: affective attitudes negatively ($\beta = -.23$, $t = -2.14$, $p < .05$) predicting interpersonal and problem solving skills. In the final model, ageism: separation negatively, general self-efficacy positively, and ageism: affective attitudes negatively predicted 31% of the variance in interpersonal and problem solving skills.

Political awareness. We conducted a *stepwise regression* analysis with political awareness as the criterion and knowledge about aging, ageism (stereotypes, separation, affective attitudes), communication apprehension with older individuals, communication apprehension with older adults in groups, and general self-efficacy as the predictors. The first step was significant (Adj. $R^2 = .12$, $F(1,93) = 15.18$, $p < .001$), where communication apprehension with older individuals negatively ($\beta = -.36$, $t = -3.69$, $p < .001$) predicting political awareness. In the final model, communicating apprehension with older individuals negatively predicted 12% of the variance in political awareness.

Leadership skills. We conducted a *stepwise regression* analysis with leadership skills as the criterion and knowledge about aging, ageism (stereotypes, separation, affective attitudes), communication apprehension with older individuals, communication apprehension with older adults in groups, and general self-efficacy as the predictors. The first step was significant (Adj. $R^2 = .14$, $F(1,93) = 15.79$, $p < .001$), general self-efficacy positively ($\beta = .38$, $t = 3.97$, $p < .001$) predicted leadership skills. The second step produced a significant change, $\Delta R^2 = .18$, $F(2,92) = 11.54$, $p < .001$, with general self-efficacy positively ($\beta = .33$, $t = 3.48$, $p < .01$) and communication apprehension with older individuals negatively ($\beta = -.24$, $t = -2.53$, $p < .01$) predicting leadership skills. In the final model, general self-efficacy positively and communication apprehension with older individuals negatively predicted 18% of the variance in leadership skills.

Social justice attitudes. We conducted a *stepwise regression* analysis with social justice attitudes as the criterion and knowledge about aging, ageism (stereotypes, separation, affective attitudes), communication apprehension with older individuals, communication apprehension with older adults in groups, and general self-efficacy as the predictors. In the final model (Adj. $R^2 = .10$, $F(1,94) = 11.15$, $p < .001$; $\beta = -.33$, $t = -3.34$, $p < .001$) ageism: stereotypes negatively predicted 10% of the variance in social justice attitudes.

Diversity attitudes. We conducted a *stepwise regression* analysis with diversity attitudes as the criterion and knowledge about aging, ageism (stereotypes, separation, affective attitudes), communication apprehension with older individuals, communication apprehension with older adults in groups, and general self-efficacy as the predictors. In the final model, (Adj. $R^2 = .15$, $F(1,94) = 17.87$, $p < .001$; $\beta = -.40$, $t = -4.23$, $p < .001$) communication apprehension with older adults in groups negatively predicted 15% of the variance in diversity attitudes.

Discussion

This research introduces an intergenerational communication intervention (ICI) grounded in Intergroup Contact Theory (Allport, 1954; Pettigrew, 1998; Pettigrew & Tropp, 2000), Social Cognitive Theory (e.g., self-efficacy, Bandura, 1977), and the social empathy model (Segal, 2011) that aims to (a) reduce ageist attitudes and increase self-efficacy, (b) promote more effective communication between younger and older adults, and (c) teach older adults how to best utilize technology to improve health outcomes (see Figure 1). The ICI will provide a forum for students to develop an understanding of commonalities that they hold with older adults while recognizing the inter-individuality of older adults (Pinquart, Wenzel, & Sörensen, 2000). For example, students will be able to establish an understanding that they may share common interests or values despite the generational difference while disbanding simplistic either-or assessments of older adults such as: "all older adults are helpless" or "older adults can't learn to use technology." Indeed, anecdotal feedback from the students involved in this project exemplifies positively violated expectations with more than one student expressing "I learned that the seniors are awesome!" This recognition of individual differences can assist in the deconstruction of ageist attitudes and stereotypes.

Key Findings

The ICI was designed to accomplish multiple goals of positively reducing age-related biases and discrimination, decreasing communication related apprehension, and increasing older adults' ability to access social support and reliable information through mediated contexts. This paper focuses on the potential student outcomes of the ICI. Our analyses yielded several key findings that warrant future development of the ICI.

First, our analyses revealed that ageism and self-efficacy can have a meaningful impact on college students' *interpersonal and problem-solving skills*. In fact, ageism and self-efficacy accounted for 31% of the variance in these vital skill sets. Students with stronger levels of ageism had poorer interpersonal and problem-solving skills, and students with higher levels of self-efficacy reported stronger interpersonal and problem-solving skills. Our findings indicate that age-related attitudes represent a meaningful barrier in students' ability to work on collaborative projects and engage in collaborative problem-solving, while higher levels of self-efficacy can facilitate students' interpersonal and problem-solving skills.

Second, we found that self-efficacy and communication apprehension with older adults predicted 18% of the variance in college students' *leadership skills*. Students who possessed perceptions of more self-efficacy were linked to students' stronger perceptions of their own leadership skills. On the other hand, students who expressed more communication apprehension indicated poorer leadership skills. Through intergroup contact, the ICI should both increase self-efficacy and decrease outgroup-related communication apprehension, thus bolstering students' leadership skills.

In addition to interpersonal, problem-solving, and leadership skills, we examined students' political awareness, social justice attitudes, and diversity attitudes. Ageism negatively predicted 10% of the variance in *social justice attitudes*, and communication apprehension negatively predicted 15% of the variance in *diversity attitudes*. Our analyses indicated that ageist stereotypes and communication apprehension with elderly individuals accounted for 12% of the variance in students' *political awareness*. Taken together, our findings indicate that ageist attitudes and stereotypes, along with age/outgroup related communication apprehension, systematically affect students' social, cultural, and political attitudes. The ICI is designed to reduce college students' outgroup related ageism and communication apprehension; therefore, we anticipate that the ICI will foster more positive attitudes about social justice, diversity, and political awareness.

Finally, we investigated how age-related attitudes, beliefs, communication apprehension, and self-efficacy affected students' desire to participate in civic engagement. The results of this sample indicate that self-efficacy positively predicted 8% of the variance in students' intentions to participate in civic activities within the next year. Our findings indicate that students who are more confident in the their abilities to meet goals and accomplish tasks are more likely to get involved in community-oriented projects and pursue volunteer opportunities. By facilitating positive intergroup contact and bolstering social empathy, the ICI should positively affect students' self-efficacy, which will in turn affect their intentions to be involved in their communities.

It is important to note that our sample had a surprisingly low level of knowledge about aging. On average, students in this study who completed Harris and Changas' (1994) Facts of Aging Quiz earned a score of 46 out of 100 points. Although these scores are slightly better than a sample of sociology students in prior research (Harris & Changas, 1994) where the average score was 44/100, participants' poor scores indicate students' lack of awareness and understanding of older adults. A closer look at the individual items illustrates the media as a possible source of misinformation, for example, only 3% of students correctly identified that older persons have less injuries in the home than younger persons. Other explanations involve egocentrism, for example, almost 80% of students indicated that the majority suffer from "empty nest syndrome" when the last child leaves home compared to the 16% who correctly identified the higher levels of life satisfaction. Educating college students about older adults through the ICI represents a viable mechanism for reducing age-related prejudice and dispelling age-related stereotypes and miscommunication, as well as potentially decreasing detrimental future stereotype embodiment and self-fulfilling prophecy.

Collectively, the findings from this study indicate that ageism, self-efficacy, and communication apprehension can affect college students' skills, social attitudes, and intention to engage in civic behaviors. Previous studies have shown how ageism can negatively impact older adults' health and well-being (Levy, Slade, & Kasl, 2002; Wurm, Tesch-Romer, Tomasik, 2007). The results from this project reveal how ageism, self-efficacy, and communication apprehension with older adults can impact the lives of college students, who will one day be caring for the growing baby boomer generation whether through personal contact, taxes, or voting on issues. These findings highlight the importance of intergroup contact and interventions like the ICI that provide a valuable and necessary service to an underserved population while significantly affecting important attitudes and skills, most notably, students' interpersonal and problem solving skills, leadership skills, and attitudes about diversity.

Practical Implications

Today's young adults will play a key role in the promotion of older adults' health and well-being as they enter the workforce in occupations ranging from health professionals, to working professionals, and community leaders. Whether interacting with older adults in these capacities or simply providing social and informational support to their loved ones, the reduction of ageist attitudes may help in the prevention of discriminatory communication practices (e.g., patronizing, dismissive, or controlling speech), that is perpetuated by these stereotypes. The ICI has the potential to increase the quality of communication between older and younger adults, provide needed skills training, and thus improve the quality of life for older adults (Lagacé, et. al, 2012) and reduce the internalization of ageist stereotypes that propagate older adults' belief that they are incompetent and frail (Levy, 1996; Levy, Hausdorff, Hencke, & Wei, 2000; Levy, Slade, & Kasl, 2002; Wurm, Tesch-Romer, Tomasik, 2007). This intervention directly affects not only the quality of life and wellbeing of older adults, but vastly improves younger adults' understanding, comfort level, and communicative success with older adults. These are invaluable skills when considering that nearly one out of five Americans will be 65 years or older by the year 2030 as well as the projected 25% increase in older adults entering the workforce (i.e., communicating with older adults as coworkers; National Institute on Aging, 2006; Ford & Orel, 2005).

Limitations

The findings from this study, along with prior research on communication and aging, underscore the importance of reducing ageist attitudes and beliefs in college students. Intervention programs, such as the ICI, have the potential to reduce students' age-related biases and foster more positive interactions between younger and older adults. Although the results of our research are promising, several limitations must be noted. First, we had a relatively homogenous sample from only one university. Future research should include the perspectives of more diverse college samples across the United States. Second, the social justice subscale (of the Civic Attitudes and Skills questionnaire) had lower reliability than desired. Finally, this exploratory study introduced the ICI and provided a strong rationale for the continued development of intervention programs that will reduce age-related biases in college students and promote effective intergroup contact between younger and older adults; however, this study described the results of a cross-sectional survey. Future research should implement the ICI and test its effectiveness for both college students and seniors through pre- and post- test measures, and with control groups, as well as seeking to understand and explain counterarguments, causality, and confounding variables.

Future Directions

This paper focused on potential student outcomes of the ICI. Given our promising findings and methodological limitations, future research should continue to refine the ICI and explore how communication interventions can reduce ageism and enhance young adults' self-efficacy. We encourage scholars to draw from more diverse samples across that nation to include more perspectives from people who have different ethnic, racial, and socio-economic backgrounds.

In addition to exploring broadly how communication interventions can lead to desirable social and psychological outcomes in young adults, future research should continue to use theory to develop the ICI as it pertains to potential outcomes for older adults. We propose a theory-based logic model to explain how the ICI might affect technology skills and health related outcomes for older adults (see Figure 2). In the model, we draw from the Unified Theory of Acceptance and Use of Technology (UTAUT) (Venkatesh, Morris, Davis, & Davis, 2003; Wang & Wang, 2010), Theory of Planned Behavior (TPB) (Ajzen, 1991; Ajzen & Fishbeing, 1980), Social Cognitive Theory (SCT) (Bandura, 1977), and extant research on social support to explain how the ICI affect health related outcomes.

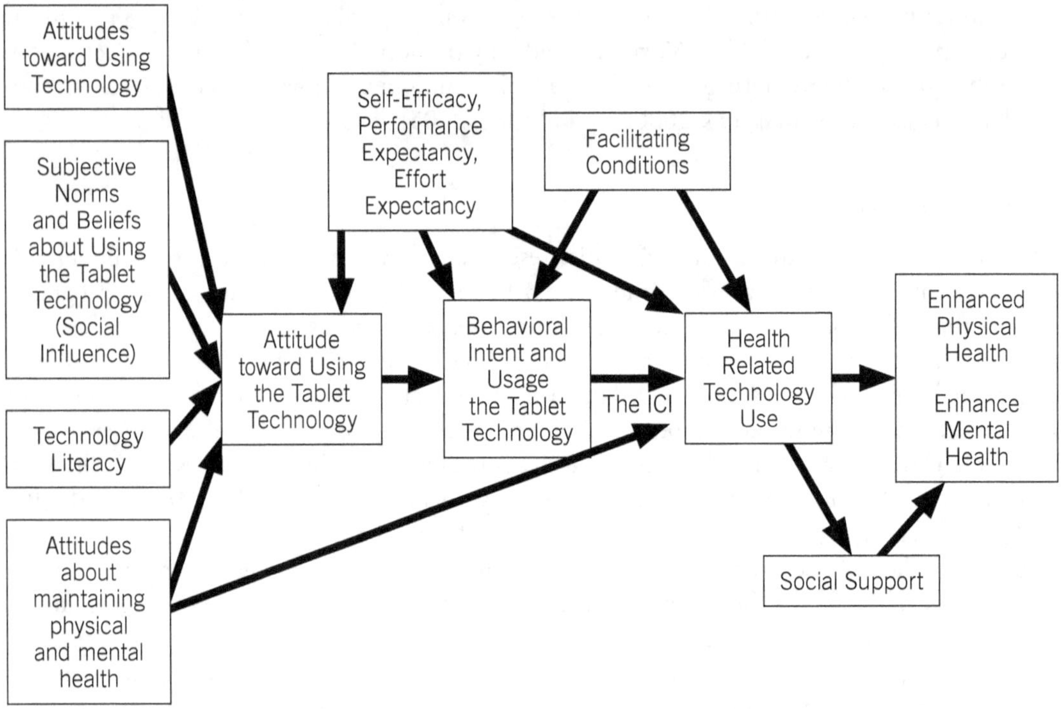

Figure 8.2 *Conceptual Framework for improving Older Adults' Health and Technology Skills related Outcomes using UTAUT, Behavior Change Theory and the Intergenerational Communication Intervention*

UTAUT. First, the model is guided by the UTAUT, which draws from multiple technology and health behavior theories (Theory of Reasoned Action, Innovation Diffusion Theory, Technology Acceptance Model, Social Cognitive Theory, Motivational Model, Model of PC Utilization) to address why some social groups adopt specific technologies or digital media (Venkatesh et al., 2003; Wang & Wang, 2010). The UTAUT consists of four key constructs that are determinants of behavioral intention and actual use of technology: performance expectancy, effort expectancy, social influence, and facilitating conditions. Gender, age, experience, and voluntariness of use moderate the impact of the four constructs on intention and use of technology (Venkatesh et al., 2003). **Performance expectancy** is the expectation of what adopting technology will allow the user to accomplish. **Effort expectancy** is whether the technology is easy to use; the time required learning how to operate the technology; and the belief of whether or not learning to use this technology is worthwhile. **Social influence** is the belief that influential individuals in the user's life (e.g. family, friend, employer) believe the potential user should adopt or utilize the technology. **Facilitating conditions** are the resources and barriers necessary to using the technology (e.g. physical resources, knowledge, and compatibility with lifestyle) (Venkatesh et al., 2003). UTAUT has been used to describe why users adopt technology in their daily lives, including for the use of health information (Venkatesh et al., 2003; Wang & Shih, 2009). UTAUT explains up to 70% of variance in behavioral intention to use technology and roughly 50% of the variance in technology use (Venkatesh et al., 2003).

Behavior change theories. Theories of behavioral change examine how key factors influence individuals to alter their behaviors (O'Keefe, 2002). Many health researchers have employed behavioral change theories to persuade individuals to adopt better eating habits (Conner, Norman, & Bell, 2002), exercise more frequently (Conn, Tripp-Reimer, & Maas, 2003), and complete health screenings (Sheeran, Conner, & Norman, 2001).

Attitudes refer to people's positive or negative feelings toward a specific behavior, issue, person, organization, or object (Petty, Wegener, & Fabrigar, 1997). Researchers have found that attitudes can impact individual's intentions to engage in specific behaviors (McEachen, Conner, Taylor, & Lawton, 2011). More positive attitudes and beliefs about technology should increase older adults' likelihood of using technology and apps, which should lead to enhanced physical and mental health outcomes. **Subjective norms** are similar to social influence and refer to people's "perceived social pressure to perform or not perform [a specific] behavior" (Ajzen, 1991, p. 188).

Social Support. Supportive communication is the "verbal and nonverbal behavior produced with the intention of providing assistance to another person perceived as needing that aid" (Burleson, MacGeorge, Knapp, & Daly, 2002, p. 374). Social support has been linked to a variety of positive physical and mental health outcomes, such as reduced stress (Uchino, 2004), decreased anxiety and depression (Ryff & Singer, 2001), and increased relational satisfaction (Sullivan & Davila, 2010). Support groups can play a key role in the maintenance of healthy behaviors (Mullin, 2010). The Internet itself provides new opportunities for access to social support (Gray, 2013; Smithson et al., 2011; Tanis, Das, & Fortgens-Sillmann, 2011). Online social capital has the potential to mediate the association between self-concealment and well-being, and technology addiction and well-being, such that perceptions of online social wealth help reduce the negative effects of self-concealment and technology addiction on mental well-being (Magsamen-Conrad & Billotte, under review). Research suggests that the type of virtual communities older adults are likely to participate in (e.g., interacting with loved ones on Facebook) are effective at extending the shared sense of community previously established by place-based groups (Lev-On, 2010), that they reduce individual social isolation (McKenna, 2008), and that they can help reduce feelings of stress (Welbourne, Blanchard, & Wadsworth, 2013). Finally, in the ICI older adults receive/experience social support from the students who become their teachers during technology instruction period.

Future research may be able to apply the logic model presented in Figure 2 to refine the ICI and understand older adults' technology adoption and utilization behaviors. Researchers may design studies that explore a number of different new communication devices and both their utility for this population (especially as related to health maintenance behaviors) as well as potential barriers to use. For example, research might explore the function of technology use related "support groups" comprised of seniors who have completed ICI and other technology-related courses or instruction together.

CONCLUSIONS

Given substantial demographic shifts (e.g., Hoyert & Xu, 2012) and the emergence of new communication technologies (e.g., Xie, 2012), younger adults will become increasingly important in the promotion of older adults' health and well-being. Unfortunately, a collection of factors impede effective communication and collaboration between older and younger adults. Drawing from the literature, this study showed how ageism and communication apprehension can impede productive intergenerational interactions, and it underscored the importance of self-efficacy in promoting college students' interpersonal, leadership, and problem-solving skills. Moreover, we introduced an intergenerational communication intervention that has the potential to reduce ageist attitudes, increase students' self-efficacy, and promote more effective communication between younger and older adults. Overall, the results offer qualified support for the continued development and implementation of a communication based intervention program and the pursuit of future research on communication, aging, and health.

REFERENCES

Ajzen, I. (1991). The theory of planned behavior. *Organizational behavior and human decision processes, 50*(2), 179–211.

Ajzen, I, & Fishbein, M. (1980). *Understanding attitudes and predicting social behaviour.* Englewood Cliffs, NJ: Prentice Hall.

Allport, G. W. (1954). *The nature of prejudice.* Reading, MA: Addison Wesley.

Auter, P. (2007). Portable social groups: Willingness to communicate, interpersonal communication gratifications, and cell phone use among young adults. *Int. J. Mobile Communications, 5*, 139–156.

Bandura, A. (1997). Self-efficacy: The exercise of control. New York: W.H. Freeman.

Barnes, L., L., de Leon, C. F., Lewis, T. T., Bienias, J. L., Wilson, R. S., & Evans, D. A. (2008). Perceived discrimination and mortality in a population-based study of older adults. *American Journal of Public Health, 98*, 1241–1247.

Bentler, P. M. (1990). Comparative fit indexes in structural equation models. *Psychological Bulletin, 107*, 238–246.

Bickmore, T. & Paasche-Orlow, M. (2012). The Role of Information Technology in Health Literacy Research. *Journal of Health Communication: International Perspectives, 17*, 23–29.

Bosscher, R. J., & Smit, J. H. (1998). Confirmatory factor analysis of the general self-efficacy scale. *Behavior Research and Therapy, 36*, 339–343.

Browne, M. W., & Cudeck, R. (1993). Alternative ways of assessing model fit. In K. A. Bollen & J. S. Long (Eds.), *Testing structural equation models* (pp. 136–162). Newbury Park, CA: Sage Publications.

Bugental, D., & Hehman, J. (2007). Ageism: A review of research and policy implications. *Social Issues and Policy Review, 1*, 173–216.

Burgoon, J. K. (1976). The unwillingness to communicate scale: Development and validation. *Communication Monographs, 63*, 60–69.

Burleson, B. R., MacGeorge, E. L., Knapp, M. L., & Daly, J. A. (2002). Supportive communication. In M. L. Knapp, & G. R. Miller, (Ed.), *Handbook of interpersonal communication* (Vol. 3, pp. 374–424). Thousand Oaks, CA: Sage.

Cody, M., Dunn, D., Hoppin, S., & Wendt. (1999). Silver surfers: Training and evaluating internet use among older adults learners. *Communication Education, 48*, 269–286.

Conn, V. S., Tripp-Reimer, T., & Maas, M. L. (2003). Older women and exercise: Theory of Planned Behavior beliefs. *Public Health Nursing*, –(2), 153–163.

Conner, M., Norman, P., & Bell, R.. (2002). The Theory of Planned Behavior and healthy eating. *Health Psychology*, 21(2), 194–201.

Cuddy, A. J. C, Norton, M. L., & Fiske, S. T. (2005). This old stereotype: The stubbornness and pervasiveness of the elderly stereotype. *Journal of Social Issues, 61*, 265–285.

Cummings, S., & Galambos, C. (2002). Predictors of graduate students' interest in aging-related work. *Journal of Gerontological Social Work, 39*, 77–94.

Curtis, J. J. (2006). Ageism and kidney transplantation. *American Journal of Transplantation, 6*, 1264–1266. doi: 10.1111/j.1600-6143.2006.01318

Dennis, H., & Thomas, K. (2007). Ageism in the workplace. *Generations, 31*(1), 84–89.

Damiano, P., Momany, E., Williard, J., & Jogerst, G. (1997). Factors affecting primary care physician participation in Medicare. *Medical Care, 35*, 1008–1019.

de Waal, F. (2009). The age of empathy: Nature's lessons for a kinder society. New York, NY: Harmony Books.

Dovidio, J. F., Gaertner, S. L., & Kawakami, K. (2003). Intergroup contact: The past, present, and the future. *Group Processes and Intergroup Relations, 6*, 5–21.

Flanagan, C., & Bundick, M. (2011). Civic engagement and psychosocial well-being in college students. *Liberal Education, 97*(2), 20–27.

Ford, R., & Orel, N. (2005). Older adult learners in the workforce: New dimensions to workforce training needs. *Journal of Career Development, 32*, 139–152. doi: 10.1177/084845305279165

Fox, S., & Fallows, D. (2003) Internet health resources. Washington, DC: Pew Internet & American Life Project; 2003. July 16.

Fraboni, M., Saltstone, R., & Hughes, S. (1990). The Fraboni Scale of Ageism (FSA): An attempt at a more precise measure of ageism. *Canadian Journal on Aging, 9*, 56–66.

Giles, H., & Gasiorek, J. (2011). Intergenerational communication practices. In K. W. Schaie & S. L. Willis (Eds.), *Handbook of psychology and aging* (pp. 233–248). London, UK: Academic Press.

Glick, P. (2002). Sacrificial lambs dressed in wolves' clothing: Envious prejudice, ideology, and the scapegoating of Jews. In L. S. Newman & R. Erber (Eds.), *Understanding genocide: The social psychology of the Holocaust* (pp. 113–142). New York, NY: Oxford University Press.

Glick, P. (2005). Choice of scapegoats. In J. F. Dovidio, P. Glick, & L. A. Rudman (Eds.), *On the nature of prejudice: 50 years after Allport* (pp. 244–261).Malden, MA: Blackwell Publishing.

Glick, P. (2008). When neighbors blame neighbors: Scapegoating and the breakdown of ethnic relations. In V. M. Esses & R. A. Vernon (Eds.), *Explaining the breakdown of ethnic relations.*

Grant, L. D. (1996). Effects of ageism on individual and health care providers' responses to healthy aging. *Health and Social Work, 21*, 9–17.

Gray, J. (2013). Feeding on the web: Online social support in the breastfeeding context. *Communication Research Reports, 30*(1), 1–11. doi: 10.1080/08824096.2012.746219

Gutheil, I., Chernesky, R., & Sheratt. (2006). Influencing student attitudes toward older adults: Results of a service-learning collaboration. *Educational Gerontology, 32*, 771–784.

Harris, D.K., & Changas, P.S. (1994). Revision of Palmore's second facts on aging quiz from a true-false to a multiple choice format. *Educational Gerontology, 6*, 743–754.

Harwood, J. (1998). Young adults' cognitive representations of intergenerational conversations. *Journal of Applied Communication Research, 26*, 13–31.

Harwood, J., & Williams, A. (1998). Expectations for communication with positive and negative subtypes of older adults. *The International Journal of Aging and Human Development, 47*, 11–33.

Hehman, J. A., Corpuz, R., & Bugental, D. (2012). Patronizing speech to older adults. *Journal of Nonverbal Behavior, 36*, 249–261. doi: 10.1007/s10919-012-0135-8

Hoffman, M. L. (2000). *Empathy and moral development: Implications for caring and justice.* London, England: Cambridge University Press.

Hoyert, D. L., & Xu, J. (2012). Deaths: Preliminary data for 2011 (National Vital Statistics Report, Trans.) (Vol. 61). Hyattsville, MD.

Hummert, M. L., Garstka, T. A. Shaner, J. L., & Strahm, S. (1994). Stereotypes of the elderly held by young, middle-aged, and elderly adults. *Journal of Gerontology: Psychological Sciences, 49,* 240–249.

Hunter, J. E., & Gerbing, D. W. (1982). Unidimensional measurement, second order factor analysis, and causal models. In B. M. Staw & L. L. Cummings (Eds.), *Research in organizational behavior* (Vol. 4, pp. 267–320). Greenwich, CT: JAI Press.

Kane, R. L., & Kane, R. A. (2005). Ageism in healthcare and long-term care. *Generations, 29,* 49–54.

Kline, R. B. (1998). *Principles and practice of structural equation modeling.* New York: Guilford.

Knapp, T., Fisher, B., & Levesque-Bristol, C. (2010). Service-learning's impact on college students' commitment to future civic engagement, self-efficacy, and social empowerment. *Journal of Community Practice, 18*(2/3), 233–251. doi:10.1080/10705422.2010.490152

Kodadek, L., Bettendorf, B., Uihlein, J., Derse, A. (2010). The memory art project: Medical students and older adults. *Wisconsin Medical Journal, 109,* 311–316.

Kreps, G. L., & Sparks, L. (2008). Meeting the health literacy needs of vulnerable populations. *Patient Education and Counseling,* 71(3), 238–332.

Kurzban, Robert, & Leary, Mark R. (2001). Evolutionary origins of stigmatization: The functions of social exclusion. *Psychol Bull, 127*(2), 187.

Lagacé, M., Tanguay, A., Lavallée, M., Laplante, J., & Robichaud, S. (2012). The silent impact of ageist communication in long term care facilities: Elders' perspectives on quality of life and coping strategies. *Journal of Aging Studies, 26,* 335–342.

Lev-On, A. (2010). Engaging the disengaged: Collective action, media uses, and sense of (virtual) community by evacuees from Gush Katif. *American Behavioral Scientist, 53*(8), 1208–1227.

Levy, B. (1996). Improving memory in old age by implicit self-stereotyping. *Journal of Personality and Social Psychology, 71,* 1092–1107.

Levy, B., Hausdorff, J., Hencke, R., & Wei, J. Y. (2000). Reducing cardiovascular stress with positive self-stereotyping of aging. *Journal of Gerontology: Psychological Sciences, 55,* 205–213.

Levy, B., Slade M. D., & Kasl, S. V. (2002). Increased longevity by positive self-perceptions of aging. *Journal of Personality and Social Psychology, 83,* 261–270.

Logan, R. (2000). *The Sixth language: Learning a living in the internet age.* Toronto, ON: Stoddart Publications.

Magsamen-Conrad, K., & Billotte, C. (under review). *The interaction of technology addiction, information sharing, and social capital to predict well-being.*

Mazziotta, A., Mummendey, A., & Wright, S. C. (2011). Vicarious intergroup contact effects: Applying social-cognitive theory to intergroup contact research. *Group Processes & Intergroup Relations, 14*(2), 255–274.

McCann, R., Dailey, R. M., Giles, H., & Ota, H. (2005). Beliefs about intergenerational communication across the lifespan: Middle age and the roles of age serotyping and respect norms. *Communication Studies, 56*, 293–311.

McCroskey, J. C. (1978). Validity of the PRCA as an index of oral communication apprehension. *Communication Monographs, 45*, 192–203.

McEachan, R. R. C., Conner, M., Taylor, N. J., & Lawton, R. J. (2011). Prospective prediction of health-related behaviours with the Theory of Planned Behaviour: A meta-analysis. *Health Psychology Review, 5*(2), 97–144.

McKenna, K. (2008). Influences on the nature and functioning of online groups. In A. Barak (Ed.), *Psychological aspects of cyberspace: Theory, research, applications* (pp. 228–242). Cambridge, New York: Cambridge University Press.

Mo, P. K. H., Malik, S. H., & Coulson, N. S. (2009). Gender differences in computer-mediated communication: A systematic review of online health-related support groups. *Patient Education and Counseling, 75*, 16–24.

Moely, B., Mercer, S., Ilustre, V., Miron, D., & McFarland, A. (2002). Changes in college students attitudes and intentions for civic involvement as a function of service-learning experiences. *Michigan Journal of Community Service Learning*, 18–26.

Morrell, M. E. (2010). *Empathy and democracy: Feeling, thinking, and deliberation*. University Park, PA: Pennsylvania State University Press.

Mullin, G. E. (2010). Patient education: The value of support groups. *Nutrition in Clinical Practice, 25*(5), 555–557.

National Institute on Aging. (2006). Dramatic changes in U.S. aging highlighted in new census, NIH report. Retrieved from http://www.nia.nih.gov/newsroom/2006/03/dramatic-changes-us-aging-highlighted-new-census-nih-report

National Institute on Aging. Fiscal Year 2005 Budget. Retrieved from http://www.nia.nih.gov/about/budget/2004/justification-narrative/behavioral-and-social-research

Neuhauser, L., & Kreps, G. L. (2003). Rethinking Communication in the E-health Era. *Journal of Health Psychology, 8*(1), 7–23. doi: 10.1177/1359105303008001426

Nussbaum, J. F., Pitts, M. J., Huber, F. N., Krieger, J. L., & Ohs, J. E. (2005). Ageism and ageist language across the life span: Intimate relationships and non-intimate interactions. *Journal of Social Issues, 61*, 287–305.

O'Keefe, D. (2002). Theories of behavioral intention. *Persuasion Theory and Research* (2nd Edition ed.). London: Sage Publications.

Pancer, S. M., & Pratt, M. W. (1999). Social and family determinants of community service involvement in Canadian youth. In M. Yates & J. Youniss (Eds.), *Roots of civic involvement: International perspectives on community service and activism in youth* (pp. 32–55). Cambridge, England: Cambridge University Press.

Palmore, E. B. (1980). The Facts On Aging Quiz: A review of findings. *The Gerontologist, 20*, 669–672.

Palmore, E. B. (1980). The Facts On Aging Quiz: Part Two. *The Gerontologist, 21*, 431–437.

Palmore, E. B. (1988). The Facts On Aging Quiz: A handbook of uses and results. New York: Springer Publishing Company.

Palmore, E. B. (1980). Knowledge about aging: What we know and need to know. *The Gerontologist, 32*, 149–150.

Pettigrew, T. F. (1998). Intergroup contact theory. *Annual Review of Psychology, 49*, 65–85.

Pettigrew, T. F., & Tropp, L. R. (2000). Does intergroup contact reduce prejudice? Recent meta-analytic findings. In S. Oskamp (Ed.), *Reducing prejudice and discrimination: Social psychological perspectives* (pp. 93–114). Mahwah, NJ: Erlbaum.

Pettigrew, T. F., & Tropp, L. R. (2006). A meta-analytic test of intergroup contact theory. *Journal of Personality and Social Psychology, 90*, 751–783. doi: 10.1037/0022-3514.90.5.751

Pettigrew, T. F., & Tropp, L. R. (2008). How does intergroup contact reduce prejudice? Meta-analytic tests of three mediators. *European Journal of Social Psychology, 38*, 922–934. doi: 10.1002/ejsp.504

Petty, R. E., Wegener, D. T., & Fabrigar, L. R. (1997). Attitudes and attitude change. *Annual review of psychology, 48*(1), 609–647.

Phillips, G. M. (1968). Reticence: Pathology of the normal speaker. *SM, 35*, 40.

Pillemer, K. (1985). The dangers of dependency: New findings in physical abuse of the elderly. *Social Problems, 33*, 146–158.

Pinquart, M., Wenzel, S., & Sörensen, S. (2000). Changes in attitudes among children and elderly adults in intergenerational group work. *Educational Gerontology, 26*, 523–540.

Rice, R. R. (2001). The Internet and health communication. In R. E. Rice & J. E. Katz (Eds.), *The Internet and health communication: Experiences and expectations* (pp. 5–46). Thousand Oaks, CA: Sage.

Roscigno, V. J., Mong, S., Byron, R., & Tester, G. (2007). Age discrimination, social closure and employment. *Social Forces, 86*(1), 313–334.

Rothenberg, J. Z., & Gardner, D. S. (2011). Protecting older workers: The failure of the age discrimination in employment act of 1967. *Journal of Sociology & Social Welfare, 38*(1), 9–30.

Rupp, D. E., Vodanovich, S. J., & Credé, M. (2005). The multidimensional nature of ageism: Construct validity and group differences. *Journal of Social Psychology, 145*, 335–62.

Ryff, C. D., & Singer, B. (2001). *Emotion, social relationships, and health.* Oxford University Press, USA.

Segal, E. A. (2011). Social Empathy: A model built on empathy, contextual understanding, and social responsibility that promotes social justice. *Journal of Social Service Research, 37*(3), 266–277.

SeniorNet (2013). Retrieved March 27, 2013 from http://www.seniornet.org

Sheeran, P., Conner, M., & Norman, P. (2001). Can the theory of planned behavior explain patterns of health behavior change? *Health Psychology, 20*(1), 12–19.

Sherer, M., Maddux, J. E., Mercadante, B., Prentice-Dunn, S., Jacobs, B., and Rogers, R. W. (1982). The self-efficacy scale: Construction and Validation. *Psychological Reports, 51*, 663–671.

Smithson, J., Sharkey, S., Hewis, E., Jones, R., Emmens, T., Ford, T., & Owens, C. (2011). Problem presentation and responses on an online forum for young people who self-harm. *Discourse Studies, 13*(4), 487–501.

Sparks, L., & Nussbaum, J. F. (2008). Health literacy and cancer communication with older adults. *Patient Education and Counseling, 71*(3), 345–350.

Stalberg, P., Yeh, M., Ketteridge, G., Delbridge, H., & Delbridge, L. (2008). E-mail access and improved communication between patient and surgeon. *Archives of Surgery, 143*, 164–168.

Street, R. L. (1991). Information-giving in medical consultations: The influence of communicative styles and personal characteristics. *Social Science and Medicine, 32*, 541–548.

Sullivan, K. T., & Davila, J.. (2010). *Support processes in intimate relationships.* New York: Oxford University Press.

Tanis, M., Das, E., & Fortgens-Sillmann, M. (2011). Finding care for the caregiver? Active participation in online health forums attenuates the negative effect of caregiver strain on wellbeing. *Communications: The European Journal of Communication Research, 36*(1), 51–66.

Tropp, L. R., & Pettigrew, T. F. (2005). Relationships between intergroup contact and prejudice among minority and majority status groups. *Psychological Science, 16*, 951–957.

Uchino, B. N. (2004). *Social support and physical health: Understanding the health consequences of relationships.* New Haven, CT: Yale University Press.

U.S. Census Bureau. (2011). The older population: 2010. U.S. Department of Commerce. Retrieved from http://www.census.gov/prod/cen2010/briefs/c2010br-09.pdf

U.S. Department of Health and Human Services. (2011). 90+ in the United States: 2006–2008. U.S. Department of Commerce. Retrieved from http://www.census.gov/prod/2011pubs/acs-17.pdf

Venkatesh, V., Morris, M. G., Davis, G. B., & Davis, F. D. (2003). User acceptance of information technology: Toward a unified view. *MIS quarterly*, 425–478.

Wagaman, M. (2011). Social Empathy as a Framework for Adolescent Empowerment. *Journal of Social Service Research, 37*(3), 278-293. doi:10.1080/01488376.2011.564045

Wang, H-Y, & Wang, S-H. (2010). User acceptance of mobile internet based on the Unified Theory of Acceptance and Use of Technology: Investigating the determinants and gender differences. *Social Behavior and Personality: An International Journal, 38*(3), 415–426.

Wang, Y-S, & Shih, Y-W. (2009). Why do people use information kiosks? A validation of the Unified Theory of Acceptance and Use of Technology. *Government Information Quarterly, 26*(1), 158–165.

Welbourne, J. L., Blanchard, A. L., & Wadsworth, M. B. (2013). Motivations in virtual health communities and their relationship to community, connectedness and stress. *Computers in Human Behavior, 29*(1), 129–139.

Wiener, J. M., & Tilly, J. (2002). Population ageing in the United States of America: Implications for public programmes. *International Journal of Epidemiology, 31*, 776–781.

Wurm, S., Tesch-Römer, C., & Tomasik, M. J. (2007). Longitudinal findings on aging-related cognitions, control beliefs and health in later life. *Journals of Gerontology Series B: Psychological Sciences and Social Sciences, 62*,156–164.

Xie. B. (2012). Improving older adults' e-health literacy through computer training using NIH online resources. *Library & Information Science Research, 34*, 63–74.

Xie, B., Watkins, I., Golbeck, J., & Huang, M. (2012). Understanding and changing older adults' perceptions and learning of social media. *Educational Gerontology, 38*(4), 282–296.

Zucchero, R. (2010). Share your experience and I'll lend you my ear: Older adult outcomes of an intergenerational service-learning experience: *Gerontology & Geriatrics Education, 31*, 383–402.

Chapter 9:

Spousal caregiver narratives and credible authority: Uncertainty in illness of spousal caregivers

Karen Sodowsky
Valdosta State University

INTRODUCTION

Imagine you have had an accident. You stumbled down your apartment stairs and now you have a broken wrist and a sprained ankle. Because your wrist is immobile you have difficulty using the crutches the Emergency Room doctor prescribed for you. Basically, you are confined to your apartment and struggling to do the everyday activities you normally do without thinking. Your friend stops by and offers to go to the store for you. A little later your mom drives in from your hometown to stay with you. She will cook, clean, and most importantly help you bath and use the restroom. Your mom and friend have now become your caregivers, doing things for you that you have been doing independently for many years. You will only need their help temporarily, but what if that was not the case? This is true for millions of adults and their families, friends, volunteers, and paid caregivers in the United States. Now add other problems like memory loss and confusion. Your caregivers will not only provide physical care at your direction, but they will need to make decisions for you because you no longer understand what is happening to you.

As the American population ages, so does the awareness of chronic illnesses that predominantly affect older adults. Older adults are more likely to experience illnesses affecting their cognitive functioning, such as Alzheimer's disease and other forms of dementia. Currently, sources estimate that 5.1 million Americans over 65 years old have Alzheimer's disease or dementia and are cared for by 11 million unpaid caregivers composed mostly of family members (Alzheimer's Association, 2010). The research over the last decade of family caregivers of people with dementia revealed an increased risk of emotional and physical well-being measured through levels of stress, depression, and medical problems (Bond, Clark, & Davies, 2003; Gaugler, Kane, Kane, & Newcomer, 2005; Sanders, 2005). Caregivers of people with dementia face another level of stress created by being surrogate decision-makers for care recipients who can no longer contribute to deciding their own physical care.

My Social Service Experience with Caregivers

During a home visit as a medical social worker to a client and her spouse, I realized that, during most of my social service career, I listened to stories from patients and their family members. This particular visit brought that into focus because, over the course of approximately ten years, I had met with this couple at least three times. The husband had suffered multiple strokes, which left him physically and cognitively disabled; subsequently he was diagnosed with Alzheimer's disease. His wife, Evelyn (pseudonym) had decided for various reasons to keep Edward (pseudonym), her husband, at home and use minimal formal support in caring for him. She was a full-time caregiver for about ten years and had experienced Edward's slow, but inevitable decline.

Evelyn was telling me her story once again. Some of the story was familiar and some of the story was new. The story, however, was the focal point of this meeting. I was listening to the history of this couple and this spousal caregiver's journey over the last ten years. Listening to the story was the most important part of the visit to her. I already knew the probable outcome of this visit. Evelyn would and indeed did continue to care for her husband in their home. Although I suspected that no physical change would be made, I did not discount the necessity of my visit. The need to make meaning of loss and suffering was the reason Evelyn had asked to speak to the social worker. The piece of the story that stands out in my memory was the Evelyn telling me about Edward's recent final decline into cognitive oblivion. Through the years, although Edward did not respond to other people, Evelyn always felt that he responded to her. Finally even that spark of recognition was gone. It was like a door closing in their relationship. She summed up the experience by saying "I could be just another nurse's aide to him."

This event had been the reason for my visit. She had turned another page in her book of caregiving and was once again evaluating her options. The biggest decision facing many spousal caregivers is nursing home placement. I had recited the basic financial and institutional processes involved with nursing home placement. This was an obligatory duty, because Evelyn had been given this information by many health and social service professionals through the years. It was not the need for information that had caused her to ask me to her home again. It was my status as an empathetic and knowledgeable listener, a counselor. This led me to several questions: Why was telling the story important when facing uncertainty producing decisions? Why was listening to the story important?

Moreover, while working as a medical social worker in this community, I found myself caring for my mother-in-law who suffered from Alzheimer's disease, as well as significant cardiac problems. My husband was his mother's healthcare power of attorney and he depended on me for information and resource recommendations. As we worked to provide his mother with a safe and comfortable living arrangement, we were constantly balancing her desire to maintain her independence with her diminishing cognitive capacities. We were required to make many decisions guided by the directions of her advance directives and previous discussions with her when she was still able to express her health care wishes. Eventually we were required to make the ultimate decision about life prolonging care, when the physician stated there were no longer any curative treatments available.

Caregiver Uncertainty in Illness

Uncertainty in illness is created through the many unknowns of dealing with disease, treatment, and the medical community (Mishel, 1988, 1990). Choosing to take medications, whether or not to undergo surgery and changing daily routines like diet and exercise are just a few examples. Uncertainty was documented among many groups of people dealing with chronic illnesses such as AIDS (Brashers et al., 1999; Brashers et al., 2000; Brashers, Neidig, Reynolds, & Haas, 1998; Folkman, 2001), end-stage renal disease (Hines, Babrow, Badzek, & Moss, 2001), cancer (Ford, Babrow, & Stohl, 1996), and other chronic illnesses requiring nursing home care (Singer, Martin, & Kelner, 1999). The patients' appraisal of the uncertainty and adaptive communication helped them manage the uncertainty produced by the health problems and subsequent treatments (Babrow, Kasch, & Ford, 1998; Brashers & Babrow, 1996; Hines, Babrow, Badzek, & Moss, 1997; Hines, Moss, & Badzek, 1997; Mishel, 1988, 1990; Mishel & Braden, 1988). According to Mishel (1988, 1990), the patient's confidence in the source of information is considered credible authority. The health care providers' knowledge is one piece of the patients' confidence level in the information they provide. In a study of people living with HIV, Brashers, Heish, Neidig, & Reynolds (2006) found that the participants considered the health professionals' knowledge of the disease and their communication skills as qualities of credible authority. Simply having knowledge is not enough to create relational confidence in the health professional; the health care providers must be able to establish professional credibility through effective and appropriate communication.

Caregivers face the uncertainty described in Mishel's (1988) model and that uncertainty is complicated by the need to make substituted judgments for their care recipients who are cognitively impaired. Deciding intimate and complicated health care choices on behalf of someone else is a difficult task. Studies indicate cognitively alert care recipients prefer their family make decisions about health problems (Hines et al., 1999; Moore & Sherman, 1999; Moore, Sparr, Sherman, & Avery, 2003), but this is not as simple a resolution as it sounds. The preference does not then equate to caregivers having confidence in their decision-making capacity (Hines et al., 2000) or that caregivers' substituted judgments coincide with older adults' choices (Hummert & Morgan, 2001; Sanesone & Phillips, 1995). Often health care choices are not addressed by an individual until an illness occurs. If people have difficulty making decisions for themselves, it is immensely more complicated to make decisions for a care recipient. It is impossible to include people who are suffering from an illness that interferes with their ability to comprehend what is happening to them.

Although numerous researchers have studied the use of formal advance directives (end-of-life decisions legal documents) and the caregiver role (Hines et al., 1999; Mutran, Danis, Bratton, Sudha, & Hanson, 1997; Rosenfeld, Wenger, & Kagawa-Singer, 2000; Sanesone & Phillips, 1995), there are many incremental changes, such as functional impairments and changing emotional roles, that require caregiver decisions not specifically covered by advance directives (Hooker, Frazier, & Monahan, 1994; McCarty 1996; Vernooij-Danssen, Persoon, & Felling, 1996). Cultural concerns (Carrese & Rhodes, 1995; Germino et al., 1998; Hopp & Duffy, 2000), the caregiver's health status (Sanders, 2005), physical intimacy (Baikie, 2002; Svetlik, Dooley, Weiner, Williams, & Walters, 2005), choosing nursing home care (Nolan & Dellasega, 2000), and managing social and financial responsibilities (Jansson, Nordberg, & Grafstrom, 2001; Perry, 2002) can all create caregiver uncertainty. The question is then how important is the credible authority to the caregiver of a person with dementia. The knowledge and communication skills of the professional health care provider may be essential to the caregiver's feelings of social support. Also the acceptance of the caregiver's narrative by a representative of the health care services adds a level of emotional support not available from informal social support given by family and friends.

Caregiver Narratives and Professional Audiences

Charmaz (1999) and Charmaz and Olsen (1997) chronicled the theoretical movement from previous theory based on structuralism to later researchers who based their narrative research on symbolic interactionism and social constructionism. Charmaz (1999) viewed this theoretical shift as a move to the study of the personal experiences of patients: "In contrast to the sick role, the narrative turn toward storytelling shifts attention from objectivity to subjectivity, from acts and facts to thoughts and feelings, and from portrayals of prescribed roles to images of past, present, and future selves" (p. 211).

In the discipline of communication, Fisher (1984) proposed the narrative paradigm. The heart of this perspective is that people are storytellers. Narratives contain commonly understood symbols of communication that evaluate and consolidate social stories. Fisher (1985, 1997) expanded on the narrative paradigm; narratives are more than stories shared between speakers and listeners. Narratives are the means by which reason is assigned and decisions are made in communities. Themes of caregiver narrative studies have included reframing lives, coping mechanisms, and reciprocity of social support (Aryes, 2000; Bennett & Vidal-Hall, 2000; Harris, 1998; Russell, 2001). These narratives become part of the community narrative of caregiving. When the researcher interviews a participant to obtain his or her story, the researcher becomes the audience (Luborsky, 1987).

The interaction between audience and narrator in illness narratives and life stories has been established (Bochner, 2001; Charmaz, 1999; Singer, 2004). The listener interacts with the storyteller and becomes a part of the story; therefore, who the audience is and what identity and role the listener plays is intricately tied to the construction of the narrative. Docherty and McColl (2003) defined the professional audience in relational terms. The interaction between the social worker (the audience) and the patient as (the narrator):

> *This process of coexploring the familiar (i.e., the client's story, view of the problem, and meanings) and codeveloping the new (i.e., meanings, realities, and narratives), marks shift away from problem definition and a move toward new ways of making sense of behavior, feelings and events. (p. 22)*

This same narrator/audience relationship has been noted between physicians and patients in the construction of illness narratives (Eggly, 2002), and it has been encouraged in therapeutic relationships with the chronically ill (Sollod, 2002). In contrast, the physicians' failures to acknowledge the patients' narratives have led to limited communication between patients and physicians (Beach, Easter, Good, & Pigeron, 2005; Waitzkin, Britt, & Williams, 1994). Narratives shared with support group members (Hsieh, 2004), life reviews shared with hospice workers (Price, 1995), even participant interviews shared with researchers (Bennett & Vidal-Hall, 2000; Miczo, 2003; Pennebaker & Keogh, 1999) have been told to audiences who acknowledge the importance of the illness and caregiver narratives. These professional listeners who represent Fisher's (1997) concept of a greater societal narrative incorporate qualities of Mishel's (1988) credible authority. Physicians, nurses, nursing home administrators, counselors, clergy, and social workers compose an official reference point for what is appropriate and acceptable in health care and caregiving because of their position of knowledge. These professionals are the gatekeepers to treatment and services and therefore create an idea of what it means to be a "good patient" or "compassionate caregiver."

Methods

This article represents research taken from a larger study. The study used triangulation of multiple interviews, a survey, and statistical information about the caregivers in one community. This chapter focuses on interviews with spousal caregivers of partners with dementia. Although there are many theoretical perspectives used to analyze narrative research, the selection for the interview portion of this study was based on the journey of the researcher to find a theoretical framework that fits the narratives heard over a career in social work. Phenomenology is a philosophy that allows the exploration of human interactions in order to extract the full meaning from the experience (Moran & Mooney, 2002; Moustakas, 1994). The objective of a study based on a phenomenological perspective has been to describe the meaning of complex and richly layered human interactions (Bailey, 1997; Moustakas, 1994). The researcher's goal has been to elucidate the underlying structures of the event, allowing the participants to be co-researchers in the mutual exploration of the narrated event (Moustakas, 1994). Researchers have used this method to interpret illness narratives in order to describe the emotional and physical interactions of patients with health care professionals (Ekman, Lundman, & Norberg, 1999; Monks, 2000). Butcher and Buckwalter (2002) also used a phenomenological interpretive analysis to explore one spouse's meaning of caregiving. The narrative was the pathway for the researchers to find the caregiver's construction of what it meant to care for her husband who was suffering from Alzheimer's disease.

My study was exploratory in targeting not only caregiver narratives, but also participants in one community who share the role of spouse. This form of analysis also allowed a description of uncertainty in illness through caregiver narratives. Although the research material was not the equivalent of the immersion of a researcher in ethnography, the descriptive nature of the analysis did allow for my professional history and my knowledge of the community to be included. This information placed the narratives into the context of the caregivers' social world and increased the description of the caregiving experience in the caregivers' own words.

These are the two research questions addressed by the material in this chapter:

RQ: What meaning do spousal caregivers of partners with dementia ascribe to the professional listener as an audience for their narratives?

RQ: How do spousal caregivers experience the uncertainty created in caregiving for a person with dementia?

The caregivers in this study were recruited from a caregiver program located within the senior services of the local county health department, where I was also employed as the caregiver counselor. The participants included four women (two white, ages 80 and 82; two African American, ages 58 and 80) and two men (both white. ages 88 and 70). All of the caregivers were married with adult children and like the majority of the community ranged from middle to lower socioeconomic statuses. The names and specific family details have been altered to protect the participants' privacy, but the substituted information is reflective of the participants' actual demographics. The narratives were analyzed using basic steps of phenomenological method of analysis proposed by Giorgi (1979). The steps incorporated the researcher's full and deep exploration of the participant's expressed meaning of the caregiving experience followed by the researcher's analysis of the derived underlying structures or universal meanings of spousal caregiving including uncertainty, credible authority, and the professional listener as the preferred narrative audience.

I have revealed my position as researcher and caregiver counselor in each participant's history. Disclosure was important, because it clearly positions me within the narratives as a credible authority. Other narrative studies have acknowledged the position of the researcher as a sympathetic or friendly audience (Harden, 2000; Irvine, 2000; Luborsky, 1987). The researcher as a sympathetic listener has been used to provide an insider perspective into the experiences of the participants (Anderson & Martin, 2003; Gibbs & Franks, 2002). This provided rapport between the researcher and the participants that encouraged the revelation of what is meaningful in the participants' experiences. It is then essential as researchers to recognize these possibilities and the effect the researcher has as the audience.

Findings

During the three years I was a caregiver counselor; I would walk into homes and meet caregivers experiencing many challenges. Although at first I was expecting to sit down and provide information as I had in past positions, but I found that an hour or two later I would leave the home having spoken perhaps 15 to 20 minutes throughout the entire visit. Most visits ended with the caregiver thanking me for all the help I had provided. What had I done? I had listened. One of the findings in the survey of caregivers from the larger study was the majority preference for on-on-one counseling as opposed to the other two services offered by the caregiver support program: support groups and educational presentation.

It was the need to tell their journey of caregiving often going back to the beginning 5, 10, or 15 years ago. When beginning this research I asked the caregivers to tell me about being a caregiver. I did not direct the multiple interviews with each caregiver in the study, other than to clarify information or emotions expressed to be sure I accurately understood the individual caregiver narrative. The caregivers choose to tell me about times of uncertainty, doubt, and confusion in the past, present, and future.

In the next sections I discuss the narratives told to me as a credible authority in diagnoses, care recipient safety, end-of-life decisions, and spousal caregivers' health. I end with a discussion of caregivers' perception of people as credible authority. Throughout these descriptions you will hear the caregivers seeking reassurance in their decisions that they have made, as well as the ones they are facing. Their choice of these details emphasized the significance of making decisions for themselves and their spouse. It also reinforced the desire to tell someone who represented the greater societal narrative of what it means to be "a good caregiver." You will also hear the other credible authorities that they appealed to during their times of uncertainty.

Uncertainty in Diagnosis

The beginning of chronic illnesses may start with minor symptoms or a significant traumatic event. In either circumstance the spousal caregiver faces uncertainty in observing the illness and in interacting with the medical community. The importance of the medical professional's expertise as the credible authority is significant. Bob Walker had cared for his wife for approximately 14 years. She suffered from Lewy body's disease which is a form of dementia associated with Parkinson's disease. He spoke about the first simple changes in Barbara Jean's physical condition:

> *So we thought it was arthritis and went to the arthritis specialist and he said no it was something else. It wasn't arthritis and he sent us to a neurologist and he right off told us it was Parkinson's disease.*

Finding the correct specialist and having faith that the medical referral process will successfully provide the caregiver with credible information is related to reducing uncertainty in diagnosis. For Bob and Barbara Jean her Parkinson's disease diagnosis was soon complicated by another. Following the discovery of breast cancer, the Walkers moved to this community "and all the trauma of a new hospital, new doctors, radiation, you know all the rest of the stuff." As the observer of his wife's illness, he reported her symptoms to the medical community, and depended on them for analysis and advice. Once again the credible authority of the medical professionals in this new treatment process was a factor in the Bob Walker's uncertainty in treating his wife's illnesses. He looked until he found a physician who shared his desire to protect his wife's dignity and independence far as long as possible.

Betty Harrison was also a long-term caregiver to her husband who suffered from a variety of health problems; the last and most difficulty to deal with was dementia. She stated that her husband "was showing signs of disorders, not common to what he had been doing. And he was leaving the house early walking and coming back." A stranger who found her husband wandering several miles from their home recommended Betty take her spouse to the Veterans hospital. After an extensive stay at the Veterans hospital, her husband was diagnosed with dementia. It was a very upsetting time for Betty because she was unfamiliar with the disease and was not used to being away from her husband, but the medical and social service professionals provided support and understanding when she told them of her husband's unusual behavior and how she must learn to cope with his symptoms. She trusted the medical professionals and found comfort from their responses to her concerns.

Irene Teller started her caregiving career with a similar unexpected first episode with her husband's illness. While the couple was eating out, her husband became pale and unresponsive, eventually fainting. By the time she and her friends were able to get him to the hospital he was recovering from the incident. The family physician ran numerous tests, but was unable to give a definitive diagnosis. A series of episodes led to the diagnosis of low blood pressure related to Parkinson's disease. Throughout this process of episodes, testing, and a series of specialists, Irene gathered information, evaluated the effectiveness of medications, and acted as a liaison with medical community treating her husband. Her husband was unaware of the significant changes in his health and in his spouse's role of reporter and health care advocate on his behalf.

She valued her relationship with their long time physician who listened carefully to her reports and praised her ability to be her husband's "nurse."

In all of these stories the caregivers' trust of the credible authority reduced uncertainty and supported the caregivers with their attention to their explanations, descriptions, and fears when discussing their spouses' illnesses. These same caregivers all expressed appreciation for my listening to their stories even though these situations had happened at the beginning of their caregiver journey they continued to look for affirmation of their decisions and the care they had given to their spouses.

Care Recipient's Safety

When the partner's cognitive decline results in behavior that is hazardous, the spousal caregiver is forced into the position of limiting the spouse's independence. Once again the caregiver must assess and respond to the uncertainty producing health situation which is occurring not to the caregiver, but the patient who does not perceive a change in his or her well-being. Alma Williams stated that even after her husband was diagnosed with Alzheimer's disease he was still able to do many of his usual activities:

> *So he started going downhill mentally, but not physically. So he was okay. He use to walk around and all. Play cards. He could cut the grass until about three years ago. He thought he was the best grass cutter in [the city's name]. The lawnmower had to go a certain way and come back a certain way or the grass wasn't right. [Alma laughs] But then last year, a couple of years ago he got where he'd be smoking and putting gas in the lawnmower and I was scared he was going to get blown up. He was very, very mean.*

Although she laughed as she recounted this clash between the caregiver's concerns and the care recipient's behavior, the actual event was stressful as reflected in her last sentence, because her husband could not comprehend his wife's explanation of concern. She also expressed the relief it is to talk with someone (myself) who understands what it is like to be a caregiver.

Robert Walker recounted an incident with his wife that reflects the same tension between caregiver and care recipient:

> *When it [the dementia] got progressively worse, one of the biggest battles we had is when I sold her car. Uh, I mean she got really mad at me. But I'd let her drive from church home and we was coming down Union and then on route 44 and uh she wouldn't stay in her lane and I was grabbing the wheel. Oh, and any time I ever would do that it would just make her furious.*

He was keenly aware of the loss of independence that taking away the vehicle represented. "But that was probably the hardest on her, because then she didn't have her independence. She couldn't go by herself, or do anything by herself." Even though he told the story as a decision he had made and lived with for years, there was the desire to have the weight of his responsibility recognized by a person who knew what it means to limit another person's independence.

In each example the caregiver assessed the progression of the illness and the risk to the spouse's safety. This continues to be a more complicated model of uncertainty in illness than that experienced by a patient alone or for caregiver whose care recipient cannot cognitively participate in making decisions. Although both of these stories were told years after their occurrences, the caregivers were seeking affirmation from another credible authority, the researcher, about their decisions to limit their spouses' behaviors.

End-of-life decision making

The uncertainty of end-of-life care was represented in different ways according to the care recipients' severity of illness. Robert Walker, who lost his spouse during the course of the study, spoke specifically and adamantly about advance directives and choices at the time of imminent death. His actions at the time of her death were consistent with his previously stated intentions. In the first interview he declared, "There's not going to be any tubes in Barbara Jean." Because he had witnessed advance directives being ignored by health care providers when taking care of friends and relatives, he knew that his role as Barbara Jean's advocate was more important than any legal documents. He stated, "So living wills are all right maybe, but you can't trust some of those doctors might not do what it says so I figure I'm her living will." Bob Walker stated that he had found a physician who shared his belief system and supported his desire to make Barbara Jean comfortable. The physician stated that he do would what was necessary and "leave the rest in God's hands." Robert chose a credible authority that understood his perspective of end-of-life care and stated that it would be honored. He repeated various versions of this story at each of his three interviews. The last interview took place after his wife had died and reviewed everything he had done. It was his final chapter in caring for his wife and wanted me to know that he had kept all of his promises to her.

Naomi Turner expressed similar concerns over the future loss of her husband's ability to swallow. She also had witnessed other people with dementia entering the final stages of the disease:

> *I know that he might reach that place one day where he might not be able to swallow. Sometimes now he has a hard time swallowing sometime at night. But ah, when that day come I be able to handle it cause I have Jesus. Who knows one day what will come cause I don't know whether he will have a tube feed or not.*

She had not come to a point of resolution as had Bob Walker, but she was aware of the decisions that she might have to make in the future. This was an uncertainty producing event and even though thinking about the possibilities of losing her husband was painful she wanted to share her thoughts with a credible authority.

Although the other spousal caregivers had not come to this type of end-of-life decision at the time of their interviews, they had addressed the idea of nursing home placement for their spouse. Irene Teller commented on the constant tension between her ability to care for her husband and the need for more assistance.

> *And each year he progresses a little more it seems like. I really had to fight the depression. I didn't tell either one of my girls cause they kind of give me a talking to "Mother you really need to put him in a home." And I just, I'm doing okay. I don't get everything done in my house like I want to.*

Other caregivers still expressed uncertainty after their spouses had entered the nursing home. The caregivers frequently referenced talking with health care professionals to confirm their decisions. Paul Brown mentioned several conversations like the one below:

> *I asked one of the other ladies in charge of the nursing home about number three in command. I asked if I could talk to her and she said yes. So we went to her office. This was a different lady than I had spoken to previously. I asked her if I did the right thing and she told me that only God knows that, but in her opinion I did.*

Making the decision to change the living arrangement of a spouse continues to produce uncertainty for the caregiver especially when the spouse questions the arrangement as in Alma Williams' case:

> *Yeah, every now and then he'll say well I want to know what I'm supposed to do. I know what's coming. So I'll say what do you mean? Well*

about being in this place. So well I say I can't take care of you; that's the reason you got to be in here.

The spousal caregiver may also question the consequences of separation from the care recipient. Breaking up the couple's home creates difficulties, as well as relieving responsibility. Betty Harrison expressed the burden of being alone, "It's very stressful. I'm by myself, he's by his self. But he's got people around him." Whether making decisions about heroic care or nursing home care each caregiver had to evaluate the progressive deterioration of their spouses. The duality of their decisions in these situations is evidenced by the consequences for both the caregivers and the care recipients. In each case the caregivers sought credible authorities to talk about their concerns. As the caregiver counselor I was included in Betty, Alma, and Paul's decisions about nursing home care. Paul also consulted with the nursing home administrative staff and his minister, people who he trusted and represented credible authority.

The spousal caregiver's health

Finally the spousal caregivers mentioned uncertainty because of their own health concerns. The caregivers were all aware that their health and well-being was tied to their spouses. For the three caregivers who were caring for their spouses at home, they recognized that if their own health failed their spouses would not remain at home. Both Bob Walker and Irene Teller stated that they did not expect their children to care for their spouses, if something were to happen to them. They both acknowledged that a nursing home would be the only level of appropriate care if they could no longer fulfill their role as primary caregiver. Naomi Turner continued to rely on her faith to give her strength and avoid the thought of nursing home care for her husband. Although she is the youngest spousal caregiver in this study, she had several serious health conditions that ultimately could impair her caregiving ability.

For the other three caregivers whose spouses were currently in nursing homes, their health had been the major reason for making that choice. Alma Williams was advised by her physician that providing the twenty-four care needed to supervise her husband would be too overwhelming for a person of her age. Betty Harrison's family intervened to facilitate the placement of their father into a nursing home, because of concern for her health and their father's safety. Paul Brown's minister, however, summed up the ultimate uncertainty about caregivers' health. Paul said:

> *I had several people, including the minister of the church; tell me, even before I put Leona in the nursing home, that if I wasn't careful he knew of several instances where the spouse did pass away before the person that was sick.*

The caregivers' and care recipients' health and well-being are intertwined; therefore the uncertainty of illness is equally enmeshed between the spouses. In each case the spousal caregiver discussed their uncertainty with a person they considered a credible authority.

The Professional Audience as Credible Authority

Irene Teller confided in her daughters for assistance with medical treatments for her husband, but did not share her own health concerns about depression and declining physical strength. Instead she shared this information with me, as the researcher. She was already well aware of their opinion that her husband required more care than Irene could safely provide for him in their home. In similar comments Bob Walker was critical of family support. He, however, expressed the importance of telling his story in great depth to the researcher. Likewise, Paul Brown found mixed support and criticism from his children when making the decision to move his wife to a nursing facility. His need for social support in this health care crisis caused him to speak with several nursing home staff members who provided him a credible authority as an audience. He was still telling this story in the course of the interviews to a new audience (the researcher) who was another credible audience.

Each of the participants, either during or after the interview was completed, made some comment stating that just talking had been helpful. Some of the participants made comments about talking to me in my role as a counselor and as a researcher. In each example, their statements reflected the importance of being able to tell their story to an interested and compassionate individual, a credible authority.

Bob Walker's statement was one example:

> *So it was [nice to talk with the researcher] and also it helps crystallize some things. When you talk about it, you know some things are there and if you ask me more questions some things might come out that I don't even know or realize. And that's why interviews like this I enjoy, because if I try to explain something to somebody, I have to figure it out up here [points to head] before I can tell it to somebody. Sometimes the insights I had I didn't know I had.*

He stated that he found that sharing his story helped him clarify his feelings about what he had learned and how he had grown. Other caregivers did not elaborate to the same extent but declared in simple ways that talking helped them when they were in uncertainty producing circumstances.

Alma Williams and Naomi Turner both referred to times in the past that talking with me as a counselor had been beneficial. Alma stated in both interviews that she felt I was trying to understand things from her point of view. She also stated that she felt I was being compassionate, "so I was talking to you at that time and you gave me a lot of encouraging words." She was referring to a time when she was deciding whether or not to place her husband in a nursing home. Naomi Turner was caring for her husband with no formal support services when we first met as client and counselor. In the interview, she referred to the informational and emotional support during our meetings:

> *Karen Sodowsky, she brought to my attention if I need more help I could get it. And finally I came to a point where I said, "Yes I do." And just knowing that I could get more help that was a big help to me, because I was doing it all by myself.*

She asked me not to record our last visit, because she felt her husband's condition was something private between the two of them. Although she did not want our conversation recorded, she wanted me to stay and talk with her as she faced the uncertainty producing circumstances of end-of-life care.

Paul Brown expressed both current and past importance of talking with me as a counselor and now as a researcher:

> *I can count on you and I do rely on you. When you called me yesterday evening, I couldn't wait to have you come out and talk. Just talking to you means so much to me and it does most other people that have spouses in a nursing home. I have no one to talk to except like now, even the darn dog. I talk to myself like I told you. I just hope that there is no one around, but I do talk to the dog too.*

He made this statement in the second interview, but in a briefer statement in the first interview he made a similar statement about the interviews. He said, "I am supposed to be helping you and you are helping me." In every case, the spousal caregivers placed some sense of satisfaction in being able to tell their story to someone who was informed and compassionate i.e. a credible authority audience. The value of the narrative in counseling and research was voiced in the course of the interviews.

CONCLUSION

The main limitation with the study comes first and most importantly from using participants from one community. Although the triangulation of three sources of information was used to broaden the ability to generalize the information, further research should be conducted in diverse communities with a greater variety of participant relationships. For example gay and lesbian couples were not readily accessible in this community and should be included in this type of study. Second because all of the participants were aware of my role in the community as a caregiver counselor it made my role as the audience for their narratives unique. Caregivers are usually talking with health care professionals who have as their first priority, the patient. Therefore having the audience ask specifically about their needs and concerns may make this research different.

I believe that although the second point is a limitation, it is also an area that requires more research. Services for caregivers have traditionally been focused on getting physical relief for the many responsibilities that consume their time and energy. Although these services are important, the need to express their unique experiences may provide a valuable support that is viewed as just a side effect of meeting with service providers. For the many years that I worked as a medical social worker supplying services to patients, I also talked with countless caregivers. It was not my primary role, but often it was one that I wished I had time to offer.

More program evaluation of services for caregivers should investigate the importance of counseling as one of the options available to caregivers. As the 11 million unpaid, informal caregivers continue to grow over the next several decades in U.S., using precious resources in the most effective manner will be essential. More research may make a case for listening, as well as doing in caring for aging adults. The need to communicate is magnified for caregivers who are with care recipients who cannot interact with them. Caregiving is both physically and emotionally challenging and it becomes even more complicated when the care recipient is not able to contribute to the discussion of what is best for him or her. The uncertainty produced by illness is enhanced for caregivers experiencing that illness with someone who is unable to interact with the caregiver and express choices about limitations of physical and cognitive independence. The caregiver's ability to tell their story to a health care professional viewed as a credible authority can reduce the uncertainty. Whether choosing to use nursing home care, deciding that daily tasks are no longer safe, or protecting the caregiver's health social support can be gained from the caregiver's narrative when told to the audience of credible authority in the health care field.

REFERENCES

Alzheimer's Association. (2010). *Alzheimer's disease: Facts and figures* [Brochure]. Chicago.

Anderson, J. O., & Martin, P. G. (2003). Narrative and healing: Exploring one family's stories of cancer survivorship. *Health Communication, 15*, 133–143.

Aryes, L. (2000). Narratives of family caregiving: Four story types. *Research in Nursing & Health, 23*, 359–371.

Babrow, A., Kasch, C., & Ford, L. (1998). The many meanings of uncertainty in illness: Toward a systematic accounting. *Health Communication, 10*, 1–23.

Baikie, E. (2002). The impact of dementia on marital relationships. *Sexual and Relationship Therapy, 17*, 289–299.

Bailey, P. H. (1997). Finding your way around qualitative methods in nursing research. *Journal of Advanced Nursing, 25*, 18–22.

Beach, W. A., Easter, D. W., Good, J. S., & Pigeron, E. (2005). Disclosing and responding to cancer "fears" during oncology interviews. *Social Science & Medicine, 60*, 893–910.

Bennet K. M., & Vidal-Hall, S. (2000). Narratives of death: A qualitative study of widowhood in later of life. *Ageing and Society, 20*, 413–428.

Bochner, A. (2001). Narrative's views. *Qualitative Inquiry, 7*, 131–157.

Bond, M. J., Clark, M. S., & Davies, S. (2003). The quality of life of spouse dementia caregivers: Changes associated with yielding to formal care and widowhood. *Social Science and Medicine, 57,* 2385–2395.

Brashers, D. E., & Babrow, A. S., (1996). Theorizing communication and health. *Communication Studies, 47,* 243–251.

Brashers, D. E., Hsieh, E., Neidig, J. L., & Reynolds, N. R. (2006). Managing uncertainty about illness: Health care providers as credible authorities. In R. M. Dailey & B. A. Le Poire (Eds.), Applied interpersonal communication matters (pp. 219–240). New York: Peter Lang.

Brashers, D. E., Neidig, J. L., Cardillo, L. W., Dobbs, L. K., Russell, J. A., & Haas, S. M. (1999). "In an important way, I did die": Uncertainty and revival in persons living with HIV or AIDS. *AIDS Care, 11,* 201–219.

Brashers, D. E., Neidig, J. L., Hass, S. M., Dobbs, L. K., Cardillo, L. W., & Russell, J. A. (2000). Communication in the management of uncertainty: The case of persons living with HIV or AIDS. *Communication Monographs, 67,* 63–84.

Brashers, D. E., Neidig, J. L., Reynolds, N. R., & Haas, S. (1998). Uncertainty in illness across the HIV/AIDS trajectory. *Journal of the Association of Nurses in AIDS Care, 9,* 66–78.

Butcher, H. K., & Buckwalter, K. C. (2002). Exasperations as blessings: Meaning-making and the caregiving experience. *Journal of Aging and Identity, 7,* 113–132.

Carrese, J. A., & Rhodes, L. A. (1995). Western bioethics on the Navajo reservation: Benefit or harm? *JAMA, 274,* 826–829.

Charmaz, K. (1999). Stories of suffering: Subjective tales and research narratives. *Qualitative Health Research, 9,* 362–382.

Charmaz, K., & Olesen, V. (1997). Ethnographic research in medical sociology. *Sociological Methods & Research, 25,* 452–494.

Docherty, D., & McColl, M. A. (2003). Illness stories: Themes emerging through narrative. *Social Work in Health Care, 37,* 19–39.

Eggly, S. (2002). Physician-patient co-construction of illness narratives in the medical interview. *Health Communication, 14,* 339–360.

Ekman, I., Lundman, B., & Norberg, A. (1999). The meaning of hospital care, as narrated by elderly patients with chronic heart failure. *Heart & Lung: The Journal of Acute and Critical Care, 28,* 203–209.

Fisher, W. R. (1984). Narration as a human communication paradigm: The case of public moral argument. *Communication Monographs, 51,* 1–22.

Fisher, W. R. (1985). The narrative paradigm: An elaboration. *Communication Monographs, 52,* 347–367.

Fisher, W. R. (1997). Narration, reason, and community. In L. P. Hinchman & S. K. Hinchman (Eds.), *Memory, identity, community: The idea of narrative in the human sciences* (pp. 307–327). Albany, NY: State University of New York Press.

Folkman, S. (2001). Coping with chronic illness: Lessons from AIDS caregivers. In S. G. Funk, E. M. Tornquist, J. Leeman, M. S. Miles, & J. S. Harrell (Eds.), *Key aspects of preventing and managing chronic illness* (pp. 307–315). New York: Springer Publishing Company.

Gaugler, J. E., Kane, R. L., Kane, R. A., & Newcomer, R. (2005). The longitudinal effects of early behavior problems in the dementia caregiving career. *Psychology & Aging, 20*, 100–116.

Germino, B. B., Mishel, M. H., Belyea, M., Harris, L., Ware, A., & Mohler, J. (1998). Uncertainty in prostate cancer: Ethnic and family patterns. *Cancer Practice, 6*, 107–113.

Gibbs, R. W., & Franks, H. (2002). Embodied metaphor in women's narratives about their experiences with cancer. *Health Communication, 14*, 139–165.

Giorgi, A. (1979). The relationships among level, type, and structure and their importance for social science theorizing: A dialogue with Shutz. In A. Giorgi, R. Knowles, & D. L. Smith (Eds.), *Duquesne studies in phenomenological psychology* (pp. 81–92). Pittsburgh: Duquesne University Press.

Harden, J. (2000). Language, discourse and the chronoscope: Applying literary theory to the narratives in health care. *Journal of Advanced Nursing, 31*, 506–512.

Harris, P.B. (1998). Listening to caregiving sons: Misunderstood realities. *Gerontologist, 38*, 342–352.

Hines, S. C., Babrow, A. S., Badzek, L., & Moss, A. H. (1997). Communication and problematic integration in end-of-life decisions: Dialysis decisions among the elderly. *Health Communication, 9*, 199–217.

Hines, S. C., Babrow, A. S., Badzek, L., & Moss, A. H. (2001). From coping with life to coping with death: Problematic integration for the seriously ill elderly. *Health Communication, 13*, 327–342.

Hines, S. C., Glove, J. J., Holley, J. L., Babrow, A. S., Badzek, L. A., & Moss, A. H. (1999). Dialysis patients' preferences for family-based advance care planning. *Annals of Internal Medicine, 130*, 825–828.

Hines, S. C., Moss, A. H., & Badzek, L. (1997). Being involved or just being informed communication preferences of seriously ill, older adults. *Communication Quarterly, 45*, 268–281.

Hines, S. C., Toale, M. C., Heisel, A. D., Baringer, K., Amos, R. D., Burkett, J. S., et al. (2000). Communication in advance care planning: Preferences for surrogate involvement. *Southern Communication Journal, 66*, 27–39.

Hsieh, E. (2004). Stories in action and the dialogic management of identities: Storytelling in transplant support group meetings. *Research and Language and Social Interaction, 37*, 39–70.

Hooker, K., Frazier, L. D., & Monahan, D. J. (1994). Personality and coping among caregivers of spouses with dementia. *Gerontologist, 34*, 386–392.

Hopp, F. P., & Duffy, S. A. (2000). Racial variations in end-of-life care. *Journal of the American Geriatrics Society, 48*, 658–663.

Hummert, M. L. & Morgan, M. (2001). Negotiating decisions in the aging family. In M. L. Hummert & J. Nussbaum (Eds.), *Aging communication and health: Linking research practice for successful aging* (pp. 177–201). Mahwah, NJ: Lawrence Erlbaum.

Irvine, L. (2000). "Even better than the real thing": Narratives of the self in codependency. *Qualitative Sociology, 23*, 9–28.

Jansson, W., Nordberg, G., & Grafstrom, M. (2001). Patterns of elderly spousal caregiving in dementia care: An observational study. *Journal of Advanced Nursing, 34*, 804–812.

Kelly, M. P., & Dickinson, H. (1997) The narrative self in autobiographical accounts of illness. *The Sociological Review, 45*, 255–278.

Luborsky, M. R. (1987). Analysis of multiple life history narratives. *Ethos, 15*, 366–381.

McCarty, E. F. (1996). Caring for a parent with Alzheimer's disease: Process of daughter caregiver stress. *Journal of Advanced Nursing, 23*, 792–803.

Miczo, N. (2003). Beyond the "fetishism of words": Considerations on the use of the interview to gather chronic illness narratives. *Qualitative Health Research, 13*, 469–490.

Mishel, M. H. (1988). Uncertainty in illness. *Image: Journal of Nursing Scholarship, 20*, 225–232.

Mishel, M. H. (1990). Reconceptualization of the uncertainty in illness theory. *Image: Journal of Nursing Scholarship, 22*, 256–262.

Mishel, M. H., & Braden, C. J. (1998). Finding meaning: Antecedents of uncertainty in Illness. *Nursing Research, 37*, 98–103.

Monks, J. A. (2000). Talk as social suffering: narratives of talk in medical settings. *Anthropology & Medicine, 7*, 15–38.

Moore, C. D., & Sherman, S. R. (1999). Factors that influence elders' decisions to formulate advance directives. *Journal of Gerontological Social Work, 31*, 21–39.

Moore, C. D., Sparr, J., Sherman, S., & Avery, L. (2003). Surrogate decision-making: Judgment standard preferences of older adults. *Social Work in Health Care, 37*, 1–16.

Moran, D., & Mooney, T. (2002) *The phenomenology reader*. New York: Routledge.

Moustakas, C. (1994). *Phenomenological research methods*. Thousand Oaks, CA: Sage.

Mutran, E. J., Danis, M., Bratton, K. A., Sudha, S., & Hanson, L. ((1997). Attitudes of the critically ill toward prolonging life: The role of social support. *The Gerontologist*, 37, 192–199.

Nolan, M., & Dellasega, C. (2000). "I really feel I've let him down": Supporting family carers during long term care placement for elders. *Journal of Advanced Nursing, 31*, 759–767.

Pennebaker, J. W., & Keogh, K. A. (1999). Revealing, organizing, and reorganizing the self in response to stress and emotion. In R.J. Contrada & R.D. Ashmore (Eds.), *Self, social identity,* and *physical health*, (pp. 101–121). New York: Oxford University Press.

Perry, J. (2002). Wives giving care to husbands with Alzheimer's disease: A process of interpretive caring. *Research in Nursing, 25*, 307–316.

Price, L. J. (1995). Life stories of the terminally ill: Therapeutic and anthropological paradigms. *Human Organization, 54*, 462–468.

Rosenfeld, K. E., Wenger, N. S., & Kagawa-Singer, M. (2000). End-of-life decision making: A qualitative study of elderly individuals. *Journal of General Internal Medicine, 15*, 620–625.

Russell, R. (2001). In sickness and in health: A qualitative study of elderly men who care for wives with dementia. *Journal of Aging Studies, 15*, 351–367.

Sanders, S. (2005). Is the glass half empty or half full? Reflections on strain and gain in caregivers of individuals with Alzheimer's disease. *Social Work in Health Care, 40*, 57–73.

Sanesone, P., & Phillips, M. (1995). Advance directives for elderly people: Worthwhile cause or wasted effort? *Social Work, 40*, 397–401.

Singer, J. A. (2004). Narrative identity and meaning making across the adult lifespan: An introduction. *Journal of Personality, 72*, 439–459.

Sollod, R. N. (2002). Beyond a sense of safety: A psychologist's tale of serious chronic illness. *Psychotherapy in Practice, 58*, 1397–1409.

Vernooij-Danssen, M. J. F. J., Persoon, J. M. G., & Felling, A. J. A. (1998). Predictors of sense of competence in caregivers of demented persons. *Social Science Medicine, 43*, 41–49.

Waitzkin, H., Britt, T., & Williams, C. (1994). Narratives of aging and social problems in medical encounters with older persons. *Journal of Health and Social Behavior, 35*, 322–348.

Chapter 10:

Ensuring a good death: Where communication can intervene

Emily M. Cramer
University of Wisconsin-Milwaukee

INTRODUCTION

One does not need to search the website of the Centers for Disease Control and Prevention (CDC) or browse the database of the *Journal of the American Medical Association* to learn that the mortality rate for death across the lifespan is 100%. The experience of dying will touch each of our lives: this scientific truth is recognized at some level of human consciousness from the moment we are born. At the same time, dying is—quite literally—a morbid topic from which we would prefer to shy away. From research conducted primarily over the past two decades, we know that individuals avoid end-of-life conversations because of embarrassment, worry, stigma, or the desire to conceal pain or difficult emotions; people may refrain from sharing preferences for end-of-life care on account of false hope or the inability to accept the illness prognosis (Larson & Tobin, 2000). Conversations about life-threatening or chronic illness among families are often constrained by either worry about risk/unexpected events or concerns about conflict (Tapp, 2001). Oftentimes, patients, families and clinicians collectively avoid mention of death or dying, even in the midst of a patient's severe suffering or poor prognosis (Quill, 2000).

As we avoid talking about dying—much less thinking about death—we may overlook some emerging trends associated with dying in the modern world. The 20th century was marked by a transition from a focus on death due to infectious disease to death from chronic disease (Conway, 2007), a trend continuing in the 21st century. Preliminary data from the CDC (National Vital Statistics Reports, 2012) reveals the top three causes of death in 2011 were due to chronic disease: heart disease, cancer, and chronic lower respiratory disease. Because people are increasingly dying from degenerative diseases today, the experience of death takes longer than it did in pre-modern societies, where death typically happened quickly due to infectious disease (Conway, 2007). Though a longer dying process may give patients the opportunity to connect with family members and settle affairs, a prolonged death does not necessarily imply a better death.

An extended life may translate into more medical procedures and additional costs that do not impact patients' health in essential ways. For example, in 2009, Medicare spent 64% of its total hospital spending on just 10% of Medicare patients who received hospital care; 6.6% (1.6 million) Medicare patients ended up dying in the hospital despite costly expenditures —23% of hospital spending—aimed at keeping them alive (Adamy & McGinty, 2012). Additionally, decreased quality of life is associated with spending the final weeks in an intensive care unit and dying in the hospital (Zhang, Nilsson, & Prigerson, 2012). The prevalence of chronic disease, combined with medical progress in managing chronic disease, has led to prolonged treatments, increased costs, and decreased quality of life at the end of life. At the center of the push-and-pull between cure and care is the patient and family—participants who often remain voiceless as a chronic disease reaches its final trajectory.

Giving patients a voice at the end of life requires effective communication. Patients who discuss dying preferences with a physician are more likely to accept an illness as terminal and choose less aggressive medical care (Mack et al., 2013; Wright et al., 2008). Patient-provider conversations between patients and physicians increase the likelihood a patient will receive palliative care and other less-intensive treatments during the final days of life (Trice & Prigerson, 2010). End-of-life discussions also are associated with reduced costs at the end of life and refraining from conversations about death can decrease patient quality of life at the end of life (Zhang et al., 2009).

To help enhance the dying experience for patients, most interventions focus on improving communication in the healthcare context. Researchers at the Dana Farber Cancer Institute are exploring the effectiveness of a checklist approach to end-of-life care planning between patient and provider (Block, 2012; O'Reilly, 2012). The Conversation Project (2012) is a national initiative to encourage families to share end-of-life wishes with each other. Respecting Choices, a collaborative effort of healthcare organizations in La Crosse, Wisconsin, involves patient communication about end-of-life wishes and assistance with advance care planning process (Hammes, Rooney, & Gundrum, 2010). Each of these solutions warrants competent communication.

The purpose of this chapter is to examine communication as a conduit for improving the end-of-life experience. First, conceptualizations of good and bad death are examined within three salient dialectical tensions found in the literature: isolation-community, constraint-control, and suffering-opportunity. Next, communication-based solutions to improve the end-of-life experience are explored in the contexts of patient-provider and patient-family interactions as well as advance care planning initiatives. The chapter concludes by suggesting an agenda for future research using theoretical and practical applications and grounded in the discipline of communication.

CONCEPTUALIZATIONS OF DEATH

Ensuring A Good Death

Conceptualizations of a good and bad death are grounded in the changing nature of disease. The World Health Organization notes that "vaccination has greatly reduced the burden of infectious disease" in our time (Andre et al., 2012, para. 1). Conversely, rates of chronic disease continue to rise, according to a report by the Partnership to Fight Chronic Disease (PFCD, 2009): 45% of the U.S. population, or more than 133 million Americans, have at least one chronic disease and

26% have multiple chronic conditions. PFCD estimates that healthcare costs related to treating chronic disease reach about $1.7 trillion annually. Rising rates of chronic disease can be attributed to a combination of factors including poor lifestyle choices, childhood obesity, and lack of focus on preventive care. Moreover, the future of chronic disease in our country is worrisome: PFCD projects that by 2023, the U.S. will see a 50% increase in cases of cancer, mental illness, and diabetes and a 40% increase in heart disease and hypertension. Pulmonary conditions and stroke will increase by approximately 30%.

Chronic diseases are the causes of 70% of all deaths in the U.S. (PCFD, 2009) and 63% of deaths worldwide (WHO, 2013). We conjecture, therefore, that the prevalence and nature of chronic disease very much influences not only what we die of but also how we die. Conway (2007) points out that death today typically does not happen quickly; death due to degenerative, chronic disease often takes several years and largely affects older populations. Chronic disease may also require numerous, expensive medical interventions that compel patients to stay in hospitals "with their bodies attached to machines by tubes, pipes and wires, surrounded, not by families and friends, but by nurses and junior doctors" (Conway, 2007, p. 197).

The intersection of chronic disease and death in the modern healthcare context influences what we conceptualize a good or bad death to be. Before describing some emerging, communication-based interventions to promote a positive dying experience, we can first identify some trends in what a good death and bad death due to chronic or prolonged illness are generally understood to signify. Recent literature on conceptualizations of death can be organized into three dialectical tensions—strained moments in the dying process where the patient and family often find themselves grappling amid extreme conditions: (a) *isolation-community*; (b) *constraint-control*; and (c) *suffering-opportunity*.

Isolation-Community

Patients often die in settings perceived to be isolated, such hospitals or other acute-care settings, despite wishes to die in a familiar, communal location, such as the home. A survey by the National Hospice and Palliative Care found that 80% of patients want to die at home (Johnson, Wang, & Metz, 2010), resonating with past research (see Grunier et al., 2007). For example, a study by Tang (2003) reported that nearly 90% of patients with a terminal illness preferred home to be the location of death; factors influencing the decision included "quality of life, availability and ability of family caregivers, concerns of being a burden to others, long-standing relationships with healthcare providers, and quality of healthcare" (p. 245). Overall, dying at a location preferred by a patient is regarded an important quality indicator at the end of life (Last Acts, 2002). However, recent CDC data (Hall, Levant, & DeFrances, 2013) show nearly one-third of all deaths in the United States occur in a hospital. Although the death rate in hospitals decreased by 8% from 2000 to 2010, the number of total hospitalizations increased by 11%. Seventy-five percent of inpatients who died in a hospital were age 65 and over, according the CDC, and the percentage of hospital deaths for individuals under 65 increased by 9%.

The statistics support Conway's (2007) contention that, despite patient wishes, many deaths today occur "offstage" with patients hooked up to machines and in institutions away from family and friends. Patient quality of life at the end of life is negatively associated with hospital stays: decreased quality of life is associated with more time in the ICU during the last week of life (Zhang et al., 2012). Additionally, a mortality follow-back survey (Teno et al., 2004) was conducted with family members about the quality of care provided at the last place where the patient received care before death. The researchers found that the last place of care had substantial influences on family members' perceptions of patient care at the end of life. More than a third of informants whose loved one died in an institution (e.g., home health agency, nursing home, or hospital) reported insufficient emotional support for the patient as well as concerns about family members' emotional support. In comparison, family members of patients receiving home hospice services were generally more satisfied with the quality of care (71%) than family members of patients who died in institutions (50%). (Hospice care is discussed in greater detail later in the chapter.)

The location of a death not only impacts patient outcomes; caregivers report more mental problems when their loved ones die in an institutional setting. A prospective, longitudinal, multisite study (Wright et al., 2010) followed 342 patients with advanced cancer and their caregivers through the patients' deaths. Results indicated that patients who died in ICU and hospital settings experienced decreased quality of life at the end of life. Furthermore, patient ICU deaths contributed to bereaved caregivers' likelihood of experiencing post-traumatic stress disorder and patient hospital deaths increased the tendency for prolonged grief.

In contrast to dying in an isolated, institutional setting, notions of a good death are community-centered and "place great stress upon sociality" (Conway, 2007, p. 199). Patients want to be able to interact with family during the dying process to resolve conflicts, spend time together, and say good-bye during the final moments of life (Steinhauser et al., 2000). For elderly adults, dying at home may be perceived as more conducive to feelings of comfort and familiarity as well as the presence of friends and family (Gott et al., 2004).

Constraint-Control

Not only does a good death tend to take place in a familiar, community-based setting, but also a good death involves the ability of the patient or family members to assert personal control and choice in the healthcare context. Nurse participants working in a primary care context emphasized that a good death is promoted when patients' preferences for end-of-life care are respected and supported (Griggs, 2010). Patients who feel prepared for death tend to experience increased quality of life at the end of life (Zhang et al., 2012). Bad deaths are conceived to be occasions when patients' treatment preferences are constrained or unclear: "patients felt disregarded, family members felt perplexed and concerned about suffering, and providers felt out of control and feared that they were not providing good care" (Steinhauser et al., 2000, p. 827).

If the patient can no longer make decisions, family members are burdened with making the "right choice" about discontinuing treatments (Fine, 2005). When end-of-life preferences have not been shared among families, physiological decline, emotional stress, and the inability to make effective end-of-life choices may ensue (Scott & Caughlin, 2012). A lack of discussion about end-of-life care also is associated with an increase in stress and a decreased likelihood of following a patient's wishes (Seymour, Bellamy, Ahmedzar, & Clark, 2003). A recent qualitative, grounded-theory study of family physicians (Tan & Manca, 2013) identified several barriers to promoting a patient's good death among family members and physicians. Barriers included family discord and dysfunction, unattainable goals and expectations, and denial of the patient's condition. A good death was facilitated for the patient when family members and the physician established mutual trust and support, understood one another, and made informed, shared decisions.

To avoid saddling family members with making end-of-life decisions on a patient's behalf, the choices of a patient can be articulated through advance directives, which are legal documents that enable patients to convey healthcare decisions about end-of-life care ahead of time (Medline Plus, 2012). A 2006 survey by the PEW Research Center (Span, 2009) found that only 26% of Americans had a living will. The reasons individuals did not complete advance directives ranged from not wanting to place limits on their healthcare to perceiving advance directives as difficult and expensive to complete. Possessing documentation about end-of-life preferences, however, may lead to improved outcomes for patients and families facing a terminal illness. For example, a mortality follow-back survey (Teno, Gruneir, Schwartz, Nanda, & Wetle, 2007) found family members of decedents with advance directives were less likely to report their loved died in a hospital, had a feeding tube, or used a respirator during the last 30 days of life. Family members of deceased patients without an advance directive were more likely to indicate problems with physician communication and uncertainty about what to expect during the dying process.

Beyond advance directives, a crucial element of ensuring patient control over end-of-life decision-making involves effective communication between the patient and physician. In a multi-site longitudinal study, Wright and colleagues (2008) found patients with advanced cancer who discussed end-of-life preferences with a physician were more inclined to accept a terminal prognosis and choose less aggressive medical care at the end of life. A more recent prospective cohort study by Mack and colleagues (2012) found that patients who had end-of-life conversations with their doctor before the last 30 days of life were less likely to receive aggressive measures, such as chemotherapy and acute care, and more likely to receive hospice care. Another study (Zhang et al., 2009) found that cancer patients who had conversations with their physicians about end-of-life preferences had significantly lower health care costs during the final weeks of life. Costs were aggregated for ICU and hospital stays, hospice care, and life-sustaining procedures.

Nevertheless, when it comes to discussing death, hospital physicians may be uncomfortable, or worse, ineffective (Gillotti, Thompson, & McNeilis, 2002; Kirk, Kirk, Kuziemsky, Wagar, 2010). Studies have indicated that physicians perceive difficult conversations to be impacted by emotional expression, feelings of failure, and lack of training. Doctors also may fear the ethical and legal implications of talking with patients about complex issues, such as discontinuing treatments (Baile et al., 2000). When these conversations go badly, negative repercussions may ensue for patient in terms of understanding of prognosis, hope, emotions and concerns, and health outcomes (Barclay, Blackhall, & Tulsky, 2007).

Though the physicians' authority and inadequate communication skills may be contributing factors to a bad death, research reveals that many healthcare professionals would like to know and follow the wishes of patients at the end of life. For example, a survey of critical care nurses indicated that participants wanted a fuller understanding of their patients' wishes for end-of life care (Beckstrand, Callister, & Kirchoff, 2006).

Suffering-Opportunity

In addition to feeling out of control, patients, family members, and providers alike envision a bad death as one involving pain and suffering (Beckstrand et al., 2006; Bratcher, 2010). Many patients fear dying in pain such as breakthrough pain or shortness of breath (Steinhauser et al., 2004). Anxiety about pain often arises from previous experience with cure-directed therapies perceived as aggressive. Aggressive treatments such as the use of a feeding tube and undergoing chemotherapy during the last week of life are negatively associated with quality of life at the end of life (Zhang et al., 2012). Moreover, such treatments at the end of life account for 5.1 percent (17.6 billion) of all hospital inpatient costs (Zhao & Encinosa, 2009). Conversely, a good death is perceived to involve the use of general analgesia, commitment to patient comfort, treatment of other symptoms that cause discomfort, such as dyspnea (Bratcher, 2010).

Patient pain and suffering at the end of life can have harmful impacts on healthcare professionals and family members as well. Hospital nurses in the UK described a bad death as one where the patient experiences a traumatic death due to pain or unrelieved symptoms (Costello, 2005). Critical care nurses reported focusing on the provision of comfort measures to manage patient pain and discomfort and, more importantly, to eliminate painful, aggressive procedures (Beckstrand et al., 2006). Family members, particularly spouses, may experience elevated anxiety, yearning, and intrusive thoughts when a patient dies a death that is perceived to be painful (Carr, 2003).

Nearly two decades ago, Ira Byock, MD, a widely-recognized palliative care physician contended that opportunities exist for dying patients to emerge from a place of suffering to a place of wellness (Byock, 1996). He argued that hospice and palliative care programs—then in their infancy—promoted personhood, life review, as well as the search for meaning and transcendence. The number of palliative care teams in hospital settings increased by nearly 150% from 2000 to 2012 (CAPC, 2012), and approximately 53,000 hospice programs exist in the country today (National Hospice and Palliative Care Organization, 2012).

Enrollment in hospice or palliative care programming offers opportunities to relieve suffering while promoting patient comfort. Palliative care is used "across the spectrum of disease severity" (Fine, Reid, Shengelia, & Adelman, 2010, p. 595)—from diagnosis with a serious or chronic illness and throughout the disease progression. Palliative care can be delivered alongside aggressive, cure-oriented treatments, such as chemotherapy or radiation. Hospice care offers comfort measures at the end of life to patients in the form of pain and symptom relief; emotional and spiritual support; practical assistance with tasks of daily living, medical supplies and medication management; and coordination of care.

Abiding by the principles of care rather than cure presents opportunities to improve quality of life and even lengthen life. A 2010 study by Temel and colleagues discovered that combining palliative care at an early stage with standard cancer treatments results in better quality of life, reduced symptoms of depression and longer survival rates for patients. Team-based, palliative care addresses the patient's physical, psychosocial and practical needs by managing symptoms, providing social and emotional support and assisting with decision making. A study by Connor and associates (2007) looked at the survival rates of 4,493 patients with congestive heart failure and five types of cancer and found that the mean survival for patients enrolled in a hospice program was 29 days longer than non-hospice patients. The researchers speculated that increased survival rates among hospice patients could be attributed to the avoidance of overtreatment, improved symptom monitoring, and treatment, and increased psychosocial support. Zapka et al. (2006) also suggest that, because the Medicare Hospice Benefit requires a physician to confirm that a patient has a prognosis of six months or less, discussion about end-of-life topics between patients and physicians are more likely in a hospice program. For patients with terminal cancer, hospice enrollment is associated with reduced rates of hospitalization and hospital deaths (Carlson et al., 2010). Furthermore, patients with a terminal illness who are not enrolled hospice tend to higher Medicare expenditures: a study by researchers at Duke University (Taylor et al. 2007) found that Medicare expenditures were, on average, $2,309 less per hospice user than for the non-hospice control group.

WHERE COMMUNICATION CAN INTERVENE

Emerging conceptualizations of a good death generally describe the patient as being surrounded by others, having his or her preferences honored, and being free from pain and suffering. Initiatives to ensure that the experience of dying is improved for individuals with chronic, terminal illness are grounded in communication. Indeed, effective communication between patients and providers as well as between patient and families has increasingly been heralded as a primary solution to a bad death. Below are examples of communication-based programs with aims to facilitate better deaths for patients facing the end of life. Solutions range from web-based resources to the inclusion of important documents in the patient chart to communication training programs for patient and physicians.

Patient-Provider Communication

Patient-physician communication is an important determinant in end-of-life care; conversations between patients and physicians increase the likelihood of a patient acknowledging a terminal illness, indicating a preference for comfort care over life-extending measures, and receiving palliative care and other less-intensive treatments during the final days of life (Trice & Prigerson, 2010). Researchers also have found that open communication between physician and patient help to bridge racial disparities in end of life care (Sacco, 2012). Moreover, most cancer patients desire to engage in conversations with physicians about whether a prognosis is terminal (Kaplowitz, Campo, & Chiu, 2002).

Accordingly, several programs have been developed to improve end-of-life communication between patient and provider. Data is now being collected by the Dana Farber Cancer Institute, an affiliate of Harvard Medical School, to gauge the effectiveness of using the Serious Illness Communication Checklist in end-of-life care planning (Block, 2012; O'Reilly, 2012). The study will enroll 450 cancer patients and 60 oncologists who will be trained on using the checklist, which includes the following discussion items:

- Patient understanding of prognosis.
- How much information patients want shared with loved ones.
- Patient goals of care, should their health seriously worsen.
- Patients' biggest fears and what functional abilities they could not imagine living without.
- How much medical intervention patients are willing to undergo to gain more time.
- How much patients want family members to know about their priorities and wishes. (O'Reilly, 2002)

The study will ascertain patient satisfaction and treatment scores in light of the checklist approach. Communicating patient values and goals associated with the end of life, the checklist will be located in patients' electronic medical records (Block, 2012).

Additionally, the Supportive Care Plan (SCP) is a tool that has demonstrated improved outcomes for ensuring that patients die in the first choice of place of care (Thompson-Hill, Hooley, Salt, & O'Neill, 2009). Developed by researchers in Great Britain, the SCP is a "patient-held document that provides a framework for initiating communication and making the plans and wishes of each individual patient known to all healthcare professionals involved in their care" (p. 250). The SCP is written in the third person to emphasize that its completion is a collaborative process. Examples of questions in the SCP include: "What discussions have taken place around where the patient would like to be cared for now or in the future?" and "What would they like or not like to happen?" In a pilot study, 50% of patients who completed a SCP died in the place they had chosen.

Some communication-based interventions have attempted to train patients to be more assertive in the medical encounter. Previously, Cegala and colleagues (2001) found that older adults who received communication skills training prior to a primary care interview sought and obtained more information than untrained study participants. More recently, Health Dialog, a London-based healthcare management company that collaborates with the Informed Medical Decisions Foundation, made available a decision aid to encourage patients to become more actively engaged in their medical care (BusinessWire, 2012). The aid, entitled *Choices for Medical Care when You are Seriously Ill*, provides resources for information and support for patients making decisions about their care.

Finally, communication skills training is now a standard component of a medical student's education, although the time dedicated to its instruction may be minimal (Cegala & Broz, 2002). A review of postgraduate training programs for physicians in end-of-life education (Weissman & Block, 2002) found that ethics and psychosocial care were the most common required domains of study; training in end-of-life communication was one of the least-often required areas of instruction. The authors of the study argue that the lack of communication skills training could influence the delivery of end-of-life care by some physicians. To remedy this, research on the benefits of offering physicians a short, intensive course in end-of-life communication skills training (Alexander, Keitz, Sloan, & Tulsky, 2006) as well as other experienced-based interventions, such as the Palliative Care Clinical Evaluation Exercise (CEX; Han, Keranen, Lescisin, & Arnold, 2005) have shown positive, albeit preliminary, results.

Patient-Family Communication

Some families may eschew conversations about the end-of-life because they fear the conversation may remove hope, cause pain, prompt negative emotional reactions, and even lead to disagreement (Scott & Caughlin, 2012). To get family members talking, ABCNews has partnered with the Institute for Healthcare Improvement to develop The Conversation Project (2012), a national initiative to encourage families to share end-of-life preferences with each other. The Conversation Project website (Figure 1) features a "Starter Kit" including tools and tips for starting the end-of-life conversation with loved ones. For example, the kit features a section where individuals can check off the people with whom they want to have the conversation and when a good time to talk might be. The kit contains examples of ice-breaker statements, such as ""I need your help with something," as well as some content areas to touch on during the conversation. The website also includes opportunities for visitors to share stories of conversations that went well.

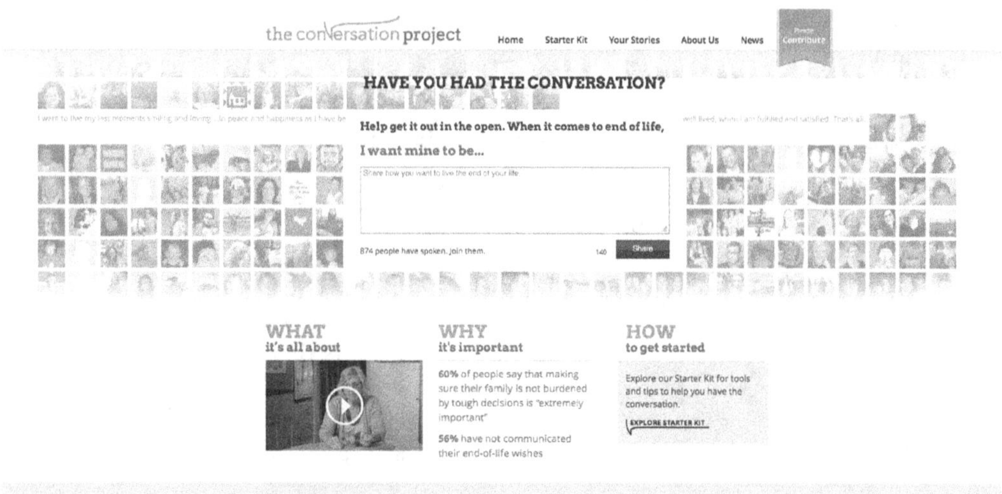

Figure 10.1 *The Conversation Project website: www.theconversationproject.org.*

Another web-based resource for families is Prepare, a website developed by researchers at the San Francisco Veterans Affairs Medical Center and University of California-San Francisco (Painter, 2013). The aim of Prepare is to simplify, using how-to videos, large type, voice overs, and 5th-grade language, the task of making and communicating medical decisions. The website encourages users to browse it in the company of friends and family and features specific steps for telling others about medical preferences (Prepare, 2013).

Completing Advance Directives

According to qualitative focus groups with care managers from the Area Agency on Aging (Baughman et al., 2012), patients and families have limited understanding of advance directives and may feel frightened or overwhelmed when communicating about end of life issues. Additional barriers to understanding advance care planning include: lack of knowledge, language barriers and cultural differences.

To increase understanding and utilization of advance directives, programs such as Respecting Choices have been established (Hammes et al., 2010). Fully implemented in 1993, Respecting Choices (RC) is a collaborative effort of healthcare organizations in La Crosse, Wisconsin to promote advance care planning within the community. The purpose of the project is to encourage the communication of end-of-life preferences through advance directives. As such, RC involves the integration of six primary goals into routine patient care:

1. Adult patients are invited to understand, to reflect on, and to discuss plans for future healthcare relevant to their stage of illness.
2. Adult patients are provided competent assistance by trained nonphysicians in the planning process.
3. Written plans (however documented) are accurate, as specific as possible, and understandable to all stakeholders.
4. Written plans are stored, transferred, and retrievable wherever the patient is being treated
5. Plans are updated and become more specific as illnesses progress
6. Plans are reviewed and honored at the right time.

   (Hammes, Rooney, & Gundrum, 2010, pp. 1249–50)

Since RC measures were put in place nearly two decades ago, a study found that 90% of patients who died in 2007 and 2008 had completed advance care planning documents, and 99% of those documents were available in the patient's medical record at the time of death (Hammes et al., 2010). Overall, researchers have found that end-of-life costs in La Crosse are lower, residents spend half as many days in the hospital, and the life-expectancy outpaces the national average by a year (Gawande, 2010). These outcomes are attributed primarily to efforts associated with RC.

Another nationwide effort to increase the completion of advance directives is National Healthcare Decisions Day (NHDD, 2012), a day dedicated to informing and empowering individuals about advance care planning. The sixth-annual National Healthcare Decisions day took place on

April 16, 2013 and the movement reports participation of 110 national organizations and 1,200 state and local organizations (NHDD, n.d.). From 2008 to 2011, over 17,500 advance directives were completed on National Healthcare Decisions Day. The movement is committed to increasing awareness of the benefits of advance directions, launching a national media campaign to increase access to advance directives, and mobilizing national, state, and community organizations to organize outreach and educational efforts.

To ensure effective communication of end-of-life preferences, more and more states also have recognized and implemented the use of the Physician Orders for Life Sustaining Treatment (POLST) form (Tolle, Tilden, Nelson, & Dunn, 1998). The POLST is a comprehensive physician order form that outlines patient preferences for resuscitation when the patient is transferred from one site of care to another. When the form was initially developed, results from a prospective pilot study involving 180 nursing home residents found that CPR preferences for residents were universally respected and that the utilization of aggressive, life-prolonging treatments was low. Today, 15 states have adopted POLST forms and 28 states are developing initiatives surrounding the use of POLST (New York Times, 2012).

DIRECTIONS FOR COMMUNICATION RESEARCH

Communication researchers can offer practical guidance, grounded in theoretical principles, about the timing, content, and format of initiatives surrounding end-of-life conversations. The discipline can play a vital role in assessing why some programs and interventions may be more successful than others. Communication research also can examine the messages and information-seeking behaviors that preclude or encourage individuals, family members, and healthcare providers to engage in conversations about death and dying. Some suggestions for theoretical and practical applications in research on good deaths are summarized next.

Theoretical Applications

The theory of motivated information management (TMIM; Afifi & Afifi, 2009) contends that individuals engage in a complex process of managing information; the decision to seek or avoid information about a topic is related to (a) the discrepancy between what one knows and what one desires to know; (b) negative emotions associated with the discrepancy; (c) expected outcomes of seeking information; and (d) perceived efficacy in information-seeking. Fowler and Afifi (2011) used the TMIM to examine adult children's information-seeking about parents' elder-care preferences. More recently, Becker and colleagues (2013) examined spousal communication about end-of-life preferences using the TMIM. The researchers discovered that the uncertainty discrepancy between what an individual knows and desires to know about a spouse's end-of-life preferences is associated with negative emotions and a greater inclination to seek information in the future. Initiatives promoting a good death, therefore, may highlight the discrepancy between what one apprehends and desires to learn about a loved one's wishes surrounding death. Future study should ascertain the usefulness of TMIM in understanding information management practices between patient and provider, especially when a prognosis is terminal.

In a qualitative study of hospice chaplains, Tenzek, Cramer, and Allen (2013) used a coordinated management of meaning (CMM) perspective to examine chaplain narratives associated with helping patients achieve a good death. CMM (Pearce, 1989, 1999; Cronen, 1994) views communication as a dual process of coordinating action and managing meanings; conversation is regarded as central to constructing social realities. Through the lens of CMM, the researchers found chaplains to view a good death to be comprised of delivering quality spiritual care, serving as a supportive presence, and fostering personal and professional growth. In future research, CMM may be useful in examining patient-provider communication or discussion among spouses about end-of-life preferences. Decision-making at the end of life may be conceptualized as an iterative process of coordinating action and managing meaning in conversations among loved ones in order to promote a good death.

Some additional, time-honored, communication-focused theoretical perspectives, among many, may guide future studies of a good death might include: relational dialectics (Baxter & Montgomery, 1996), cognitive dissonance (Festinger, 1957), and uncertainty management (Brashers et al., 2000). Relational dialectics can explore the tensions, particularly between connection and autonomy, among family members engaged in end-of-life decision making. Cognitive dissonance may help explain why some patients may find themselves in healthcare situations that are dissonant with their health-related beliefs. Uncertainty management may offer further understanding as to why some individuals prefer to avoid conversations about death and dying. Surely, researchers in the discipline must be compelled to lend their expertise and insights to improve the experience dying patients, lest we be perceived as communication experts avoiding a difficult conversation altogether.

Practical Applications

From a practical perspective, exploring the nuances and dynamics of real-time, end-of-life conversations between patients and families, patients and providers, and families and providers is crucial to learning more about how interactions can be improved. However, easing into these difficult, delicate moments can be challenging for researchers and subjects alike—it is not surprising that a considerable amount of research surrounding communication at the end of life is retrospective. One way to gather more information about end-of-life interactions may be to observe and talk with hospice patients and family members. Patients enrolled in hospice program must possess a prognosis of six months or less of life. A logical conclusion might be that patients who have accepted a terminal illness prognosis would be more amenable to participating in research. Communication researchers thereby might be able explore expressions of community, control, and opportunity at the end of life. Extreme sensitivity would be required of researchers during the interview process given the fragility and uncertainty that patients may be experiencing.

Future research also must examine the influence of demographic factors, specifically ethnicity, on the shaping of end-of-life experience. When it comes to pain and suffering, racial disparities exist in the experience of death. Research demonstrates that African Americans undergo more aggressive treatments at the end of life and are less likely to have Do Not Resuscitate (DNR) orders in their charts (Sacco, 2012). In a cross-sectional sample of 90 patients with advanced heart failure or cancer, African Americans were also less likely to report pain and symptom management that patients of other ethnicities (Zapka et al., 2006). Gruneir et al. (2007) also found that minority individuals with low educational attainment are more likely to die in hospitals, whereas individuals who are White are more likely to die at home. It is incumbent on communication researchers to identify barriers to conversations about pain and preference for care. Studies need to focus on how patient and provider characteristics constrain or enable interactions in the end-of-life context. Perhaps mistrust, negative health experiences, and provider assumptions may influence the initiation of important communication interventions.

Finally, technological advancements cannot be ignored, even when it comes to death and dying. Future communication-based research should examine how individuals integrate computer-mediated communication technologies such as e-mail, social media, electronic charting, video-chatting, and Smartphones into the process of dying. Might conversations about end-of-life preferences take place in mediated channels? If so, how might the features of a particular technology enhance or detract from the conversation? Examining the effectiveness of mediated communication tools such as Prepare, Serious Illness Communication Checklist, and *Five Wishes* Online, an online advance care planning document (Aging with Dignity, n.d.), may be helpful jumping-off points for research. Moreover, as identities become more integrated into technology, researchers should ascertain just how one's online presence influences decision-making and human interaction in the context of a terminal prognosis.

CONCLUSION

Patients, especially those coping with chronic diseases, continue to die in hospitals after rounds of aggressive treatments aimed at prolonging life. Some patients want all extreme medical measures to be taken, regardless of trajectory: their wishes can and should be honored. However, research reveals that most people want to die at home, surrounded by the *community* in which they built their lives; they want to exert some semblance of *control* in making decisions at the end of life; and they want to take advantage of *opportunities* to reduce pain and suffering. Advances in medicine in combination with disease trends have made it more difficult for such a death to occur.

Even at the end of life, health in the form of quality of life can be promoted, threats of dying painfully or in isolation can be mitigated, and unacceptable conditions can be avoided. To do this, researchers should continue to develop a thorough understanding a good death in light of ever-increasing medical advances and the rising rates of chronic disease. Communication-based research also can inform theoretical and practical solutions to address the comprehensive, interactional needs of the dying. From there, we can begin to start or expand upon efforts to preserve the dignity and health of those who are living, even as they die.

REFERENCES

Adamy, J., & McGinty, T. (2012, July 6). The crushing cost of care. *The Wall Street Journal.* Retrieved from http://online.wsj.com/article/SB10001424052702304441404577483050976766184.html

Afifi, W. A., & Afifi, T. D. (2009). Avoidance among adolescents in conversations about their parents' relationship: Applying the Theory of Motivated Information Management. *Journal of Social and Personal Relationships, 26,* 488–511.

Aging with Dignity. (n.d.). Welcome to My Five Wishes Online. Retrieved from https://fivewishesonline.agingwithdignity.org/

Alexander, S. C., Keitz, S. A., Sloane, R., & Tulsky, J. A. (2006). A controlled trial of a short course to improve residents' communication with patients at the end of life. *Academic Medicine,* 81(11), 1008–1012.

Andre, F.E., Booy, R., Bock, H.L., Clemens, J., Datta, S.K., John, T.J., Lee, B.W., Lolekha, S., Peltola, H., Ruff, T.A., Santosham, M., & Schmitt, H.J. (2012, November). Vaccination greatly reduces disease, disability, death and inequity worldwide. *Bulletin of the World Health Organization.* Retrieved from http://www.who.int/bulletin/volumes/86/2/07-040089/en/

Baile, W.F., Buckman, R., Lenzi, R., Glober, G., Beale, E.A., & Kudelka, A.P. (2000). SPIKES: A six-step protocol for delivering bad news: Application to the patient with cancer. *The Oncologist, 5,* 302–311.

Barclay, J.S., Blackhall, L.J., & Tulsky, J.A. (2007). Communication strategies and cultural issues in the delivery of bad news. *Journal of Palliative Medicine, 10*(4), 958–977.

Baughman, K.R., Aultman, J., Hazelett, S., Palmisano, B., O'Neill, A., Ludwick, R., & Sanders, M. (2012). Managing the trenches of consumer care: The challenges of understanding and initiating the advance care planning process. *Journal of Gerontological Social Work, 55*(8), 721–737.

Baxter, L. A., & Montgomery, B. (1996). *Relating: Dialogues and dialectics.* New York: Guilford.

Becker, K., Cramer, E., & Priddis, D. (2013). *In sickness and in health: Seeking information about spousal end-of-life preferences.* Unpublished manuscript.

Beckstrand, R. L., Lynn Clark Callister, & Kirchhoff, K. T. (2006). Providing a "good death": Critical care nurses' suggestions for improving end-of-life care. *American Journal of Critical Care, 15*(1), 38–45.

Block, S. (2012). Involving physicians in upstream conversations: The Serious Illness Communication Checklist. *BMJ Supportive & Palliative Care, 2*(2), 187.

Brashers, D.E., Neidig, J.L., Haas, S.M., Dobbs, L.K., Cardillo, L.W., Russell, J.A. (2000). Communication in the management of uncertainty: The case of persons living with HIV or AIDS. *Communication Monographs, 67*(1), 63–84.

Bratcher, J. R. (2010). How do critical care nurses define a "good death" in the intensive care unit? *Critical Care Nursing Quarterly, 33*(1), 87–99.

BusinessWire. (2012, November 15). Health Dialog makes decision aid available for National Hospice and Palliative Care Month. Retrieved from http://www.businesswire.com/news/home/20121115006927/en/Health-Dialog-Decision-Aid-National-Hospice-Palliative

Byock, I. R. (1996). The nature of suffering and the nature of opportunity at the end of life. *Clinics in Geriatric Medicine, 12*(2), 237.

Carlson, M.D.A., Herrin, J., Du, Q., Epstein, A.J., Barry, C.L., Morrison, R.S., Back, A.L., & Bradley, E.H. (2010). Impact of hospice disenrollment for patients with cancer. *Journal of Clinical Oncology, 28*(28), 4371–4375.

Carr, D. (2003). A "good death" for whom? Quality of spouse's death and psychological distress among older widowed persons. *Journal of Health and Social Behavior, 44*(2), 215–232.

Cegala, D.J., & Broz, S.J. (2002). Physician communication skills training: a review of theoretical backgrounds, objectives and skills. *Medical Education, 36*, 1004–1016.

Cegala, D. J., Post, D. M., & McClure, L. (2001). The effects of patient communication skills training on the discourse of older patients during a primary care interview. *Journal of the American Geriatrics Society, 49*(11), 1505–1511.

Center to Advance Palliative Care (CAPC). (2012). Growth of palliative care in U.S. hospitals 2012 snapshot. Retrieved from http://www.capc.org/capc-growth-analysis-snapshot-2011.pdf

Connor, S.R., Pyenson, B., Fitch, K., Spence, C., & Iwasaki, K. (2007). Comparing hospice and nonhospice patient survival among patients who die within a three-year window. *Journal of Pain and Symptom Management, 33*(3), 238–246.

Conway, S. (2007). The changing face of death: Implications for public health. *Critical Public Health, 17*(3), 195–202.

Costello, J. (2006). Dying well: nurses' experiences of "good and bad" deaths in hospital. *Journal of Advanced Nursing, 54*(5), 594-601. doi:10.1111/j.1365-2648.2006.03867.x

Cronen, V.E. (1994). Coordinated management of meaning: Practical theory for the complexities and contradictions of everyday life. In J. Siegfried (Ed.), *The status of common sense in psychology*, (pp. 183–207). Norwood, NJ: Ablex Press.

Festinger, L. (1957). *A theory of cognitive dissonance.* Stanford, CA: Stanford University Press.

Fine, E., Reid, M.C., Shengelia, R., & Adelman, R.D. (2010). Directly observed patient-physician discussions in palliative and end-of-life care: A systematic review of the literature. *Journal of Palliative Medicine, 13*(5), 595–603.

Fine, R.L. (2005). From Quinlan to Schiavo: medical, ethical, and legal issues in severe brain injury. *Proceedings of Baylor University Medical Center, 18*(4), 303–310.

Fowler, C., & Afifi, W. A. (2011). Applying the theory of motivated information management to adult children's discussions of caregiving with aging parents. *Journal of Social and Personal Relationship, 28*(4), 507–535

Gawande, A. (2010, August 8). Letting go: What should medicine do when it can't save your life? *The New Yorker.* Retrieved September 18, 2012 from http://www.newyorker.com/reporting/2010/08/02/100802fa_fact_gawande

Gillotti, C., Thompson, T., & McNeilis, K. (2002). Communicative competence in the delivery of bad news. *Social Science & Medicine, 54,* 1011–1023.

Gott, M., Seymour, J., Bellamy, G., Clark, D., & Ahmedzai, S. (2004). Older people's views about home as a place of care at the end of life. *Palliative Medicine, 18*(5), 460–467.

Griggs, C. (2010). Community nurses' perceptions of a good death: A qualitative exploratory study. *International Journal of Palliative Nursing, 16*(3), 140–149.

Gruneir, A., Mor, V., Weitzen, S., Truchil, R., Teno, J., & Roy, J. (2007). Where people die: a multilevel approach to understanding influences on site of death in America. *Medical Care Research and Review, 64*(4), 351–378.

Hall, M.J., Levant, S., DeFrances, C.J. (2013, March). Inpatient hospital deaths: National Hospital Discharge Survey 2000-2010. *NCHS Data Brief, 118,* 1–8. Retrieved from http://www.cdc.gov/nchs/data/databriefs/db118.pdf

Hammes, B.J., Rooney, B.L., & Gundrum, J.D. (2010). A comparative, retrospective, observational study of the prevalence, availability, and specificity of advance care plans in a county that implemented an advance care planning microsystem. *Journal of the American Geriatrics Society, 54,* 1249–1255.

Han, P. K., Keranen, L. B., Lescisin, D. A., & Arnold, R. M. (2005). The palliative care clinical evaluation exercise (CEX): An experience-based intervention for teaching end-of-life communication skills. *Academic Medicine, 80*(7), 669–676.

Johnson, T., Wang, J., & Metz, J. (2010, December 27). End-of-life care at home can improve quality of life for patients and families. *ABCNews.* Retrieved from http://abcnews.go.com/Health/physician-recommends-end-life-conversations-patients/story?id=12458914

Kaplowitz, S. A., Campo, S., & Chiu, W. T. (2002). Cancer patients' desires for communication of prognosis information. *Health Communication, 14*(2), 221–241.

Kirk, I., Kirk, P., Kuziemsky, C., & Wagar, L. (2010). Perspectives of Vancouver Island hospice palliative care team members on barriers to communication at the end of life: A preliminary study. *Journal of Hospice & Palliative Nursing, 12*(1), 59–68.

Larson, D.G., & Tobin, D.R. (2000). EOL conversations: Evolving practice and theory. *JAMA*, *284*, 1573–78.

Last Acts. (2002). *Means to a better end: A report on dying in America today.* http://www.rwjf.org/

Mack, J.W., Cronin, A., Keating, N.L., Taback, N., Huskamp, H., Malin, J.L., Earle, C.C., & Weeks, J.C. (2012). Associations between end-of-life discussions characteristics and care received near death: A prospective cohort study. *Journal of Clinical Oncology*, *30*, 1–9.

MedlinePlus. (2012). Advance directives. Retrieved from http://www.nlm.nih.gov/medlineplus/advancedirectives.html

National Healthcare Decisions Day. (n.d.). Case statement. Retrieved from http://www.nhdd.org/storage/47970757-NHDD-Case-Statement.pdf

National Healthcare Decisions Day. (2012). Home page. Retrieved from http://www.nhdd.org/

National Hospice and Palliative Care Organization. (2012.). *NHPCO facts & figures: Hospice care in America.* Retrieved from http://www.nhpco.org/sites/default/files/public/Statistics_Research/2012_Facts_Figures.pdf

National Vital Statistics Reports. (2012). Deaths: Preliminary data for 2011. Retrieved from http://www.cdc.gov/nchs/data/nvsr/nvsr61/nvsr61_06.pdf

New York Times, Editorial. (2012, November 24). Care at the end of life. Retrieved from http://www.nytimes.com/2012/11/25/opinion/sunday/end-of-life-health-care.html?nl=todaysheadlines&emc=edit_th_20121125&_r=0

O'Reilly, K.B. (2012, June 13). Checklist approach to be tested in end-of-life care planning. *American Medical News.* Retrieved from http://www.ama-assn.org/amednews/2012/06/11/prsc0613.htm

Quill, T.E. (2000). Initiating end-of-life discussions with seriously ill patients. *JAMA 284*(19), 2502–2507.

Painter, K. (2013, January 3). Projects get people talking about end-of-life care. *USA Today.* Retrieved May 15, 2013 from http://www.usatoday.com/story/news/nation/2013/01/04/prepare-health-care-conversations/1807963/

Partnership to Fight Chronic Disease (PFCD). (2009). The impact of chronic disease on U.S. health and prosperity: A collection of statistics and commentary. *2009 Almanac of Chronic Disease.* Retrieved November 27, 2012 from http://www.fightchronicdisease.org/sites/fightchronicdisease.org/files/docs/2009AlmanacofChronicDisease_updated81009.pdf

Pearce, B. W. (1989) *Communication and the human condition.* Carbondale, IL: Southern Illinois University Press.

Pearce, B.W. (1999). Using CMM, the coordinated management of meaning, Pearce Associates Seminar, CA.

Prepare. (2013). Home page. Retrieved May 15, 2013 from https://www.prepareforyourcare.org/

Sacco, J. (2012, August 6). At the end of life, talk helps bridge racial divide. *New York Times*. Retrieved from http://www.nytimes.com/2012/08/07/health/views/at-the-end-of-life-talk-helps-bridge-a-racial-divide.html?_r=3smid=tw-share&

Scott, A.M. & Caughlin, J.P. (2012). Managing multiple goals in family discourse about end-of-life health decisions. *Research on Aging, 34*(6), 670–691.

Seymour, J., Gott, M., Bellamy, G., Ahmedzar, S.H., & Clark, D. (2003). Planning for the end of life: The views of older people about advance care statements. *Social Science & Medicine, 59*, 57–68.

Span, P. (2009, April 20). Why do we avoid advance directives? *New York Times*. Retrieved September 18, 2012 from http://newoldage.blogs.nytimes.com/2009/04/20/why-do-we-avoid-advance-directives/

Steinhauser, K.E., Clipp, E.C., McNeilly, M., Christakis, N.A., McIntyre, L.M., & Tulsky, J.A., M.D. (2000). In search of a good death: Observations of patients, families, and providers. *Annals of Internal Medicine, 132*(10), 825–832.

Tan, A., & Manca, D. (2013). Finding common ground to achieve a "good death": family physicians working with substitute decision-makers of dying patients. A qualitative grounded theory study. *BMC Family Practice, 14*(1), 14.

Tang, S.T. (2003). When death is imminent: Where terminally ill patients with cancer prefer to die and why. *Cancer Nursing, 26*(3), 245–251.

Tapp, J.M. (2001). Conserving the vitality of suffering: Addressing family constraints to illness conversations. *Nursing Inquiry, 8*(4), 254–63.

Taylor, D.H., Osterman, J., Van Houtven, C.H., Tulsky, J.A., Steinhauser, K. (2007). What length of hospice use maximizes reduction in medical expenditures near death in the U.S. Medicare program? *Social Science and Medicine, 65*, 1466–1478.

Temel, J.S., Greer, J.A., Muzikansky, A.M., Gallagher, E.R., Admane, S., Jackson, V.A., Dahlin, C.M., Blinderman, C.D., Jacobsen, J., Pirl, W.F., Billings, J.A., & Lynch, T.J. (2010). Early palliative care for patients with metastatic non-small-cell lung cancer. *The New England Journal of Medicine, 363*, 733–42.

Tenzek, K., Cramer, E.M., & Allen, M. (2013). *Spiritualty and coordinated management of meaning: Examining the chaplain's role in a "good death."* Unpublished manuscript.

Teno, J.M., Clarridge, B.R., Casey, V., Welch, L.C, Wetle, T., Shield, R., & Mor, V. (2004). Family perspectives of end-of-life care at the last place of care. *Journal of the American Medical Association, 291*(1), 88–93.

Teno, J. M., Gruneir, A., Schwartz, Z., Nanda, A., & Wetle, T. (2007). Association between advance directives and quality of end-of-life care: A national study. *Journal of the American Geriatrics Society, 55*(2), 189–194. doi: 10.1111/j.1532-5415.2007.01045.x

The Conversation Project. (2012). Homepage. Retrieved from http://theconversationproject.org/

Thompson-Hill, J., Hookey, C., Salt, E., & O'Neill, T. (2009). The supportive care plan: A tool to improve communication in end-of-life care. *International Journal of Palliative Nursing, 15*(5), 250–255.

Tolle, S.W., Tilden, V.P., Nelson, C.A., & Dunn, P.M. (1998). A prospective study of the efficacy of the physician order form for life-sustaining treatment. *Journal of the American Geriatrics Society, 46*, 1097–1102.

Trice, E. D., & Prigerson, H. G. (2009). Communication in end-stage cancer: review of the literature and future research. *Journal of Health Communication, 14*, 95–108.

Weissman, D.E., & Block, S.D. (2002). ACGME requirements for end-of-life training in selected residency and fellowship programs: a status report. *Academic Medicine, 77*(4), 299–304.

World Health Organization (WHO). 2013. Chronic diseases. Retrieved from http://www.who.int/topics/chronic_diseases/en/

Wright, A.A., Keating, N.L., Balboni, T.A., Matulonis, U.A., Block, S.D., & Prigerson, H.G. (2010). Place of death: Correlations with quality of life of patients with cancer and predictors of bereaved caregivers' mental health. *Journal of Clinical Oncology, 28*(29), 4457–4464.

Wright, A.A., Zhang, B., Ray, A., Mack, J.W., Trice, E., Balboni, T., Mitchell, S.L., Jackson, V.A., Block, S.D., Maciejewski, P.K., Prigerson, H.G. (2008). Associations between EOL discussions, patient mental health, medical care near death, and caregiver bereavement adjustment. *JAMA, 300*(14), 1665–1673.

Zapka, J.G., Carter, R., Carter, C.L., Hennessy, W., Kurent, J.E., DesHarnais, S. (2006). Care at the end of life: Focus on communication and race. *Journal of Aging and Health, 18*(6), 791–813.

Zhang, B., Nilsson, M.E., Prigerson, H.G. (2012). Factors important to patients' quality of life at the end of life. *Archives of Internal Medicine, 172*(15), 1133–1142.

Zhang, B., Wright, A.A., Huskamp, H.A., Nilsson, M.E., Maciejewski, M.L., Earle, C.C., Block, S.D., Maciejewski, P.K., & Prigerson, H.G. (2009). Health care costs in the last week of life: Associations with end-of-life conversations. *Archives of Internal Medicine, 169*(5), 480–8.

Zhao, Y., & Encinosa, W. (2009, November). Procedures with the most rapidly increasing hospital costs, 2004-2007. *The Costs of End-of-Life Hospitalizations, Statistical Brief #81.* Retrieved November 26, 2012 from http://www.hcup-us.ahrq.gov/reports/statbriefs/sb81.pdf

Chapter 11:

Family communication patterns, illness attitudes, and the willingness to disclose symptoms to parents

Nathan Miczo and Lisa Miczo
Western Illinois University

INTRODUCTION

Research in health communication frequently revolves around either interactions between patients and caregivers (including contact with doctors, nurses, pharmacists, etc.), or how individuals process and incorporate messages about health and illness via various media (including media portrayals of health issues, as well as health campaigns targeting attitudes and/or behaviors). According to Cline (2003), what these two areas have in common is that they approach health and illness from an institutional standpoint. In viewing health using such a framework, the individual as patient is often left out of the equation. That is, ill persons typically enter the clinic, and the caregiver/patient interaction becomes the focus of the illness experience; or, it is assumed that health messages created by media specialists will influence individuals with little consideration for the environments in which those individuals find themselves. As anyone who has ever had health issues knows, there is much more to dealing with illness than simply dealing with healthcare professionals; moreover, even symptoms themselves may intrude upon relationships between people. So it is important that this focus be widened to take into consideration that a large part of our response to health issues and symptoms of illness is managed through self-care and is influenced by those we have relationships with and other nonprofessionals in our network (i.e., the lay network). To address this, many health communication scholars advocate an approach to health and illness that takes into account the individual on the physical, psychological, and social levels, thereby acknowledging that individuals are active agents in their own management of illness. As Mishler (1984) pointed out, from the standpoint of the patient, the visit to the clinic may be only a small part of the overall illness experience.

For the ill person, illness begins with the occurrence of symptoms, not with the visit to the clinic. Then, those symptoms are validated as illness only as we interact with and negotiate them with others (Telles & Pollack, 1981), such as when a parent takes a child's temperature and examines the child closely before accepting the claim that an illness has appeared so going to school is out of the question. Illness, therefore, is a relational phenomenon and understanding it requires drawing upon research from interpersonal literature. The study discussed in this chapter sought to explore the "neglected box" (Cline, 2003, p. 286) of interpersonal communication in the experience of health and illness. In particular, this study examined college students' willingness to disclose symptoms to their parents as that decision related to the students' family communication patterns.

Typically, because college students report fewer symptoms than older populations, they are overlooked for their everyday health experiences. Nevertheless, college students are a particularly interesting population for study because they are in a transitional state. Frequently, when they *are* the focus of health research, the emphasis of that focus is risk behaviors' impact on both mental and physical health impairment. However, examining the symptom experience adds to this approach as it identifies pathways of the risk-health outcome relationship. As college students face these issues during the transition to adulthood, variations in family environments ought to be especially relevant. Although they may not be under the direct supervision of their parents they often still rely on them for various forms of support, including emotional support and comfort, as well as more tangible elements such as parents' insurance. Thus, the family environment is often an integral influence upon college students' negotiation of health and illness experiences, even as those individuals struggle with making health-related decisions on their own for the first time (Lipnickey, 1988).

Family Communication Patterns and Symptom Disclosure

One program of communication research that examines the family environment centers on family communication patterns. Family communication patterns theory is argued to address both sense-making and decision-making in families (Koerner, LeRoy, McCarthy Veach, 2010). According to Koerner and Fitzpatrick (2006), family communication patterns can be understood utilizing two dimensions of measurement: conversation orientation and conformity orientation. Conversation orientation concerns the level or degree of openness within the family; families high on this dimension exhibit frequent interaction, shared decision-making, and the free expression of attitudes. On the other hand, conformity orientation involves the level or degree of uniformity within the family; families high on this dimension have members who are expected to share similar beliefs and opinions on matters. A recent meta-analysis of the theory's two dimensions found that, although stable modest relationships existed between the dimensions and various outcomes, the strongest relationships existed between conversation orientation and psychosocial outcomes, including both physical and mental health (Schrodt, Witt, & Messersmith, 2008). That is to say, families that are more oriented toward conversational openness have members that tend to be more physically and mentally healthy. This makes sense when one consider that if a family characteristically discusses even tough topics with one another (e.g., depression, alcohol abuse, weight loss, a relationship break-up), issues affecting health status are more likely to be addressed in positive ways before they become more serious.

Symptoms are alterations in the perception of normative bodily states. They are subjectively experienced and therefore may or may not correspond to an underlying pathology and may or may not be interpreted as illness. The persistence and seriousness of symptoms is certainly a factor that weighs heavily in interpretation (Reis, 2001), but the overall response to symptoms is invariably influenced by social and interpersonal considerations. Nevertheless, initial responses to symptoms generally involve some type of self-care. Dean (1986) posited four types of self-care: 1) do nothing, 2) self-medicate, 3) non-medication self-treatment, and/or 4) seek clinical care.

When symptoms are interpreted as illness, the decision to do nothing effectively functions as a form of denial, as one attempts to carry on one's everyday role obligations. Self-medication, insofar as most over the counter medications are not curative, may often be an attempt to mask symptoms or alleviate their subjective experience to allow for normal everyday interactions and behaviors. To the extent that interpersonal considerations impact the illness experience, these two options involve avoidance responses; that is, denial and masking of symptoms function to help one avoid interpersonal discussions of one's health state, discussions that may involve issues thought to be private or stress-inducing. By contrast, the third and fourth options are more approach-oriented. Non-medication self-treatment most often involves such things as rest, relaxation, talking with friends and family, exercising, and so forth (Dean, 1986). Engaging in these activities may involve the direct participation of close others, thereby fostering opportunities for talk about feeling states more directly. Although a visit to a health care professional may be done independently, oftentimes such a visit comes about through discussion between the person experiencing the symptoms and close others.

Family communication patterns are likely to impact this process at several points. The ability of a young adult to secure social support during times of stress and strain ought to be aided by a family environment that encourages open communication and the expression of feelings. Insofar as stress and symptoms are positively associated, the willingness to talk about "feeling states" (Telles & Pollack, 1981) ought to be related to a family's conversation orientation.

> H1: Conversation orientation is positively associated with willingness to disclose symptoms to parents.

The role of conformity orientation may manifest itself in parental attitudes toward illness. Illness may be seen as a disruption of family structure, thereby investing it with a negative status. This view of illness, as being imbued with a moral element is supported by studies examining individuals' definitions of illness as they relate to issues of strength, willpower, and worth. As an ill person, one may be made to feel that s/he has caused a disruption to the system that interferes with the family's ability to sustain normal functioning and achieve its goals, in other words letting the family down. In this way, health and illness are permeated by value judgments about strength and weakness, vulnerability, prevention, and stoicism, among other things (Gwyn, 2002; Parrott, Miller-Day, Peters, & Dillard, 2010). For the family high on conformity orientation then, negative connotations are likely to be attached to illness. As a result, children ought to be less likely to want to talk to their parents about symptoms, and/or more likely to adopt an avoidant response in their own decision-making.

> H2: Conformity orientation is negatively related to the willingness to disclose symptoms to parents.

Illness Attitudes and Symptom Disclosure

Attitudes about the interpersonal ramifications of illness are an important part of the decision-making processes involved in self-care. Parsons's (1951) sick role concept provides a coherent framework for understanding those attitudes. According to Parsons, illness causes a disruption of the social order and therefore, society must find a way to accommodate and deal with that disruption. The sick role provides a way to minimize the consequences of illness. When entering the sick role, individuals have the right to exemption from responsibility for their symptoms and the right to relinquish everyday role performances; they also have the duty to try and get well and the duty to seek competent medical care and comply with all directives. For example, one is not allowed to skip work, but if legitimately ill, would expect to be given time off to recuperate. Likewise, this person would not be expected to fulfill social obligations (e.g., attend a reunion), but this person would be socially obligated to see a healthcare provider and follow through with that provider's directives.

Although Parsons's sick role provides a useful model for the illness experience, it suffers from the assumption that the rights and duties of sick individuals are necessarily tied to one another and to the medical institution. Clearly, people are not always allowed to take off work or put off social obligations or duties. Similarly, people don't always go to the doctor or clinic when they are ill. Additionally, while this model takes into account the social order and its network of connections that must be negotiated when one takes on the "sick role," it does not adequately account for those influences at the interpersonal-relational level. To address this issue, researchers have incorporated interpersonal-relational variables in an effort to take the model from simply a defined role to a set of attitudes about illness and their interpersonal ramifications. This research has uncovered four attitudes toward illness (see Miczo, 2004; Miczo, Miczo, & Johnson, 2006). The first, *release*, indexes the extent to which individuals believe that ill persons should be freed from normal role obligations. The second, *consideration*, refers to the belief that ill persons need more comfort and attention than usual. *Burden*, the third attitude, involves a recognition that ill persons may have to depend on others to get well, which can strain those relationships. The final attitude, *deviance*, concerns beliefs that illness is due to poor habits of living and may be exaggerated to garner the secondary gains of illness (e.g., special attention, getting out of undesirable activities).

In families that value openness, members ought to feel free to express their feelings of health and illness. They are unlikely to do so if they feel that they will be treated as deviants, malingerers, or made to feel that their diminished capacity will pose an undue stress upon other family members. Conversely, discussing the experience of symptoms necessarily involves the implicit or explicit asking and granting of release from social roles and the recognition that ill persons may require additional care and consideration. Thus, the third hypothesis is advanced.

> H3: Conversation orientation is positively related to the (a) release and (b) consideration illness attitudes, and negatively related to the (c) burden and (d) deviance attitudes.

On the other hand, in families that exhibit a more authoritarian structure, illness ought to be more likely to be viewed as weakness, or moral failing, and the suspicion that ill persons are "milking the system" to escape the bonds of hierarchy ought to be more prevalent. Such family members ought to be more sensitive to the stress their illness places on other family members and they should therefore be less likely to believe that ill persons have the right to be released from their everyday roles or should receive extra attention and care. Based on the communication patterns theorized to accompany the conformity orientation, the fourth hypothesis was forwarded.

H4: Conformity orientation is negatively related to the (a) release and (b) consideration attitudes, and positively related to the (c) burden and (d) deviance attitudes.

Self-concealment and Symptom Disclosure

Another factor that may be related to symptom disclosure and family communication patterns is self-concealment. Self-concealment is defined "as a predisposition to actively conceal from others personal information that one perceives as distressing or negative" (Larson & Chastain, 1990, p. 440). According to Larson and Chastain, self-concealment is not simply the opposite of self-disclosure; rather, it reflects an active attempt to suppress and conceal negative information about the self. In their preliminary study, they found that self-concealment was related to both physical and psychological symptom experience, leading them to speculate that one pathway linking concealment and symptoms was the unlikelihood of gaining support from relational partners, including parents (see also Finkenauer, Engels, & Meeus, 2002). If their reasoning is correct, then a negative relationship should be obtained between self-concealment and willingness to disclose symptoms.

H5: Self-concealment is negatively related to the willingness to disclose symptoms.

This study also examines family communication patterns as an antecedent influence on the development of self-concealment; if families are more prone to conversing openly, it logically follows that members would feel less pressure or inclination to suppress potentially negative information about themselves. As such, it is expected that conversation orientation is negatively related to self-concealment. On the other hand, in high conformity orientation families, differences of attitude and opinion that threaten family stability ought to be stifled. Given the importance of transition to adulthood as a developmental stage, young adults from high conformity families are likely to have experienced some degree of self-silencing, leading to the research prediction of a positive correlation between conformity orientation and self-concealment.

H6: Self-concealment is negatively related to (a) conversation orientation and positively related to (b) conformity orientation.

Finally, the network of hypothesized relationships suggests mediating roles for both illness attitudes and self-concealment in the family communication-symptom disclosure connection. That is, family communication patterns shape illness attitudes and self-concealment behaviors and these, in turn, impact individuals' willingness to disclose symptoms to parents.

H7: Illness attitudes and self-concealment mediate relationships between family communication patterns and willingness to disclose symptoms.

METHOD

Sample

Participants were undergraduate students from a medium-sized Midwestern university. The sample (N = 352) was almost evenly split, with 54% female, reporting an average age of 21.13 years (SD = 1.72, range 18–31). The ethnic composition for the sample was 83% White/Caucasian, 8.5% Black/African-American, 2% Hispanic/Latin American, 1.4% Asian/Pacific Islander, with 3% indicating "Other." Thirty-five percent of the participants were seniors, 30% were juniors, 15% were sophomores, and 18% were freshmen. The sample also reported on the family configuration participants had in mind when responding to questions about parents and family. The majority of respondents were reporting on biological mother and father (79%), followed by biological mother only (9%), biological mother and stepfather (6%), biological father only (1.4%), adoptive parents (1%), and biological father and stepmother (1%).

Procedure

A survey instrument was created to examine the hypothesized relationships posed above. The first part of the survey asked participants to mark one of six options for family configuration. The second section contained questions concerning family communication patterns, illness attitudes, and self-concealment. These items were randomly arranged using the online Research Randomizer program, and constructed as 5-point Likert-type questions with the endpoints 1 "Strongly disagree" to 5 "Strongly agree." The next section consisted of questions concerning individuals' willingness to disclose a variety of psychological and physical symptoms/complaints to parents; these items were constructed as 5-point Likert-type questions with the endpoints 1 "Very unlikely" to 5 "Very likely." The final section of the survey contained demographic questions. The survey was approved by the university's Institutional Review Board.

Measures

Family communication patterns. Participants completed the revised family communication patterns (RFCP) instrument (Fitzpatrick & Ritchie, 1994; Ritchie & Fitzpatrick, 1990; Koerner & Fitzpatrick, 2002), which gauged the level and direction of their reported family communication patterns with regard to the dimensions of conversation and conformity. Conversation orientation refers to the degree of openness in family communication (e.g., "In our family we often talk about our plans and hopes for the future."); conformity orientation involves the extent of homogeneity expected among family members (e.g., "When I am at home, I am expected to obey my parents' rules."). Both subscales were reliable: conversation orientation (α = .88; M = 3.48, SD = .62); conformity orientation (α = .72; M = 2.90, SD = .52).

Illness attitudes. Attitudes regarding the interpersonal and relational implications of illness were assessed with the illness attitudes scale (Miczo, 2004; Miczo, Miczo, & Johnson, 2006). Thirty-five items were drawn from prior research on the sick role (Berkanovic, 1972; Kassebaum &

Baumann, 1965; Segall, 1976) and utilized to assess four illness attitudes: release (9 items, e.g., "Ill persons should be allowed to get more rest."), consideration (10 items, e.g., "Ill persons should be given more attention than usual."), burden (8 items, e.g., "When you're sick, you often have to impose on others."), and deviance (8 items, e.g., "People often claim that they're sick in order to get out of things."). A number of items were eliminated to improve measurement reliability yielding the following alpha coefficients: release (6 items, $\alpha = .56$; $M = 3.63$, $SD = .44$); consideration (7 items; $\alpha = .65$; $M = 3.17$, $SD = .50$); burden (5 items; $\alpha = .63$; $M = 2.98$, $SD = .56$); deviance (4 items; $\alpha = .62$; $M = 3.21$, $SD = .62$). Given the somewhat low reliability estimates, confirmatory factor analysis was utilized to examine the final set of subscales. Results of that analysis suggested a reasonable fit to the data, χ^2 (df = 203) = 403.97, $p < .01$, CFI = .80, RMSEA = .05 (90% CI .05, .06) and provided justification for including the results reported herein.

Self-concealment. The dispositional tendency to keep things to oneself was assessed with the self-concealment scale (Larson & Chastain, 1990). The 10-item scale was modified to refer to parents rather than the generalized other of the original version (e.g., "I have an important secret that I haven't shared with anyone." was changed to "I have an important secret that I haven't shared with my parents."). The scale was reliable ($\alpha = .76$; $M = 2.88$, $SD = .62$).

Willingness to disclose symptoms to parents. The willingness to disclose symptoms to parents was assessed with a modified version of the symptom checklist (Bartone, Ursano, Wright, & Ingraham, 1989). The instructions for the scale asked respondents to "indicate how likely you would be to talk to your parents if you were experiencing…", followed by the phrase "I would tell my parents if I was experiencing…." The twenty items of the symptom checklist contain a variety of physical (e.g., dizziness, general aches and pains) and psychological (e.g., depressed mood, crying easily) complaints. Exploratory factor analysis (EFA) was utilized to probe distinct factors. The EFA using principal axis factoring with oblique rotation revealed four factors; however only the first two explaining 52.64% of the variance were retained as meaningful variables. The first factor (45.28% of the variance) consisted of eight items assessing psychological symptoms (e.g., "difficulty concentrating"); the second factor (7.37% of the variance) contained four items revolving around physical symptoms (e.g., "general aches and pains"). Both factors were reliable: psychological symptoms ($\alpha = .92$; $M = 3.12$, $SD = 1.01$); physical symptoms ($\alpha = .80$; $M = 3.77$, $SD = .90$).

RESULTS

Hypotheses 1 and 2

Hypothesis 1 predicted a positive correlation between conversation orientation and willingness to disclose symptoms to parents. As is evident in Table 1, conversation orientation was positively related to willingness to disclose both physical ($r = .27$, $p < .01$) and psychological symptoms ($r = .42$, $p < .01$). Thus, H1 is supported.

Table 11.1 Correlations between Family Communication Patterns, Illness Attitudes, Self-concealment, and Willingness to Disclose Symptoms to Parents

	1.	2.	3.	4.	5.	6.	7.	8.
1. Conversation Orientation	—							
2. Conformity Orientation	–.28**	—						
3. Release	.21**	–.01	—					
4. Consideration	.19**	.15**	.28**	—				
5. Burden	.02	.21**	.02	.24**	—			
6. Deviance	.02	.15**	.00	–.11*	.23**	—		
7. Self-concealment	–.37**	.40**	.02	.14*	.24**	.15**	—	
8. Psychological Symptoms	.42**	–.17**	.07	.08	.01	.03	–.28**	—
9. Physical Symptoms	.27**	–.11*	.13*	.16**	–.07	.03	–.08	.54**

Note. * $p < .05$. ** $p < .01$.

The second hypothesis predicted a negative association between conformity orientation and symptom disclosure. In support of H2, conformity orientation was negatively related to willingness to disclose both physical ($r = -.11, p < .05$) and psychological symptoms ($r = -.17, p < .01$).

Hypotheses 3 and 4

Hypothesis 3 predicted conversation orientation is positively related to the (a) release and (b) consideration illness attitudes, and negatively related to the (c) burden and (d) deviance attitudes. Correlation analyses revealed that conversation orientation was positively related to the release ($r = .21, p < .01$) and consideration attitudes ($r = .19, p < .01$), but not significantly related to the burden ($r = .02, p = .71$) and deviance attitudes ($r = .02, p = .70$). H3, therefore, is partially supported.

Hypothesis 4 predicted conformity orientation is negatively related to the (a) release and (b) consideration attitudes, and positively related to the (c) burden and (d) deviance attitudes. As is evident in Table 1, conformity orientation was not significantly correlated to the release attitude ($r = -.01, p = .86$); however, it was positively associated with the consideration ($r = .15, p < .01$), burden ($r = .21, p < .01$), and deviance attitudes ($r = .15, p < .01$). H4 is partially supported.

Hypotheses 5 and 6

The fifth hypothesis predicted a negative relationship between self-concealment and the willingness to disclose symptoms to parents. This hypothesis was partially supported, in that self-concealment was significantly and negatively related to disclosure of psychological symptoms, ($r = -.28$, $p < .01$), but not physical symptoms ($r = -.08$, $p = .16$).

Hypothesis 6 predicted that self-concealment would be negatively related to (a) conversation orientation and positively related to (b) conformity orientation. Correlation analyses revealed a negative association between self-concealment and conversation orientation ($r = -37$, $p < .01$), and a positive relationship between self-concealment and conformity orientation ($r = .40$, $p < .01$), providing support for H6.

Hypothesis 7

The final hypothesis predicted that illness attitudes and self-concealment mediate relationships between family communication patterns and willingness to disclose symptoms to parents. To examine this hypothesis, Hayes's Mediate macro for SPSS was employed (Hayes, 2011). Hayes's program allows for the estimation of the total, direct, and indirect influence of a set of independent variables on an outcome variable through a set of mediator variables. The total effects model estimates the impact of the independent variables upon the outcome variable (in this study, family communication patterns' affect on symptom disclosure). The direct effects model assesses the impact of independent variables and mediators upon the outcome variable (in this study, family communication patterns and self-concealment on symptom disclosure). The omnibus test of the direct effect estimates whether model fit is improved when the independent variables are added to a model containing only the mediators. In other words, in this study, the program allows for determination of whether illness attitudes and self-concealment better explains the relationship between family communication patterns and symptom disclosure. Indirect effects are then interpreted as different from zero with a given degree of confidence if zero is outside of the confidence interval. In other words, if zero is outside the confidence interval, family communication patterns exert an indirect effect on symptom disclosure via an individual's illness attitudes or self-concealment tendencies. This is taken as evidence of mediation. Because the program allows for only one outcome variable at a time, separate analyses were conducted for each symptom type.

For physical symptoms, the total effects model was significant, F (2, 348) = 13.72, $p < .01$, $R^2 = .07$. In this model, conversation orientation was a significant predictor of willingness to disclose physical symptoms, $B = .37$, *s.e.* = .08, but conformity orientation was not, $B = -.07$, *s.e.* = .09. The direct effects model was also significant, F (7, 343) = 5.78, $p < .01$, $R^2 = .11$. As can be seen in Table 2, conversation orientation and consideration were significant positive predictors, and burden was a significant negative predictor, of willingness to disclose physical symptoms. The omnibus test of the direct effect was significant, F (2, 343) = 9.10, $p < .01$, $R^2 = .05$. Inspection of the indirect effects reveals that zero fell outside of the 90% confidence interval for the effect of both conversation and conformity orientation on physical symptom disclosure through the consideration attitude; and, for the effect of conformity orientation on physical symptom disclosure through the burden attitude. In other words, the consideration attitude is the mechanism that positively influences the relationship between both conversation and conformity communication patterns and physical symptom disclosure. Additionally, the burden attitude is the mechanism that influences the conformity orientation's negative impact on disclosure of physical symptoms.

Table 11.2 Mediation Analysis for Willingness to Disclose Physical Symptoms to Parents

Variable	Role	B	s.e.	Sig.	90% CI
Self-concealment	Mediator	.05	.09	$p = .60$	
Conversation Orientation					–.06, .03
Conformity Orientation					–.04, .08
Omnibus CI					–.02, .05
Release	Mediator	.09	.11	$p = .44$	
Conversation Orientation					–.02, .05
Conformity Orientation					–.01, .02
Omnibus CI					–.01, .02
Consideration	Mediator	.27	.10	$p < .01$	
Conversation Orientation					.01, .11*
Conformity Orientation					.01, .11*
Omnibus CI					.00, .05*
Burden	Mediator	–.19	.09	$p < .05$	
Conversation Orientation					–.04, .00
Conformity Orientation					–.10, –.01*
Omnibus CI					–.02, –.00*
Deviance	Mediator	.10	.08	$p = .19$	
Conversation Orientation					–.00, .02
Conformity Orientation					–.01, .05
Omnibus CI					–.00, .01
Conversation Orientation	Predictor	.32	.09	$p < .01$	
Conversation Orientation	Predictor	–.12	.10	$p = .23$	

Note. B = unstandardized coefficient; s. e. = standard error; Sig. = significance; CI = confidence interval; * indicates significant indirect effect.

For psychological symptoms, the total effects model was significant, $F\,(2, 348) = 37.18, p < .01$, $R^2 = .18$. In this model, conversation orientation was a significant predictor of willingness to disclose psychological symptoms, $B = .66$, *s.e.* = .08, but conformity orientation was not, B = –.11, *s.e.* = .10. The direct effects model was also significant, $F\,(7, 343) = 12.03, p < .01$, $R^2 = .44$. As can be seen in Table 3, conversation orientation was a significant positive predictor, and self-concealment was a significant negative predictor, of willingness to disclose psychological symptoms. The omnibus test of the direct effect was significant, F (2, 343) = 19.91, p < .01, R^2 = .09. Inspection of the indirect effects reveals that zero fell outside of the 90% confidence interval for the effect of both conversation and conformity orientation on psychological symptoms through self-concealment. As such, family communication patterns had opposite associations with self-concealment; in turn self-concealment impacted participants' willingness to disclose psychological symptoms. Overall, H7 received minimal support.

Table 11.3 Mediation Analysis for Willingness to Disclose Psychological Symptoms to Parents

Variable	Role	B	s.e.	Sig.	90% CI
Self-concealment	Mediator	–.27	.09	*p* < .01	
Conversation Orientation					.03, .13*
Conformity Orientation					–.17, –.04*
Omnibus CI					–.10, –.02*
Release	Mediator	–.03	.12	*p* = .83	
Conversation Orientation					–.04, .03
Conformity Orientation					–.02, .01
Omnibus CI					–.02, .01
Consideration	Mediator	.08	.11	*p* = .48	
Conversation Orientation					–.02, .06
Conformity Orientation					–.02, .06
Omnibus CI					–.01, .03
Burden	Mediator	.05	.10	*p* = .62	
Conversation Orientation					–.01, .02
Conformity Orientation					–.03, .05
Omnibus CI					–.01, .01
Deviance	Mediator	.08	.08	*p* = .32	
Conversation Orientation					–.01, .02
Conformity Orientation					–.01, .05
Omnibus CI					–.00, .01
Conversation Orientation	Predictor	.56	.09	*p* < .01	
Conversation Orientation	Predictor	–.04	.11	*p* = .68	

Note. B = unstandardized coefficient; s. e. = standard error; Sig. = significance; CI = confidence interval; * indicates significant indirect effect.

DISCUSSION

Given the potential disruptiveness of illness, the interpretation of, and response to, symptoms are particularly meaningful consequential actions. College students faced with stressors, and possibly engaging in risk behaviors, must make decisions when they experience symptoms about whether or not to discuss those subjective feeling states with parents. This study revealed that family communication patterns do impact that decision-making process. Additionally, this study investigated specific mediators of the family communication-symptom disclosure link. The implications and potential limitations of this study, as well as fruitful avenues for future research will be discussed.

Family Communication Patterns and Disclosure of Symptoms

The family has been characterized as the crucible for learning and transformation. It is with interest that the influence of family communication processes on decisions regarding health may be examined. Koerner et al. (2010) argue "shared understanding is affected by the degree of openness and frequency of communication . . . and the extent to which authority shapes meaning... The resulting family communication patterns affect interactions with health-care practitioners as well as many family processes" (p. 184). This study supports their contention with evidence that a family's level of conversational openness (orientation) positively impacted collegians' willingness to disclose perceived symptoms of illness (in this case to parents), thus opening up the channel for various types of social support to take place. In this circumstance, the openness and frequency of communication within the family has promoted a context of freedom to disclose personal health issues. Koerner et al. (2010) describe the goal of open communication in the family setting as "co-discovering the meaning and symbols and objects that constitute reality" (p. 188). This study would indicate that in the case of illness, the open pattern of communication (conversation orientation) provides a safe environment for disclosing concerns about health issues, raising what may be very personal and sensitive topics concerning well-being, and potentially requesting social support. At the same time, results reveal that the conformity orientation pattern, whereby parents who typically "define the meaning of things, and thus the social reality, for the family" (p. 188) construct an atmosphere where young adults are deterred from discussing health concerns, and, in the process, are dissuaded from seeking guidance or support regarding signs of illness they may perceive.

While families vary considerably in terms of structure and functionality, there is nevertheless a broad-based cultural expectation that family should provide care and emotional support to its members. It appears, however, that the cognitive schemata endorsed in high conformity families and manifested in their communication patterns influence members to disbelieve such functions will be fulfilled for them when it comes to the experience of illness. Rather, young adults of such families demonstrate beliefs that family interests are privileged above the interests of the individual needs of its members. This is in line with Koerner and Fitzpatrick's (2002) observation that high conformity families are more regulatory in nature and display less confirming behaviors, less empathy, and less perspective-taking than those families scoring lower on conformity.

Considering that the experience of symptoms is the first stage of illness, the response to symptoms is liable to impact the course of the illness itself. Consequently, the suppression of symptom disclosure to parents by these young adults is disquieting, in that for many college students this time of their life represents their first real encounter with having control over their own health-related behaviors and decisions. Moreover, as past research evidences, this transitional stage between adolescence and adulthood can be fraught with opportunities to engage in risk-taking behaviors that may have serious (even fatal) outcomes for health, making open communication of health and health concerns overall even more important. Two conceivable motivations for the inhibition to disclose symptoms are probable. First, it is contended that the very nature of family structure in families who are high in conformity orientation lends itself to the stifling of family communication and other behaviors that break with ritual and routine. In this environment, the family system is preserved through the enforcement of uniformity and harmony, and to discuss health concerns is likely to be perceived as a bid for change to those preserving forces (therefore a potential threat), and produce disconfirming or negative responses. A second motivation that would explain the decision of young adults in these families to conceal symptoms of illness relates to the potential disclosure of risk and/or other behaviors unsanctioned by parents. As in the first context, such information is almost certain to be perceived as threatening to the unity and self-image so prized by these families.

Family Communication Patterns and Illness Attitudes

The examination of illness attitudes in this study extended research on the role of family environment on students' responses to signs of illness (see Miczo, Miczo, & Johnson, 2006). Miczo et al. (2006) state, "family interactions affect the formation of illness attitudes, which then subsequently influence decisions regarding care-seeking, as well as the everyday experience of life's aches and pains" (p. 114). In this case, the communication orientation of families was found to be associated with illness attitudes. Specifically, conversation orientation was significantly and positively related to both the release and consideration illness attitudes; c that is, the beliefs that ill persons should be exempted from everyday obligations and should be given comfort and care because of their ill state. Therefore, those young adults in families where open conversation was encouraged and affirmed, viewed illness as a part of life, not as a moral failing of the sick person. Such a view strongly suggests that these college students were products of an environment where they experienced support and confirmation when faced with illness. This interpretation effectively echoes findings from Miczo et al. (2006), whereby, "students who receive support more readily admit to illness" (p. 114).

The picture formed for young adults in high conformity families, however, is markedly different. These students demonstrated illness attitudes endorsing negative views of those who enter the sick role, reporting significant positive associations with both seeing illness as a burden to others and as an enactment of deviance (exploiting the sick role). While these participants also reported significant positive associations with the illness attitude of consideration, in light of the attached negative connotations to illness reported, this result may be interpreted as begrudging admittance that illness is a fact of life and not always under one's control. Another plausible explanation is that this attitude reflects a desire on the part of these students for social support in these circumstances (see also Miczo et al., 2006). Put in the context of family, these results would indicate a family environment where sickness was typically seen as a disruption to the system, interfering with the family's normal operations and functioning, thereby putting stress on the family network. In this way, these family members developed attitudes about health and illness tainted by value-laden judgments. These attitudes are reflected in their unwillingness to disclose symptoms to parents; this coincides with findings that college students will downplay symptoms of illness in situations where desires or expectations of support are not met (Miczo et al., 2006).

Self-Concealment and Illness Attitudes as Mediators of Family Communication-Symptom Disclosure Link

The final set of hypotheses established a context for examining illness attitudes and self-concealment as mediators of the family communication-symptom disclosure link. Students who concealed more overall from their parents were also less likely to reveal psychological symptoms to them. Insofar as symptoms such as depressed mood and loss of interest in the world involve mental health problems, they may be especially likely to impair interpersonal and relational functioning (Segrin, 2001). The resultant loss of support from parents by withholding self-disclosure may thus create a vicious cycle of experiencing mental health symptoms, doing nothing and/or attempting to cope on one's own, encountering stressor pile-up, which then leads to the exacerbation of psychological symptoms. This cycle may be especially likely among adolescents from high conformity families. Openness, on the other hand, may mitigate this pattern through the garnering of social support and other forms of self-treatment (Dean, 1986), as well as encouragement to seek medical care.

Physical symptoms were more sensitive to illness attitudes. Participants from families high in either conversation or conformity orientation were more likely to believe that ill persons need extra care and comfort, and this, in turn was related to greater willingness to reveal physical symptoms. On the other hand, those from families higher in conformity were more aware of the burdens of illness, an attitude that dissuaded its members from disclosing even physical symptoms to parents. The emphasis on parental authority and control, as well as familial structure, appears to place young adults in a double bind. On the one hand, they recognize that ill persons require consideration from the lay network, but they are also aware of the burden that illness poses on that same network. Future research might explore this double bind as an example of an "integrative dilemma" as outlined in problematic integration theory (Babrow, 2001).

The fact that different variables emerged as relevant to the disclosure of physical versus psychological symptoms requires comment. In some respects, it is not surprising that illness attitudes played a role in the disclosure of physical symptoms. It has long been argued that the sick role works best for acute illness episodes, where one cannot be held responsible for falling ill, and getting better is often as much desired by the ill person as by caregivers (Arluke, 1988; Gallagher, 1976; Segall, 1988). However, there is no well-defined social role for those coping with psychological symptoms (e.g., depression, loneliness), not to mention the negative social connotations often associated with mental health problems (as recent public service announcement campaigns attempt to combat). In the absence of such a role, the rights and the obligations of the sufferer are unclear. Individuals and their social networks are left to fend for themselves, navigating and negotiating such conditions on the basis of personality dispositions (e.g., self-concealment) and familial experiences. These results emphasize the importance of the sick role construct as a sociocultural and societal resource that can be drawn upon by both the ill person and the social network in the management of illness. It is clear that such a construct would be beneficial for those suffering from psychological symptoms.

Limitations

One characteristic of this study that is often seen as a limitation concerns the use of a college student population. Nevertheless, the nature of this study's focus was aimed at just that population of young adults transitioning into adult independence whose disclosure of symptoms could be conceived of as primarily voluntary (out of the household). Thus, this could also be seen as a strength of this study. However, though young adults were the focus of the research, clearly, not all young adults attend colleges and universities or live at home during this transition period. Future research should attend more closely to structural issues such as whether or not the young adult lives at home, has a job, pays for his/her own insurance, etc., that are likely to reflect the degree of ongoing involvement on the part of parents. Segall (1988), for example, found that individuals from higher socioeconomic strata were more likely to endorse the belief that sick persons should be released from everyday social roles, and were more likely to talk to others about health concerns. A second limitation concerns the lack of a measure of actual experience of symptoms. The focus was principally on the communication of symptoms, but this investigation is unable to speak to differences in the experience of symptoms based on family communication patterns. Finally, reliabilities for some of the measures in this study were low. In particular, the illness attitudes scale should be improved to increase its utility for future research.

Conclusions and Future Directions

This investigation has established a role for family communication in the study of everyday health and illness experiences. Specifically, family communication patterns were related to the willingness to disclose symptoms to parents. Future research might explore how different family configurations, by crossing the dimensions of conversation and conformity orientations, might foster differences in illness attitudes and symptom disclosure. Family communication patterns also exhibited some associations with illness attitudes. It would be interesting to examine the specific verbal and nonverbal messages conveyed by parents that contribute to illness attitude formation. The role of self-concealment, especially in the suppression of disclosure of psychological symptoms, also warrants further attention. Researchers and practitioners need to open the "neglected box" (Cline, 2003, p. 286) of the role of interpersonal relationships in health and illness. Those relationships are often antecedent factors shaping the quality of patient-caregiver interaction, as well as the processing of media messages.

REFERENCES

Arluke, A. (1988). The sick-role concept. In D. S. Gochman (Ed.), *Health Behavior: Emerging Research Perspectives* (pp. 169–180). New York: Plenum Press.

Babrow, A. S. (2001). Uncertainty, value, communication, and problematic integration. *Journal of Communication*, *51*, 553–573.

Bartone, P. T., Ursano, R. J., Wright, K. M., & Ingraham, L. H. (1989). The impact of a military air disaster on the health of assistance workers. *Journal of Nervous and Mental Disease*, *177*, 317–328. doi: 10.1097/00005053-198906000-00001

Berkanovic, E. (1972). Lay conceptions of the sick role. *Social Forces*, *51*, 53–64.

Cline, R. J. W. (2003). Everyday interpersonal communication and health. In T. L. Thompson, A.

M. Dorsey, K. I. Miller, & R. Parrott (Eds.), *Handbook of Health Communication* (pp. 285–313). Mahwah, NJ: Lawrence Erlbaum.

Dean, K. (1986). Lay care in illness. *Social Science and Medicine*, *22*, 275–284. doi: 10.1016/0277-9536(86)90076-6

Finkenauer, C., Engels, R. C. M. E., & Meeus, W. (2002). Keeping secrets from parents: Advantages and disadvantages of secrecy in adolescence. *Journal of Youth and Adolescence*, *31*, 123–136.

Fitzpatrick, M. A., & Ritchie, L. D. (1994). Communication schemata within the family: Multiple perspectives on family interaction. *Human Communication Research*, *29*, 275–301. doi: 10.1111/j-1468-2958.1994.tb00324.x

Gallagher, E. B. (1976). Lines of reconstruction and extension in the Parsonian sociology of illness. *Social Science & Medicine*, *10*, 207–218. doi: 10.1016/0037-7856(76)90001-9

Gwyn, R. (2002). *Communicating health and illness*. London: Sage.

Hayes, A. F. (2011). Mediate macro for SPSS. [Computer software]. Retrieved from http://afhayes.com/spss-sas-and-mplus-macros-and-code.html

Kassebaum, G. G., & Baumann, B. O. (1965). Dimensions of the sick role in chronic illness. *Journal of Health and Human Behavior*, *6*, 16–27. doi: 10.2307/2948615

Koerner, A. F., & Fitzpatrick, M. A. (2002). Understanding family communication patterns and family functioning: The roles of conversation orientation and conformity orientation. *Communication Yearbook*, *26*, 37–69.

Koerner, A. F., & Fitzpatrick, M. A. (2006). Family communication patterns theory: A social cognitive approach. In D. O. Braithwaite & L. A. Baxter (Eds.), *Engaging theories in family communication: Multiple perspectives* (pp. 50–65). Thousand Oaks, CA: Sage.

Koerner, A. F., LeRoy, B., & McCarthy Veach, P. (2010). Family communication patterns. In C. L. Gaff & C. L. Bylund (Eds.), *Family communication about genetics* (pp. 184–198). New York, NY: Oxford Univ. Press.

Larson, D. G., & Chastain, R. L. (1990). Self-concealment: Conceptualization, measurement, and health implications. *Journal of Social and Clinical Psychology, 9*, 439–455.

Lipnickey, S. C. (1988). University students' knowledge and use of health resources. *Health Values, 12*, 18–26.

Miczo, N. (2004). Stressors and social support perceptions predict illness attitudes and care-seeking intentions: Re-examining the sick role. *Health Communication, 16*, 347–361.

Miczo, N., Miczo, L. A., & Johnson, M. (2006). Parental support, perceived stress, and illness-related variables among first-year college students. *Journal of Family Communication, 6*, 97–117.

Mishler, E. G. (1984). *The discourse of medicine: Dialectics of medical interviews.* Norwood, NJ: Ablex.

Parrott, R., Miller-Day, M., Peters, K., & Dillard, J. (2010). Societal, expert, and lay influences. In In C. L. Gaff & C. L. Bylund (Eds.), *Family communication about genetics* (pp. 34–67). New York, NY: Oxford Univ. Press.

Parsons, T. (1951). *The social system.* Glencoe, IL: The Free Press.

Reis, J. (2001). Consumers' self-care algorithms for the common cold: Implications for health education interventions. *Journal of American College Health, 50*, 27–32.

Ritchie, L. D., & Fitzpatrick, M. A. (1990). Family communication patterns: Measuring intra-personal perceptions of interpersonal relationships. *Communication Research, 17*, 523–544.

Schrodt, P., Witte, P. L., & Messersmith, A. S. (2008). A meta-analytical review of family communication patterns and their associations with information processing, behavioral, and psychosocial outcomes. *Communication Monographs, 75*, 248–269.

Segall, A. (1976). Sociocultural variation in sick role behavioural expectations. *Social Science & Medicine, 10*, 47–51.

Segall, A. (1988). Cultural factors in sick-role expectations. In D. S. Gochman (Ed.), *Health Behavior: Emerging Research Perspectives* (pp. 249–260). New York: Plenum Press.

Segrin, C. (2001). *Interpersonal processes in psychological problems.* New York: Guilford.

Telles, J. L., & Pollack, M. H. (1981). Feeling sick: The experience and legitimation of illness. *Social Science and Medicine, 15A*, 243–251.

Chapter 12:

The Ventria Venture: Communicating health risks and rewards of genetically modified crops

Roy Schwartzman
University of North Carolina at Greensboro

INTRODUCTION

In November 2004 the sun shone brightly on more than the cornstalks and livestock populating most of the landscape in rural northwestern Missouri. Ventria Bioscience, a company engaged in "biopharming," the production of pharmaceuticals from genetically modified plants, announced a joint venture with Northwest Missouri State University to move its headquarters from California to bucolic Maryville, Missouri. Ventria's intention to relocate promised to brighten the economic future of a sparsely populated region that remained in the doldrums of a stagnant agrarian economy. The story might have ended mundanely, with a ribbon-cutting ceremony and sunny optimism beaming from the smiles of corporate executives and local dignitaries. Instead, Ventria's plan to cultivate genetically modified rice embroiled corporate scientists, academic administrators, politicians, farmers, and the nation's largest beer brewer in a scorching controversy that vaporized Ventria's venture. The heated debate over transgenic rice illuminates the discursive landscape of how the potential health risks and benefits of genetically modified organisms (GMOs) are presented and interpreted.

The Ventria case sheds light on a broader and increasingly troublesome issue in health communication. The controversy encapsulates the persistently conflicting ways that different stakeholders construct and perceive the health implications of new technologies. This chapter examines the dispute as an instance of a more general tension between bifurcated narratives that frame emergent biotechnologies as promising panaceas that cure dreaded diseases or as menacing monstrosities that upset the balance of nature.

This chapter confronts the following questions via the case at hand:

1. How do the arguments regarding the implications of biotechnology coalesce to form persuasive master narratives that frame scientific innovations as helpful or hazardous to human health?
2. What factors within the narrative frameworks generate outrage against emergent biotechnologies sufficient to outweigh their projected medical and economic value?

When such questions become concretized in specific cases, the central issue tends to crystallize into a more fundamental question: How much risk to human health is acceptable to yield a potential benefit?

THEORY AND METHOD

This chapter uses intuitive risk heuristics to unpack the decision-making criteria that weigh the merits of health-related arguments. Risk heuristics acknowledges that people often do not make purely rational, scientifically justified decisions about how technologies will affect human health. These unscientific means of evaluating arguments about technology do not simply reflect ignorance or laziness. Instead, many apparently inexplicable decisions arise from the activation of simple, intuitively appealing, apparently commonsensical judgments (Kahneman, 2011; Slovic, 2000). Faced with the challenge of interpreting esoteric, often confusing and inconsistent health and medical data, people substitute simpler, more familiar argumentative routes to render decisions (Gardner, 2008). Scholars easily discard these heuristics as the detritus of arguments, mere fallacies that indicate misguided thought or misapplied rules of logic. Heuristics rehabilitates these largely dismissed or ignored shortcuts as important risk assessment tools that do play a crucial role in judgment. Heuristically formulated judgments can infuse the decisions of even highly trained scientific experts, suggesting that this aspect of decision-making should be taken into account as a factor that can affect all stakeholders (Kahneman, 2011).

The Ventria controversy strengthens the growing awareness that many decisions about health do not proceed according to a standard statistical cost-benefit analysis. Instead of weighing the probabilities of food contamination and other dangers attendant to cultivating genetically altered crops, stakeholders often construct their perceptions of health hazards based on factors extrinsic to the sheer probability and magnitude of a projected outcome (Schwartzman, Ross, & Berube, 2011). Rather than employ a calculus to weigh risks versus benefits, those who deliberate about potential health hazards invoke several heuristic devices to determine acceptable levels of risk and obtainable levels of rewards from emergent technologies. These heuristics provide useful lessons as to why reliance on the power of science alone may not carry the day in providing reassurances about the safety of emergent technologies.

Three types of heuristic devices undergird the arguments at critical junctures in the controversy: availability, framing, and insistence on certainty. These heuristics worked synergistically, permitting Ventria's opponents to build a more persuasive case that prevented the company's plans from materializing. The availability heuristic describes the tendency to judge the likelihood of a risk by the ease with which instances of it (actual or hypothetical) can be brought to mind. An event becomes especially imaginable when conjoined with a powerful affect, establishing a strong emotional association with the hazard or its avoidance (Keller, Siegrist, & Gutscher, 2006). Availability, therefore, gains traction as a purported risk becomes more realistic (i.e., immediate and vivid) and emotion-laden. The availability heuristic becomes especially potent if it can link risks to events within an audience's range of experience. If a risky event—or an analogous one—has occurred in the past, the perception grows that the event could be repeated in the future regardless of how miniscule its statistical likelihood may be (Keller, Siegrist, & Gutscher, 2006). In this case, the availability heuristic adjudicated whether the risks or the benefits of GMOs seemed more immediate, more relevant, and more understandable. In the sense that a health-related decision becomes consequential only to the extent that it can be conceptualized clearly, availability may qualify as a necessary precondition for risk assessment (Kuran & Sunstein, 1999).

Framing deals with how decisions are influenced by the ways choices are presented in discourse. Ample evidence shows that human decision making often does not follow a strict cost-benefit logic, even when deciding about issues that have a direct impact on personal health. Lakoff (2010) recommends focusing more attention on how framing, especially through metaphors and narratives, reflects and shapes emotional allegiances to a cause. The alignment of terminology and narrative traditions regarding an issue can replace more calculated risk assessments, especially when the exact risks are difficult to quantify.

In the absence of clearly quantifiable harms or benefits and amid unknown probabilities of risk, decision makers may resort to the convenience of thinking in absolutes. Seeking the greatest degree of protection and unable to process what infinitesimally small differences in degree of risk might mean in practice, they establish zero risk as the desired standard. Categorical rejection of risk offers a simple benchmark that, even if unachievable in practice, offers the comfort of complete safety. Although seemingly irrational in a risk-filled world, embracing a no-risk position arises as the logical extension of a pervasive desire to avoid losses whenever possible. In situations when one feels little control (e.g., inadvertent exposure to food contamination), the desire to flee from risk becomes especially acute (Simon, Houghton, & Aquino, 1999).

The saga of Ventria's attempt to establish biopharming in Missouri shows how the lure of profit could not vanquish the fear of health risks. Table 1 lists the crucial events in the unfolding controversy. To track the relevant discourse, the LexisNexis Academic database was searched using the keyword "Ventria" for the years 2004 through 2006. In addition, news releases and promotional publications from Northwest Missouri State University that discussed the university's relationship with Ventria were examined. Congressional testimony from Ventria's CEO (Scott Deeter) was included as an indicator of the company's approach to direct interaction with policymakers.

Table 12.1 Timeline of Key Events

April 2004	Ventria Bioscience announces plans to move headquarters to Maryville, Missouri, cultivate commercial plots of transgenic rice in the state, and process it in a facility at Northwest Missouri State University
November 2004	Ventria and Northwest Missouri State University agree to create center for plant biologics, anchored by Ventria's transgenic rice processing operations.
January 2005	Dean Hubbard, President of Northwest Missouri State University, joins Ventria Board of Director as an unpaid member
April 2005	April 7: Anheuser-Busch threatens to boycott all Missouri-grown rice if Ventria proceeds with cultivating transgenics April 15: Threatened boycott withdrawn when Ventria agrees not to grow transgenic rice within 120 miles of commercial rice
September 2005	Ground broken for plant biologics center at Northwest Missouri State University
December 2005	Missouri Economic Finance Board refuses to fulfill state's pledge of $10 million to the Ventria project, but would support a loan later if federal grant support comes through. December 30: Ventria cancels plans for transgenic rice crops and processing in Missouri
January 2006	Ventria and Northwest Missouri State University terminate agreement for the company's processing facilities and relocation

This chapter explores the heuristically infused argumentation that fueled competing narratives about the safety and desirability of biopharmaceuticals. These major argumentative *topoi* traverse familiar ground in the ongoing debates surrounding GMOs. Thus far, scholarly literature has not sufficiently addressed the ways that heuristics can interface with the formation (or erosion) of trust in specific sources of information and in the institutions they represent. Recognizing the role of heuristics can cultivate trust at the social (interpersonal) and epistemic (institutional) levels (Sjöberg & Herber, 2008) to prevent dialogue from devolving into diatribe.

ALTRUISM VERSUS AVAILABILITY

Ventria built its justification for biopharming on a foundation of altruistic arguments, touting the purportedly lifesaving potential of the proteins derived from transgenic rice. Ventria CEO Scott Deeter regularly reiterated slight variations on the humane refrain: "We're solving world problems...we want to save two million kids a year. That's what gets us out of bed in the morning"

(Mulvaney & Zivian, 2013, p. 167). This selfless spirit would presumably "shade out naysayers and help to immunize the company against consumer revolt" (Weasel, 2009, p. 188).

Strategically, Ventria's advocacy for saving millions of dysentery-plagued children in the third world could render objections from the local community insignificant in two ways. First, in terms of scope and severity of impact, the prospect of alleviating the suffering or saving the lives of millions of vulnerable children clearly outweighed the unquantified impact of unknown effects of ingesting transgenic rice. Deeter remarked, "Our production technology enables the cost-effective addition of Lactiva and Lysomin to oral-rehydration solution for the benefit of millions of children worldwide" (Different Applications, 2005). He also linked Ventria's products to national security concerns by claiming potential reductions in diarrhea that incapacitated American combat troops. Treatment with Ventria's proteins would defend against this "silent enemy attacking American troops" (Different Applications, 2005). Second, on a scale of values the preservation of defenseless children would seem to reduce the fears of local farmers to selfish refusal to lend their crops to more noble causes. Northwest Missouri State University president Dean Hubbard—who also was serving on Ventria's board of directors—succinctly contrasted the competing value systems. Referring to beer brewer Anheuser-Busch's opposition to Ventria's project (a topic that will be addressed later), Hubbard quipped, "What this boils down to is beer or babies" (Canon, 2005).

The availability heuristic is driven by socially constructed devices that infuse an argumentative position with a sense of salience and vividness (Kuran & Sunstein, 1999). Salience describes the degree to which a point seems immediately relevant. A risk or a benefit gains salience with an audience to the extent that its occurrence seems imminent, in close proximity, has great magnitude, or has affected people similar to that audience. Vividness refers to sensory impact and the affect that it induces. Verbally constructed vividness has long been the province of rhetoric, as it concerns the discursive tools of influence that encompass emotion as well as logic.

Compassion Confronts Salience and Vividness

On a cost-benefit level, Ventria's position seems convincing, but only when approached from deliberative reasoning that calculates net gains and losses. Social determinations of health risks and benefits, however, incorporate many factors beyond the probability and magnitude of helpful or harmful outcomes. The way that health dangers or benefits are communicated outweighs the absolute probability and magnitude of events in forming perceptions of risk (Kasperson et al., 2010). As heuristics for decision making enter consideration, arguments based on sheer projected health impacts carry less weight. The argumentation tactics exemplified by Ventria failed to address the richly layered public construction of risks.

The availability heuristic comes into play when the likelihood or impact of an event seems greater not because of its high statistical probability but because instances come to mind readily (Tversky & Kahneman, 1973). The potential health payoff promised by Ventria seemed remote to many observers. The "lifesaving" drugs that could rehydrate victims of diarrhea remained in the indefinitely distant future (Weasel, 2009)—plus their primary benefits were targeted at geographically distant third world countries where diseases such as dysentery still ran rampant.

Ventria's opponents propagated a seemingly endless set of possible contamination scenarios. Fears of contamination had some foundation. In 2004, Ventria was cited by the USDA for growing test plots of bioengineered rice within 100 feet of human food crops (Carolan, 2010). As these scenarios proliferated, they activated the availability heuristic rendering contamination as actualizable even if its statistical probability were miniscule. The health risks of biopharming, while not quantified, detailed circumstances readily within a rural resident's or farmer's realm of experience. Seeds or pollen being scattered by ordinary means such as birds, rats, or wind invoked familiar natural processes of botanical propagation. Even casual gardeners could identify with the intrusion of "volunteer" plants. New technologies often face an uphill battle with the availability heuristic because few if any identifiable precedents exist to ground claims of safety. The sealed plots that Ventria touted as secure might have prevented laboratory contamination, but they were beyond any concrete experiential reference point for non-scientists. The proposed health advantages of biopharming were imprecise, conjectural, and both temporally and geographically remote.

The wayward bird scenarios, by contrast, employed specific visual images that created vivid narratives in news coverage. One Missouri bootheel rice farmer who worked on his family farm mocked Ventria, casting them as technologically savvy but lacking agricultural common sense.

> *They've got a good grasp on the technology. But what they don't have a good grasp on is dirt clod-kicking, grass-roots farming in southern Missouri. Those blackbirds will be all over that rice, carrying it and tracking it away—and ducks, too, with those big, webbed feet. (Lambrecht, 2005b)*

Precise images of waddling duck and throngs of blackbirds made the mechanisms of contamination immediately salient to the general public. One environmentalist assessed the ease of contamination: "Just washing away in a big rain-storm in enough" (Barrionuevo, 2005). The sense of immediacy and normality that was crafted rhetorically (Perelman & Olbrechts-Tyteca, 1969) outweighed the remote, hypothetical benefits of biopharming.

Wherever one turned, possible transmission mechanisms arose that could transport genetically modified grains to "pure" foods: rain, wind, birds, mice, rabbits, lizards. By contrast, Ventria never gave a persona to its arguments. The beneficiaries of biopharming remained aggregated as millions of children or battalions of soldiers, never an identifiable face or name. Research has revealed an astonishingly low threshold for so-called "compassion fatigue," the point where people become desensitized to suffering (Vedantam, 2010, p. 254). Paradoxically, as the absolute number of people harmed increases, the sense of personal connection with victims and the desire to help them decline (Slovic, 2007). While this effect is not linear, Slovic's (2007) research finds that psychic numbing to pain and suffering begins to activate as soon as the victims exceed a single individual. The personal testimony of one recovered child might have begun to activate the availability heuristic and shifted sympathies in favor of biopharming. Concentration of impact onto one person magnifies its significance beyond sheer numbers, as that individual's concrete immediacy amplifies the scope of her or his suffering within a limited perceptual field.

Beer to the Rescue?

In April 2005, Anheuser-Busch entered the fray. As one rice farmer observed, Anheuser-Busch's involvement represented a tipping point: "Anheuser-Busch holds the trump card" (Canon, 2005). The St. Louis-based company, the largest rice buyer in the nation, threatened to boycott buying any Missouri rice if the biopharmed rice were planted (Canon, 2005). Within a few weeks, the beer giant relented after Ventria agreed to move its test plots 120 miles away from the nearest rice crops cultivated for food (Yount, 2008). The negotiations with Anheuser-Busch lasted long enough to cause Ventria to miss the optimum growing season, derailing plans to implement the test plots in 2005.

Although Anheuser-Busch justified its decision by citing fears of crop contamination, their opposition to the Ventria project served important trust-building functions for the beer brewery. Unlike the rice processing and marketing companies that opposed Ventria, Anheuser-Busch's objections could not be dismissed as fear of economic competition. Instead, Anheuser-Busch could appeal to more noble motives and a firmer foundation for earning public trust. Ventria and Anheuser-Busch took on contrasting institutional personae. Whereas Ventria offered optimistic conjectures about economic benefits, Anheuser-Busch had been an economic engine in the state since its founding in 1852. The brewery (still a family-owned American company at that time) was founded in St. Louis and never relocated its headquarters, positioning it as the champion for Missouri rice farmers. Ventria was promoting microscopic particles explained in scientific esoterica and not yet in commercial production. Anheuser-Busch manufactured the most popular beer in the nation, a familiar beverage culturally linked with middle-class enjoyment.

FRAMING AND AFFECT: NATURE VERSUS FRANKENRICE

Extensive research on risk communication demonstrates that the way that choices are phrased directly influences which position or action gets chosen as preferable (Kim et al., 2005; Tversky & Kahneman, 1981). When the phenomena under discussion are poorly understood or difficult to concretize, decision makers may rely on framing to guide their choices according to the affect that the frames generate (McElroy & Seta, 2003). In this case, the intervention of Anheuser-Busch clearly illustrates how the credibility of genetic modification was undercut by framing it as unnatural, rendering it fearful and morally suspect.

Among the institutional actors, Anheuser-Busch occupied a potentially paradoxical position. Given the linkages between alcohol and all sorts of social ills ranging from drunk driving to homicide, breweries could more likely be cast as merchants of death than as protectors of purity and guardians of public safety. Anheuser-Busch, however, already was immersed in a rich symbolic vocabulary that identified it with the natural roots of its beverage rather than with the consequences of its misuse. Beer advertisements consistently link beer with images of unspoiled nature (Strate, 1991). The ubiquitous Budweiser Clydesdales plus the symbol of Busch beer (a rearing horse), symbolically connect to the American frontier (cowboys). The horses nostalgically associate beer with untamed and unadulterated Nature (Strate, 1991). These symbols reinforced the stature of Anheuser-Busch as the guardian of tradition while Ventria had no visual representations of its products aside from diagrams of molecular structures. This visual disparity reinforces the difficulty Ventria encountered in invoking the availability heuristic. The symbolic aura of Anheuser-Busch also tapped into the affect heuristic (Slovic, 2007), wherein emotional attachments assume more importance than dispassionate calculations of probable outcomes. Anheuser-Busch's longstanding record of geographical loyalty, the scale of its economic impact, and its associations with natural purity offered ample grounds for positive emotional associations.

Ventria attempted to ease anxieties by casting its operations as extensions of natural substances rather than human-engineered alterations of nature. A phrase that originated in Ventria news releases became the company's stock description of its genetically enhanced proteins. The substances, which "occur naturally in human tears, saliva and breast milk" (Stafford, 2005; Evo, 2006), still failed to register as benign natural substances necessary for human survival.

Ventria CEO Scott Deeter attempted to naturalize biopharmaceuticals by linking their transgenic proteins to the most wholesome of all foods.

> *Ventria's first two health products are proteins called Lactiva and Lysomin. These two proteins are found naturally in mother's milk, saliva, tears, and they contribute to the improved health status that has widely been reported for breast-fed children when compared to their infant formula-fed counterparts. (*Different Applications, *2005)*

In the same Congressional hearing, Deeter asserted that, far from harmful, the company's rice-derived proteins were nutritious dietary supplements.

> *The member asked the question, what would happen if there was a contamination? Well, I cannot speak for every product, but I can speak for Ventria's products. You know, it is in mother's milk. These proteins are in saliva. They are in our tears. What would happen? You might be healthier." (*Different Applications, *2005)*

The biological evidence casts doubt on this dismissive claim (Rehbinder et al., 2008). The human lactoferrin that Ventria planned to splice into its rice plants could be an allergen, as it bears molecular similarities to bovine lactoferrin, a known allergen. In addition, the iron in lactoferrin serves as a food source to harmful microbes, which could proliferate when ingested by livestock. Furthermore, since chicken fed this protein reproduced at higher rates, wild birds that consume the rice might induce population imbalances that disrupt ecosystems.

Issued from sources that the public did not deem trustworthy (i.e., those who held a financial stake in the venture), Ventria's reassurances rang hollow. Ventria encountered a double bind. Stressing the pot of gold that biopharming promised might lure investors, but it did little to assure local farmers that the company considered them and the surrounding communities as anything other than means for generating profits.

Ventria offered pecuniary rewards to farmers rather than dialogue with them. By increasing the value of rice far beyond what it could earn from commodity uses alone, Ventria's biopharming project dangled a tempting economic lure to the depressed northwest Missouri economy (Evo, 2005). The company estimated that farmers could double their profits by growing transgenic strains of rice compared to what they had been earning from conventional crops (*Different Applications*, 2005). The lure of rewards, however, could not override the fear of scientifically spawned monstrosities.

The idealized sanctity of nature contrasted directly with claims that unintended cross-pollination of crops would yield genetic monstrosities. This line of argument revisits the "Frankenfood" mythos that associates genetically modified foods with the Frankenstein monster, metaphorically implying that tampering with nature will have drastic negative consequences (Zinken, Hellsten, & Nerlich, 2008). The Frankenfood frame had particular resonance in this instance. Ventria's transgenic rice was the first known case of a GM food crop that contained human genes. "The rice is a major step in so-called Frankenstein Foods, the first mingling of human-origin genes and those from plants" (Poulter, 2007).

Threats of genetically modified plants accidentally mixing with traditional crops loomed large due to the availability heuristic, which rendered such scenarios imminent and realizable. The Frankenrice angle, however, struck directly at the credibility of Ventria and by implication genetic engineering itself. Far from unintentional transmission of GMOs, the implantation of human genetic material into rice represented a deliberate violation of the boundaries between human an non-human. Splicing together two such radically different organisms as rice and human fit neatly into the Frankenstein narrative of the mad scientist patching together a monstrous creation from discordant parts. The moral implications were detailed in the cinematic introduction to viewers of the 1931 Frankenstein film: "We are about to unfold the story of Frankenstein, a man of science who sought to create a man after his own image without reckoning upon God" (Whale, 1931). Within this framework, transgenic modifications were branded as moral and metaphysical transgressions, perversions of the divine creative process. Powell and Leiss already concluded in 1997: "Genetic engineering has now replaced nuclear energy as the primary example of 'science-out-of-control' in popular culture" (p. 129).

The prefix "Franken-" had been affixed to all sorts of biogenetic modifications, especially those that combined genes from different species. Ventria's transgenic rice quickly acquired the label "Frankenrice" from environmental groups, organic farmers, and other opponents. The name provided a convenient mnemonic to energize links between Ventria's biopharming, mad scientists, moral transgression against the laws of natural propagation (Rushing & Frentz, 1989), and unforeseen medical disasters. Absent specification or quantification of the negative outcomes, the consistently disturbing metaphoric associations and narrative implications of Frankenstein references have served as a rallying point against GMOs (Zinken, Hellsten, & Nerlich, 2008). Frankenfood references condense the various fears about genetic engineering into a familiar narrative that defies scientific refutation

(Gusterson, 2005). The legacy of Frankenstein recalls the inherent moral corruptibility of humans, an incipient danger that science and regulatory agencies cannot expunge.

How could the Frankenfood narratives and clusters of unflattering metaphors gain traction against scientific research? The answer lies in loss aversion, the persistent preference for minimizing negative outcomes rather than maximizing gains (Lehrer, 2009). Rephrased in terms of argumentation, only a compelling rationale can overcome the presumption that things should be left as they are. Kahneman (2011) summarizes the impact on decision making: "Loss aversion is a powerful conservative force that favors minimal changes from the status quo in the lives of both institutions and individuals." The threat of loss or harm looms disproportionately large in decision making. Given a choice between realizing a benefit and incurring a loss of equivalent value, people show a widespread and consistent preference for preventing loss (Kahneman & Tversky, 1979). Across a wide array of situations and contexts, motivation to avoid bad outcomes (whatever they may be) outweighs the desire to achieve good outcomes (Baumeister et al., 2001). Regardless of why loss aversion exercises such force, its power as a heuristic explains why the appeal of financial prosperity does not necessarily trump even infinitesimally small risks of ruining existing crops and food supplies. Since the region had no extensive track record with GMOs, it seemed more prudent to safeguard tangible crops already being harvested than to embark on an experiment whose processes and economic prospects were poorly understood by the local population.

THE QUEST FOR CERTAINTY

In Congressional testimony given in June 2005 while the Missouri rice controversy was at full steam, Ventria CEO Scott Deeter made a rare departure from scientific circumspection and momentarily shed all qualifiers to his claims. He asserted that the biopharmed crops "can easily achieve the necessary geographic isolation from their food crop counterparts to eliminate any concerns of cross-contamination with the food supply" (Different Applications, 2005). As environmentalists and other opponents continually stressed, there can be no guarantees of preventing all contamination. With the level of acceptable risk set at zero, anything short of absolute certitude conceded argumentative ground to Ventria's adversaries. In fact, Deeter attempted to assuage public fears of cross-contamination with an reassurance that hardly inspired confidence: "Ventria will work hard to keep its rice isolated" (Murphy, 2007, p. 205). Avowal of hard work presumed that stakeholders would trust the company to be vigilant—not a likely bet in rural areas suspicious both of outsiders (Ventria was relocating from California) and of corporate greed (in the wake of the 2001 Enron scandal).

Back in March 2005, *Delta Farm Press* already expressed the frustration local farmers felt with Ventria's approach to communication with the agricultural community. The transcript of a written question and answer exchange with Ventria CEO Scott Deeter illustrated the disconnects between researchers and the local farmers who risked contaminated crops. Throughout the interview, the farm publication sought certainty against contamination, translated as a risk probability of zero. The first question set a challenging tone: "Can Ventria guarantee that its pharma-rice (or its pollen) won't somehow find its way into neighboring (conventional) rice fields?" (Ventria Bioscience response, 2005). The question's phrasing raises three noteworthy points. First, the question invested the rice itself with agency uncontrollable by humans. Its pollen may simply "find its way" into the wrong places regardless of human vigilance. In effect, the question asked whether Ventria could control the uncontrollable. Second, the question set an unreachably high bar for safety, implying zero risk tolerance. The question was loaded, since no technology can offer absolute guarantees of safety. The failure, however, appeared to arise from Ventria's reluctance to issue a no-risk guarantee, which insinuated the company's lack of trustworthiness in protecting the public or lack of competence in managing risk.

Third, and most important, this interview reveals the conflicting conceptions of risk communication displayed by the farmers' representative and the Ventria CEO. Responding to the request for assuring no risk, Deeter replied by detailing the company's reliance on self-pollinating plants, which "significantly reduces the risks from cross-pollination." He then described "Ventria's commitment to sound stewardship" by listing four basic safety practices and stressing compliance with all USDA standards. The next question demonstrated fundamental distrust by dismissing Ventria's reassurances, asking: "[I]s Ventria's guarantee backed by anything more than words?" Deeter's laconic response was: "Please see above," referring to the same technical procedures and legal compliances that had just been labeled "mere words" (Ventria Bioscience response, 2005). The next two questions, dealing with Ventria's willingness to pay for lost farm income and to insure against losses from contamination, generated the same deferrals to procedural safeguards.

The core of this interchange lies in factors that tap into deeper epistemological and ethical conflicts. Each interlocutor understood risk communication as a unitary phenomenon. Deeter interpreted risk communication as risk management, whereby Ventria as the researcher bore sole responsibility to minimize the likelihood of harm and monitor progress to that end. He failed to recognize that Ventria could not earn the confidence of farmers unless the company established trust. Deeter understood trust as confidence in the technical capacity to reduce probability of harm. The agricultural journalists sought reasons to trust Ventria as placing the best interests of farmers foremost. Deeter responded that farmers should read the technical data, even offering citations of two articles in agricultural research journals. Scientific and regulatory precision provides scant comfort to audiences searching for definitive declarations of safety, not detailed degrees of probability (Berube, 2008).

Deeter asked farmers to place their faith with two institutions not renowned for stellar levels of trustworthiness: corporate researchers (Ventria) and the federal government (the USDA). Deeter referred to "sound stewardship" in partnership with the USDA, yet failed to identify any stewardship that had been developed collaboratively with local farmers. Local farmers received glowing promises about what Ventria would do for them, but minimal input in deciding or discussing what stewardship would involve other than Ventria's customary corporate practices.

IMPLICATIONS AND RECOMMENDATIONS

The following section suggests how lessons gleaned from the Ventria case could generate more common discursive ground by recognizing and responding to the sources of concern about genetic modifications. While the present case study illustrates divergent views regarding GMOs, it highlights a more profound cognitive and rhetorical disconnection that confronts the implementations of new technologies. Referring to public objections to GMOs, Wynne (2001) urges health communicators to recognize opposition that runs deeper than cost-benefit calculations: "These judgements are less a (mis)judgement of the risks per se, than a deeper public rejection of this very discourse which expert institutions use to define and give meaning to the issues and to the public" (p. 647).

Especially in cases where the exact degree of health risk is difficult to quantify, consumers and policy makers tend to place more weight on the trust they have for specific sources (e.g., Ventria) or in institutions (e.g., corporate entities or the authority of science) than on factual assessments of safety (Powell & Leiss, 1997; Siegrist, Earle, & Gutscher, 2007). In short, judgments of health risks are filtered through perceptions of social and institutional trust. The activation of several heuristics created an atmosphere of mistrust that promoted polarization and categorical rejection of opposing claims.

Availability and Engagement

Technological innovators face an uphill climb against the availability heuristic. With little precedent for performance and as yet unrealized benefits, new technologies often pit vague promises against the concrete reality of the status quo. Health communicators might, however, embrace the novelty of a technology as an opportunity to engage the public more directly with how new technologies are deployed and regulated. Pervasive media generalizations of GMOs as threats to health and safety might carry less weight with constituencies who participate more directly in policy discussion and implementation. Experience with a wide range of technological innovations worldwide shows that early involvement with concerned stakeholders increases public satisfaction with outcomes (Frewer et al., 2004). Many opportunities for constructive engagement were available. Instead of recruiting the university's president to a board of investors, Ventria might have established an independent advisory board comprised of consumer advocates and leaders of concerned organizations. The company also could have made biopharming more vivid and salient by offering demonstrations of its technologies, thereby offering greater transparency as an antidote to suspicion.

Ventria positioned itself as an entrepreneurial innovator promising pro-social benefits of its biopharmaceuticals. To many local rice farmers, Ventria appeared as an interloper—an upstart and intruder motivated by potential profit rather than altruistic medical concerns or genuine regard for local communities. Although its CEO was a Kansas native, Ventria as a corporation seemed willing to relocate wherever it could find the acreage and financial incentives to expand its test plots. Social trust suffered from misgivings that Ventria sought to relocate to Missouri because it was dodging more stringent regulatory practices in its home state of California (Lambrecht, 2004; Lee, 2004).

Failure to include local agricultural communities early in the deliberations aroused suspicion and resentment. One rice farmer in rural Missouri opined: "Those people [Ventria] came into Missouri through the back door and cut a deal before we even knew anything was going on" (Lambrecht, 2005b). In science communication research, momentum has been building for "upstream engagement" in technological innovations, or involvement of immediate stakeholders as early in the deliberative process as possible, to counteract precisely these sorts of suspicions (Pidgeon & Rogers-Hayden, 2007).

Although Ventria had successfully courted the local university's leadership, the company steadfastly adhered to a deficit model of public scientific understanding. The deficit model deems the public deficient in scientific knowledge and therefore incompetent to render rationally grounded judgments. The solution, according to the deficit model, is to inject a healthy dose of scientific literacy into public consciousness and let science guide policy decisions (Schwartzman & Carlone, 2008). By implication, the preferred mode of communication becomes unidirectional and patriarchal (Gross, 1994). Key decisions about public health should be entrusted to the scientific experts who employ reason untarnished by emotion to arrive at optimal outcomes on behalf of the lay public. Scott Deeter's Congressional testimony echoed this attitude, treating local opposition as sheer irrationality: "We have been able to consider the scientific facts, and we are not swayed as much by the emotional arguments that are really meant to stymie the innovator and arrest progress in these important areas" (Different Applications, 2005). As mere obstructionists, Ventria's opponents did not merit a more direct response. Such an attitude distanced Ventria from its opponents, allowing contamination scenarios to spread unabated and thus become a dominant public perception.

Attention to Framing

Deetz, Tracy, and Simpson (2000) point to the importance of any organization anticipating how discursive framing tools—imagery, figures of speech, emotionally charged terminology, myths and legends, and traditions—construct narratively driven perceptions of that organization and its representatives. Beyond the specific choices of terminology and crafting a coherent narrative, the current study suggests that health communicators must more thoroughly acknowledge and adapt to the ways that emotion-laden terminology drives public decision making and policy formation. Repeatedly invoking the authority of science carries little weight with audiences whose trust in science as an impartial intellectual institution has been undermined by its affiliation with presumably profiteering corporations. Instead of simply reiterating the sovereignty of science, health communicators would serve themselves and their constituencies better by recognizing how to maneuver rhetorically within the heuristically infused risk analytics employed by non-specialist.

The university's position in the controversy illustrates the need for conscious consideration of an institution's perceived persona. Given the entrenched cultural narrative of Frankenstein's monster and the moral hazards of interloping on nature's territory, the university had a chance to assume the role of the moral guardian and protector of public health. The university could have positioned itself as a bulwark against fears of the unknown "alien rice" (Weintraub, 2005) and suspicions surrounding Ventria's profit-driven motives. While still supporting Ventria's project, Northwest and its president could consistently redirect the terms of discussion toward more positive framing as continuing a long, familiar tradition of crop hybridization.

Unfortunately for Ventria and its supporters, the framing of genetic modification solidified before it could be cast in a more positive light. Unevenly valenced oppositional pairings such as conventional/unconventional, pure/contaminated, natural/monstrous became firmly rooted as descriptors. Had advocates of genetic engineering been more proactive with crafting their discourse, they might have adopted and popularized terminology linking GM crop cultivation with innovation or enhancement that offered a helping hand to natural processes. By treating genetic alterations as extensions of, rather than threats to, the "wisdom of nature," GMOs could become an ally to nature rather than presumptuous disruption of nature's architecture (Bostrom & Sandberg, 2008).

Northwest Missouri State University President Dean Hubbard seemed to miss the entire framing issue in his response to Anheuser-Busch's threatened boycott. Steadfastly operating within the academic, rational decision-making model, he laconically replied: "Any concerns have been addressed thoroughly to the satisfaction of the scientific community" (Associated Press, 2005). The problem was that other constituencies aside from the scientific community—the legislature, agricultural communities, and corporate enterprises—also demanded satisfaction. Those non-scientist stakeholders were unwilling to cede decision making on potential health risks to scientists, some of whose research Ventria was funding.

Trust and Risk Tolerance

Both Ventria and Northwest Missouri State University seemed to dismiss the cloud of controversy that had enveloped not only GMOs in Europe, but in previous ventures of the same company's attempts to cultivate transgenic rice in California. These public concerns, regardless of their unscientific nature, contributed to insistence on zero risk tolerance—an impossible standard for Ventria or any other company to meet. As Aven and Renn (2010) observe, consumers unable to calculate precise levels of GMO risks insist that nothing short of zero risk will suffice from companies that cannot be trusted to act in the public interest.

Replying that people engage regularly in far more risky behaviors than exposure to GMOs (e.g., riding in an automobile) carries little weight in these situations. Individuals feel they can exert some control over their own risk exposure (e.g., by driving carefully), but become more risk averse as they cede control to a third party whose main concern is profit over protection. Citing the lapses in trust that accrue from "hints or cues related to conflicts of interest," Aven and Renn (2010, p. 170) conclude: "For example, if one depends upon information provided by third parties for the assessment of such risks, and these third parties are not considered trustworthy, then one does not accept any cost-benefit calculation."

A foundation of trust, therefore, becomes a necessary condition for constituencies to entertain any concept of what might constitute an acceptable level of risk. In order for discussions of acceptable risk to occur in the first place, a responsible health communicator must convince stakeholders—and not only shareholders or investors—that it places paramount importance on their safety and protection.

Ventria was not alone in failing to build a foundation of trust that would encourage dialogue. The partnership with Northwest Missouri State University was tainted by the university and its president behaving more as entrepreneurial investors than as responsible custodians of public safety. The uncritical endorsement of every action and announcement by Ventria left no distance between the educational institution and the opportunistic genetic engineers. Given the cozy relationship between Northwest Missouri State University and Ventria, the university's endorsements no longer carried the force of impartial third-party assessments. Not only was Northwest's president serving on Ventria's board of directors, but the university received a 4% share in Ventria as part of the negotiations to relocate the company (Lambrecht, 2005). The more Northwest's president touted the value of Ventria's projects, the more distrust of the company transferred to the university. Northwest began to serve more as an advocate, an extension of Ventria's public relations, than as a guardian of the community serving as both host and watchdog of a potential economic engine. By December 2005, budget allocations for the biopharmaceutical processing center at the university had been slashed in half (Hollingsworth, 2005). Within a month, Ventria officially terminated its plans for biopharming in Missouri.

What, then, could be done in an atmosphere of zero risk tolerance? If public perceptions prevent any engagement with the concept of acceptable levels of risk, a discursive impasse results. Even if Ventria could not cultivate sufficient trust either in its own credibility or in that of the institutions it represented (science and business), it still could have developed a rapport with its constituencies by holding itself more accountable to them. As Sandman (1993) observes, willingness to be held accountable—perhaps empowering independent observers as monitors and watchdogs—can lay the groundwork for open and honest communication even when trust is minimal. The implicit plea to entrust public health to profit-seeking business or esoteric science can be replaced by the willingness to be answerable to the stakeholders who will hold the product developers accountable. "Giving the public 'permission' not to trust you is virtually the only way out of widespread mistrust" (Sandman, 1993, p. 54). Following some of Sandman's (1993) suggestions, Ventria could have enlisted local farmers, environmental groups, and academics unaffiliated with the project as part of the monitoring process to check for cross-pollination. Even better, Ventria could have involved similar parties in the design or quality control of its various crop containment technologies, in effect inviting its potential opponents to ally in its self-policing.

Cultivating fertile discursive ground for communication about health risks of GMOs should have begun long before the grandiose announcements that transgenic rice promised, as Hubbard hoped, a "rural economy [that] has been transformed" (Barrionuevo, 2005). Several questions required answers if Ventria had any prospect of earning sufficient public trust to allow for some discussion of acceptable risk levels. First, how would Missouri's land and its rice farmers be configured as inherently valuable, as something more than instruments for Ventria to generate profits? Second, how could Ventria partner with impartial, respected local institutions (educational, agricultural, and scientific) with no vested financial interests to enlist their participation as watchdogs and monitors? Third, how could the benefits from GMOs be presented as more salient to the local community, as imminent public goods that differed from the GMOs already understood as monstrous contaminants?

Only after such questions had been answered to the satisfaction of relevant stakeholders could discussions be rechanneled toward tolerable levels of risk rather than futile pursuit of risk-free guarantees (Derby & Keeney, 1981). Cultivating a more trusting discursive environment could enable discussion of risk acceptability instead of risk avoidance. Rather than trying to silence objections by invoking the authority of science, developers of genetically engineered crops could work alongside relevant stakeholders to maintain levels of risk proportionate to the benefits. This dialogical partnership, however, requires sufficient trust to enable tolerance of some level of risk in the first place.

As a public educational institution, Northwest Missouri State University might have been in a position to negotiate a collaborative critical encounter with technological innovation. The university's status as an economic driver for a depressed agricultural economy, as a center for scientific research, and as an advocate for its community as well as a guardian of its interests (including safety) positioned it to be an impartial broker. Casting aside the tempered, cautionary tone characteristic of science, President Hubbard recast the educational institution as an opportunist. Instead of asserting the importance of being a vigilant watchdog of the Ventria facilities that would be housed adjacent to the Northwest campus, Hubbard simply dismissed the issue of risk by foregrounding the economic advantages. Rather than enact the traditional charge of universities to encourage impartial deliberation, Hubbard instead shifted the locus of institutional trust to the corporate developers of genetically modified crops. The institutional trust usually granted to an educational institution was ceded to the much more dubious level of trust the public placed in an outside corporation.

CONCLUSION

The case of Ventria illustrates how social and institutional trust interface with narratively embedded heuristics to sow seeds of suspicion or generate cooperative dialogue. Ventria's biopharming project was vanquished in Missouri, but the argumentative *topoi* that infuse the protagonists' narratives persist in the ongoing debates over health implications of biotechnologies. As one analyst noted, "The economic and academic ambitions of the Missouri project make it unique, but the arguments echo those heard in similar disputes in Europe and, increasingly, in the United States" (Barrionuevo, 2005). Currently farmers in Uganda are weighing the potential for transgenic, disease-resistant bananas and cassavas to reduce famines from low crop yields (Doucleff, 2013).

Ugandan farmers worry about their lack of knowledge or control regarding the future use of GM crops, especially if private corporations begin supplying GM seeds for other plants. As the pace of technological innovations accelerates, the encounters among the various stakeholders will become more frequent. The discursive directions of such controversies are sobering and justify additional attention from researchers.

One troubling practice gleaned from GMO snafus has been to pre-empt conflict by constricting communication. The desire to protect patentable and profitable technologies has accelerated "global drives towards new forms of proprietary knowledge" that are difficult to regulate or control due to their confidentiality (David & Thompson, 2008, p. 114). Declaration of an emergent medical or agricultural innovation as a trade secret insulates it from well-informed public critique. Proprietary innovations are legally protected from detailed ingredient or procedural disclosures, making it more difficult for the public to access information needed to assess the potential health risks.

Ultimately any collaborative engagement with bioengineered crops must balance the need to protect against health risks with the desire to maximize the health benefits that may accrue from genetic technologies. Ventria charted its own course of innovation after its embroilment in controversies. In June 2005, after the argumentative climate in Missouri became too heated, Ventria quietly planted 75 acres of the same transgenic rice in North Carolina, where no commercial rice crops grow (Weintraub, 2005). By 2006, Northwest and Ventria had parted company. Meanwhile the North Carolina test plots still flourish, attracting little attention in a state courting biotechnology as its rescue from recession.

REFERENCES

Associated Press. (April 13, 2005). The "king of beer" comes out against genetically engineered rice. *Organic Consumers Association*. Retrieved from http://www.organicconsumers.org/ge/beer041405.cfm

Barrionuevo, A. (August 16, 2005). Can gene-altered rice help rescue the farm belt? *New York Times*. Retrieved from LexisNexis Academic database.

Baumeister, R. F., Bratslavsky, E., Finkenauer, C., & Vohs, K. D. (2001). Bad is stronger than good. *Review of General Psychology*, *5*(4), 323–370.

Berube, D. (2000). Debunking mini-max reasoning. *Contemporary Argumentation and Debate*, *21*, 53–73

Berube, D. M. (2008). Intuitive toxicology: The public perception of nanoscience. In F. Allhoff & P. Lin (Eds.), *Nanoethics: Emerging debates* (pp. 91–108). London: Springer.

Bostrom, N., & Sandberg, A. (2009). The wisdom of nature: An evolutionary heuristic for human enhancement. In J. Savulescu & N. Bostrom (Eds.), *Human enhancement* (pp. 375–416). New York: Oxford University Press.

Canon, S. (April 12, 2005). Busch to boycott state's rice if genetic alterations allowed. *Kansas City Star*. Retrieved from LexisNexis Academic database.

Carolan, M. S. (2010). *Decentering biotechnology: Assemblages built and assemblages masked.* Ashgate Publishing Company. Surrey, UK: Ashgate.

David, K., & Thompson, P. B. (2008). *What can nanotechnology learn from biotechnology? Social and ethical lessons for nanoscience from the debate over agrifood biotechnology and GMOs.* Burlington, MA: Elsevier.

Deetz, S. A., Tracy, S. J., & Simpson, J. L. (2000). *Leading organizations through transition: Communication and cultural change.* Thousand Oaks, CA: Sage.

Derby, S. L., & Keeney, R. L. (1981). Risk analysis: Understanding "how safe is safe enough?" *Risk Analysis, 1*(3), 217–234.

Different applications for genetically modified crops. Hearing before the Subcommittee on Rural Enterprises, Agriculture, and Technology of the Committee on Small Business. *House of Representatives*, 109th Cong. 1 (2005, June 29) (testimony of Scott Deeter). Retrieved from http://www.gpo.gov/fdsys/pkg/CHRG-109hhrg23179/html/CHRG-109hhrg23179.htm

Doucleff, M. (June 25, 2013). Will GMOs help protect Ugandan families against hunger? *The Salt*. Washington, DC: National Public Radio. Retrieved from http://www.npr.org/blogs/thesalt/2013/06/17/192789454/will-gmos-help-protect-ugandan-families-against-hunger?utm_medium=Email&utm_source=share&utm_campaign=

Evo, A. B. (August 16, 2005). Can gene-altered rice rescue the farm belt? *New York Times*. Retrieved from LexisNexis Academic database.

Frewer, L., Lassen, J., Kettlitz, B., Scholderer, J., Beekman, V., & Berdal, K. G. (2004). Societal aspects of genetically modified foods. *Food and Chemical Toxicology, 42*, 1181–1193.

Gardner, D. (2008). *Risk: The science and politics of fear.* Toronto: McClelland and Stewart.

Gross, A. G. (1994). The roles of rhetoric in the public understanding of science. *Public Understanding of Science, 3*(1), 3–23.

Gusterson, H. (2005). Decoding the debate on "Frankenfood." In B. Hartmann, B. Subramaniam, & C. Zerner, C. (Eds.), *Making threats: Biofears and environmental anxieties* (pp. 109–133). Lanham, MD: Rowman and Littlefield.

Hollingsworth, H. (December 30, 2005). Biopharming company won't come to Northwest Missouri State. *Associated Press State and Local Wire*. Retrieved from LexisNexis Academic database.

Kahneman, D. (2011). *Thinking, fast and slow* [Kindle version]. New York: Random House. Retrieved from Amazon.com

Kasperson, J. X., Kasperson, R. E., Pidgeon, N., & Slovic, P. (2010). The social amplification of risk: Assessing fifteen years of research and theory. In P. Slovic (Ed.), *The feeling of risk: New perspectives on risk perception* (pp. 317–344). London and Washington, D.C.: Earthscan.

Keller, C., Siegrist, M., & Gutscher, H. (2006). The role of the affect and availability heuristics in risk communication. *Risk Analysis, 26*(3), 631–639.

Kim, S., Goldstein, D., Hasher, L., & Zacks, R. T. (2005). Framing effects in younger and older adults. *Journals of Gerontology: Series B: Psychological Sciences and Social Sciences, 60B*(4), P215–P218.

Lakoff, G. (2010). *Moral politics: How liberals and conservatives think* (2nd ed.). Chicago: University of Chicago Press.

Lambrecht, B. (December 2, 2004). Company's move here may reflect relaxed climate. *St. Louis Post-Dispatch*, p. B1. Retrieved from LexisNexis Academic database.

Lambrecht, B. (April 24, 2005a). Firm races against clock to plant rice in Missouri. *St. Louis Post-Dispatch*, p. B1. Retrieved from LexisNexis Academic database.

Lambrecht, B. (March 26, 2005b). GMO rice for drug firms being sought. *The Tribune* (Port St. Lucie/Fort Pierce, FL). Retrieved from LexisNexis Academic database.

Lehrer, J. (2009). *How we decide.* Boston: Houghton Mifflin.

McElroy, T., & Seta, J. J. (2003). Framing effects: An analytic–holistic perspective. *Journal of Experimental Social Psychology, 39*(6), 610–617.

Mulvaney, D., & Zivian, A. (2013). Sowing seeds of hope in California's fields of resistance to pharm rice and Frankenfish. *Journal of Political Ecology, 20*, 159–179.

Murphy, D. (2007). *Plant breeding and biotechnology: Societal context and the future of agriculture.* Cambridge, UK: Cambridge University Press.

Perelman, Ch., & Olbrechts-Tyteca, L. (1969). *The new rhetoric: A treatise on argumentation.* (J. Wilkinson & P. Weaver, Trans.). Notre Dame, IN: University of Notre Dame Press.

Pidgeon, N., & Rogers-Hayden, T. (2007). Opening up nanotechnology dialogue with the publics: Risk communication or "upstream engagement"? *Health, Risk and Society, 9*, 191–210.

Poulter, S. (March 6, 2007). The rice with human genes. *Mail Online.* Retrieved from http://www.dailymail.co.uk/news/article-440302/The-rice-human-genes.html

Powell, D., & Leiss, W. (1997). *Mad cows and mother's milk: The perils of poor risk communication.* Montreal: McGill-Queen's University Press.

Rehbinder, E., Engelhard, M., Hagen, K., Jørgensen, R. B., Pardo-Avellaneda, R., Schnieke, A., & Thiele, F. (2008). *Pharming: Promises and risks of biopharmaceuticals derived from genetically modified plants and animals*. Ethics of Science and Technology Assessment, Vol. 35. London: Springer.

Rushing, J., & Frentz, T. (1989). The Frankenstein myth in contemporary cinema. *Critical Studies in Mass Communication*, *6*(1), 61–80.

Sandman, P. M. (1993). *Responding to community outrage: Strategies for effective risk communication*. Fairfax, VA: American Industrial Hygiene Association.

Schwartzman, R., & Carlone, D. (2008). A rhetorical reconsideration of knowledge management: Discursive dynamics of nanotechnology risks. In A. Koohang, K. Harman, & J. Britz (Eds.), *Knowledge management: Foundations and principles* (pp. 1–39). Santa Rosa, CA: Informing Science Press.

Schwartzman, R., Ross, D. G., & Berube, D. M. (2011). Rhetoric and risk. *Poroi 7*(1). Retrieved from http://ir.uiowa.edu/poroi/vol7/iss1/9

Siegrist, M., Earle, T. C., & Gutscher, H. (Eds.). (2007). Trust in risk management: *Uncertainty and scepticism in the public mind*. Sterling, VA: Earthscan.

Simon, M., Houghton, S. M., & Aquino, K. (1999). Cognitive biases, risk perception, and venture formation: How individuals decide to start companies. *Journal of Business Venturing, 15*(2), 113–134.

Sjöberg, L., & Herber, M. W. (2008). Too much trust in (social) trust? The importance of epistemic concerns and perceived antagonism. *International Journal of Global Environmental Issues*, *8*(1/2), 30-44.

Slovic, P. (Ed.). (2000). *The perception of risk*. London: Earthscan.

Slovic, P. (2007). "If I look at the mass I will never act": Psychic numbing and genocide. *Judgment and Decision Making*, *2*(2), 79–95.

Slovic, P., Finucane, M. L., Peters, E., & MacGregor, D. G. (2007). The affect heuristic. *European Journal of Operational Research*, *177*(3), 1333–1352.

Strate, L. (1991). The cultural meaning of beer commercials. In R. H. Holman & M. R. Solomon, *Advances in consumer research, vol. 18* (pp. 115–119). Provo, UT: Association for Consumer Research.

Tversky, A., & Kahneman, D. (1973). Availability: A heuristic for judging frequency and probability. *Cognitive Psychology*, *5*(2), 207–232.

Tversky, A., & Kahneman D. (1981). The framing of decisions and the psychology of choice. *Science*, *211*(4481), 453–458.

Vedantam, S. (2010). *The hidden brain*. New York: Spiegel and Grau.

Ventria Bioscience response. (March 22, 2005). *Delta Farm Press*. Retrieved from http://www.deltafarmpress.com/ar/050322-ventria-pharmrice2/index.html

Weasel, L. H. (2009). *Food fray: Inside the controversy over genetically modified food*. New York: Amacom.

Weintraub, A. (July 31, 2005). What's so scary about rice? *Bloomberg Businessweek Magazine*. Retrieved from http://www.businessweek.com/stories/2005-07-31/whats-so-scary-about-rice

Whale, J. (Director). (1931). *Frankenstein* [Film]. Universal City, CA: Universal Studios.

Wynne, B. (2001): Creating public alienation: Expert cultures of risk and ethics on GMOs. *Science as Culture, 10*(4), 445–481.

Yount, L. (2008). *Biotechnology and genetic engineering* (3rd ed.). New York: Facts on File.

Zinken, J., Hellsten, I., & Nerlich, B. (2008). Discourse metaphors. In R. M. Frank, R. Dirven, T. Ziemke, & E. Bernárdez (Eds.), *Body, language, and mind. Volume 2: Sociocultural situatedness* (pp. 363–386). Berlin: Mouton de Gruyter.

Chapter 13:

Using the right cues: Directions and implications for communication of health related information through social media

Patric R. Spence
University of Kentucky

Kenneth A. Lachlan
University of Massachusetts Boston

Xialing Lin
University of Kentucky

INTRODUCTION

As technology continues to evolve so too must communicators using technology. This is particularly relevant for the broad area of healthcare. However, healthcare organizations have been slower to adopt social media than other business organizations (GIEHP, 2010). Although many organizations may use new media for goals related to professional collaboration, marketing, workforce recruitment, and brand management, health related information seekers may be turning to these sites for health education, wellness, care management, or information on any number of health care issues. Therefore the correct adoption and use of new media, specifically social media should be of concern to healthcare organizations attempting to communicate to stakeholders.

As Hollan and Stornetta (1992) note, new media can facilitate communicative goals in ways not possible in face-to-face communication, by providing additional peripheral cues. When health concerns manifest, individuals seek health related information in a number of ways and look for information about a number of health related issues. This idea of health information seeking is defined as the search for messages that help "to reduce uncertainty regarding health status" and "construct a social and personal (cognitive) sense of health" (Tardy & Hale, 1998) addressing both active and passive information acquisition. Moreover it suggests that people can seek information about health related information from a variety of sources. It is estimated that about 113 million Americans, (accounting for 80% of American Internet users) have used online resources to obtain health related information (Fox, 2006). As social media is gaining popularity as a means of medical and health related information seeking, the ways in which people make judgments about the information they obtain is of specific importance. One area for health related organizations to be mindful of is the cues provided by the media itself.

A substantial body of research promotes the notion that online channel technologies can offer more information than traditional media (e.g., Cassell, Jackson, & Cheuvront, 1998; Neuhauser & Kreps, 2003; Noar, Clark, Cole, & Lustria, 2006; Street & Rimal, 1997). When comparing several media types on a variety of factors, Street and Rimal (1997) reported that new media scored "high" on features including interactivity, sensory vividness, networkability, and modifiability, whereas traditional media scored lower on the same attributes. In the realm of social media, Social Information Processing Theory (SIPT; Walther, 1992) provides a widely accepted approach to explain the effects of communication among individuals in mediated environments. SIPT posits that online communication can convey affective information and relational communication, despite the reduced availability of nonverbal cues; this notion should also be applied in online health messages.

One key assumption of SIPT is that individuals have similar offline and online goals, including impression formation and judging information. SIPT posits that in instances in which a channel does not provide familiar cues, users will make social judgments anyway, using whatever information is available. Users with sufficient cognition will tailor their messages to generate and detect health message dissemination, to identify affective information, and to manipulate emotional and cognitive perceptions (Walther, 1992). The numerous cues throughout social media can be distinguished into three sources: self-generated cues, other-generated cues, and system-generated cues (Tong, Van Der Heide, Langwell, & Walther, 2008). System-generated cues are information on a user's profile chosen by the social media system; other-generated cues are sources of information from others posted on a user's profile; and self-generated cues are fully controlled by a profile owner. Those cues given off by the environment provide a lens for people to be able to perceive underlying interaction structures indirectly (Brunswik, 1956; Gosling, Ko, Mannarelli, & Morris, 2002).

Moreover research outlines that people tend to seek the most value, such as reliability or credibility of online information, from a higher source of warranty cues; both other-generated and system-generated cues may have the highest warranting value in a social media page (Antheunis & Schouten, 2011; Walther & Parks, 2002). Individuals will adapt their perceptions based on information cues that the system generates "to achieve the same goals online as they do offline" if the social media "do not allow for the usual cues used" (Westerman et al., 2012). As a platform or broad category of media, the central tenant of Web 2.0 is embodied (the notion of harnessing collective intelligence O'Reilly & Battelle, 2009). Social media allow users to produce and disseminate content, evaluate this content, and collaborate in efforts to create better content, all with the goal of returning to a shared understanding of this content. Several popular examples of such platforms include Facebook, Twitter, YouTube, Flickr, and live journal. One area that healthcare organizations need to be aware of is how their potential stakeholders will perceive and use the organizations' social media presence.

System generated cues and credibility

Source credibility has been defined as "judgments made by a perceiver…concerning the believability of a communicator" (O'Keefe, 1990, p. 181). A significant corpus of research has aimed to define the characteristics of senders and messages that constitute source credibility (see O'Keefe, 1990 for review). Although there is still debate about the precise factor-structure of the construct, a common factor structure includes three general dimensions of perceived source credibility: expertise/competence (i. e., the degree to which a perceiver believes a sender to know the truth), trustworthiness (i. e., the degree to which a perceiver believes a sender will tell the truth as he or she knows it), and goodwill (i. e., the degree to which a perceiver believes a sender has his or her best interests at heart.) A few studies have examined the role of source credibility, social media, and health information seeking. Although a variety of information is available on Twitter, perceived source credibility is an important process to understand in learning about the usefulness of health related information.

Specifically looking at Twitter, Westerman, Spence, & Van Der Heide (2012) examined the ways in which information concerning a user's position in a social network impacted others' judgments of their source credibility. This was done through the manipulations of the number of followers, the number of people followed (follows), and the ratio between followers and follows. Results suggest that the number of followers a person has and the number of people a person follows affect assessments of that person's source credibility. First, the extent to which someone obtaining information from a Twitter page believes that a target is competent, and the degree to which an observer believes that a target will can be trusted, are related curvilinearly to the number of people following the profile. In this pattern, too few or too many followers actually make a Twitter user less believable. In addition, Westerman, et al. (2012) found that trustworthiness and competence were curvillinearly related to the number of people a Twitter profile owner follows such that following too few or too many people causes people to judge a profile owner to be less credible. Last, the authors argue that the ratio between followers and the number of people one follows affects perceptions of competence in specific subject matter. That is, if one has many followers, but does not follow many others, that person is regarded as less of an expert.

In the Westerman et al. (2012) study participants viewed one of six mock Twitter pages. The pages were constructed to appear as if the profile owner was attempting to disseminate information and recent updates about H1N1, a heath related threat that was relevant at that time. Also, the H1N1 outbreak was a health threat which could affect the college audience, making the content of the Twitter page particularly salient for members of the sample.

A second study extending that research examined the role of credibility and speed of posts to a Twitter feed. Westerman, Spence, and Van Der Heide (in press) argued that another system-generated cue that could be important is for credibility is the speed of postings or updates displayed on social media. Social media caters to information consumers who want to obtain information in real time. As Levinson (2009) has pointed out, one of Twitter's central features is message immediacy.

The Westerman et al. (In Press) study found that the speed of updates on a Twitter feed did not have a direct impact of source credibility, but rather cognitive elaboration was a mediator in the relationship between speed of updates and credibility. The updates in the study were face (less than a minute since the most recent update), medium (the most recent update was an hour), and slow (the most recent update was over posted one day previous). The results bolster Sundar's (2008) notion of the machine heuristic may which may operate in part because system generated cues can create a situation that consumers of information need to think more about, and this thinking leads to increased judgments of credibility.

More broadly the Westerman et al. (2014) results support the notion that there are cues that people attend to when making credibility judgments about information presented through social media. The speed of new technologies allow the public to obtain information faster and under circumstances that even a few years ago was virtually impossible; therefore using these system generated cues to enhance credibility can be a best practice for health communication.

The ability of system generated cues to influence credibility was also studied by Edwards, Spence, Gentile, Edwards, & Edwards (2013), with findings adding support to the studies by Westerman et al. (2012; In Press). Edwards et al. (2013) manipulated Klout scores on a Twitter page to determine the impact of Klout score on credibility. Klout is a system-generated tool for measuring an individual's online influence and is measured with three components: true reach (the number of people a user influences), amplification (the level of influence), and network impact (the influence of the user's network). Information is collected and updated daily an each morning Klout scores are updated. The scores have a range of 1–100, with a higher score indicating a higher level of influence. The study had participants view one of three conditions with either a low, medium, or high Klout score (all other information was constant). Findings suggest that the Twitter feeds with a high Klout scores were perceived as higher in competence and character than feeds with lower Klout scores.

Taken together, the findings of this these three studies (Edwards et al., 2013, Westerman et al., 2012; 2014) outline the persuasiveness of system generated cues in social media, and provide several implications for use in healthcare. The findings become particularly important as the use of social media continues to rise for health related information seeking. The changing nature of information consumption has contributed to the raising concerns about the best ways various publics can obtain information. Healthcare organization that use and promote a social media page to communicate to stakeholders need to be aware that the cues provided by the medium itself will influence perceptions of credibility and potentially actions of the public. Being too slow to update social media causes credibility to decrease; a social media page may then be seen as unprofessional, untimely, or sophomoric. Therefore health related information provided on social media by organizations, muse be sent out via social media frequently enough to sustain credibility. It may be wise for organizations to have multiple individuals with access to the account and training to provide updates. Or there are several tools with bulk schedule features which will allow organizations to schedule pre-written tweets to go out at specific times of the day. This will allow the social media owner to appear active and engaged. This does not make up for the transactional benefits that social media provides and is based off from, but it can help an organization bolster credibility, especially when resources may be limited and having a person dedicated to social media is not feasible. The findings concerning the relationship between speed of updates and credibility comes back to a central point of social media; it is important to be active (Kaplan & Haenlein, 2010). Social media is designed to be social. It is about sharing and interaction; thus keeping content new, timely and engaging with stakeholders will ensure that the speed of the updates on a social media page is recent.

Moreover, several lessons can be learned and applied from the Westerman et al. (2012) findings. The results suggest a curvilinear pattern in the shape of an inverted "U" for the relationship between followers, follows, and credibility. More specifically, there may be an "unbelieveability" heuristic that leads others to doubt the credibility of those who have amassed extensive (and perhaps superfluous) social connections. It would be wise for health care organizations to work to obtain followers. Although several tactics for collecting followers exist, it may be best to try to partner with other organizations to co-promote and gain more attention. Another way to obtain followers is to be interesting (Kaplan & Haenlein, 2010). If a health care organization wants potential stakeholders to engage, participate in conversations and build a relationship, the organization must give them a reason to do so. An organization must learn what its potential stakeholders are looking for and provide it.

Credibility, User and Other Generated Cues

Hinyard and Kreuter (2007) note that "traditional persuasion research indicates a positive relationship between similarity of the source and receiver of a persuasive message and perceived expertise of the source on the persuasive topic generally facilitate persuasion (Alpert & Anderson, 1973; Rogers & Bhowmik, 1970; Simons, Berkowitz, & Moyer, 1970; Wilson & Sherrell, 1993)" (p. 785). Indeed, a rich history of media research has suggested that messages targeted at members of specific groups can be effective in promoting health behavior modification. Of particular note, ethnicity and perceived similarity has been a central component of this research. For example, Herek et al. (1998) found that African Americans evaluated AIDS educational videos as more favorable when delivered by an African American spokesperson. Anderson and McMillion (1995) similarly found that African American women responded more favorably to breast cancer messages when presented by an African American female, as opposed to males or members of other ethnic groups.

Appiah (2003; 2004) has extended this work into new media health campaigns. His 2003 study indicated that African- American respondents spent more time with health websites targeted at the black community, and were better able to recall information delivered on these sites. The 2004 study further indicated that these results were even stronger for respondents who expressed high degrees of ethnic identity. This is consistent with research suggesting that perceptions of similarity may have a similar impact on responses to computer mediated interactions. Behrend and Thompson (2011) found that those who perceived computer mediated agents as similar in appearance and behavior learned more through online training programs. Nass, Moon, Fogg,

Reeves, and Dryer (1995) also found greater user satisfaction with computer mediated characters who appeared to match the personality of the user, while Nass and Lee (2001) reported similar findings for both perceptions of personality type and vocal matching between avatar and user.

Moreover, the findings reported by Appiah (2004) lead one to consider the role of ethnic identity in these processes. Past studies have suggested that self-perception is a key component of the notion of ethnicity (Turner, Hogg, Oakes, Reicher, & Blackwell, 1987). Through ethnic identity, individuals form a sense of community and connectedness through common ideas and behaviors. This self-categorization carries with it a number of assumptions. First, that an individual self-identifying with a specific ethnicity can express themself (Yogeeswaran, Dasgupta, Adelman, Eccleston, & Parker, 2011), making this identity clear to the public. Second, it is assumed that a person with high ethnic identity will express a sense of belonging to the community (Phinney, 1990).

When applied to social media environments, ethnicity can be viewed in a way as a sort of impression management and can be communicated several ways, but most often through user generated cues. Other generated cues however, can be used to bolster and reinforce perceptions of ethnic identity and attachment (Gosling et al., 2002). This would be consistent with Walther and Parks' (2002) "warranting hypothesis," which states that other generated cues are typically judged as more credible and reliable since they are not the product of the individual under scrutiny. Warranting likely plays a critical role in evaluating personal characteristics. Several experiments have examined the impact of other-generated cues on impression formation, and uniformly indicate that other-generated information that an individual is attractive leads to higher impressions of both physical and social attractiveness, reliability, and task attractiveness (Walther, Van Der Heide, Hamel, & Shulman, 2009; Walther, Van Der Heide, Kim, Westerman, & Tong, 2008).

Spence, Lachlan, Westerman, and Spates (2013) examined the impact of user generated cues, and the role of ethnicity in perceptions of the credibility of people delivering health messages. Examining health related content on Facebook, the authors found that African American respondents indicated very high source credibility appraisals when interacting with Caucasian avatars offering formation regarding heart disease. The authors offer that there may be a kind of expectation violation, whereby a message targeted at the African American community may be seen as more genuine when delivered by a Caucasian spokesperson, because this is unexpected and indicative of a level of genuine concern. The authors also offer that the role of ethnic identity should be examined given past research suggesting that African Americans would favorably to spokespersons with high ethnic identity.

In order to further explore this, another research team replicated the study, but this time manipulated the self-expressed ethnic identity of the African American avatar through either user or other generated cues on Facebook (Spence, Lachlan, Spates, & Lin, 2012; Spence, Lachlan, Spates, Lin, Shelton & Gentile, 2013). The results indicated that that African American avatars with high ethnic identity were in fact found more credible by African American respondents. Alternately, Caucasian respondents reported the highest levels of perceived credibility for African American spokespersons with low ethnic identity.

The authors this time offer that the use of high ethnic identity may push audience members to the margins of perceived opinion, and that high levels of ethnic identity in African American avatars may evoke negative stereotypes and biases among Caucasian audiences. While Caucasian respondents may attempt to outwardly indicate that that they are unbiased, unconscious attitudes and beliefs may rise to the surface when making abstract evaluations of credibility and intent. This finding is consistent with past research indicating that patients hold higher opinions of Caucasian doctors than those of other ethnicities (Corbie-Smith, Thomas, Williams, & Moody-Ayers, 1999). It is also consistent with research concerning the expression of ethnic identity among both Caucasian and African American individuals. Past research offers evidence that Caucasians may be less likely to identify with minorities (non-White) when those individuals publically express their ethnic identity (Yogeeswaran et al., 2011). This data also indicates that as others indicate more ethic identity, Caucasians are less likely to accept those individuals as members of mainstream culture.

The authors also offer that issue involvement may be a key moderator to consider. In this particular study, the health messages in question were related to Lyme disease, in a deliberate attempt to use a stimulus that was not particularly germane to either the Caucasian or African American community. They add that the findings of the previous study had substantially different responses and that the results of responses to Caucasian and African American avatars may be more predictable when issue involvement is fairly benign.

Another contributing factor to the observed differences is a lack of cultural transcendence and willingness to interact with others (see Hendrix, 1997). When Caucasians are unfamiliar with other cultures or have had limited interactions with members of said cultures, lower credibility may be ascribed to an unfamiliar individual, particularly when a high degree of ethnic identity is outwardly expressed.

Taken together, the findings of this these three studies (Spence et al., 2013; Spence et al., 2013; Spence et al., 2013) outline the persuasiveness of user and other generated cues in social media, and provide several implications for use in healthcare. The findings support the need to design messages targeted at the audience in question. In the noted studies (Spence et al., 2013; Spence et al., 2013), all respondents indicated concern for the health risk in question that was well above the midpoint of the scale. In other words, targeting a health message using underrepresented spokespersons seemed to be somewhat effective in inducing risk awareness among the audience members, regardless of the perceptions of spokesperson's credibility or their own ethnicity. Communicating these issues with the use of other or user generated cues is effective.

However, the findings become particularly important as the use of social media continues to rise for health related information seeking. Source credibility and persuasiveness can be bolstered through cues from the user or others. Thus healthcare organizations should be mindful of this and use appropriate cues to bolster the message. If healthcare organizations desire potential stakeholders to be active information consumers engaged in the healthcare dialogue, the organization must allow them to do so. Ensuring potential stakeholders can post online comments and respond to the comments provided by the organization goes a long way in establishing credibility and trust. The organization then must work to ensure the other generated cues and user generated cues support each other and the message.

Contending with other sources

Finally, the continued growth of social media has meant that information consumers are now far less beholden to what passes through traditional gatekeepers. As stated earlier, social media is built upon the concept of Web 2.0, which was developed upon the notion of harnessing collective intelligence to allow users to create content, discuss that content, and collaborate to create better content (O'Reilly & Battelle, 2009). With advances in new media and technology, information consumers may now bypass traditional gatekeepers altogether and turn directly to primary information sources, many of whom are information consumers themselves. Because information provided in social media channels has the ability to circumvent traditional gatekeeping, consumers become more responsible for making decisions concerning the accuracy of information they find online (Kovach & Rosenstiel, 1999). This change has created a shift from the traditional notion of "gatekeeping" to what Bruns (2008) has referred to as "gatewatching." Gatewatchers are unable to control the gates through which information passes, but instead keep a constant eye at the gates, and pass what flows through those gates onto others who then make the choice about the topic relevance and usefulness. Gatewatchers fundamentally promote or diffuse information by making sources or stories known to others in the new media environment. Rather than publishing unique information, they make others' information known and add to it. This can be seen in social media such as Facebook or Twitter through the reposting and sharing of links. However, now that information consumers have more responsibility to determine the veracity of information provided, healthcare organizations also have a added responsibility to ensure that their message are represented and to promote a sense of credibility that information consumers perceive.

The gatewatching process involves the promotion of user generated and other generated cues, and in some instances these individuals can be through of as opinion leaders (Rogers, 2010). Identifying these potential partners and making them part of the dialogue can also bolster credibility for the message and help the healthcare organization promote its message. As potential sources of information expand, healthcare organizations must consider how to partner with others to promote the common goal. With increases in technology organizations must be mindful not to try to dominate or "win" a conversation in new media environments, but rather how to increase reach and influence the direction of communication.

REFERENCES

Alpert, M.I., & Anderson, W.T. (1973). Optimal heterophily and communication effectiveness: Some empirical findings. *Journal of Communication*, *23*, 328–343.

Anderson, R.B., & McMillion, P. Y. (1995). Effects of similar and diversified modeling on African American women's efficacy expectations and intentions to perform breast self-examination. *Health Communication*, *7*, 327–343.

Appiah, O. (2004). Effects of ethnic identification on web browsers attitudes toward, and navigational patterns on, race-targeted Sites. *Communication Research*, *31*(3), 312–337.

Appiah, O. (2003). Americans online: Differences in surfing and evaluating race-targeted web sites by Black and White users. *Journal of Broadcasting and Electronic Media*, *47*(4), 534–552.

Antheunis, M. L., & Schouten, A. P. (2011). The effects of other-generated and system-generated cues on adolescents' perceived attractiveness on social network sites. *Journal of Computer-Mediated Communication*, *16*, 391–406

Behrend, T. S., & Thompson, L., F. (2011). Similarity effects in online training: Effects with computerized trainer agents. *Computers in Human Behavior*, *27*, 1201–1206.

Bruns, A. (2008). The active audience: Transforming journalism from gatekeeping to gate-watching. In C. Paterson & D. Domingo (Eds.) *Making online news: The ethnography of new media production*. New York: Peter Lang.

Brunswik, E. (1956). *Perception and the representative design of psychological experiments*. Berkeley: University of California Press.

Cassell, M. M., Jackson, C., & Cheuvront, B. (1998). Health communication on the Internet: An effective channel for health behavior change? *Journal of Health Communication*, *3*, 71–79.

Corbie-Smith, G., Thomas, S.B., Williams, M.V., & Moody-Ayers, S. (1999). Attitudes and beliefs of African Americans toward participation in medical research. *Journal of General Internal Medicine*, *284*, 567–546.

Global Institute for Emerging Healthcare Practices (2010). *Should healthcare organizations usesocial media?* Retrieved May 16 2013 from http://assets1.csc.com/health_services/down loads/CSC_Should_Healthcare_Organizations_Use_Social_Media.pdf

Edwards, C., Spence, P. R., Gentile, C. J., Edwards, A., & Edwards, A. (2013) How much Klout do you have. . . A test of system generated cues on source credibility. *Computers in Human Behavior*, *29*, A12–16. doi: 10.1016/j.chb.2012.12.034

Fox, S. (2006). Online health search 2006. Pew Internet and American Life Project. Retrieved From http://www.pewinternet.org/~/media//Files/Reports/2006/PIP_Online_Health_2006.pdf.pdf

Gosling, S. D., Ko, S. J., Mannarelli, T., & Morris, M. E. (2002). A room with a cue: Personality judgments based on offices and bedrooms. *Journal of Personality and Social Psychology*, *82*, 379 –398.

Hendrix, K. (1997). Student perceptions of verbal nonverbal cues leading to images of black and white professor credibility. *Howard Journal of Communications, 8* (3), 251–273.

Herek, G.M., Gillis, J., Glunt, E.K., Lewis, J., Welton, D., & Capitanio, J.P. (1998). Culturally sensitive AIDS educational videos for African American audiences: Effects of source, message, receiver, and context. *American Journal of Community Psychology, 26* (5), 705–743. doi:10.1023/A:1022157914906

Hinyard, L. J., & Kreuter, M. W. (2007). Using narrative communication as a tool for health behavior change: A conceptual, theoretical, and empirical overview. *Health Education and Behavior, 34* (5), 777–792.

Hollan, J., & Stornetta, S. (1992). Beyond being there. In P. Bauersfeld, J. Bennett, & G. Lynch (Eds.), CHI '92 conference proceedings: *ACM conference on human factors in computing systems* (pp. 119–125). New York: Association for Computing Machinery.

Kaplan, A. M., & Haenlein, M. (2010). Users of the world, unite! The challenges and opportunities of social media. *Business Horizons, 53*, 59–68.

Kovach, B., & Rosenstiel, T. (1999). *Warp speed: America in the age of mixed media*. New York: Century Foundation Press.

Levinson, P. (2009). *New new media*. Boston, MA: Allyn and Bacon.

Nass, C., Moon, Y., Fogg, B. J., Reeves, B., & Dryer, D. C. (1995). Can computer personalities be human personalities? *International Journal of Human-Computer Studies, 43*, 223–239.

Nass, C., & Lee, K. M. (2001). Does computer-synthesized speech manifest personality? Experimental tests of recognition, similarity-attraction, and consistency-attraction. *Journal of Experimental Psychology: Applied, 7*(3), 171–181. doi:10.1037/1076-898X.7.3.171

Neuhauser, L., & Kreps, G. L. (2003). Rethinking communication in the e-health area. *Journal of Health Psychology, 8*, 7–22.

Noar, S. M., Carlyle, K., & Cole, C. (2006). Why communication is crucial: Meta-analysis of the relationship between safer sexual communication and condom use. *Journal of Health Communication, 11*, 365–390.

O'Keefe, D. J. (1990). *Persuasion: Theory and research.* Thousand Oaks, CA: Sage.

O'Reilly, T., & Battelle, J. (2009). *Web squared: Web 2.0 Five years on*. Retrieved May 16, 2013 from http://assets.en.oreilly.com/1/event/28/web2009_websquared-whitepaper.pdf

Phinney, J. S. (1990). Ethnic identity in adolescence and adulthood: A review of research. *Psychological Bulletin, 108*, 499–514.

Rogers, E. M., & Bhowmik, D. K. (1970). Homophily-heterophily: Relational concepts for communication research. *Public Opinion Quarterly, 34*(4), 523–538.

Rogers, E. M. (2010). *Diffusion of innovations.* Free press.

Simons, H. W., Berkowitz, N. N., & Moyer, R. J. (1970). Similarity, credibility, and attitude change: A review and theory. *Psychological Bulletin, 73*(1), 1–16.

Spence, P. R., Lachlan, K. A., Spates, S. A., Shelton, A. K., Lin, X., & Gentile, C. J. (2013). Exploring the impact of ethnic identity through other-generated cues on perceptions of spokesperson credibility. *Computers in Human Behavior, 29*, A3–11. doi: 10.1016/j.chb.2012.12.026

Spence, P. R., Lachlan, K. A., Spates, S. A., & Lin, X. (2013) Intercultural differences in responses to health messages on social media from spokespeople with varying levels of ethnic identity. *Computers in Human Behavior, 29* (3), 1255–1259.

Spence, P. R., Lachlan, K. A., Westerman, D. K., & Spates, S. (2013). Where the gates matter less: Ethnicity and perceived source credibility in social media health messages. Howard *Journal of Communication, 24* (1), 1–16.

Street, R. L., & Rimal, R. N. (1997). Health promotion and interactive technology: A conceptual foundation. In R. L. Street, W. R. Gold, & T. Manning (Eds.), *Health promotion and interactive technology: Theoretical applications and future directions* (pp. 1–18). Mahwah, NJ: Lawrence Erlbaum Associates, Inc.

Sundar, S. S. (2008). The MAIN model: A heuristic approach to understanding technology effects on credibility. In M. J. Metzger & A. J. Flanagin (Eds.), *Digital media, youth, and credibility* (pp. 73–100). Cambridge, MA: The MIT Press.

Tardy, R. W., & Hale, C.L. (1998). Getting "plugged in": A network analysis of health-information seeking among "stay-at-home moms". *Communication Monographs, 65*, 336–57

Tong, S. T., Van Der Heide, B., Langwell, L., & Walther, J. B. (2008). Too much of a good thing? The relationship between number of friends and interpersonal impressions on Facebook. *Journal of Computer-Mediated Communication, 13*, 531-549.

Turner, J. C., Hogg, M. A., Oakes, P. J., Reicher, S. D., & Wetherell, M. S. (1987). *Rediscovering the social group: A self-categorization theory.* Oxford: Basil Blackwell

Walther, J. B. (1992). Interpersonal effects in computer-mediated interaction: A relational perspective. *Communication Research, 19*, 52–90.

Walther, J. B., & Parks, M. R. (2002). Cues filtered out, cues filtered in: Computer-mediated communication and relationships. In M. L. Knapp & J. A. Daly (Eds.), *Handbook of interpersonal communication* (3rd ed., pp. 529–563). Thousand Oaks, CA: Sage.

Walther, J. B., Van Der Heide, B., Hamel, L. M., & Shulman, H. C. (2009). Self-Generated versus other-generated statements and impressions in computer-mediated communication: A test of warranting theory using Facebook. *Communication Research, 36*(2), 229-253.

Walther, J. B., Van Der Heide, B., Kim, S. Y., Westerman, D., & Tong, S. T. (2008). The role of friends' appearance and behavior on evaluations of individuals on Facebook: Are we known by the company we keep? *Human Communication Research, 34*, 28–49.

Westerman, D. W., Spence, P. R., & Van Der Heide, B. (in press). Social media as an information source: Recency of updates and credibility of information. *Journal of Computer Mediated Communication.*

Westerman, D., Spence, P. R., & Van Der Heide, B. (2012). A social network as information: The effect of system generated reports of connectedness on credibility on Twitter. *Computers in Human Behavior, 28*(1), 199–206.

Wilson, E. J., & Sherrell, D. L. (1993). Source effects in communication and persuasion research: A meta-analysis of effect size. *Journal of the Academy of Marketing Science, 21*(2), 101–112.

Yogeeswaran, K., Dasgupta, N., Adelman, L., Eccleston, A., & Parker, M. T. (2011). To be or not to be (ethnic): Public vs. private expressions of ethnic identification differentially impact national inclusion of white and non-white groups. *Journal of Experimental Social Psychology, 47,* 908.

Chapter 14:

Toward a framework for the study of communication and ocular health and disease: Lessons from a personal narrative of vision loss

Peter M. Kellett
University of North Carolina at Greensboro

INTRODUCTION

"Going blind, especially later in life, presents one with a huge, potentially overwhelming challenge: To find a new way of living, of ordering one's world, when the old way has been destroyed" (Sacks, 2010, p. 755).

Macular degeneration and other eye diseases that negatively affect vision—particularly central visual acuity—have received little attention in communication studies. Understandably so, perhaps, given that this area of study remains primarily the bailiwick of medical and related fields (Ong & Cruz, 2012; Tombran-Tink & Barnstable, 2006; Vader, 1992). Yet vision loss and other sensory loss (particularly hearing) are a significant challenge to, and defining feature of, the human communicative experience of everyday life of many people, particularly those over 50 years of age (Ainlay, 1989; Boerner, 2012; Kleinschmidt, 1995). As many as a third of the U.S. population will experience significant vision loss after 50 years of age. As the above quote from Sacks's own account of profound vision loss illustrates, vision loss (even mild impairment) can have a deep impact on how people communicate; on their ability to participate in and maintain relationships; and on key aspects of their identity—such as their sense of self and their capacity for independent living (driving, for example). As the U.S. population continues to grow in the post 50 age group, and as visually oriented technology continues to grow in its predominance in everyday life, the ability to adapt to visual impairment as a *health communication* issue will only grow in importance. As such, ocular health and disease as it impacts communication ought to be further developed as an area of interest and concern to health communication researchers and practitioners.

On the other side of this health communication issue, we have spent little time researching the relationship between communication and the promotion and maximization of ocular health among our population (Wason & McMillen, 1998). How people can protect and maintain healthy eyes, and related vision, as well as minimize the impact of risk factors so that the chances and dangers of vision loss are minimized later in life, are important concerns not just to health care professionals but also to the health communication field.

In order to anchor these issues of communication and vision loss in lived experience, this chapter, first, presents a concise personal narrative account of my own experience of vision loss and progressive visual impairment (see also Putnam, 1974; Sacks, 2010). The personal narrative of the first year of the experience engages the reader with a vivid first-hand account of the communication and identity challenges, everyday struggles and miscommunications, and the adaptations involved in living through the early stages of vision loss/impairment.

Then, the themes and questions that emerge from my personal narrative are used to promote our understanding of the relationship of vision loss to ocular health and related communication strategies. In short, we explicate what can be learned from my own personal narrative towards developing guidelines and strategies for promoting ocular health, and for understanding and relating to others living with vision loss.

Finally, the implications for developing a framework for studying vision, vision loss, eye health and its relationship to communication are explored, and a communication framework for generating further research questions is created. The chapter carefully connects to existing work in health communication, and other fields, as well as offers points of departure to suggest the development of new and compelling avenues of scholarship.

Lessons from a Personal Narrative

(From the journal notes of Pete Kellett)

In May of 2011 I was diagnosed with cone-dystrophy—a degenerative disease affecting the photoreceptors (cones) of the retina (Trabouli, 2012). Related to this, in December of that year, I developed the additional complication of retinal edemas that caused macular degeneration (Wason & McMillen, 1998). I received a course of seven injections of Avastin into my right eye, which stabilized the decline by the middle of 2013. My left eye did not develop edemas, but both eyes have vision loss from the cone-dystrophy, and in addition my right eye has significant retinal scarring from the edemas that blurs central vision. In May of 2013, as I finish writing this chapter, I am mildly visually impaired, but am fortunately in a period of stability for both conditions. The following experiences are taken from my own personal notes on the experiences of the first year of living with retinal disease, and related vision loss. I represent the experiences chronologically as they happened, and then develop the central themes of the experience and key communication questions that emerged within each theme.

The First Year in Review—Mid May 2011 to Mid May 2012

> *"Have you ever been a sun gazer?" She asked.*
>
> *"What's that?" I responded.*
>
> *"Someone who gazes at the sun." She said, seriously and without even the slightest irony.*
>
> *(Kellett, personal journal notes)*

The above quote from my journal notes captures the poignant moment in the conversation when my optometrist first disrupted my comfortable world to indicate that something was quite wrong with my eyes—specifically my retinas. It was mid-May 2011. And what an odd moment of disruption it was. She had noticed dark "bulls-eye" circles around my optic nerve in the macula, and I suppose, had no other way of beginning the conversation. She hadn't seen this condition before in someone like me under 50 years old (48 at the time), and had no real sense of how to explain it to me. But asking me about being a "sun gazer" was the best place to begin? I had no idea what a sun gazer was until I looked it up online later. I was immediately confused, worried, and left wanting to know more. How bad was this news? What would it mean? Was sun exposure a factor in causing this, as her question implied? Thus, with this very odd conversation I began my journey into visual impairment with wide information gaps and uncertainties that were filling and roiling with confusion, fear, and shock. Kindly in some ways, the optometrist refused to give me a revised prescription to purchase new glasses until I had visited with an ophthalmologist they recommended, and until he indicated in writing to them that new glasses would be "worth it" for me. More fear and shock filled me and swirled in my body…"worth it"? WOW...what a turn of phrase…was I going…*blind*?

After many tests, my ophthalmologist named my condition as "Bulls-eye cone dystrophy." I wrote the name down on a notepad I had brought for note taking and committed to doing research on it. He gave the condition a positive frame—perhaps it was stable, or very slow in decline. I may have had it my whole life. It gave me some hope, and now I had a name for it. Then he told me that they did not know what caused this condition and that there was "No known treatment." These words were heavy, very heavy. They led to lots more questions in my mind but I wasn't quite sure how to formulate them or ask the doctor what this all meant. It was such an alien conversation for me. He went on to tell me that there was probably a genetic component which swung my mind to my family. Mum and dad were close to 80 years old and didn't even wear glasses. Where were the genes coming from, I wondered? How could this be called "treatment" when we were just keeping things under observation and going back in three months? When I told my dad, he was sad for me and deeply concerned but said he wasn't surprised as I had always had "bad eyes." I was shocked as I never thought of myself in this way.

I searched online for research and advice that I did not get in the health care communication. The disease was consistently described as attacking central vision—impacting detail such as face recognition and reading, and causing color blindness and light sensitivity. I told myself I must be in the very early stages as I felt ok except for night driving, and some detail vision challenges. I found research linking antioxidant rich foods to positive outcomes and followed up with some dietary changes. There were lists of "good" foods and "bad" foods in online sources and I resolved to change my diet in that direction. Blood pressure could be a factor so I stepped up workouts. Some, none, or all of this might help but I had no way of knowing, so I did what I could. I found research about stem cell treatment that was promising, but that also pointed out the enormous expense and early stages of that possible treatment. Talking to a friend with other health problems he told me that everything you need is always five years away. The phrase stuck with me. He had a point and, darkly, my mind wandered to the fact that we could blow the world up several times over, but not cure a simple eye condition. Irony helped for brief bursts.

That summer I found myself hanging onto, and reveling in, activities that were important to me. Gardening, lapidary-arts work (gem stone cutting which requires good vision), playing music, and reading took on a new poignancy as I didn't know when any of them would change and be a struggle. How many years would I be able to see the flowers bloom and the fruit trees I had planted fruit were questions that filled me with sadness. I also met Hema, my future wife, and jumped into a relationship. I found myself wondering how long I would be able to see her face before going blind, although I don't think I voiced these questions to her in the first year together. Dramatic and gloomy reactions perhaps, but I had no way of knowing the answers. As the relationship progressed, Hema began to move things around in the kitchen—symbolically inserting herself deeper into my life--and I found myself angry at the changes. Part loss of bachelor routine and part protection of having things in familiar places, the conflicts were minor but curious in that I could still see well. One evening we watched a documentary about a blind American mountaineer who took children climbing in Tibet (a place where blindness is often seen as a curse). He was inspiring, and I realized I should stop feeling sorry for myself. He also said he liked things in specific places, and—affirming my new preoccupation—momentarily I felt a strong connection to him.

I wondered how long I would be able to read, and when should I switch to audio books. I began zooming to 200% on my computer but noted, ironically, that the zoom command itself doesn't zoom. I also noticed many websites for visual aid products were difficult to read and rarely were designed for the people who needed the products. Something I had never noticed before is that the world is designed by people with a "normal" vision range. In late summer I remember saying out loud while alone, "Today I can drive, today I can read, today I can see my sweetheart's face." I was reminding myself to focus on the positive by speaking these facts into the air. My thoughts, behavior, and talk were marked by a struggle between the positive and negative—the bright and dark sides of communication.

In November, around daylight savings time change, I began to experience difficulty seeing. I was feeling nauseated one evening in PF Chang's. I had to get outside to breathe the cold air and I stared down at the ground sitting on the bench outside—taking in big lung-fulls of air. Faces on television, and in real life, began to look horribly distorted. I began averting my eyes from people because of this. I knew something was wrong but, when I called the doctor's office, I was told to wait until my appointment in December.

As the days grew shorter, I relinquished driving to Hema, especially at night. But I was a bad back seat driver and annoyed her with constant commands and sound effects that indicated I was frightened by her driving choices. She understood, thankfully. I would get angry, and shout and curse if I couldn't see the keys to punch in the code to enter Hema's apartment community. I began relying on routines for driving which sometimes annoyed Hema who liked to vary routes. I would get annoyed if Hema used my computer and didn't return to the correct zoom size. I wanted to return to the familiar, but it was slipping out of control, and I wasn't good at communicating these struggles. I felt like I needed a vision loss coach but there was nobody to help me understand what to do and how to have these new—and very alien—conversations. I wondered if I would be disabled, abandoned, even homeless, if I couldn't do my job anymore. Hema always told me not to worry, that things would be all right and I wanted to believe her. "I will be your eyes my love…" she would say to me often…"don't worry."

Just before Christmas, I dropped off some cards at the post office. As I walked outside, a man was coming in. His face appeared completely blank to me. This was the first frightening sign of this common symptom. I was stunned and found myself caught between wondering if I knew him and acting as if I was simply passing close by a friendly stranger. Billy Idol's song, "Eyes without a face" came to me later as I lay in bed and thought about this surreal moment. When faces would all be blank, and how I would adapt to this enormous disruption in one of the basics of non-verbal communication, I had no idea.

My friend Bud Goodall became a great source of supportiveness through this vision loss process as he always had been in our 20 year friendship. He was dying of pancreatic cancer and we began to have regular online conversations in which we actively supported each other (see Kellett, 2013). Here is one moment that brought me to tears:

> *Bud: "I will pray for you my friend"*
>
> *Me: "And I will pray for you"*
>
> *Bud: "We always did make a good team"*
>
> *Me: "Yes and we're still in the game…"*

I went back to my ophthalmologists on December 23rd for the check-up. Based on tests, he began injections into my right eye immediately. I remember I was the last patient there before the holidays, and I held his staff up from their office Christmas photograph and lunch. I now had macular degeneration, and I had needles going into my right eye, and had no real understanding of how this was connected to the dystrophy. Online it was listed as a "possible complication," which sounded so clinical looking at it from the existential intensity of this moment.

I bought Hema an engagement ring early in our relationship so that I could see it on her hand, and enjoy the happiness it brought to her face for as long as possible before I couldn't see it sparkle anymore. I gave it to her on Christmas Eve in front of the Christmas tree I had insisted on putting up by myself just to know I could do it.

I began to notice language use around blindness and other disabilities. It bothered me now when people used deaf, dumb, and blind as pejoratives. I began to identify with other visually impaired and disabled people in this way, as I slowly became one. I wanted to connect with others and hear their stories. I often wondered if their struggles, fears, and hopes were the same as mine, and how they coped with the changes in their lives.

I insisted on driving us to the beach for New Years as 2012 arrived. The medication was making a difference and I was encouraged and wanted to drive the familiar route to Wilmington, NC. We got up at dawn and, bundled up, we photographed the sunrise over the ocean every minute until it was up—reveling in the visual experience of the colors and light of the emerging first sun of the new year. We were hopeful of my having good sight for a long time to come, but on that trip we began to make something like a bucket-list of the visual experiences we might share as if things might degenerate sooner rather than later. After all, they could degenerate quickly. The visual (ocular) began to be tied to our shared dreams in interesting ways. We would visit our respective homelands of England and India and see where we both were born, where we grew up, where went to school—see the places and people that were formative for us. This felt like a healthy way of engaging with the experience and building it into a positive and happy life narrative that worked for both of us.

Communicating with family about my condition was interesting and revelatory. Dad said several times, "I'd give you one of mine (eyes) if I could, son." This was poignant as well as incredible touching. I had never experienced him talking to me on quite this emotional level before. It was a dramatic change. Yet, he has told me several times that, as a baby twin, he took charge of taking care of me while mum focused on my brother. He was feeling my struggle deeply. My mother was concerned but didn't say much except to empathize about medications and side-effects, something that was central to her world of daily pains and struggles with arthritis. My twin brother didn't say much either, and yet in the second year of the experience he began to have similar problems, signaling a genetic origin. I committed to being there for him on his (perhaps parallel) journey—advising and encouraging in a way I never could when he had cancer, twice, several years before. I just didn't know what to say then. Now I could empathize, and be supportive. My younger and closest brother kept in touch on the condition but I knew he couldn't relate to it. My older brother simply gave me brief, big brotherly advice, and told me to push for the best treatment possible and I never heard from him on the topic again.

I reconnected with a blind student—Kolby—from a semester ago. We got together and walked around campus with Sunny her dog, catching up. She was concerned and interested in my experience and my story so far. She announced that she wanted to be "captain of my support team!" She was an inspiration to me and many others. She was totally blind, and made it through college full of positivity and finished with a 4.0 GPA. Her positive energy in the face of struggle helped to keep me going.

There were many ups and downs. After my second injection at the end of January I had bad side effects including a dramatically bloodshot eye, choking feelings from anaphylaxis which lasted for a few days, and the feeling of having the flu. Hema was upset and kept saying over and over, "I just want you to be all right, I just want you to be all right." I didn't know what to say. I wanted to be all right but I knew I wasn't. She said I looked "pitiful." The time immediately after this injection was a low point emotionally. However, the next morning I could see the date window on my watch well enough to know it was off by a day, and probably had been for a while! It filled me with hope. I emailed friends Art and Steve saying, "Ain't hope grand!" Steve wrote back saying, "Yes, hope is grand. I can't imagine life without it." We began to freely share medical updates among the three of us—supporting and celebrating each other with health at the center of our talk when the times arose. Steve joked that such talk among people over 50 was known as an "organ recital"! These, and so many other positive communication moments, spurred me to design and teach a course in Fall 2012, called "Positive Communication" in which I was able, in part, to talk about the powerful impact of relational communication in helping me through the difficult experiences. It was a successful course and a new area of teaching and scholarly interest for me. Again I wanted to turn the experience into something positive—something healthy.

Having said this about being positive, I still struggled with moments of deep disappointment and despair that I kept private. I remember hugging a pillow one night as the dark possibilities struck me and just said over and over to myself, "Oh no! Oh no! Oh no!...Not knowing why I was experiencing this, and not knowing how it would progress, and what that would mean for me were gaps that continued to dig and scratch at my mind. I also struggled with outbursts of anger when I couldn't see something well enough to complete a previously simple task. I remember going into a rage while online trying to book a hotel room in England. The dates would not go in the boxes. I stormed away cursing, which surprised even me. Hema was scared by my anger. It turns out I was putting the dates in in the U.S. order—month then day, instead of day then month as in the U.K. I was punching in dates that had already passed! Perhaps there is a fruitful link to the notion of emotional intelligence for those experiencing sensory loss that is worth researching here, I wondered in retrospect? I just didn't know how to control or express the incredibly difficult emotions and things I was experiencing.

Sharing with others, and how to share, was a prominent decision by spring 2012. Some I told, such as family and close friends. People varied enormously in their level of empathy and their ability to communicate about my condition. Some worked in much needed humor to our talk. Jon, a friend of mine, had been out of the country for a while. He emailed me to ask how my condition was progressing, but added a welcome playful twist. He said that if I didn't respond to the email, he would know I was no longer able to read email, and would therefore feel very bad for me! Some I didn't burden with the problem. One day my hair stylist noticed I had hacked a piece of hair while trimming sideburns a few days before. She was laughing at me. I didn't want to embarrass her by saying I was visually impaired so missed the mark with the trimmers! These conversations and many like them led me to begin thinking about how health communication is as much an issue of conversational competence as anything. Knowing how to have conversations about health is a crucial communication skill. I noted to myself that I would come back to this notion and write about it sometime.

At the end of this first year, after five injections, my vision loss had begun to stabilize. I craved connection with others with similar experiences. I talked with my ophthalmologist about doing some research using his patient list which consisted of many people just like me. He was agreeable. I was excited at the prospect of connecting with others. I began to research historical and famous people who had lived with these diseases. Standing out for me were Stephen King the contemporary writer and painter Edgar Degas. On losing some of his central vision, King's take on it was that, as a writer, and as a man, he values peripheral vision more than central. This was definitely a positive and pithy take on it. Edgar Degas the French painter suffered the same diseases I did. His painting changed dramatically when he developed vision loss. Without the same treatment I have now, he had lost much of his vision by my age. As a result, however, he became a prominent member of the impressionist movement. He lamented his vision loss bitterly but it had, ironically, become part of his success. I bought a print of his painting, "Peasant girls bathing in the sea at dusk" because it captures something about vision loss for me. It is painted at dusk when it is more comfortable to see outside without the bright sun of day. It captures the beauty of life and human movement even through the low detail impressionist strokes of a visually impaired person. It hangs just above my computer in the office where I write. I look at it often and draw inspiration from the fruits of his struggle. He found a way to express himself—to communicate, and so would I in my own albeit much less famous way.

Towards the end of the first year, just before "back to school" advertisements heralded fall classes I began to wonder what teaching would be like if I were to become blind. The small gestures, inside jokes, connections made through eye contact, that formed the fabric of relating to students, would be wiped away. I started to wonder about when and how I would tell students about my visual impairments and what it would mean for them in terms of how they would have to adapt to make our relationship effective. My first attempts were clumsy and ineffective as they were when I was learning how to tell friends and colleagues. In the fall of 2013, when I returned to teaching after a research leave, I remember one day walking into a chair close to the front of class and hearing them laugh at my blundering into the object they could clearly see. I took the opportunity and told them it was because I was visually impaired and they laughed again—thinking I was joking. The communicative moment failed and I knew I would have to develop better ways of talking to people about my issues.

Fast forward to the second year of my vision loss experience, I reached a point where I simply described my condition to a class and outlined what it meant in terms of my limitations and things they would need to know. They were shocked, but more easily understood some of the things I did in class. I would control the lighting, and had other peculiarities like sometimes blanking out as I read the roll to take attendance. I would need to pause until my vision clunked back into focus, and they should not be alarmed or uncomfortable at such a momentary pause and silence. Sometimes I would have to look just over someone's face to see them clearly. I was searching for a bit of good retina to focus on the face details but they wouldn't know this unless I told them. I would walk into things and sometimes knock things over. I would eventually insist on going paperless by spring 2013 so I could read everything on screen. They reacted positively to this as it cut down on printing costs and meant they didn't have to make a special trip to the office to drop off papers.

I knew when I returned to teaching that fall I had to become proactive in avoiding and averting misunderstandings associated with non-verbal impacts of my vision loss. Specifically, by spring 2013 I would tell classes that if I saw them outside of their familiar spots in class—walking down the corridor for example, that I may not recognize them as their faces may appear blank to me. I had to be careful to ask them not to misinterpret my lack of recognition of them as this was easily done. Was I being standoffish or was I ignoring them? No, I couldn't see them! I began asking them to initiate hello's when passing by, and to announce who they were if standing in my doorway waiting for me to invite them in. Some took note and some let it brush by them without taking much notice. Some, I remember, did not shift their interpretive frameworks and still assumed I was completely "normal." I remember telling one student from a previous semester in May 2013 just before graduation when she came by to say goodbye that I hadn't forgotten who she was, I just couldn't see her face as she stood in the doorway. She came into my office assured that I knew her and appreciated her coming by. She had forgotten my explanations from when she was in my class, but it was ok; I understood that generalizing things from one class to somewhere else is often a challenge. How easy it is to miscommunicate and misunderstand the visual. These conversations began clumsily, but I got better at scripting and performing them, and the clearer I was the better students got at understanding what I was telling them and adapting to my impairment. Through trial and error I got better at communicating about my vision health.

Currently, I am beginning notes on my third year of communicative adaptations to vision loss and the health communication challenges and opportunities it brings. I openly welcome discussion of the topic of my personal experiences, and am busy working on publications and papers around this topic. The following issues and framework are central to organizing my current and future work.

Central Themes and Emerging Health Communication Questions

From this abbreviated account of one year of vision loss from diagnosis to end of the first year we draw the following main narrative themes, and list some of the key questions that we will use to build a scholarly agenda around communication, vision, and vision loss.

New communicative scripts: Teaching and learning from communication and miscommunication

> What impact does vision loss have on everyday communication and on miscommunication?

How are miscommunications opportunities for health communication and learning?

What are effective strategies for explaining visual impairments to others and necessary accommodations from others?

What new ways of communicating are necessary for effective adaptation and everyday healthy functioning?

Narrating and making sense of the experience of vision loss

What are "healthy" ways of understanding and narrating vision loss?

What patient narratives (their storying of past, present, and future) predict effective adaptations to, and understanding of, vision loss?

How are shifts in identity related to the process of vision loss, and what are "healthy" ways to manage and communicate about identity adaptations?

Learning and adapting

How can people beginning to lose vision learn from the narratives and lives of others who have experienced vision loss (historical, inspirational, and the everyday)?

How can poignant moments of communication and change be sources of learning about health communication?

How can the struggles, shock, emotional difficulties, and other adaptive issues be sources of learning about vision loss and health communication?

Embracing positive communication

What forms of supportive communication, listening, empathy, and so on, are important for people experiencing vision loss?

How are humor and playfulness an important role in managing vision loss experiences and challenges?

What are "positive" and "negative" patterns of talking about vision loss for patients, and what do these tendencies impact in the experience and in relationships with others not experiencing vision loss?

Interconnections of health, family, and relational history

How can family health history and early life experiences be understood as significant to vision loss?

How do family and relational patterns and dynamics affect adaptation to and experience of vision loss?

How does vision loss change and reify family relationships?

How is one's communication about health, and specifically vision loss, dependent on the specifics of one's familial relationships prior to the health decline?

Effective communication about vision loss and implications

What are effective strategies for seeking information, questioning health care professionals, dealing with gaps in information, and understanding information as a whole?

How can critical and dialogic listening positively affect relationships to various and often competing information sources, and people during vision loss?

What are effective ways to disclose and discuss experiences and implications of vision loss with loved-ones, in the workplace, and with friends?

What conflicts are common during vision loss (intrapersonal, identity, and relational) and how can they be effectively understood and managed?

How can eye health be better promoted as a personal and public health issue?

Toward a Communication Framework for Ocular Health

The above themes and questions, derived from my own experience, provide a rich source of possibilities for research linking health communication and the experience of vision loss and ocular health promotion. More broadly, connecting the two threads of vision loss and ocular health, and bringing them into a communication centered framework requires us to have openness to forwarding several key components of a research agenda or framework.

First, and perhaps most importantly, we will need to recognize the importance of, and further develop research on, ocular health as an area of health communication. Understanding the relationship between behavior, communication, and the centrality and importance of the health and performance of our eyes is a key necessary development. Through my own experience I became acutely aware that my own field of study had little to offer in terms of theories or even case studies I could draw on for insight or comfort. I also became aware of what little information I had ever come across, except for the Occuvite television advertisement, relating to eye health as something that could have a behavioral plan or course of action. Eye health is something that we can talk about, be mindful of, and strategic about promoting (Kitchen, 2007). These gaps are, I believe, a significant health communication opportunity.

Second, we will need to embrace more longitudinal and life-span approaches to studying eye health and communication. Genetics and early life experiences can have profound effects on vision loss and ocular health later in life. Understanding the relationship between genetic factors and the habits of younger people (sun related behavior, diet, smoking, and other risk factor awareness), and the personal and collective experiences of older people struggling with vision loss as it connects to other factors (diabetes, high blood pressure, and others), will both need to be part of the framework of study (Fuchs &Packer, 2001).

As I struggled to piece together the clues and develop at least a working narrative of how my disease came about, and how my own behaviors and health choices might have combined with genetic factor, I began to realize that a clear, explanatory account was elusive, perhaps even mythical. But I still needed and desired a story of some kind that held together. I also began to wonder how my later years would be affected, and what I could learn from the experiences of others. Again, I believe these narrative and experiential dimensions to be significant health communication scholarship opportunities.

Third, we will need to embrace the fact that many people operate in their everyday lives with some degree of sensory loss. Much of our research in communication studies assumes, largely unproblematically, that everyone operates with five full or "perfect" senses. This is not true for many people. In fact, it would be interesting to consider how everyday life is often about adapting to and working around the fact that people do not have five fully functioning senses. Communication theory ought to engage with this facticity, and we ought to be open to engaging with experiences of vision loss through a variety of methods, including personal narrative, auto-ethnographic, qualitative interviewing and surveys, as well as valuable quantitative and behavioral approaches. Visual impairment can have a profound impact on many aspects of our communicative lives, and the qualitative and personal experience of adapting to and living around such health problems is a rich area of possible research, and valuable insight (Kellett, 2013).

Finally, in health communication we will need to embrace more of a connection to the study of impairments and to relevant areas of disability studies. Encouragingly, the study of disabilities as they pertain to communication is now an official NCA caucus, and rich interconnections with research and theory building around impairments and disabilities are emerging. Among our student demographic, there are fruitful areas of research around the impact of learning disabilities, ADD, ADHD, bipolar conditions, emotional intelligence, and so on, on communication. Among the broader population this fruitfulness expands to include the impact of disabling sensory loss on communication. The lack of real knowledge in my workplace, among my students and colleagues, and people generally about the experience and implications of visual impairment for communication was, well…eye opening. I was also surprised to realize that our own communication theories bore little connection to the reality of making do, of struggle, and adaptation necessary to function as a visually impaired person. Perhaps most revealing to me was my own complete lack of awareness of these gaps in our scholarship until I became a visually impaired person myself.

In conclusion, I note that I would love to have told more of my story. I would love to engage the reader with the stories of others with similar experiences. Hopefully, this brief glimpse into my personal experience is enough to engage the reader with a world we may not typically think of as one relevant to health communication. Hopefully through the questions generated we can "see" the possibilities of further engagement with this important topic, and hopefully there will be substantially more work in health communication that focuses on the eyes, their health, and impact on our communication and our lives. In closing I note that the macula—a part of the body I hadn't heard of before mine became diseased—represents only about 4% of the inner surface of the eyes, a tiny part of the body, and yet its health is central to much of how we function communicatively in our everyday lives as sighted people. This is a poignant fact about the human body, and its health, worth pondering.

REFERENCES

Ainlay, S.C. (1989). *Day brought back my night: Aging and new vision loss.* New York: Routledge.

Boerner, K., & Wang, S-W. (2012). Goals with limited vision: A qualitative study of coping with vision-related goal interference in midlife. *Clinical rehabilitation*, *26*, 1: 81–93.

Fuchs, J., & Packer, L. (2001). *Environmental stressors in health and disease.* New York: Dekker.

Kellett, P.M. (2013). *Mutually supportive communication and relational narratives: Creating connection between two friends in declining health.* Unpublished manuscript.

Kitchen, C.K. (2007). *Fact and fiction of healthy vision: Eye care for adults and children.* Westport, Conn: Praeger.

Kleinschmidt, J.J. (1995). *The impact of vision loss in the elderly.* New York: Garland.

Ong, J.M., & Cruz, L da (2012). A review and update on the current state of stem cell therapy and the retina. *British Medical Bulletin*, *102*, 1: 133–146.

Putnam, W.D. (1974). *On becoming partially sighted: A personal account of the loss of sight.* Santa Monica, CA: Rand.

Sacks, O.W. (2010). *The mind's eye.* New York: Knopf.

Tombran-Tink, J, & Barnstable, C.J. (2006). *Ocular angiogenesis: Disease mechanisms and therapeutics.* Totoura, NJ: Humana Press.

Trabouli, E.I. (2012). *Genetic disease of the eye.* New York: Oxford University Press.

Vader, L.A. (1992). Vision and vision loss. *The nursing clinics of North America*, *27*, 3: 705–714.

Wason, B., & McMillen, J.J. (1998). *Macular degeneration: Living positively with vision loss.* Alameda, CA: Hunter House.

Chapter 15:

The moderating role of empathy in patient outcomes: A proposed model to reframe the debate between biomedical and patient-centered approaches

Patricia E. Gettings
Purdue University

INTRODUCTION

Patient-centered approaches have taken center stage over the past 40 years and have nearly replaced traditional biomedical approaches in representing the ideal form of physician-patient interaction (Mead & Bower, 2000). These patient-centered approaches have been linked to a host of positive outcomes including improved recovery from symptoms (e.g., Stewart et al., 2000), patient satisfaction (e.g., Roter, 1989), physician satisfaction (Roter, Steward, Putnam, Lipkin, Stiles, & Inui, 1997), and others. As further support of their popularity, many medical education organizations now include patient-centeredness in their learning objectives or unit descriptions. For example, the Accreditation Council for Graduate Medical Education defined internal medicine as "the discipline encompassing the study and practice of patient-centered care from adolescence to old age, during health and all stages of illness" (ACGME, 2005, p. 1).

However, patient-centered approaches to physician-patient interaction are not without critics. Scholars have issued cautions warning against the unquestioning acceptance of such models as superior to biomedical approaches due to issues such as the lack of conceptual clarity surrounding the term and, thus, its measurement (Mead & Bower, 2000), a lack of research focused on the actual communicative qualities of the interactions (Elwyn, Edwards, Kinnersley, & Grol, 2000), and a tendency to gloss over the complexities of both the medical context and the patients themselves in empirical work (e.g., Levinson & Chaumeton, 1999). Although proponents of biomedical models typically agree with some aspects of patient-centered approaches, they are hesitant to abandon traditional approaches so readily.

Careful analysis of the debate between these two approaches to medical care, however, reveals that such high-level discussion about overarching medical philosophies overlooks significant interpersonal factors that might serve as points of similarity and impact patient outcomes. Empathy is one such factor that may moderate the link between physician-patient interaction and outcomes, ultimately playing a big role in a host of critical patient outcomes (e.g., satisfaction, likelihood to follow health advice of physician). And, since biomedical and patient-centered approaches to physician-patient interaction conceptualize empathy differently, any attempts at synthesis must be able to account for these differences.

Given these broad propositions, the goal of this paper is to advance a tentative model that begins to reframe the debate surrounding biomedical versus patient-centered approaches to medical interactions by theorizing about the role empathy plays in moderating the link between physician-patient interactions and, ultimately, patient outcomes (see Figure 1).

In what follows, I first briefly define traditional and patient-centered approaches to patient-physician communication and review some of the critiques frequently leveled at patient-centered approaches. Next, I explicate empathy as it can be conceptualized in each of the two approaches. The remaining sections elaborate on the constructs included in the model, providing empirical and theoretical support for implied relationships. I conclude by pointing to potential limitations of the model as well as offering areas for future research directions.

Traditional versus Patient-centered Approaches to Physician-Patient Communication

The traditional approach to patient-physician interactions, often called the biomedical model, is most often associated with a focus on reducing a patient's illness and, arguably, reducing the patient herself, to a set of disease-signaling symptoms (Mead & Bower, 2000). Hence, once a physician is able to accurately identify an illness she can go about applying appropriate treatments and/or therapies in an effort to improve the patient's medical condition, ideally returning him to a "normal" or original state. Sometimes conceptualized as paternalistic in nature, the focus in this approach is on the highly knowledgeable physician transmitting information to a relatively naïve patient (Coulter, 1999). In sum, biomedical approaches are characterized by an overall emphasis on biomedical issues, physician control over much of the interaction and decisions, and an assumption of passivity and/or compliance on the part of the patient (Haan, 1979; Smith & Pettegrew, 1986).

In contrast to traditional biomedical approaches, patient-centered approaches refer to interactions in which there is increased focus on the physician coming to understand the whole patient (not just disease symptoms) and engaging her as an active participant in decision-making processes. In other words, the interaction should take on a sense of "partnership" between physician and patient (Coulter, 1999, p.719). Thus, patient-centered models reflect more power-sharing between the doctor and patient and presuppose that the physician is able to frame current conversations using knowledge of the patient's lifestyle, values, and understanding of his/her own health condition (Vanderford, Stein, Sheeler, & Skochelak, 2001). Various definitions have been offered within the literature. For example, Levenstein, McCracken, McWhinney, Stewart, & Brown (1986) described a patient-centered approach as one in which "the physician tries to enter the patient's world, to see the illness through the patient's eyes" (p. 25). This definition highlights the notion of the physician working with the "whole" patient—taking a more holistic account of her health. Other definitions stress the importance of patients being well-informed and making them an integral player in health decisions (e.g., Grol, de Maeseneer, Whitfield & Mokkink, 1990; Winefield, Murrell, Clifford, & Farmer, 1996).

Critiques of Patient-centered Approaches

This chapter is not the first to assert that there are shortcomings to assuming that patient-centered interactions are always the best approach with every patient in every medical encounter. Three primary critiques will be discussed here. A first critique of patient-centered approaches is that their application may be fundamentally hampered by a lack of conceptual clarity. Mead and Bower (2000), for example, argued that there is "considerable ambiguity concerning the exact meaning of the term [patient-centered] and the optimum method of measuring the process and outcomes of patient-centered care" (p. 1087). Elwyn, Edwards, Kinnersley, and Grol (2000) similarly noted that "one difficulty (among many) is that the involvement of patients in decisions has been left undefined. It is usually conceptualized as "patient-centredness," which is a broad and variably interpreted concept" (p. 892). Finally, Bensing (2000) described patient-centered medicine as a "fuzzy concept" (p. 21). He continued, "with fuzzy concept is meant a global concept, that everybody will recognize in its overall meaning, but yet can have a quite different connotation for different people when going into more detail" (p. 21). In sum, discussion and examination of patient-centered approaches is difficult because scholars are often not on the same page (or even similar pages in some accounts) when it comes to defining the term itself.

A second and related critique is that there has been little examination of the qualities of patient-centered interactions (e.g., Elwyn, Edwards, Kinnersley, & Grol, 2000). That is, from a communicative perspective, not much is known about how these dyadic interactions actually sound in practice. More often patient-centeredness is studied as if it is a monolithic concept (i.e., absent or present) than attended to as a complex, multidimensional construct. So, for example, many scales used to measure patient-centered behaviors focus solely on the actions of the physician and ignore patient responses (e.g., Langewitz, Eich, Kiss, & Wossmer, 1998; Ockene et al., 1988). Few take into account the dyadic, mutual influence processes that undoubtedly undergird physician-patient interactions.

Finally, more work is needed to examine how patient-centered approaches impact different types of patients across a range of encounters. Much of the research assumes that all patients are equally—and positively, of course—impacted by patient-centered approaches. For instance, Coulter (1999) noted that "little is known about the readiness of patients to take on decision making responsibility," indeed "some patients may not want to have an active role thrust on them" (p. 719). Rowland and Holland's (1989) research demonstrated this point by finding four types of responses from patients with breast cancer: Type 1 "You decide for me doctor"; Type 2 "I demand you do procedure X"; Type 3 "I cannot decide"; and Type 4 "Given the options, your recommendations and my preferences I choose treatment X." Clearly not all of these patients were interested only and/or wholly in a patient-centered approach.

Moreover, while there is empirical evidence to support the notion that patients desire patient-centered consultations in *some* medical contexts (e.g., primary care; Little, Everitt, Williamson, Warner, Moore, Gould, Ferrier, & Payne, 2001), the complexities of applying this approach to other areas of medicine have been virtually ignored. For example, analyses of patient-centered approaches in surgical settings are all but missing from the literature. Although there are likely many reasons for this absence, one explanation might be that the nature of surgery itself (especially sudden or emergency surgeries) makes it extremely difficult for physicians to exercise patient-centeredness. Perhaps the communication dynamic in many surgical contexts is best likened to that in traditional medical settings. Levinson and Chaumeton (1999) supported this notion in a study examining communication between surgeons and patients during routine office visits found that surgeons talked more than patients during encounters, discussion tended to focus on biomedical issues, and that the overall tone of the visits was positive (although surgeons rarely expressed empathy or engaged in social talk). Might this suggest that surgeons lack training in patient-centered approaches or perhaps that biomedical approaches to physician-patient communication are best suited for surgical contexts? Further examination is clearly needed.

The Role of Empathy in Traditional and Patient-centered Models

The importance of empathy in the medical setting has been long recognized and remains undisputed (e.g., Bertakis, Roter, & Putnam, 1991; Hojat et al., 2011; Mercer & Reynolds, 1984). Indeed, the Association of American Medical Colleges states in their Learning Objectives for Medical Student Education that, "physicians must be compassionate and empathetic in caring for patients" (p. 4, 1998). Higher levels of physician empathy in medical interactions have been associated with a host of positive outcomes including higher levels of patient satisfaction and compliance (Kim, Kaplowtiz, & Johnston, 2004), reduced likelihood of patient malpractice litigation (Levinson et al., 1997), and greater physician job satisfaction (e.g., Suchman, Roter, & Lipkin, 1993), to name only a few. However, there are two conceptualizations of empathy that seem to coincide with the patient-centered and biomedical approaches outlined above.

The first school of thought proposes that empathy includes a crossing over phase in which one individual genuinely becomes one with an interlocutor during an interaction (Davis, 1990). This perspective contends that "the art of healing is, in part, made up of a therapeutic use of oneself or a therapeutic presence for patients" (Davis, 1990, p. 711). In this way, then, the goal of the physician is to connect with the patient (and, arguably, vice versa) during an interaction as both a way to facilitate understanding of the patient's experience of illness *and* as a part of the healing process itself. Patient-centered approaches to medical encounters make these same demands of physicians. Although perhaps extreme, Berwick (2009) situated empathy in these approaches as follows: "ask patients today what they dislike about health care, and they will mention distance, helplessness, discontinuity, a feeling of anonymity. . ." (p. 562). He further claimed that "threats . . . come far more from denying our [health care professionals] basic instincts to help than from embracing them" (p. 563). This form of empathy will be called PC empathy.

The second school of thought frames empathy as the cognitive ability to understand another's perspective of the world (Nightingale, Yarnold, & Greenberg, 1991). In doing so, an important distinction is made between empathy and *sympathy*, (for these authors, the latter entails the capacity to join in the feelings of another) (Hojat et al., 2002). Put somewhat differently, Stepien and Baernstein defined empathy in the medical setting as ". . . appreciation of the patient's emotions and expression of that awareness to the patient" (2006, p. 524). Others have called this state compassionate detachment (Blumgart, 1964). Conceptualized in this way, then, empathy, allows for greater distance between the physician and patient, and involves the capacity (i.e., cognitive ability) to *appreciate* the emotions and experiences of a patient. On one hand physicians are expected to relate to what their patients are experiencing. On the other, they must maintain sufficient distance so as to avoid inappropriate displays of emotion that could cloud technical judgment. This perspective of empathy fits easily into the biomedical approach to physician-patient interaction. For clarity, this construct will be referred to as BM empathy in the discussion that follows.

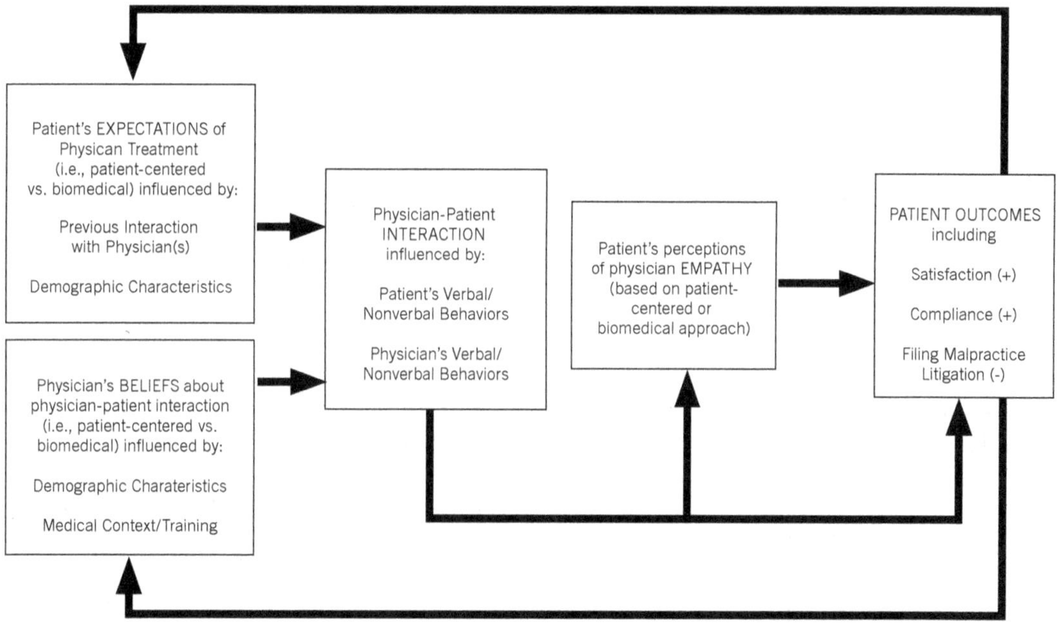

Figure 15.1 *Model of Physician-Patient Interaction with Empathy as a Moderating Variable*

A PROPOSED MODEL: EMPATHY AS A MODERATOR

Given this conceptual background and broad strokes treatment of the variables included in the proposed model (Figure 15.1), I will consider each suggested relationship in turn.

Patient's Expectations

This construct refers to the preconceived notions that the patient brings to every physician-patient interaction. Indeed, there are likely an infinite number of factors that shape an individual's ideas about what should occur during an encounter with a physician (e.g., family history, stories from close others, nature of the medical issue). Two categories in particular are included in the proposed model: previous interaction with a/the physician(s) and demographic characteristics. Although little longitudinal research has been conducted on this topic, there are suggestions in the literature that a patient's previous interactions with a particular physician (physicians in general or even media depictions of physicians) influence their expectations for a current or future physician-patient encounter. Even if a patient is visiting a given physician for the first time, he or she may be influenced by *previous* interactions with other physicians and approach this new interaction with these expectations (i.e., those shaped by a previous encounter) in mind. In line with this thinking, a previous negative encounter with a physician may influence how a patient approaches a new physician and shape his/her expectations going into this new encounter. In turn, a second negative encounter with a new (or perhaps the same) physician could solidify negative expectations, while a second encounter that is positive may begin to shift expectations in a positive direction (such that the following encounter would be framed with different—more positive—expectations). For example, Wright, Holcombe, and Salmon's (2004), research indicated that more enduring doctor characteristics such as whether the doctor had formed an individual relationship with them or whether the doctor respected them were important factors for breast cancer patients. Patient's trust in a physician also impacted their preferences for interaction style (Arora & McHorney, 2000). Moreover, general trends in the research suggest that younger patients, women, and those with higher levels of education preferred to take a more active role in physician-patient interactions (e.g., Arora & McHorney, 2000; Thompson, Pitts, & Schwankovsky, 1993). Thus, there may be demographic differences in the expectations of patients who are younger adults, parents of young children, elderly, etc.

The patient's verbal and nonverbal behaviors during these interactions, thus, are shaped by his/her expectations for these types of encounters. Despite complexities when it comes to the particularities of why and how various characteristics shape patient expectations for physician-patient interactions one thing is clear: different patients want different things. The proposed model accounts for such disparities. Measurement of this construct could include a standard demographic questionnaire, including questions aimed at understanding a patient's past experiences with physicians.

Physician's Beliefs

Just as the patient brings ideas about how physician-patient interactions should proceed to a medical encounter, so too does the physician. Again, there is an innumerable list of influences to this end including the physician's demographic characteristics and the medical context/training of their particular area of expertise. There is a surprising lack of research on the ways in which physician characteristics impact their interaction preferences with patients. One example is a meta-analysis Roter, Hall, and Aoki (2002) conducted (26 studies total), aimed at uncovering physician gender effects. Overall, their findings suggested that female physicians engaged in significantly more active partnership behaviors, positive talk, psychosocial questioning, and emotionally focused talk compared to male physicians.

In terms of medical context, then, the nature of the surgical setting as addressed above may indicate that surgeons' beliefs fall more in line with biomedical approaches than with patient-centered ones (Levinson and Chaumeton, 1999). A perspective that surgeons should transmit only necessary information to patients, coupled with an overall emphasis for taking control and on resolving medical issues would shape a physician's actions during engagement with patients.

Based on this brief review, then, it is clear that physician beliefs about how physician-patient interactions *should* proceed influence how the physician behaves during such encounters and so is included in the proposed model. Measurement of this construct could include a standard demographic questionnaire, as well as questions intended to learn more about a physician's training background and medical area of expertise.

Mutual Influence Processes and Patient's Perceptions of Physician Empathy

The core of the proposed model is the interpersonal interaction that occurs during the patient's visit with the physician. It is during these encounters that the bulk of communication occurs, impressions are formed, and decisions are made about future courses of action. Importantly, the nature of the mutual influence processes that occur during this interaction is what develops empathy as a moderating variable.

Physician-patient interaction. The model includes one direct path and one moderated path emanating from the physician-patient interaction. This construct speaks to the interpersonal nature of the medical encounter in that the verbal and nonverbal cues of the physician influence those of the patient and vice versa. The direct path indicates that there are some patient outcomes that are the direct result of the interaction. Often, however, and in the cases of the dependent variables included in this model, it is proposed that outcomes are moderated by the degree of empathy. Evidence that suggests what occurs during physician-patient interactions that accounts for various levels of patient-perceived empathy will also be addressed.

It is important to point out that measurement of biomedical interaction and patient-centered interactions are most often conceptualized as representing two ends of a spectrum (i.e., the absence of patient-centeredness is assumed to indicate the presence of biomedical approaches), yet the accuracy of this assumption is debatable. Additionally, the critiques of patient-centered approaches have resulted in questions surrounding the utility of some measures (Epstein, 2005). For example, a lack of conceptual clarity could make it difficult to know what is being measured and why. Still, measurement of the quality of physician-patient interaction has typically taken one of three primary approaches.

First, there are studies that consist of direct observations of clinical interactions and utilize tools such as coding systems, checklists, or rating scales to measure the degree to which they are patient-centered (Epstein et al., 2005). A second approach to classifying interaction patterns still uses direct observation, but includes standardized patients (instead of actual patients). The rating scales used in these are similar to those used with actual patients and, importantly, since physicians often do not know the individual is a standardized patient, evidence has suggested that these are highly correlated with actual patient encounters (Glassman, Luck, O'Gara, & Peabody, 2000). The third grouping of measurement techniques utilizes physician and/or patient self-report. That is, scales assessing various aspects of a recent encounter are thought to indicate whether a patient-centered approach was employed or not.

Biomedical approaches. Generally speaking, interaction here would be characterized by increased physician and decreased patient talk time, the majority of questions being asked by the physician and answered by the patient, and shorter total duration. In terms of content, the overall emphasis would be a series of questions and answers aimed at the physician understanding the patient's symptoms as a means to provide diagnosis. In the sense of "paternalism" described by Coulter (1999) the communication patterns in these interactions might be likened to traditional parent-child communication in that patients generally speak only when spoken to by the physician.

For instance, an elderly individual who has become accustomed to interacting in ways prescribed by the biomedical approach (i.e., not interested in taking an active role or being involved in decision-making) would likely volunteer little information about how a current illness is impacting his life and instead wait quietly for the doctor to ask questions aimed at a diagnosis. In turn, if the interaction is with a physician who believes the biomedical model is most appropriate (or necessary) she is unlikely to ask questions beyond those aimed at understanding the symptoms and diagnosing the illness. The above description and example, of course, assumed that both the physician and patient were aligned with the biomedical approach.

Patient-centered approaches. Interaction in these encounters would be characterized in ways that are essentially the opposite of those described for biomedical approaches. Thus, interaction here would be characterized by both physician and patient asking and answering questions, approximately equal talk time—if not more by the patient, and longer total duration. In terms of content, the primary focus would be on the physician garnering a complete understanding of the patient's experience of illness and the two discussing a possible range of outcomes. Again, this brief description assumed that both the physician and patient were aligned with the patient-centered approach.

Empathy as a moderating variable. The moderated link between interaction and patient outcomes is a unique contribution of this model. It suggests that empathy changes the degree to which interaction influences patient outcomes (exemplified here by satisfaction, compliance, and litigation). It is not entirely clear in the literature, however, which specific aspects of an interaction lead to patients' perceptions of empathy. Speculatively, though, physicians who match their involvement with patients' expectations for involvement might result in patients' heightened experiences of empathy. Illustratively, Street and Buller (1987) demonstrated two distinct nonverbal communicative patterns in physician-patient communication. First, physicians "nonverbally exerted greater dominance and control by employing longer speaking turns, more social touch, and more pauses while speaking than did the patients" (p. 234). The second pattern exhibited matching in which "patients tended to reciprocate nonverbal behaviors signaling affiliation including gaze, response latencies, body orientations, and gestures (p. 234). As expected, the second pattern was significantly and positively correlated with patient satisfaction. Importantly, though, the first pattern (i.e., dominance) was *not* significantly negatively correlated with satisfaction. The authors purported that "although some physician-patient interactions may be characterized by greater nonverbal expressiveness than others. . . physician-patient matching of these behaviors likely reflects the joint establishment of acceptable displays of nonverbal involvement" (p. 248).

One possible explanation offered stems from Expectancy Violations Theory in suggesting that there are potentially "acceptance regions" for what patients deem as appropriate physician behaviors (and, thus, behavior or levels of intensity above or below these ranges would be deemed inappropriate) (e.g., Burgoon, 1983; Street & Brady, 1982). Is it possible that patients who have expectations in line with biomedical approaches to physician-patient approaches experience (BM) empathy as conceptualized in this model and have a corresponding region of acceptance indicating empathic behaviors? Similarly, patients with expectations in line with patient-centered approaches experience (PC) empathy as conceptualized in this model and have an associated region of acceptance. Heightened levels of empathy, thus, are experienced when physician verbal and nonverbal behaviors match patient expectations. Lower levels of empathy, then, result from mismatches. Although there are an infinite number of paths that could demonstrate moderation between interaction and outcomes, I will focus on four in particular.

First, consider a physician and patient who interact in ways prescribed by the patient-centered approach. Patients would likely report high levels of PC empathy and low levels of BM empathy. The outcomes would be improved in this case: increased levels of satisfaction and compliance and decreased likelihood of filing malpractice suits.

The second combination runs counter to much of the current literature on physician-patient interactions that might suggest that empathy is absent in biomedical encounters. Imagine an interaction in which both the physician and patient interact in ways concordant with the biomedical approach. Importantly, given the conceptualization of empathy in the biomedical approach, a patient in this interaction *might* report high levels of BM empathy (but likely lower levels of PC empathy). In this case, still, the patient would enjoy increased levels of satisfaction and compliance (i.e., compared to both an individual who perceived average or low levels of BM empathy and/or an individual who reported high levels of PC empathy).

Third, consider the case in which the physician attempts to communicate in patient-centered ways but the patient idealizes biomedical approaches. Here the patient who perceived high levels of PC empathy *but low levels of BM empathy* is likely to experience worsened outcomes such as decreased satisfaction, lessened compliance, and increased likelihood of filing malpractice litigation.

Finally, imagine an interaction during which the physician interacts in line with the biomedical approach, yet the patient is expecting a patient-centered approach. Similar to case three, this individual will likely perceive high levels of BM empathy but *low levels of PC empathy* and, thus, experience worsened outcomes. In sum, cases three and four demonstrate instances in which the physician's behaviors do not fall within the patient's region of acceptance and are perceived as a lack of empathy.

Admittedly, measurement of empathy viewed in this dichotomous manner would need future refinement. That is, there are a variety of tools currently used to measure empathy (e.g., Interpersonal Reactivity Index). However, analysis of individual scale items would be needed to support the creation of factors for BM and PC empathy.

Patient Outcomes and Feedback Loops

There are a host of possible patient outcomes of physician-patient interaction. Included in the proposed model are patient satisfaction, compliance with suggested regimen, and likelihood of patient's filing malpractice suits because these three are frequently noted in the literature (Mead & Bower, 2002). The sign next to the label on the proposed model indicates which direction is desirable. Satisfaction is often measured using a self-scale (e.g., The Medical Interview Satisfaction Scale; Wolf, Putnam, James, & Stiles, 1978), which includes items such as "After talking to the doctor, I felt much better about my problems" or "The doctor seemed to know what he was doing during the examination" (p. 397). Examples of measurements for patient compliance include both subjective approaches (i.e., asking patient's about missed doses) and using a pill count (which was carried out without prior explanation to the patient) (e.g., Stewart, 1984). Likelihood of malpractice litigation is usually assessed retrospectively.

In addition, as indicated by the feedback loops in the proposed model from patient outcomes back to patient's expectations of physician treatment and physician's beliefs about physician-patient interaction, this model purports a cycle of influence that occurs over time instead of viewing physician-patient interaction in isolation. That is, more than likely the outcomes of a patient's or physician's most recent medical interaction would influence his/her expectations and/or beliefs for the next occasion. Indicative of this line of thinking, the Accreditation Council for Graduate Medical Education (2007) included "create and sustain a therapeutic, ethical relationships with patients" as a competency requirement for physicians (Swing, p. 649). Moreover, longer physician-patient relationships were associated with greater levels of trust (Kao, Green, Davis, Koplan, Cleary, 1998). Although speculative, these feedback loops represent an important element of the proposed model and a potentially productive area for future study.

Limitations and Future Research

Given the speculative nature of this initial model, it is important to discuss at least two potential limitations. First, this model is an attempt to synthesize two very different paradigms in the health communication literature into a single model. As such, the goal was to show how an interpersonal construct (i.e., empathy), albeit conceptualized differently, can result in similar outcomes based on patterns of moderation. This focus, however, might have been purchased at the cost of some of the model's range and/or predictive power. Future additions might look to expand the model's range by finding other areas of overlap between biomedical and patient-centered approaches to medical interactions (e.g., trust, liking). Similarly, adding a construct to account for physician outcomes would further expand the model's range and predictive power.

Second, the proposed model assumes that patient's expectations and physician's beliefs shape their behavior during interaction in consistent ways. In many instances this is the case. However, the model does not thoroughly account for changes—however incremental—that might occur over the course of one given interaction in either the physician or patient's perspectives or communicative behaviors. Put somewhat differently, further model development would work to provide additional explanation of possibilities that, for example, a patient who comes in expecting a biomedical interaction begins to shift this opinion based upon the physician's patient-centeredness.

Despite these limitations, the proposed model makes three unique contributions to our understanding of physician-patient interaction that can also serve as important areas for future research. First, this model underscores the importance of physicians remaining flexible and, ideally, trying to work with each patient in a unique way that best reflects his or her preferences. Much of the literature seems to suggest that patient-centered approaches are *always* best for patients, often to the detriment of biomedical approaches. A primary thrust of patient-centered approaches is that physicians first understand the beliefs, values and experiences of the patients before moving forward in an interaction. The insistence that patient-centered approaches are what all patients will (or should?) want, then, runs counter to the very core ideas of the patient-centered approach. The implication of such theorizing for the medical community is that flexibility is paramount.

Part of physician training, for example, ought to highlight the idea that different patients might prefer different approaches and that there is great value in exploring these possibilities. More research that examines which patients are likely to want biomedical versus patient-centered approaches, for instance, would help untangle some of the complexities. Does everyone want to be treated in the patient-centered manner? If not, how might a physician communicatively uncover this preference and adjust his/her own ideas?

Second, the inclusion of mutual influence processes in the proposed model speaks to the importance of viewing physician-patient interactions as dynamic relationships. That is, although in most cases individuals meet with a single physician (or team of physicians) over extended periods of time, research tends to focus on isolated interactions. This model begins to account for the influence of repeated encounters between two individuals in relation to one another by including feedback loops. However, the interpersonal nature of the physician-patient dyad has yet to be adequately explored. For example, in what ways do a patient's expectations for physician behaviors during an interaction change over time? In what ways do the patient's behaviors change? What might account for these changes? Does empathy (BM or PC) increase or decrease over time? Why?

Finally, continued empirical work is needed to uncover the qualities of both biomedical and patient-centered interactions. The default assumption that patient-centered approaches are superior to biomedical approaches has hindered the development of rich, nuanced understanding of either. That is, much of what we know of patient-centered approaches is based on or in reaction to biomedical approaches. What is the scope of verbal and nonverbal behaviors included in both approaches to physician-patient interaction? Is there a possibility for a hybrid of the two (Smith & Hoppe, 1991)?

CONCLUSION

The aim of this proposal was to offer a model that begins to reframe the debate between biomedical and patient-centered approaches to physician-patient communication. That is, instead of emphasizing the differences between the two, the proposed model is able to incorporate both approaches using empathy as a common link. The theorizing above suggested that patients' perception of physician empathy itself (and, perhaps alongside other relational aspects) moderates the relationship between physician-patient interaction and patient outcomes. Although tentative, this model offers a variety of testable claims, practical implications for medical educators, physicians and patients alike, and is useful in identifying areas of future research.

REFERENCES

Accreditation Council for Graduate Medical Education. (2005). Program requirements for graduate medical education in internal medicine: Educational innovations project. Retrieved from http://www.acgme.org/acWebsite/RRC_140/140_EIP_PR205.pdf

Association of American Medical Colleges. (1998). *Learning objectives for medical student education: Guidelines for medical schools*. Retrieved from https://www.aamc.org/

Axelrod, D.A., & Goold, S.D. (2000). Maintaining trust in the surgeon-patient relationship: Challenges for the new millennium. *Archives of Surgery, 135*, 55–61.

Bensing, J. (2000). Bridging the gap: The separate worlds of evidence-based medicine and patient-centered medicine. *Patient Education and Counseling, 39*, 17–25.

Bertakis, K.D., Roter, D., & Putnam, S.M. (1991). The relationship of physician medical interview style to patient satisfaction. *The Journal of Family Practice, 32*, 175–181.

Berwick, D.M. (2000). What "patient-centered" should mean: Confessions of an extremist. *Health Affairs, 28*, 555–565.

Bosk, C.L. (1979/2003). *Forgive and remember: Managing medical failure.* The University of Chicago Press: Chicago, IL.

Burgoon, J.K. (1983). Nonverbal violations of expectations. In J.M. Wiemann, & R.P. Harrison (Eds.), *Nonverbal interaction* (pp. 72–112). Beverly Hills, CA: Sage.

Coulter, A. (1999). Paternalism or partnership? *British Medical Journal, 319*, 719–720.

Davis, C. M. (1990). What is empathy, and can empathy be taught? *Physical Therapy, 70* (11), 707–711.

Elwyn, G, Edwards, A., Kinnersley, P., & Grol, R. (2000). Shared decision-making and the concept of equipoise: the competences of involving patients in healthcare choices. British *Journal of General Practice, 50*, 892–897.

Epstein, R.M., Franks, P., Fiscella, K., Cleveland, G.S., Meldrum, S.C., Kravitz, R.L., & Duberstein, P.R. (2005). Measuring patient-centered communication in patient-physician consultations: Theoretical and practical issues. *Social Science & Medicine, 61*(7), 1516–1528.

Grol, R., deMaeseneer, J., Whitfield, M., & Mokkink, H. (1990). Disease-centred versus patient-centred attitudes: Comparison of general practitioners in Belgium, Britain and the Netherlands. *Family Practice, 7*(2), 100–103.

Haan, N. G. (1979). Psychosocial meanings of unfavorable medical forecasts. In G.C. Stone, F. Cohen, & N.E., Adler (Eds.) *Health psychology—A handbook: Theories, applications, and challenges of a psychological approach to the health care system* (pp. 113–140). San Francisco: Jossey-Bass Publishers.

Hojat, M., Gonnella, J.S., Nasca, T.J., Mangione, S., Vergare, M., & Magee, M. (2002). Physician empathy: Definition, components, measurement, and the relationship to gender and specialty. *American Journal of Psychiatry, 159*, 1563–1569.

Hojat, M., Louis, D.Z., Markham, F.W., Wender, R., Rabinowtiz, C., & Gonnella, J.S. (2011). Physicians' empathy and clinical outcomes for diabetic patients. *Academic Medicine, 86*, 359–364.

Kao, A.C., Green, D.C., Davis, N.A., Koplan, J.P., & Cleary, P.D. (1998). Patients' trust in their physicians: Effects of choice, continuity and payment method. *Journal of General Internal Medicine, 13*(10), 681–686.

Kim, S. S., Kaplowitz, S., & Johnston, M. V. (2004). The effects of physician empathy on patient satisfaction and compliance. *Evaluation & the Health Professions, 27*, 237–251.

Langewitz, W.A., Eich, P., Kiss, A., & Wossmer, B.W. (1998). Improving communication skills—a randomized controlled behaviorally oriented intervention study for residents in internal medicine. *Psychomatic Medicine, 60*(3), 268–276.

Levenstein, J.H., McCracken, E.C., McWhinney, I.R., Stewart, M.A., & Brown, J.B. (1986). Patient-centred clinical method: A model for the doctor-patient interaction in family medicine. *Family Practice, 3*(1), 24–30.

Levinson, W., & Chaumeton, N., (1999). Communication between surgeons and patients in routine office visits. *Surgery, 125* (2), 127–134.

Levinson, W., Gorawara-Bhat, R., & Lamb, J. (2000). The study of patient clues and physician responses in primary care and surgical settings. *The Journal of the American Medical Association, 284*(8), 1021–1027.

Levinson, W., Roter, D., Mullooly, J.B., Dull, V.T., & Frankel, R.M. (1997). The relationship with malpractice claims among primary care physicians and surgeons. Journal of the American *Medical Association, 277,* 553–559.

Little, P., Everitt, H., Williamson, I., Warner, G., Moore, M., Gould, C., Ferrier, K., & Payne, S. (2001). Preferences for patient centred approach to consultation in primary care: observational study, *British Journal of General Practice, 322*, 1–7.

Mead, N., & Bower, P. (2002). Patient-centred consultations and outcomes in primary care: a review of the literature. *Patient Education and Counseling, 48*(1), 51–61.

Mead, N., & Bower, P. (2000). Patient-centredness: a conceptual framework and review of the empirical literature. *Social Science & Medicine, 51,* 1087–1110.

Mercer, S.W., & Reynolds, W.J. (2002). Empathy and quality of care. *British Journal of General Practice, 52*, S9–12.

Ockene, J., Quirk, M., Goldberg, R., Kristeller, J., Donnelly, G., Kalan, K., Gould, B., Greene, H., Harrison-Atlas, R., Pease, J., Pickens, S., & Williams, J. (1988). A residents' training program for the development of smoking intervention skills. *Archives of Internal Medicine, 148*, 1039–1045.

Roter, D. (1989). Which facets of communication have strong effects on outcome?: A meta-analysis. In M. Steward & D. Roter (Eds.), *Communicating with medical patients.* Newbury Park, CA: Sage.

Roter, D., Stewart, M., Putnam, S.M., Lipkin, M., Stiles, W., & Inui, T.S. (1997). Communication patterns of primary care physicians. *Journal of the American Medical Association, 227,* 350–356.

Rowland, J.H., & Holland, J.C., (1989). Breast Cancer. In *The Handbook of Psycholoncology*, J.H. Rowland and J.C. Holland (Eds), New York: University Press.

Smith, R., & Hoppe, R. (1991). The patient's story: Integrating the patient and physician centered approaches to interviewing. *Annals of Internal Medicine, 115*, 470–477.

Smith, D.H., & Pettegrew, L.S. (1986). Mutual persuasion as a model for doctor-patient communication. *Theoretical Medicine, 7,* 127–146.

Stewart, M., Brown, J.B., Donner, A., McWhinney, I.R., Oates, J., Weston, W.W., & Jordan, J. (2000). The impact of patient-centered care on outcomes. *The Journal of Family Practice, 49*(9).

Street, R.L., Jr., & Brady, R.M. (1982). Speech rate acceptance ranges as a function of evaluative domain, listener speech rate, and communication context. *Communication Monographs, 49*, 290–308.

Suchman, A.L., Roter, D., Green, M., Lipkin, M., and the Collaborative Study Group of the American Academy on Physician and Patient (1993). *Physician satisfaction with primary care office visits, 31* (12), 1083–1092.

Swing, S. (2007). The ACGME outcome project: Retrospective and prospective. *Medical Teacher, 29*, 648–654.

Vanderford, M.L., Stein, T., Sheeler, R., & Skochelak, S. (2001). Communication challenges for experienced clinicians: Topics for an advanced communication curriculum. *Health Communication, 13*, 261–284.

Winefield, H., Murrell, T., Clifford, J., & Famer, E. (1996). The search for reliable and valid measures of patient-centredness. *Psychology & Health, 11*, 811–824.

Wolf, M., H., Putnam, S. M., James, S.A., & Stiles, W.B. (1978). The medical interview satisfaction scale: Development of a scale to measure patient perceptions of physician behavior. *Journal of Behavioral Medicine, 1*(4), 391–401.

Chapter 16:

Forms and facets of effective support provision from friends and family: Recipient perspectives among people coping with eating disorders

Jessica E. Akey
The State University of New York at Fredonia

Hsin Lin
University at Buffalo – The State University of New York

I-Hsuan Chiu
University at Buffalo – The State University of New York

Lance Rintamaki
University at Buffalo – The State University of New York

INTRODUCTION

According to The National Association of Anorexia Nervosa and Associated Disorders (2008), or ANAD, 24 million people are currently managing an eating disorder. Eating disorders are significantly correlated with psychological disturbances, such as mood, anxiety, impulse-control, and substance use disorders (Hudson et al., 2007). Eating disorders have been identified as one of the most deadly psychiatric disorders among young women (Fairburn, 2001) and are marked by chronicity and relapse (Fairburn, Cooper, Doll, Norman, & O'Connor, 2000). There has been a substantial rise in the incidence rate of bulimia nervosa during the past second half of the 20th century (Hoek, 2006; Hoek & van Hoek, 2003). Eating disorders have become a growing problem yet a low proportion of individuals with eating disorders seek clinical treatment (Hudson, et al., 2007). It is of paramount importance to recognize mechanisms that would contribute to the treatment and recovery of eating disorders.

An eating disorder can be viewed as a perpetual eating behavior disturbance that is intended to control weight but leads to serious physical and psychosocial impairment (Fairburn, 2001). Body concerns and disturbed eating patterns such as the use of purging tactics are highly correlated with feelings of shame and secrecy, which cause further withdrawal (Basile, 2004; Silberstein, Striegel-Moore, & Robin, 1987). This withdrawal reduces the opportunity for individuals managing eating disorders to form open and trusting relationships, and/or it can aggravate existent relationships (Quiles Marcos & Terol Cantero, 2009). Women suffering from anorexia and bulimia nervosa have been found to show high levels of social anxiety, insecurity, and social isolation (Rorty, Yager, Buckwalter, & Rossotto,1999; Striegel-Moore et al., 1993). Involvement in social relationships is frequently difficult for individuals with eating disorders and social maladjustment may remain even after symptomatic recovery (Rorty et al., 1999; Yager, Landsverk, & Edelstein, 1987).

Research indicates that individuals managing eating disorders tend to perceive the social support they receive as inadequate and show great dissatisfaction with it (Grissett & Norvell, 1992; Limbert, 2010; Rorty et al., 1999; Tiller, Sloan, Schmidt, Troop, Power, Treasure,1997; Troop, Holbrey, & Treasure, 1998). Although the causal direction is unclear, the characteristics of individuals managing eating disorders (e.g. poor social skills or feelings of isolation and shame) might weaken these individuals' abilities to develop supportive networks that meet their needs, which in turn induces dissatisfaction and deterioration of health (Grissett & Norvell, 1992; Rorty et al., 1999).

Social support is widely acknowledged as a mechanism to help individuals manage physical and emotional strain and it is thought to be related with positive health outcomes (Cohen & Wills, 1985; Patterson, Garwick, Bennett, & Blum, 1997). Both the presence of enacted social support and the perception of availability of social support are related to improved well-being (Schafer, Coyne, & Lazarus, 1981). A growing interest in the field is to find out to what degree the presence of social support influences the development of eating disorders. Some researchers suggest that received social support can offer a safeguard to protect individuals from developing disordered eating behavior (Stice & Whitenton, 2002). Perceived support from one's family, partner, or friends is found to be important to the quality of life of individuals with eating disorders as well as those who have formerly been affected with eating disorders (de la Rie, Noordenbos, Donker, & van Furth, 2007). Furthermore, successful recovery for individuals managing eating disorders is found to be associated with the act of seeking social support (Bloks, van Furth, Callewaert, & Hoek, 2004).

So far no efforts have been directed at reviewing the effectiveness of the forms of social support perceived by individuals with eating disorders. Knowing what facets of support are helpful to people managing eating disorders can aid their loved ones in helping them get through, and possibly recover from, a debilitating mental illness. Accordingly, the aim of the current study is to map out a typology of effective and problematic forms of social support that individuals managing eating disorders perceive from their family members and friends. A systematic evaluation of the perceived social support from family and friends can provide a guide for deciding how to best offer support to individuals with eating disorders.

METHOD

Participants

As part of a larger on-going study on eating disorder management, 34 men and women with eating disorders were interviewed concerning their experiences coping with their disorders. Recruitment was conducted through two channels: (a) flyers posted in facilities providing eating disorder recovery and support programs in a mid-sized city in the mid-eastern United States and (b) postings to websites devoted to offering useful resources to help individuals managing eating disorders.

Participants were aged between 18 and 53 (M = 25, SD = 8.3) and twenty-three (68%) identified as Caucasian, eight (23%) as Other, two (6%) as Asian, and one (3%) as African American. Thirty-one (91%) participants were women, which correspond to national estimates that indicate men constitute approximately 10% of the eating disorder population in the United States (National Institute of Mental Health, 2001). The mean height of the participants was 5'4½" (SD = 3.3) and mean weight was 138 pounds (SD = 38.8) with their lowest lifetime adult weight averaging 115 pounds (SD = 29.6). The wide range of body types presented in the study reflected the extent of disordered behaviors and stages of recovery.

Coding procedure

Interviews with the participants were conducted either face-to-face or via the phone, contingent on participants' availability and convenience. After giving informed consent and enrolling in the study, participants were asked questions regarding their demographic profile and completed an Eating Attitudes Test (EAT-26; Garner, Olmstead, Bohr, & Garfinkel, 1982), which is the most widely used measurement of symptoms and behaviors specific to eating disorders. The EAT-26 produced a general diagnostic description of the study's participants and their eating disordered behaviors. At the conclusion of the interview, all participants received debriefing materials about accessing treatment and support through local or online resources.

This study adopted a grounded theory approach (Glaser & Strauss, 1967) in which themes were discovered and coded by a three-person research team. Throughout the data collection process, interview questions were refined to attend to recurring themes and emergent lines of inquiry. Follow-up questions were included, when needed, to clarify issues and validate the interviewer's interpretations of responses Researchers utilized semi-structured questions and covered a range of topics, including asking participants what support they have experienced regarding the management of their eating disorders and whether that support was perceived as helpful or unhelpful. The average time of the interviews was 65 minutes (SD = 29.8). Interviews were audio recorded, transcribed verbatim, and de-identified using pseudonyms.

Latent content analysis and constant comparative techniques (Glaser, 1992) were employed to analyze the interview transcripts. The three members of the research team reviewed the data independently to identify fundamental themes among the participants' responses. Through consensus, they produced a unified categorical system to describe the methods of providing social support that participants deemed as helpful and unhelpful towards the management of their eating disorder. The researchers then returned to the data to independently evaluate the comprehensiveness of this categorical system and confirm that every response would fall into only one of the categorized forms.

RESULTS

Forms of effective and problematic family and friends support are categorized into four potential dimensions: informational, instrumental, appraisal, and emotional. Cutrona and Suhr (1994) outline the dimensions as informational provides information to a person in need, instrumental involves visible means of assistance, appraisal aids others in feelings of competence, and emotional expresses caring and/or empathy. Ten forms of support were deemed as effective from the participant's perspective. Instrumental forms include: facilitate treatment, participate in shared activities, model exemplar behaviors, and provide financial support. Appraisal forms of support include hold accountable, offer encouragement, and encourage elaboration. Emotional forms of support include demonstrate concern, provide acknowledgment, and convey acceptance. Six forms of supportive attempts were deemed as ineffective from the participant's perspective. Instrumental forms include enable and use coercion. Emotional forms include criticize, express contempt, repudiate, and break confidentiality.

Forms of helpful FF social support

Instrumental support. *Facilitate treatment.* Friends and family (FF) facilitate treatment by helping individuals managing eating disorders gain access to medication and courses of treatment. Stacey explains that her dad babysat her daughter, so that Stacey could take the time to go to an inpatient treatment facility. "He watched my daughter while I was at [facility X]. My dad's retired; he watches her everyday. He's been a great support system for me." By providing childcare, Stacey's father allows Stacey the opportunity to obtain the self-care she needs.

FF also facilitate treatment by assisting individuals managing eating disorders with adhering to courses of treatment. Diane's husband will come home from work during the middle of the day to eat alongside Diane. Diane's husband engages in this behavior to ensure that Diane eats lunch. As Diane says of her husband, "There are certain people I feel safe eating with and he's one of them. So he'll come home and eat with me even if it's in the middle of his day, if I need it." Having a partner in the recovery process can reduce feelings of isolation and increase likeliness of adherence. A key component within treatment management as a form of FF social support is that the friend or family member must know the support receiver's preferred coping style or courses of treatment. Once an individual managing an eating disorder reveals his/her preferences regarding food and eating disorder-related stress, then the support provider can tailor the support behavior.

Participate in shared activities. Another helpful form of instrumental FF social support is participating in shared activities with an individual managing an eating disorder. This form of support often involves invitations to engage in social encounters. Julie provides a testament to how this form of support can be enacted unknowingly when she says of her friends, "People have invited me out. That's good because usually I'll isolate. They just invite me out. I need that… If I'm out in a social environment I'll do okay... I will eat something. I don't want to stick out." Managing an eating disorder can be lonely and consume one's mental and physical resources. FF can also offer support to a loved one managing an eating disorder by providing opportunities to engage the mind and body in alternative activities, providing a distraction from the disorder.

Model exemplar behaviors. Another way that FF help individuals managing eating disorders is by modeling exemplar behaviors or, as Pearl says, "being an example by being themselves." Modeling exemplar behaviors for an individual managing an eating disorder takes the form of exhibiting desirable attitudes and behaviors towards food. Cathy explains how she attempts to copy the eating habits of her friends, whom she considers healthy:

> *It's helpful to sit with them while eating because I can watch what they're eating and try to eat at their pace or try to eat what they eat. I know that if we're both done and we've had the same thing but ¾ of it are still on my plate and theirs is done, then I know I need to keep going. Just sort of in a copying way. I'll try to copy someone who I think is healthy, that's my best bet.*

One way that friends and family members can support healthy behaviors in an individual managing an eating disorder is to recognize his/her own potential as a role model. FF can have an influence over the perceived social norms of an individual managing an eating disorder. Cathy's testimony documents that it is perceived as helpful for FF to cultivate a norm of healthy relationships with food.

Provide financial support. A resounding complaint from participants who have had some experience with professional treatment is that treatment was costly and difficult to afford. Participants cite treatment as expensive—and note that insurance either does not cover the costs of treatment or it permits too small an amount of treatment that long-term effects are unlikely. This causes extra stress for eating disordered individuals who are aware of a need for medical attention, yet are faced with financial barriers when attempting to access professional help. One way that FF are able to alleviate that stress is through providing financial support.

When FF provide financial support, this allows individuals managing eating disorders to gain access to healthcare professionals. Nora explains how her mother contributed financially to help her afford care, "My mom paid for treatments, just like therapy and meds." Providing financial support can also serve as a type of respite, while a loved one recovers from an eating disorder.

Eating disorders affect both the mental and physical functioning of those they afflict. For several of the participants this has resulted in either the complete loss of, or temporary break from, employment or education. When an individual's future is thrown off track in that way, it can be devastating. FF providing financial support is one way to alleviate the monetary devastation that can occur while managing an eating disorder.

Appraisal support. *Hold accountable.* Friends and family members can hold a loved one accountable by challenging poor behaviors and/or excuses, providing sternness when needed, or pushing individuals to engage in healthy behaviors. Another way that FF can hold a loved one accountable is to offer evaluative support by being honest. When asked how she would want FF to respond to her request for support, Sara asserts, "I would want an honest opinion." When Janice confronts her mother about money for returning to college, her mother gives an honest appraisal of Janice's situation, emphasizing that her priority should be on treatment, rather than returning to school:

> *I started to cry and she just hugged me and she was just like, "You don't need money for school, you need money for therapy." I asked her if she really thought so and she said, "Yeah." I told her to tell me why and she did.*

When asked to explain what about this conversation was helpful, Janice replied, "I guess just that Mom took the time to explain why she felt that way and she cared about my opinion." Participants repeatedly express a desire for their friends and family members to treat them with respect.

Offer encouragement. Participants also refer to offers of encouragement, which we classify as a form of appraisal support that proves helpful in the management of eating disorders. Melissa substituted healthy forms of weight management for eating disordered behaviors and her family encouraged the change. Melissa explains, "They support me with encouragement. Like last year, when I was on Weight Watchers, or when I was going to swimming. They provided me encouragement about that." Similarly, Joanne's friends encourage her when she enacts behaviors conducive to recovery. Joanne recounts:

> *Most of my friends are very supportive of my recovery for my eating disorder and when I told all of them today, "Oh, I went to a meeting", they were all so proud of me and they couldn't believe it, so I know that now they are going to be even more supportive of me.*

Positive praise and endorsement of proactive methods of change and recovery provide individuals managing eating disorders with positive feedback and support regarding their endeavors.

Compliments regarding appearance also serve as a ways to offer encouragement. Individuals managing eating disorders are sensitive to their weight and appearance and appreciate compliments regarding appearance during times of weight fluctuation. Liz enjoys that her husband proclaims his attraction regardless of her size. Liz says, "Now my husband is helping in just encouraging me that whatever size I am, I'm beautiful." Jeremy's partner similarly conveys attraction regardless of size when saying, "Jeremy, everything is going to be okay. Don't worry about it. Like I said, you look better when you're bigger." Even though the causes and performances of eating disorders are complex, all eating disorders necessarily contain an element of focus on appearance. When FF provide individuals managing eating disorders with compliments regarding appearance, it can provide a temporary reprieve from self-deprecation.

Encourage elaboration. The support form of encouraging elaboration is also identified as a helpful form of appraisal social support from FF. Encouraging elaboration involves allowing the individual with an eating disorder to discuss his or her feelings, while a friend or family member engages in perspective-giving and exploring underlying emotional triggers to eating disordered behaviors. Pearl says that her FF help just by, "Sitting down and saying, 'How are you feeling today?'" Simple prompts from FF regarding the emotional state or feelings of an individual managing an eating disorder can serve to assist in supporting the individual to be self-evaluative and expressive.

Emotional support. *Demonstrate concern.* Another repeating form of emotional social support is demonstrating concern through nonverbal acts that demonstrate caring and attentiveness, or engaging in extra effort for the individual's benefit. Melissa says about her boyfriend, "It meant a lot to me when he told my parents that he cared enough about my safety to try and get help for me." Melissa positively perceives her boyfriend's act of reaching out to her family regarding her health because it demonstrates concern. Beth reveals, "I was in patient treatment just a couple of months ago and my family came out, they flew out to visit me, and that alone was like support that I needed, just being there for support." The family's act of flying out to visit Beth is a performance of demonstrating concern.

Provide acknowledgment. Participants also refer to the helpfulness of FF in providing acknowledgment. This can include providing acknowledgment of the eating disorder. Individuals managing eating disorders may experience stress and anxiety about disclosing to their FF and once they do disclose, they do not want FF to dispute or refuse to accept the existence of the disorder.

FF can also provide acknowledgment of the struggle and difficulty of eating disorders. Many participants relate the management of their disorder to a powerful and daily addiction. For example, Karen contends, "It's a lot harder than an alcoholic is. You can stop drinking, you don't have to drink. But you have to eat, so you kind of have to slay that dragon three times a day." Just like with alcohol addiction, recovery from an eating disorder is a difficult process. When individuals managing eating disorders come to FF to discuss personal struggle and stress related to the disorder, acknowledging that hardship is documented as a helpful form of support.

Convey acceptance. FF can convey acceptance by crafting messages that communicate feelings of normalcy toward someone who has an eating disorder, rather than making his/her struggles more upsetting by focusing predominantly on problematic eating behaviors. Overall, participants express a desire to be treated justly and without judgment. Individuals managing eating disorders have to manage their own personal feelings of rejection, so it is helpful for others to express messages of caring and acceptance.

Liz has anxiety eating around other people, which is a common sentiment among participants interviewed in the current study. One way that Liz's husband conveys acceptance is by allowing Liz to eat in whatever capacity she wants, without making mention of her eating behaviors. Liz expresses how her husband's emotional support allows her to feel at ease in their home when she says, "No one is freaking out on me in my household. If I ordered a pizza and only eat one bite, everyone is okay, let that go, that pizza is gone." Individuals managing eating disorders want to feel that their FF care for them unconditionally.

Forms of unhelpful or problematic FF social support

Instrumental support. *Enable.* One form of unhelpful instrumental support is enabling behavior. FF enable the behaviors of individuals managing eating disorders by providing support that facilitates continued disordered eating. Marissa lives at home with her mother and struggles with episodes of binge-eating. She explains that her mother does the grocery shopping and she still continues to buy Marissa's trigger foods, thus providing fuel for Marissa's daily struggle with food and portion choices. Marissa is the only household member who identifies herself as eating disordered, so when she is dieting, which is a behavior she views as healthy eating, her mother still buys what is considered typical food for the rest of the house. As there are no restrictions on what family members can eat and help themselves to, Marissa finds it difficult to manage healthful eating choices on her own.

Use coercion. The use of coercion is an unhelpful display of support that places demands on the individual managing an eating disorder and/or makes the individual feel intimidated. Often use of coercion from FF comes in the form of forcing an individual to eat. Sandra recalls the repeating stressful experience of dinnertime when she lived at home with her parents:

> *My dad would not allow me to scoop my own food at dinner… I remember one time we had pasta and the plate was a big dinner plate and he just would fill the entire thing with pasta, huge. I would eat as much as I felt was necessary but you couldn't even tell that I had eaten any because he put so much on the plate and that would start a fight. That was just always the worst. It's very stressful for me and for them I think too.*

The use of coercion involves a battle for control over food and body, which are the two things individuals managing eating disorders seek to control most. Sandra indicates that this experience was likely stressful for her parents, the support providers, as well as for herself. Sandra's parents may have been aiming to facilitate treatment for Sandra by making sure that she eats food during dinnertime. However, disparities exist between the amount of food Sandra's parents deemed appropriate and the amount Sandra deemed feasible.

Sandra's example indicates that when there is an imbalance or heightened sense of power within the FF relationship, coercion can be more likely to occur. However, FF with no outward authority (i.e., no structural power) can similarly use coercion on an individual managing an eating disorder, as in Melissa's example:

> *I have a friend where I would go to eat with and she would force the food, joking around. Like eating a box of candy or something and offer me one and I would say no and she would say, "Come on, eat one! Eat one!" That is not helpful at all.*

Melissa expresses a desire for her friend to respect Melissa's refusal of the offer of candy.

Emotional support. *Criticize.* Many times FF do not understand the multi-faceted components of an eating disorder and are particularly apt to forget that it is a mental disorder. FF get frustrated with what they view as a matter of vanity and choice. Vanessa explains that it is not helpful when FF "criticize and say, 'That's not normal. Why can't you just stop?', and things like that. Just not be understanding I guess." The result of misunderstanding the disorder, or attempts at 'tough love,' can be hurtful.

In their frustration, FF may criticize an individual managing an eating disorder, further aggravating the condition. Criticism can take the form of blame, such as examples provided by Janice: "'Well, you shouldn't have done this,' or 'You are so dumb,' or 'You should have known better.'" Individuals managing eating disorders self-critique themselves ruthlessly, so it is not helpful to have a close other add to the self-denigration.

Express contempt. Similar to providing criticism, expressing contempt is an unhelpful attempt at support that likely results from FF not understanding the facts about eating disorders. Expressing contempt can take the form of mocking eating disorders or the individuals who struggle with them. When someone expresses contempt toward an individual managing an eating disorder, he or she expresses little to no tolerance of the disorder. Hillary shares the story of when she revealed her disorder to her future husband, "Before I married my husband I decided that I needed to tell him about the eating disorder…He just said, "It is so stupid. Why do you have to suck yourself up that way?" Hillary is upset that her relational partner refers to her eating disorder as "so stupid," because she feels that he is extending that judgment upon her as well.

Repudiate. Participants repeatedly mention repudiation, the opposite of providing acknowledgement, as being unhelpful from FF. Friends and family members repudiate when they invalidate the concerns of the individual struggling with an eating disorder. Katherine says, "Don't tell me that I don't look like I have a problem." When an individual managing an eating disorder seeks support from FF in an attempt to get help, that means the disease and/or the individual has reached a critical point that demands serious attention from others. It is upsetting when the individual managing an eating disorder is met with FF who suggest that a problem doesn't exist. Jessica tells the story of when she was feeling mentally and physically unwell, as a result of her eating disorder, and her mother was not a helpful source of support, "'Mom, I'm really feeling suicidal, I'm struggling, I need help.' She would simply tell me to 'Suck it up.' She didn't really understand." Jessica's mom repudiated, or denied, the severity of Jessica's experiences. Luckily, Jessica eventually got professional treatment from people who were able to understand her concerns and condition.

Break confidentiality. Participants mention the act of FF breaking confidentiality as a distressing attempt at social support. FF break confidentiality by sharing private information about an individual's experience with an eating disorder. Sometimes this includes sharing information with others in efforts to help the individual dealing with an eating disorder. Control and ownership are repeating themes in the lives of individuals managing eating disorders. When a FF betrays a secret, it becomes one more instance where the individual managing an eating disorder is not able to feel a sense of control over what is viewed as hers/his.

DISCUSSION

Taking a qualitative approach, this study developed a descriptive schema that delineates what people managing eating disorders believe to be effective and problematic forms of social support provided by their friends and family. Family and friends can benefit from learning ways to best support loved ones who suffer from disordered eating. These social supportive interactions may include: facilitating treatment, participating in shared activities, modeling exemplar behaviors, providing financial support, holding accountable, offering encouragement, encouraging elaboration, demonstrating concern, providing acknowledgment, and conveying acceptance. At the same time, those attempting to express supportive communication should attempt to avoid forms of support identified herein that our participants describe as unhelpful and likely to exacerbate stress. These forms include enabling, coercing, criticizing, expressing contempt, repudiating, and breaking confidentiality.

Testimonies from people in the current study indicate that when they seek support from friends or family to help them manage their eating disorder, it is perceived as most helpful when the support person addresses the expressed concern seriously, without providing judgment or critique. Not taking the disorder seriously can engender a negative impact over good-willed intentions. Offering support that facilitates continuing disordered eating behavior (e.g., buying junk food or avoiding the problem) can disrupt healthy routines and jeopardize the maintenance of a health regimen.

Petronio's (2002) Communication Privacy Management Theory, or CPM, offers a method of understanding the relationship between privacy and breaking confidentiality. One facet of CPM involves the principles of control and ownership. According to CPM, individuals believe they own their private information and disclosing that information leaves them vulnerable (Morr Serewicz & Petronio, 2007). Secrecy is a common facet of managing an eating disorder and individuals with eating disorders are hesitant to disclose. FF are often connected through similar networks, so it makes sense that participants prefer that FF practice discretion. Participants would prefer that support persons simply listen and provide support, rather than breaking confidentiality, and thereby trust, in the relationship.

Coded forms of helpful FF instrumental support are facilitating treatment, participating in shared activities, modeling exemplar behaviors, and providing financial support. Rather than attempting to coerce, modeling exemplar behaviors towards food, by eating according to one's own level of comfort, is a preferred form of support. Also, rather than enabling disordered eating habits, facilitating treatment is a welcome change for an individual managing an eating disorder. When sharing a home with someone, this can come in the form of cooking different meals or separating trigger foods from the groceries. A key component to promoting treatment management is the friend or family member knowing the support receiver's preferred coping style or course of treatment. Once an individual managing an eating disorder reveals his/her preferences regarding food and eating disorder-related stress, then the support provider can tailor the support behavior.

Additionally, the appraisal support type of holding an adult accountable for his or her actions can reduce disordered eating. When FF hold an individual accountable, they take the risk of expressing an opinion that may not be favorable for their loved one to hear and to which s/he could respond to with anger or by turning to isolation. However, the nature of the FF relationship suggests that FF may be the best support provider for an individual managing an eating disorder, as the concerns of FF may be taken seriously and addressed. Other helpful forms of FF appraisal support include offering encouragement and encouraging elaboration on topics important to the support receiver and his or her eating disorder.

Helpful forms of FF emotional support are conveying acceptance, providing acknowledgment, and demonstrating concern. Individuals managing eating disorders self-critique themselves ruthlessly, so it is not helpful to have a close other add to their self-denigration. Rather than providing criticism or expressing contempt, emotional support in the form of conveying acceptance helps an individual managing an eating disorder to feel less like an outcast and to feel loved unconditionally. Participants regard repudiation of their disease and suffering as problematic, and would prefer FF to provide acknowledgment.

This study makes two theoretical contributions to the literature of social support in eating disorders, as well as in chronic illness in general. First, it supports Burleson's (1994) typology of sophisticated emotional support provision. According to Burleson's hierarchy of comforting messages, messages at the bottom level practically deny the feelings and thoughts of the other. These messages are oriented to criticize and invalidate the other's feelings and are telling the other how to feel and what to do. Messages at the middle level take the other's concerns gravely. These messages are offered to express sympathy and commiseration as well as understanding about the situation. At the top level are messages that acknowledge and validate the other's feelings, assisting the other to express their feelings and offering interpretations about the origins of these feelings. The effective forms of friends-and-family social support we found in this study fall in the top level, whereas the problematic forms fall in the bottom level of the message hierarchy. This is consistent with other previous evidence (e.g., Jones & Guerrero, 2001; Kunkel & Burleson, 1999) that messages at the top level are viewed more positively and effective when practicing social support.

Second, this study broadens the application of optimal matching. Optimal matching theory (Cutrona & Russell, 1990) posits that certain types of stressful events/ stressors would entail certain types of deficiencies, which should be matched with specific social support to reach the maximum effects. Controllability is the major determinant in search of a suitable match. Uncontrollable incidents would require emotional support to help individuals to relieve negative feelings, whereas controllable incidents would demand instrumental/ tangible support to fend off consequences. A medical illness can be regarded as an uncontrollable incident that affects several domains of the patient's life, including income, interaction with others, and physical capability (Cutrona & Russell, 1990). The responses from our participants reinforced the optimal matching process. They pointed out that they would consider received support that is associated with their needs as helpful and support unassociated with their needs as unhelpful. Cutrona & Russell (1990) only refer to medical illness as a stressful incident in a broad sense, however we examined a specific type of medical illness and hence extended the application of optimal matching to a particular category of stressful incidents.

The study also provides practical contributions to practitioners, eating disorder caregivers, and associated support groups. It offers friends and family, of an individual living with an eating disorder, tools with which to help that individual manage recovery from the disease. We listed both the effective and problematic forms of social support from the participant's perspective so that friends and family of the individual managing an eating disorder can have concrete guidelines about when and how to give appropriate support. This information can be distributed via many channels, including via healthcare clinicians and individuals managing eating disorders themselves. Individuals with an eating disorder can give out the information to let their friends and family understand their real needs and potentially reduce conflicts that arise from inconsistent viewpoints of support provision. A list of effective and problematic forms of social support can be included in training materials for workshops targeted at FF support groups, such as the workshops run by Treasure and her colleagues (2007) for family caregivers of individuals with eating disorders. The information may also help to curtail exacerbation of the disease and frustration that results for friends and family members.

Several factors should be considered when interpreting the results from the current study. To begin with, the kinds of qualitative methods employed in this study are excellent for developing descriptive systems, but cannot yield information pertaining to the frequencies or magnitude of effects of these variables. As such, we cannot speculate on which of these strategies prove more helpful for participants than others, if certain variables are more helpful for specific groups of individuals with an eating disorder (i.e., individuals with anorexia nervosa, bulimia nervosa, or binge eating disorder), or the degree to which these variables differ in effectiveness when utilized alone or in tandem with other supportive strategies. Future research should seek to answer these questions, as well as exploring the frequency with which individuals managing eating disorders receive both effective and problematic support and how the prevalence of such support affects subsequent affective, behavior, and clinical outcomes.

CONCLUSION

Through interviewing individuals managing eating disorders, we developed a descriptive schema that outlines the effective and problematic forms of social support provided by friends and family members. The results of the study enrich the literature of functional aspects of social support in eating disorders. More importantly, the results provide tangible and practical guidelines for friends and family to assist in the treatment and management of eating disorders appropriately and effectively.

REFERENCES

Basile, B. (2004). Self-disclosure in eating disorders. *Eating and Weight Disorders, 9*, 217–223.

Bloks, J. A., van Furth, E. F., Callewaert, I., & Hoek, W. H. (2004). Coping strategies and recovery in patients with a severe eating disorder. *Eating Disorders, 12*, 157–169.

Burleson, B. R. (1994). Comforting messages: Features, functions, and outcomes. In J. A. Daly & J. M.Wiemann (Eds.), *Strategic interpersonal communication* (pp. 135–161). Hillsdale, NJ: Lawrence Erlbaum.

Cohen, S., & Wills, T. A. (1985). Stress, social support and the buffering hypothesis. *Psychological Bulletin, 98*, 310–357.

Cutrona, C., & Russell, D. (1990). Type of social support and specific stress: Towards a theory of optimal matching. In B. Sarason, I. Sarason, & G. Pierce (Eds.), *Social Support: An interactional view* (pp.319–366). New York: Wiley.

Cutrona, C. E., & Suhr, J. A. (1994). Social support communication in the context of marriage: An analysis of couples' supportive interactions. In B. R. Burleson, T. L. Albrecht, & I. G. Sarason (Eds.), *Communication of social support: Messages, interactions, relationships, and community* (pp. 113–135). Thousand Oaks, CA: Sage.

de la Rie, S., Noordenbos, G., Donker, M., & van Furth, E. (2007). The patient's view on quality of life and eating disorders. *International Journal of Eating Disorders, 40*(1), 13–20. doi: 10.1002/eat

Fairburn, C. G. (2001). Atypical eating disorders. In C. Fairburn & K. D. Brownell (Eds.), *Eating disorders and obesity: a comprehensive textbook* (2nd Ed.). New York: Guilford Press.

Fairburn, C. G., Cooper, Z., Doll, H. A., Norman, P. A., & O'Connor, M. E. (2000). The natural course of bulimia nervosa and binge eating disorder in young women. *Archives of General Psychiatry, 57*, 659–665.

Grissett, N. I., & Norvell, N. K. (1992). Perceived social support, social skills and quality of relationships in bulimic women. *Journal of Consulting and Clinical Psychology, 60*, 293–299.

Hoek, H. W. (2006). Incidence, prevalence and mortality of anorexia nervosa and other eating disorders. *Current Opinion in Psychiatry, 19*, 389–394.

Hoek, H. W., & van Hoeken, D. (2003). Review of the prevalence and incidence of eating disorders. *International Journal of Eating Disorders, 34*, 383–396.

Hudson, J. I., Hiripi, E., Pope, H.G., Jr., Kessler, R.C. (2007). The prevalence and correlates of eating disorders in the National Comorbidity Survey Replication. *Biological Psychiatry, 6l,* 348–58.

Jones, S. M., & Guerrero, L. A. (2001).The effects of nonverbal immediacy and verbal person centeredness in the emotional support process. *Human Communication Research, 27,* 567–596.

Kunkel, A.W., & Burleson, B. R. (1999). Assessing explanations for sex differences in emotional support: A test of the different cultures and skill specialization accounts. *Human Communication Research, 25,* 307–340.

Limbert, C. (2010). Perceptions of social support and eating disorder characteristics *Health Care for Women International, 31,*170–178. doi: 10.1080/07399330902893846

National Association of Anorexia Nervosa and Associated Disorders. (2013). *Eating disorder statistics.* Retrieved from http://www.anad.org/get-information/about-eating-disorders/eating-disorders-statistics

National Institute of Mental Health. (2007). *Eating disorders.* Bethesda (MD): National Institute of Mental Health, National Institutes of Health, U.S. Department of Health and Human Services. (NIH Publication No. 07–4901).

Patterson, J.M., Garwick, A.W., Bennett, F.C., & Blum, R.W. (1997). Social support in families of children with chronic conditions: Supportive and non-supportive behaviors. *Developmental and Behavioral Pediatrics, 18,* 383–391.

Petronio, S. (2002). *Boundaries of privacy: Dialectics of disclosure.* Albany, NY: SUNY Press.

Quiles Marcos, Y., & Terol Cantero, M. (2009). Assessment of social support dimensions in patients with eating disorders. *The Spanish Journal of Psychology, 12*(1), 226–235.

Rorty, M., Yager, J., Buckwalter, J. G., & Rossotto, E. (1999). Social support, social adjustment, and recovery status in bulimia nervosa. *International Journal of Eating Disorders, 26*(1), 1–12.

Schafer, C., Coyne, J. C., & Lazarus, R. S. (1981). The health related functions of social support. *Journal of Behavioral Medicine, 4,* 381–406.

Silberstein, L. R., Striegel-Moore, R. H., & Rodin, J. (1987). Feeling fat: A women's shame. In H. B. Lewis (Ed.), *The role of shame in symptom formation* (pp. 89–108). Hillsdale, NJ, England: Lawrence Erlbaum Associates.

Stice, E., & Whitenton, K. (2002). Risk factors for body dissatisfaction in adolescent girls: A longitudinal investigation. *Developmental Psychology, 38,* 669–678.

Striegel-Moore, R. H., Silberstein, L. R., & Rodin, J. (1993). The social self in bulimia nervosa: Public self-consciousness, social anxiety and perceived fraudulence. *Journal of Abnormal Psychology, 102,* 297–303.

Tiller, J. M., Sloane, G., Schmidt, U., Troop, N., Power, M., & Treasure, J. L. (1997). Social support in patients with anorexia nervosa and bulimia nervosa. *International Journal of Eating Disorders, 21*(1), 31–38.

Treasure, J., Sepulveda, A. R., Whitaker, W., Todd, G., Lopez, C., & Whitney, J. (2007). Collaborative care between professionals and non-professionals in the management of eating disorders: A description of workshops focussed on interpersonal maintaining factors. *European Eating Disorders Review, 15* (1), 24–34.

Troop, N. A., Holbrey, A., & Treasure, J. L. (1998). Stress, coping, and crisis support in eating disorders. *International Journal of Eating Disorders, 24*(2), 157–166.

Yager, J., Landsverk, J., & Edelstein, C. K. (1987). A 20-month follow-up study of 628 women with eating disorders. I: Course and severity. *American Journal of Psychiatry, 144*, 1172–1177.

Chapter 17:

Communication and healthy sexual practices: Toward a holistic communicology of sexuality

Jimmie Manning
Northern Illinois University

INTRODUCTION

Reviewing the small body of sex research in the communication discipline, it would appear that although many studies examine health issues related to sexuality—including disease and prevention (e.g., Basu, 2011), campaigns (e.g., Palmgreen & Donohew, 2010), and adolescent sex education (e.g., Jones & Biddlecom, 2011)—there is limited exploration about issues such as sexual pleasure, sex talk in relationships, or even what sex means to personal identity. In this essay I advocate for and work toward a *holistic* approach to communication and sexuality, one that considers all aspects of sexuality and communication as relevant to a person's well-being. The ideas explored here are a response to critiques about limited understandings of both relationships and sexuality (Foster, 2008; Manning, 2013) as well as sexual health (Baglia, 2005; Tiefer, 2004). Following Ashcraft and Mumby (2004), I label this approach as a *communicology*—specifically a *communicology of sexuality*—in hopes of establishing that a communicative approach is both disciplinary-unique (similar to a sociological or psychological approach) and yet all-inclusive of a broad range of ideas regarding sexuality and communication. As Martinez (2011), who also uses a communicology label, notes, communication studies about sexuality are largely fragmented and are in need of connection.

Addressing all of these fragments is beyond the reach of a single essay, but the overview presented in this one establishes generative links across many research traditions. This cross-tradition approach is inspired by Craig (1999, 2007) who argues that the field of communication is a *constitutive* one that connects at least seven different research traditions to look at similar (and sometimes not-so-similar) ideas and concepts through multiple lenses in order to compare knowledge claims and allow for generative perspectives. A rhetorician may examine how claims about sexuality are structured in public health debates, a cultural scholar may examine how the discourses introduced in those debates play into everyday talk about health care, and a critical scholar may examine how the rhetoric and discourses used ignore women and people of color. Together, those different traditions of communication research allow for different claims to be considered holistically, in one discipline, to make constitutive and often practical claims.

To begin considering a holistic communicology of sexuality, I offer an overview of areas of traction in sexual health studies as they relate to communication. This research primarily falls into two domains: medical approaches and critical approaches. I close that overview with an examination of interpersonal and relational aspects of sexuality and health, as sex and sexuality are constructed in most cultures as inherently relational and, as such, serve as a gateway for a holistic sense of how sex plays into physical and mental health. To further illustrate these connections, I then offer brief glimpses into three different research studies that explore some aspect of interpersonal sexuality and health. It is my hope that, collectively, the research reviewed or presented here allows for continued development of a holistic communicology of sexuality inclusive of connections between relationships and health.

AREAS OF TRACTION IN SEXUAL HEALTH STUDIES

Studies of sexual health—including studies in the communication discipline—have largely fallen into two categories: those that take a medical approach, or that are firmly rooted in scientific principles and inquiry; and critical approaches, studies that are still systematic and often empirical but that typically use more subjective methods in order to empower or give voice to marginalized communities. Questions about how the two seemingly disparate areas of inquiry can work together continue to be a part of conversations about studies of sexuality in the academy (Manning, 2009a); and yet as traction builds in both medical and critical camps still other areas of inquiry continue to develop (e.g., qualitative health studies; Morse, 2012). Embracing Craig's (1999) spirit of considering communication as a constitutive field of study and Manning's (2014) notions about how these apply to interpersonal communication in particular, these differences in perspective should not be viewed as troublesome but instead as another consideration for developing full, rich, and multilayered theoretical and practical approaches that a single research tradition would not allow. Here I briefly examine both medical and critical approaches, sharing exemplars from communication research studies when possible. As these categories and exemplars demonstrate, studies of sexual health reach far beyond doctor-patient interaction or public health campaigns.

Medical approaches

The majority of sexuality research across the academy would be categorized as falling into a medical model of sexuality (Tiefer, 1996; Tiefer, 2004). Much of this work is interdisciplinary, but as one might expect disciplines including medicine, public health, and psychology contribute a great deal to this body of research. Organizations such as the Society for the Scientific Study of Sexuality (see http://www.sexscience.org) often provide a platform for researchers who take this approach, especially as it allows for cross-disciplinary conversation. Medical-oriented studies of sexuality often use physiobiological measures for understanding body functions and sociopsychological measures for understanding behaviors and social aspects of sexuality. Examining the *Handbook of Sexuality-Related Measures* shows over 100 different instruments used to understand sexuality, ranging from measures of arousal/arousability to disability to harassment to sexually transmitted diseases (Davis, Yarber, Bauserman, Schreer, & Davis, 1998). In examining scientific approaches to sexuality, four key areas emerge.

Sexual behaviors and identities. One area of sexuality research explores sexual behaviors and identities. For example, Herbenick and colleagues conducted an extensive survey involving a national probability sample of 5,865 men and women aged 14–94 in order to consider the sexual behaviors of adolescents and adults in the United States (Herbenick et al., 2010). Such research allows a general sense of what kinds of sexual behaviors are being enacted and who is likely to be doing them. For instance, their study demonstrated that masturbation was practiced by people throughout their lifespan and was a primary source of sexual pleasure for adolescents and those over the age of 70 (Herbenick et al., 2010). Counts for those engaging in oral sex, vaginal sex, and anal sex were also obtained, and it was apparent that such behaviors were not unusual. Just because behavior is not uncommon, however, it does not mean that the majority of people practice it. For example, over 20% of men aged 25–49 and women aged 20–39 reported engaging in anal sex during the past year (Herbenick et al., 2010). That suggests it is a somewhat normal behavior, even if the majority of people are not engaging it. The same could be said for same-sex sexual behavior. Seven percent of adult women and eight percent of adult men identified as gay, lesbian, or bisexual in the study, but even more reported engaging same-sex sexual behavior (Herbenick et al., 2010). Similarly, condom use is not necessarily unusual behavior, but participants only reported using condoms about 25% of the time when having vaginal intercourse (Herbenick et al., 2010). Studies that demonstrate sexual behavior allow health practitioners and researchers a baseline understanding of what people are doing and where they might focus their efforts. It also allows communication scholars to be able to consider how language may mask or accurately reflect enacted behavior.

Oftentimes research operationalizes people in sex studies by assigning an identity to them that generally describes their sexual practices (Roberts, 2006). Many of these terms enter public discourse, such as *heterosexual, bisexual,* or *nymphomaniac*. Some of these terms are negatively perceived because they represent behavior that may be perceived as deviant (Elia, 2006). Healthy sexual behavior is not measured by deviance alone, however, as many sexual behaviors that are only enjoyed or enacted by a small percentage of the population are harmless both to the individual enacting that sexual behavior and to others (Noland, 2010). Instead, healthy sexual behavior is measured more by the harm that it causes to a person or that the person might inflict upon others (Aggrawal, 2009). The term *paraphilia* is used to mark sexual desires and behaviors that include dangerous activities (Kafka, 2001). They are also used as pejorative terms to insult or belittle another. Common paraphilias include compulsive masturbation, pornography dependence, and protracted promiscuity. Many paraphilias are listed in the *Diagnostic and Statistical*

Manual of Mental Disorders, a publication from the American Psychiatric Association, but over 500 possible paraphilias have been identified (Aggrawal, 2009).

Sex and disease. Another common area of inquiry includes sexually transmitted diseases (STDs) and infections (STIs). Many times these studies are aimed at populations that are in particular danger of acquiring such diseases, such as adolescents and young adults (Weinstock, Berman, & Cates, 2004). Sexual disease is frequently studied both in terms of how it is transmitted from one partner to another (e.g., Leone, 2005) and in terms of prevention (e.g., Lombardo & Léger, 2007). As one might imagine, studies of HIV/AIDS have been quite common over the past 30 years (Walker, Hart, D'Silva, 2012), but many studies also examine general safe sex behaviors such as condom use (e.g., Noar, Carlyle, & Cole, 2006) or the effects a disease and/or treatment has on a person's body (e.g., Mallon, Miller, Cooper, & Carr, 2003). Although it is less common, research also examines how people may cope with STDs or STIs including how they might go about seeking treatment (e.g., Gott & Hinchcliff, 2003) or where they might go for support, especially in consideration of stigma (e.g., Fortenberry, 2004). Many studies are particularly interested in online contexts, as many are seeking both information (e.g., Noar, Clark, Cole, & Lustria, 2006) and support (e.g., Peterson, 2009) via the world wide web. Given its focus on messages, meaning, and interaction, prevention of and education about sexual diseases are research areas that communication studies is especially well equipped to handle.

Sex and reproduction. Although studies about sexual reproduction have been happening for centuries, over the last few decades this work has made impressive strides toward understanding why people are not able to conceive children and in helping those interested in becoming parents conceive children and carry them to term (Centers for Disease Control and Prevention, 2012). Communication studies have explored social understandings associated with infertility, especially concerns of stigma and privacy management (Bute, 2013). Ties between sex and reproduction are often taught as part of sex education programs, both inside (Askelson, Campo, & Smith, 2012) and outside (Bute & Jensen, 2011) of the home. As such, it is not unusual to find research that addresses sex education from both reproductive and disease-preventative angles (e.g., de Irala, Urdiain, & del Burgo, 2007). Studies of sexuality and reproduction demonstrate that the topic is often tied to larger societal institutions such as marriage and family (Caldwell, Caldwell, Caldwell, & Pieris, 1998). Many research studies examine the knowledge base of those who are teaching about reproduction. For example, Veiga and colleagues examined the scientific knowledge, beliefs, and behaviors of teachers in training and found that 85% reported they were ill-equipped (and demonstrated the same via knowledge tests) to teach about human sexuality (Veiga, Teixera, Martins, & Meliço-Silvestre, 2007). Another study reviewed 12 textbooks for secondary schools related to human sexuality and found that, on average, there were 12.6 incorrect pieces of information that could be identified in each book (de Irala, Urdiain, & del Burgo, 2007). Such studies demonstrate that health communication scholars should consider ways accurate and responsible sex education programs can be put into place.

Biologies. Another path to exploring sexuality and health—one that is much more common in other disciplines than it is in communication—is biological approaches. As the label suggests, these approaches examine how bodies function in relation to sexual activities and often involve studies of brain activity, neurological systems and functions, body parts related to sexual activity, and even genetics (Bancroft, 2002). At first glance, it may appear that such research is not suited for communication inquiry, but a growing body of research related to communibiology (Beatty, McCroskey, & Pence, 2009) examines how neurological systems are related to communication behavior. For example, Denes (2012) examined the types of disclosure that often occur after sexual activity—sometimes colloquially referred to as *pillow talk*—to consider its links to oxytocin, a hormone that has been linked to physical affection and intimacy. She found that women who reported experiencing orgasm during a sexual experience, and who would also thus be more likely to experience the effects of oxytocin—were significantly more likely to disclose to their partners after sex. She also found that disclosing positive feelings for a partner after sexual activity positively correlates with relational trust, satisfaction, and closeness. As that illustrates, connections between healthy relational practices can be related to physiological functions, making it a concern for health communication scholars interested in sexuality.

Critical approaches

Another broad approach to sexual health is enacted via critical and feminist lenses. In communication studies, a critical lens examines communicative problems that arise from "material and ideological forces that preclude or distort discursive reflection" (Craig, 2007, p. 85). In other words, critical research seeks communicative voices that may be silenced and uses scholarship to emancipate those voices. One particular type of critical approach that has gained traction is the feminist tradition (Craig & Muller, 2007). This tradition places a "focus on the importance and usefulness of talk, connectedness, and relationships" (Kramarae, 1989, p. 157) especially in consideration of women's experiences and gender-based language in public, private, and public-private spheres. Similarly, queer theory (Yep, 2003) has been used to explore the well-being of lesbian, gay, bisexual, and transgender (LGBT) persons. All of these approaches are usually tied into critiques of allowing medical models to dominate health care and social perceptions of a healthy culture.

Critiques of the medicalization of sexuality. Many critical scholars critique what has come to be known as the *medicalization of sexuality*, or many of the perspectives often explored using the medical approach discussed earlier in this chapter. Critical scholars often argue that sex has been transformed from something that people do as a natural part of human existence into socially constructed identities or problems that are morally-distorted and largely-profitable endeavors (Roberts, 2006). Critiques of medicalization are varied, but one key theme is access. Turning sexuality into a medical issue makes the terminology, and thus the ability to interpret research findings about sexuality, understandable only to those who have medical expertise and who can read the highly specialized reports often published in expensive medical journals or practitioner guidebooks (Roberts, 2006). That, in turn, drives up health care costs related to sexuality and encourages pharmaceutical companies to encourage people they have sexual problems that need medication. For example, in his study of Viagra, Baglia (2006) detailed how men who were functioning in normal and healthy ways were often convinced by interactive marketing that they had problems with maintaining a healthy erection. In a similar study, Tiefer (2004) explains how pharmaceutical companies—after seeing the success of Viagra—worked to develop female sexual dysfunction in order to be able to profit from the disorder. That is, it was not that a pre-existing problem needed to be solved by medication, but rather that pharmaceutical companies were trying to create a problem so that they could convince women they needed a cure.

Critical approaches to the medicalization of sexuality often critique how American attitudes about sexuality are promoted to other cultures, particularly indigenous cultures, as a way of pushing dominant sexual values into other territories (Roberts, 2006). Many times critical sexuality studies examine how identity itself is largely a social construction. As such, sexual identities are not so much something that are inherent to people and who they are but rather are an aspect of identity that is asserted and controlled by a culture. A key theorist used by critical sexuality scholars is Michel Foucault, whose *The history of sexuality: An introduction* (1987) details the European development of the idea that people have sexual identities and that questions how sex and sexuality have become subjects for scientific research. Many times this leads to sexual behaviors being pathologized, especially if they deviate from the norm (Terry, 1999). For example, homosexuality used to be classified as a dangerous sexual behavior, but this classification was more of a result of negative attitudes toward same-sex behavior rather than any kind of potential harm (Elia, 2003). That is why *homosexual*, as an identity, is viewed by many critical scholars as a negative label for same-sex oriented individuals, as it has roots in pathologizing same-sex sexual behavior (Manning, 2009b). As all of this suggests, those examining sexuality through a critical lens are often considering ways sexuality is stifled and how individuals who have been minoritized may be freed from social control of sexuality.

Harassment, violence, and consent. Another series of critical sexuality studies includes those examining physical and mental health as individuals cope with issues such as sexual harassment, sexual violence, and issues of consent. These issues are often examined through a feminist lens, as they often involve the lived experiences of women more than they do the experiences of men, but such issues can apply to the lives of many different people from many different backgrounds (Wood, 2008). Some of these topics might not appear to be ostensibly health related at first glance. For example, sexual harassment is often studied in an organizational context or as a legal issue. Health-oriented studies of sexual harassment, however, examine the anxieties that being sexually harassed can place upon an individual. For example, Bingham and Battey (2005) examined the stresses those who are sexually harassed in a collegiate environment can face, including decreased academic performance, physiological responses such as eating disorders, and lowered self-esteem. The research demonstrated that professors can provide both instrumental and emotional support for those who experience sexual harassment, thus helping with the coping process (Bingham & Battey, 2005).

Sexual aggression and assault also plays into health studies, not only in the physical effects that can result from such encounters but also in terms of mental health. Like sexual harassment, understandings of how support can be offered to survivors of sexual assault is an important consideration (Wood, 2008). Much like physical healthcare, where preventative measures can help people avoid illness, health scholars can work to avoid the mental anguish, depression, and the sometimes self-destructive behaviors that often follow sexual harassment or sexual assault, even in intimate partner relationships (Johnson, 2006). For example, hooks (1996) suggests awareness programs in organizations can help both those who are experiencing the discomfort of sexual harassment to recognize the behaviors and to help those who might engage such behaviors to avoid them. Similar studies have examined signs of sexual assault or intimate partner violence (Roloff, 1996) as well as the sources of not understanding (Hickman & Muehlenhard, 1999) or feeling entitled to ignore (Jozkowski & Peterson, in press) a need for consent to proceed with sexual activity. Unwanted sexual attention and the mental anguish it can cause are not limited to face-to-face encounters. For instance, many adolescents have reported unwanted sexual attention via text messages or social networks, and these experiences have led to needs for counseling, disruption of family systems, and the stresses that accompany navigating legal realms (Manning, in press-b).

Queer theory. The experiences of lesbian, gay, bisexual, and transgender (LGBT) people are often minimized in health care as much as they are in other domains (Harvey & Housel, in press). As scholarly inquiry about LGBT populations continued to evolve in the academy, one particular theoretical tradition to emerge was queer theory. *Queer theory* focuses on society's tendencies to construct sexuality in ways that suggest heterosexuality is a normal and natural way of being (Yep, 2003). Not only is heterosexuality normal, but it is also normative in that those who stray from heterosexual ideals are often punished (Manning, 2009a). In his overview of the need for queer theory to facilitate healing for LGBT people and communities, Yep (2003) notes four kinds of violence that injure non-heterosexual individuals: interior-individual violence, or the anxiety, shame, fear, and internalized homophobia an LGBT individual places upon his or herself; exterior-individual violence such as verbal abuse, discriminatory behaviors, and physical violence enacted toward an LGBT person by another; interior-collective violence in the form of everyday talk that treats LGBT people as different, and usually inferior, to heterosexual people; and exterior-collective violence, or institutional policies or formations that discriminate or explicitly call for harm for LGBT people including refusal of rights for partners to visit in hospitals, refusal of marriage, or even hanging or stoning for homosexual behavior in some cultures. As this implies, queer theory seeks to understand ways the physical and mental health of LGBT people are injured and how they can be supported or protected.

ANOTHER DOMAIN: SEXUALITY AND RELATIONSHIPS

As both the medical and critical approaches to sexual health research suggest, relationships are a core part of understanding sexual practices. Of course, two people can emotionally bond without sexuality just as two people can engage sexually without emotional attachment (Diamond, 2003). Many report that their sexual expression is an important part of who they are, and that stifling it can have profound impacts on their emotional and physical health (Sprecher, Christopher, & Cate, 2006). Moreover, a sexual relationship, whether it is temporary or enduring, can have long-term impacts on one's physical and mental well-being (Sprecher & McKinley, 1993).

Linking relationships, sex, and health

Given the potential for promoting a person's well-being, it is a worthwhile endeavor to begin establishing links between relationships, sex, and health. I begin exploring those connections here, with a heightened focus on studies of interpersonal communication. Sex and relationships are connected in many ways. Looking across a variety of romantic couple types, it is clear that sexual satisfaction correlates positively with overall relationship satisfaction (Sprecher et al., 2006). Positive correlates can also be found between sexual frequency and romantic love (Yela, 2000) as well as sexual satisfaction and the likelihood that a relationship will last (Sprecher, 2002). The nature of these links is not fully understood, and causal links have yet to be established. As Sprecher et al. (2006) speculate about these understandings:

> *The causal link between sexual and nonsexual aspects of relationships may be direct (e.g., when one increases, it causes increase in the other). On the other hand, it may be that sexual dimensions affect other relationship processes (e.g., sexual communication, conflict) that in turn lead to changes in general relationship dimensions. Conversely, changes in general relationship dimensions may affect relationship processes, which then induce changes in the sexual dimensions of a relationship. Unfortunately, there is surprisingly little work that directly investigates processes that might link the sexual and emotional-pair-bonding dimensions of relationships. Researchers have only indirectly studied such processes. (p. 471)*

As that summation indicates, research that moves toward the development of those links is in order. Given the ties already established between sex and relationships, it is evident that healthy relationships are also related to healthy sex lives.

The health benefits of increased sexual activity. Research suggests that engaging in sexual intercourse yields many positive benefits, as both men and women who report more sexual activity also live longer, have better immune systems, and are less likely to face many diseases including cancer (Muise, 2011). Orgasms offer the potential for relaxation and improved sleep (Komisaruk, Beyer-Flores, & Whipple, 2006) as well as healthier blood circulation and better skin (Horstman, 2012). As most people who have experienced sex probably realize, it enhances mood—especially when accompanied by orgasm—as dopamine, oxytocin, and endorphins are released (Horstman, 2012). Preliminary research also suggests orgasm may encourage more oxygen to enter and nourish women's brains (Komisaruk & Whipple, 2005). Sex also is a form of exercise, with vigorous sex burning up to 200 calories an hour (O'Keefe, Vogel, Lavie, & Cordain, 2010). Of course, sex is also a source of pleasure for many, with many different erogenous zones providing different kinds of pleasure when stimulated by sensual touch. People in romantic relationships tend to have more sex than people who are not in relationships (Laumann, Gagnon, Michael, & Michaels, 1994), even if those in long-term relationships are likely to find periods of fluctuation where they are having more or less sex depending on life's circumstances (Sprecher et al., 2006).

Sexual dysfunction in relationships. Even though sex brings many benefits, it can also be a cause for frustration, embarrassment, and relational strain. Because sexuality is frequently socially constructed as part of a romantic relationship (Noland, 2010), when a couple is not engaging in sex it can lead to relational doubt (Sprecher et al., 2006). One cause of decreased or non-existent sexual intimacy is *sexual dysfunction*, physical and/or psychological barriers that prevent someone from engaging sex. Those in romantic relationships who are experiencing sexual dysfunction can take some relief in that research demonstrates most forms of sexual dysfunction predispose situations in a current relationship (Aubin & Heiman, 2004), and so the cause is not related to being a poor relational partner. For instance, it is not uncommon for victims of sexual assault (Heiman, 2001), those who received negative messages about sex from parents or education programs (Aubin & Heiman, 2004), and women who have been taught that the main purpose of sex is to satisfy men (Cotton-Huston & Wheeler, 1983) may experience psychological dysfunction that makes them frigid or resistant to sex or particular sexual activities. A negative body image can also cause psychological sexual dysfunction (Heiman, 2000). Many times sexual dysfunction can be managed in conjunction with therapy, medical treatment, and interpersonal work with a romantic partner (Aubin & Heiman, 2004).

Sexuality and interpersonal communication. Clearly, interpersonal relationships are tied to sexual health. Understanding the communication that constitutes those relationships would be of benefit both to a holistic understanding of sexual health and a more thorough communicology of sexuality. Such a communicology is not far out of reach. Interpersonal communication scholars have already built strong research bases exploring health (Thompson, Robinson, & Brashers, 2011), emotions (Metts & Planalp, 2011), romantic relationships (Vangelisti, 2011), biology and physiology (Floyd & Afifi, 2011), supportive communication (MacGeorge, Feng, & Burleson, 2011), and other areas that are closely related to understanding sexual health. Yet despite these advances, little work that has explicitly explored sexual health and its connections to interpersonal communication has been explored. Manning (2013) notes that the most recent edition of *The SAGE Handbook of Interpersonal Communication* (see Knapp & Daly, 2011) does not list *sex, sexuality*, nor any other ostensibly sex-oriented terms in its index. Foster (2008) notes a dearth of sexuality work in interpersonal communication studies as well, and she particularly calls for reflexive forms of research that will help to widen the scope of such endeavors. Her assertion about lack of reflexive methods is supported by a January 2013 search of the popular research database Communication and Mass Media Complete that yielded only 15 unique peer-reviewed article results when searching for combinations of the words *interpersonal, sex* or *sexuality*, and *qualitative* (Manning, 2013). Without studies of sexuality and interpersonal communication, full understandings of sexual health also falter. Communication researchers need to continue to widen perspectives so that researchers can ask questions that probe deeper and yield more reliable findings; teachers can disseminate these understandings to others; and practitioners can help people in their quest for sexual health.

WIDENING SEXUAL HEALTH PERSPECTIVES THROUGH RELATIONSHIP RESEARCH: THREE STUDIES

To help widen the perspectives about possible connections between interpersonal communication and sexual health—and also to address concerns about lack of a holistic understanding of sexuality in general—here I present data from three interpretive qualitative research studies that approach relationships and sexual health in different ways. By engaging an interpretive approach, I also avoid falling into the medical/critical binary where studies of sexual health are often placed. Brief methodological details are included with each study, and areas of research are cited to place data into context and to serve as a heuristic (Baxter & Braithwaite, 2008; Manning & Kunkel, 2014) for understanding their implications. I begin with a study exploring purity pledges.

Sex education and sexual pleasure: Families discussing purity pledges

Purity pledges are oaths young women take to refrain from sexual activity until married (Gardner, 2011). Purity pledges are frequently paired with purity rings that are worn in place of a wedding ring until marriage (Manning, 2013). Research about pledges to this point is limited to studies of efficacy (e.g., Bruckner & Bearman, 2005; Rosenbaum, 2009) and feminist critiques of the practice (e.g., Doan & Williams, 2008). In order to consider how meaning-making plays into the pledge process for families, I conducted multiadic interviews (Manning, 2010; Manning, 2013) with 13 families (57 research participants total, ethnically diverse but predominantly White; 13 mothers and fathers, 28 daughters, and 3 sons) from two United States communities. Each child interviewed signed a purity vow. Interpersonal-oriented thematic analysis (Manning & Kunkel, 2014) revealed five themes: parents should want the best for their children, sex before marriage is terrifying, young women have no sexual agency, purity rings are rich with meaning, and sex is a beautiful gift. Although all of the themes allowed interesting and notable aspects (and will continue to be explored in other research reports), two themes of particular interest to sexual health are the somewhat contradictory notion that sex can be terrifying and that it can also be a beautiful gift. Unpacking elements of these two themes further allows insights to parent-child sex education conversations.

First, it should be noted that participants in the study almost universally agreed that the conversation about sex that preceded the more direct talk about the pledge was filled with discussion where both parents were involved. In her overview of research about parent-child sex conversations, Noland (2010) notes that children receive little information about sex from parents compared to other sources, and when children do talk with parents about sex it is usually with a same-sex parent. Fathers are also less likely to provide information about sex than mothers (Noland, 2010).

Yet, the participants shared that both parents were equally contributing to the discussions. As one daughter said in a family interview, "At first it was kind of weird to hear my parents talking about this. But after we were talking for a while it was easy, and I really think they wanted to hear what I thought about it, too." Even though parents were talkative, that did not mean that the daughters were always as eager to share. As one mother stated in a family interview, "Both of our girls were more quiet, but then that makes sense since they are the ones that have a lot to learn." The imbalance shared by participants, where parents did more talking than their children, is to be expected given past research (Noland, 2010).

Second, as the two themes of *sex as terrifying* and *sex as beautiful* illustrate, both negative and positive aspects of sex were discussed in purity pledge conversations. This aspect of the purity pledge conversations differs from what past research suggests will happen. In typical parent-child conversations about sex, topics are more likely to skew toward negative aspects of sex and sexuality including diseases or infections, pregnancy, and negative social repercussions (Heisler, 2005). Those topics were discussed, especially in terms of the aftermath of having sex before marriage. Unlike typical parent-child sex conversations, however, all 13 families shared how an important part of discussing the pledge was acknowledging how great sex can be not only as a bonding force between two people in love, but also as a source of pleasure for those who are married. "Sex is great," one father shared in a family interview. "It really is. It is something that is to be shared with the person you love the most. That's why I love sex. That's why everyone should love sex!" A mother in another interview shared, "We made sure to tell her it feels good. And that we like it, and it is healthy. Because if you don't tell them that part, then you're not telling the truth. So how can they believe the rest?" Daughters were less likely to talk about this in family interviews, but as one shared, "I kind of like how they put it, telling me that it is this special built in gift that God gave us and that it is something you only want to share with someone else who loves you as God wanted you to."

A final way participant experiences differed from existing research is that taboo topics not discussed in typical parent-child sex conversations were also considered. Topics such as infidelity, peer pressure, and non-normative sexuality are commonly not included in parent-child sex conversations (Heisler, 2005; Noland, 2010), but they were regularly mentioned by families as part of purity pledge talks. These topics were often presented in a negative light, similar to how other dangers such as STDs and pregnancy were articulated. Sometimes this was articulated in vague ways, such as when a father shared, "It's not even normal sex that most of these kids are doing. It's stuff to, you know, freak out the other kids." Many times it was discussed in much more direct terms, such as the mother who in a family interview said, "Like, they needed to know about affairs, and why people have them. And why me and her father haven't. Because we were each other's first, and only, and so we don't think about others, because there's only us." Another mother offered a different perspective, stating in a private interview:

> *And we talk about everything. We tell them how boys will try to get them in bed, and how their friends will try to tell them it's okay, because they need to know. And we, I really think it is important that they know if*

they have sex before someone before marriage, it is cheating on their husband. And it is cheating themselves, because sex feels good in a lot of ways. So that should, it should be discovered with a husband, not some boy.

As that data exemplar somewhat illustrates, the taboo topics were often framed by parents in contrast with the pleasures that sex in a marriage can bring.

Reducing uncertainty: Sexting as exploratory practice

Just as purity pledges have received popular culture attention, so has sexting. Sexting, or the "willing interactive exchange of sexual-oriented messages using a digital mobile communications device" (Manning, 2013, p. 7), is largely constructed in research as a problematic adolescent behavior (e.g., The National Campaign, 2008) or as a heightened legal or political issue (e.g., Humbach, 2010; Juntunen & Valiverronen, 2010). It is not surprising that sexting research has been approached with assumptions that the behavior is problematic, as a review of media accounts of sexting (Manning, in press-b) revealed that sexting—as well as online sexuality in general—were being approached as almost inherently negative topics. That same review also pointed out that most of the news stories involving sexting were examining how youths were sexting, whether it be with each other or with an adult (Manning, in press-b). This made me wonder why so little attention has been paid to adults who are sexting each other, as the topic was largely unexplored in research and ignored by the media. To better understand adult sexting, I engaged 10 participant interviews that allowed for development of an online survey with 68 additional participants. Most participants were white (75.6%), but they were diverse in age (from 18 to 54 years), sex (55% female, 45% male), and sexual orientation (13% identified as lesbian, gay, or bisexual). Participants described their most recent and a memorable sexting experience; answered questions about their understandings, experiences, motivations, and views of sexting; and shared any text-based sext messages they had on their phones.

Health communication research has focused on uncertainty in many different contexts over the past two decades (Thompson et al., 2011), although most of these studies have focused on how illness creates uncertainty or social support for those who are ill rather than more mundane aspects of uncertainty such as sexual health. Considering sexuality, relational communication, and disclosure via the sexting data and using Babrow and Matthias's (2009) observations about uncertainty as a heuristic allows for insights about one way digitally-mediated interaction can facilitate healthy sexual relationships for adults. Babrow and Matthias's (2009) arguments about uncertainty suggest that uncertainty results from either having too little or too much information. When one has too little information, it creates situations of information seeking; and one has too much information, it might result in avoidance or selective attention to one information source (Babrow & Matthias, 2009). That was the case for research participants who shared they felt emboldened or in a safe space for sexual conversation during or following a sexting experience.

Some described this aspect of sexting in terms of information seeking. As a 21 year old gay White man shared in an interview, "My boyfriend, he's really shy, and that was his way of finding out what kinds of stuff I like. So I would text him something, and he would say that he liked it, and then he would ask me what I liked. And then I would tell him, and the next time we were together, in person, he would do it." That articulation of information seeking to reduce uncertainty was not explicitly labeled, but others shared sexting experiences that were. As a 40 year old Black bisexual woman shared in a survey, "With him it was about figuring out what we were going to do together next. He would outright tell me that he wanted to know what I liked and that was sexy to him. When I told him, he would ask me if I wanted him to do those things next time we were together." Selective attention based on too much information was also reported, although as a 38 year old Latina heterosexual woman shared in her survey this might also involve clarification:

> *He is completely random and I never know what to expect or when. It starts usually with a picture of him and he is naked. Then he will tell me what he is doing. That is where it gets wild. One second he is having sex with me then the next he is down on me then the next he is kissing me then he puts me in different positions. Sometimes it is what we do that he says and other times it is things we do not do. Usually I am confused because I get into one position or picture in my head and then he switches it to another. Then he will say what do you think of that and I go which one?*

In a member check interview, I asked if she ever attempted to resolve the random and fast-changing scenarios. She replied, "Yes. When we were together one time he told me let's try what we talked about on the phone. I said, 'Which one? You change it so fast I don't think I can keep up.' Then we told what we really wanted and really liked. And so that was nice." The combination of texting and face-to-face conversation allowed for a couple to comfortably navigate their sexual relationship.

Relational turning points: Rethinking first time sexual encounters

Events associated with passion, such as the first time two people engage sexual intercourse, are often reported as having great positive effect on relationship commitment (Baxter & Bullis, 1986). Additional research shows that the first time a couple has sex is often held as a special kind of memory, full of vivid detail and emotionally significant (Harvey, Flanary, & Morgan, 1986). Oftentimes *first sex*, as it is often referred to in studies of sex and sexuality, is embedded in research as part of a trajectory of relational closeness (Sprecher & McKinney, 1993)—almost as if it were part of a larger cultural narrative of how relationships progress. To be certain, many a popular press (e.g., Fein & Schneider, 2013) or morality-based (e.g., Phillips & Phillips, 2006) guide to doing healthy, happy relationships warns of the perils of engaging sex too soon in a relationship. These notions are turned on their head, somewhat, by reviewing the results of four multiadic (Manning, 2010) interviews that were conducted using the Retrospective Interview Technique (RIT) (Huston, Surra, Fitzgerald, & Cate, 1981), a process that has individuals or couples plot their relationships on a graph that represents time and commitment.

Instances on those graphs that are associated with change in commitment, whether they be positive or negative, are labeled as *turning points* (Baxter & Bullis, 1986). As an alternate way to generate an understanding of relational *turning points*, I asked each member of a couple to generate their turning points in a separate room and away from each other. Following that process, I interviewed each member of the couple separately and promised that I would not share anything they told me with the partner. I then joined the two back together and had them negotiate their turning points chart into one chart (recording this negotiation), and following that I interviewed them again together about their final chart. This data collection is ongoing, but to date I have collected data from 54 couples (108 participants). Most of these couples do follow a pattern where sex either followed a date or series of dates or where sex signified the beginning the relationship after a period of friendship and flirting. Four couples did not follow this pattern.

In two of the four cases, the couples were disjunctive in how they listed their first turning point. In those two cases, one of the partners listed first sex as the beginning turning point where the other included meeting at a bar (in one case) and going on a first date (in the other). After discussing the situation with their partners, first sex was listed by both couples as being the first turning point. When I asked about this, the couples offered similar answers. This interview excerpt from a couple in their 40s helps to illuminate the situation:

> ***Husband:*** *I didn't want you to get the wrong idea, and I didn't want her to be, to think that we were telling you too much. We don't usually do that.*
>
> ***Wife:*** *No.*
>
> ***Husband:*** *But we did that night!* (Laughs.)
>
> ***Interviewer:*** *So do you tell others?*
>
> ***Wife:*** *See, that's why I listed it as having sex. Because I don't even remember what we talked about in the bar. Me and my girlfriends were out, and then I saw him and that was about all there was to it until the next morning.*
>
> ***Husband:*** *So I guess I'm lucky I was good looking.* (Laughs.) *She was good looking too, and she was funny, and so there was more to it than us wanting sex.*
>
> ***Wife:*** *Obviously.*
>
> ***Husband:*** *So I guess I don't want to think of it that way either.*
>
> ***Interviewer:*** *So what do you tell others?*
>
> ***Husband:*** *We say we met in a bar, but. But we don't tell them we had sex that first night. We talk more about how we met in the bar and*

thought each other was funny. And I don't think there's anything wrong or dishonest there. Most people don't tell that.

Wife: *But really it was the sex that got me interested. I didn't get up and go the next morning.*

Husband: *And I was glad she didn't.*

Wife: *But it was the sex and us cracking jokes that kept us around.*

As the data illustrate, the couple remembers sexual attraction as the first turning point, but that turning point is socially stifled in favor of more acceptable discourses.

The couple in the previous interview did not seem to struggle much with first sex also serving as their first turning point. That was not the case with two other couples who listed first sex as first turning point. Turning to an interview excerpt from a couple in their early 30s to illustrate the struggle:

Girlfriend: *If I could change one thing, that would be it. Because it's not accepted in my family that you'd do that.*

Boyfriend: *And I'm afraid people would judge me, and her probably too.*

Girlfriend: *Me more than you. I think only whores do that.*

Interviewer: *So, just to clarify, you two met that night online and then in a couple of hours you got together?*

Boyfriend: *It was probably about four hours, and then it got late.*

Girlfriend: *But a lot happened in those four hours.*

Boyfriend: *No one gets that.*

Interviewer: *So you've told people?*

Boyfriend: *No, not really.*

Girlfriend: *Kind of. I've changed it some. I tell it like it's a first date.*

Interviewer: *So why is it not a first date?*

Boyfriend: *You can't have a first date on the internet.*

Girlfriend: *And then to have sex right after meeting someone on the internet? You're double-dinged. Only whores do that.*

Boyfriend: *So we keep it pretty secret.*

As that exemplar illustrates, context is important. In this case, meeting online changes the context of first sex in such a way that it is qualitatively distinct from the other three couples' explanations of first sex as first turning point. When asked later why the conversation online might not represent a turning point, the couple was insistent that online conversations were not real—even though they met that way and were together for over five years.

Of the four couples, none indicated they shared that first sex was their first turning point. As a member of one of the couples observed, "You don't talk about sex in your relationship in general, and so even if it is what started you can't really bring it up." A member of another couple said, "Even if we're comfortable with it, and I think we are, others probably wouldn't be." In addition to allowing a sense of the stress and discomfort some couples feel when explaining their relationships—as well as a tendency to shape the narrative to conventional norms—this research also helps to illustrate how sexual scripts are normative. This normativity can have profound impacts on one's relational and sexual health. For example, given that so many popular press books on dating and finding a soul mate stress the importance of delaying sex (Zimmerman, Holm, & Starrels, 2001), one might feel as if a relationship is doomed if that sex were to come too early. Other research suggests that those who feel uneasy about their sexuality or as if their sexual behaviors are not a part of the norm might not be honest with health care providers about their sexual activity (Manning, in press-a).

Perhaps most importantly, these data help to illustrate the understandings that can emerge from reviewing the outliers. Research demonstrates men and women both report a greater likelihood of sex in relationships when there is emotional investment (Hill, 2002), but these data indicate some develop an emotional investment because of sex. As Metts (2004) notes, gendered scripts might also have an impact on how people remember and articulate their sexual experiences, so the outliers to research findings about when sexual activity enters a relationship might not be as small as data indicate. Given culture's tendency to shame sexuality that is deviant, developing fuller understandings of the sexual outliers can help people to feel more comfortable with their sexuality or—if the non-normative behavior has negative personal consequences—consider how that behavior may be addressed.

Continuing the conversation: Toward a holistic approach

As these studies illustrate, the connections between sexuality, relationships, and health may not be as obvious as one might expect, but they are certainly worth exploring as possible links to people's sexual health, happiness, and well-being. As the broad overview of sexual health and communication literature reveals, there is room for exploration and growth as a sexual communicology continues to be established. The data analyzed in this essay seeks to expand exploration and growth in one particular area—interpersonal communication studies—to explore how cultures create meaning and social structures about healthy sexual practices via communication. Surely many other areas of sexual health await exploration in a holistic communicology of sexuality. As Manning (2014) asserts in continuing an argument for constitutive approaches to studies of interpersonal communication, "Only by reading and thinking across traditions… can we advance the field as a whole while conducting specialized work on particular topics" (p. 501). As the various traditions collected together in this essay demonstrate, the various approaches to sex and sexuality can allow multiple, rich contributions to communication research, teaching, and practice.

REFERENCES

Aggrawal, A. (2009). *Forensic and medico-legal aspects of sexual crimes and unusual sexual practices.* Boca Raton, FL: CRC.

Ashcraft, K. L., & Mumby, D. K. (2004). *Reworking gender: A feminist communicology of organization.* Thousand Oaks, CA: Sage.

Askelson, N. M., Campo, S., & Smith, S. (2012). Mother-daughter communication about sex: The influence of authoritative parenting style. *Health Communication, 27,* 439–448. doi:10.1080/10410236.2011.606526

Aubin, S., & Heiman, J. R. (2004). Sexual dysfunction from a relationship perspective. In J. H. Harvey, A. Wenzel, & S. Sprecher (Eds.), *The handbook of sexuality in close relationships* (pp. 477–517). Mahwah, NJ: Lawrence Erlbaum.

Babrow, A. S., & Matthias, M. S. (2009). Generally unseen challenges in uncertainty management: An application of problematic integration theory. In T. D. Afifi, & W. A. Afifi (Eds.), *Uncertainty, information management, and disclosure decisions* (pp. 9–25). New York: Routledge.

Baglia, J. (2005). *The Viagra ad venture: Masculinity, media, and the performance of sexual health.* New York: Peter Lang.

Bancroft, J. (2002). Biological factors in human sexuality. *Journal of Sex Research, 39,* 15–21. doi:10.1080/00224490209552114

Basu, A. (2011). HIV/AIDS and subaltern autonomous rationality: A call to recenter health communication in marginalized sex worker spaces. *Communication Monographs, 78,* 391–408. doi:10.1080/03637751.2011.589457

Baxter, L. A., & Braithwaite, D. O. (2008). *Engaging theories in interpersonal communication: Multiple perspectives.* Thousand Oaks, CA: Sage.

Baxter, L. A., & Bullis, C. (1986). Turning points in developing romantic relationships. *Human Communication Research, 12,* 469–493.

Beatty, M. J., McCroskey, J. C., & Pence, M. E. Communibiological paradigm. In M. J. Beatty, J. C. McCroskey, & K. Floyd (Eds.), *Biological dimensions of communication: Perspectives, research, and methods* (pp. 3–16). Cresskill, NJ: Hampton.

Bingham, S., & Battey, K. (2005). Communication of social support to sexual harassment victims: Professors' responses to a student's narrative of unwanted sexual attention. *Communication Studies, 56,* 131–155. doi:10.1080/0008957050078767

Blumstein, P., & Schwartz, P. (1983). *American couples: Money, work, sex.* New York: Morrow.

Bruckner H., & Bearman P.S. (2005). After the promise: The STD consequences of adolescent virginity pledges. *Journal of Adolescent Health, 36*, 271–278.

Bute, J. J. (2013). The discursive dynamics of disclosure and avoidance: Evidence from a study of infertility. *Western Journal of Communication, 77*, 164–185. doi:10.1080/10570314.2012.695425

Bute, J. J., & Jensen, R. E. (2011). Narrative sensemaking and time lapse: Interviews with low-income women about sex education. *Communication Monographs, 78*, 212–232. doi:10.1080/03637751.2011.564639

Caldwell, J. C., Caldwell, P., Caldwell, B. K., & Pieris, I. (1998). The construction of adolescence in a changing world: Implications for sexuality, reproduction, and marriage. *Studies in Family Planning, 29*, 137–153.

Centers for Disease Control and Prevention. (2012). *Assisted reproductive technology.* Retrieved from Centers for Disease Control and Prevention website: http://www.cdc.gov/ART/

Christopher, F. S., & Cate, R. M. (1985). Premarital sexual pathways and relationship development. *Journal of Social and Personal Relationships, 2*, 271–288.

Cotton-Huston, A. L., & Wheeler, K. A. (1983). Preorgasmic group treatment: Assertiveness, marital adjustment and sexual function in women. *Journal of Sex and Marital Therapy, 9*, 296–302. doi:10.1080/00926238308410916

Craig, R. T. (1999). Communication theory as a field. *Communication Theory, 9*, 119–161.

Craig, R. T. (2007). Communication theory as a field. In R. T. Craig, & H. L. Muller, (Eds.), *Theorizing communication: Readings across traditions* (pp. 63–98). Thousand Oaks, CA: Sage.

Craig, R. T., & Muller, H. L. (2007). Concluding reflections. In R. T. Craig, & H. L. Muller, (Eds.), *Theorizing communication: Readings across traditions* (pp. 495–502). Thousand Oaks, CA: Sage.

Davis, C. M., Yarber, W. L., Bauserman, R., Schreer, G., & Davis, S. L. (Eds.). (1998). *Handbook of sexuality-related measures.* Thousand Oaks, CA: Sage.

Denes, A. (2012). Pillow talk: Exploring disclosures after sexual activity. *Western Journal of Communication, 76*, 91–108. doi:10.1080/10570314.2011.651253

Diamond, L. (2003). What does sexual orientation orient? A biobehavioral model distinguishing romantic love and sexual desire. *Psychological Review, 110*, 173–192.

Doan, A. E., & Williams, J. C. (2008). *The politics of virginity: Abstinence in sex education.* Santa Barbara, CA: Praeger.

Dunn, J. C., & Manning, J. (2014). Reflecting on the study: Excerpts from an interview with Jennifer C. Dunn. In J. Manning, & A. Kunkel, *Researching interpersonal relationships: Qualitative methods, studies, and analysis* (pp. 139–144). Thousand Oaks, CA: Sage.

Elia, J. P. (2003). Queering relationships: Toward a paradigmatic shift. In G. A. Yep, K. E. Lovaas, & J. P. Elia (Eds.), *Queer theory and communication: From disciplining queers to queering the discipline(s)* (pp. 61–86). Binghamton, NY: Harrington Park.

Fein, E., & Schneider, S. (2013). *The new rules: The dating dos and don'ts for the digital generation.* London: Piatkus.

Floyd, K., & Afifi, T. D. (2011). Biological and physiological perspectives on interpersonal communication. In M. L. Knapp & J. A. Daly (Eds.), *The Sage handbook of interpersonal communication* (4th ed.) (pp. 87–127). Thousand Oaks, CA: Sage.

Fortenberry, J. D. (2004). The effects of stigma on genital herpes care-seeking behaviours. *Herpes, 11*, 8–11.

Foster, E. (2008). Commitment, communication, and contending with heteronormativity: An invitation to greater reflexivity in interpersonal research. *Southern Communication Journal, 73*, 84–101. doi:10.1080/10417940701815683

Foucault, M. (1987). *The history of sexuality: An introduction.* (R. Hurley, trans.). London: Penguin.

Gardner, C. J. (2011). *Making chastity sexy: The rhetoric of evangelical abstinence campaigns.* Berkeley, CA: University of California.

Gott, M., & Hinchliff, S. (2003). Barriers to seeking treatment for sexual problems in primary care: A qualitative study with older people. *Family Practice, 20*, 690–695. doi:10.1093/fampra/cmg612

Harvey, J. H., Flanary, R., Morgan, M. (1986). Vivid memories of vivid loves gone by. *Journal of Social and Personal Relationships, 3*, 359–373.

Harvey, V., & Housel, T. H. (In press). *Left out: Health care issues facing LGBT people.* Lanham, MD: Lexington.

Heiman, J. R. (2000). Orgasmic disorders in women. In S. R. Leiblum, R. C. Rosen (Eds.), *Principles and practice of sex therapy* (3rd ed., pp. 118–153). New York: Guilford.

Heiman, J. R. (2001). Sexual desire in human relationships. In W. Evaraerd, E. Laan, & S. Both (Eds.), *Sexual appetite, desire, and motivation: Energetics of the sexual system* (pp. 117–134). Amsterdam: Royal Netherlands Academy of Arts and Sciences.

Heisler, J. M. (2005). Family communication about sex: Parents and college-aged offspring recall discussion topics, satisfaction, and parental involvement. *Journal of Family Communication, 5*, 295–312.

Herbenick, D., Reece, M., Schick, V., Sanders, S. A., Dodge, B., & Fortenberry, J. D. (2010). Sexual behavior in the United States: Results from a national probability sample of men and women ages 14–94. *Journal of Sexual Medicine, 7,* 255–265. doi:10.1111/j.1743–6109.2010.02012.x

Hickman, S. E., & Muehlenhard, C. L. (1999). "By the semi-mystical appearance of a condom": How young women and men communicate sexual consent in heterosexual situations. *Journal of Sex Research, 36,* 258–272.

Hill, C. A. (2002). Gender, relationship stage, and sexual behavior: The importance of partner emotional investment within specific situations. *Journal of Sex Research, 39,* 228–240.

Horstman, J. (2012). *The Scientific American book of love, sex, and the brain: The neuroscience of how, when, why, and who we love.* San Francisco: Jossey-Bass.

Humbach, J. A. (2010). Sexting and the first amendment. *Hastings Constitutional Law Quarterly, 37,* 433–486.

Huston, T. L., Surra, C., Fitzgerald, N. M., & Cate, R. (1981). From courtship to marriage: Mate selection as an interpersonal process. In S. Duck, & R. Gilmour (Eds.), *Personal relationships 2: Developing personal relationships* (pp. 53–88). New York: Academic.

de Irala, J., Urdiain, I. G., & Burgo, C. L. (2008). Analysis of content about sexuality and human reproduction in school textbooks in Spain. *Public Health, 122,* 1093–1103. doi:10.1016/j.puhe.2008.01.005

Johnson, M. P. (2006). Gendered communication and intimate partner violence. In B. J. Dow, & J. T. Wood (Eds.), *The SAGE handbook of gender and communication* (pp. 71–87). Thousand Oaks, CA: Sage.

Jones, R. K., & Biddlecom, A. E. (2011). Is the internet filling the sexual health information gap for teens? An exploratory study. *Journal of Health Communication, 16,* 112–123. doi: 10.1080/10810730.2010.535112

Jozkowski, K. N., & Peterson, Z. D. (In press). College students and sexual consent: Unique insights. *Journal of Sex Research.* doi:10.1080/00224499.2012.700739

Juntunen, L., & Väliverronen, E. (2010). Politics of sexting: Re-negotiating the boundaries of private and public in political journalism. *Journalism Studies, 11,* 817–831. doi:10.1080/14616701003643996

Kafka, M. P. (2001). The paraphilia-related disorders: A proposal for a united classification of nonparaphilic hypersexuality disorders. *Sexual Addiction & Compulsivity: The Journal of Treatment and Prevention, 8,* 227–239. doi:10.1080/107201601753459937

Knapp, M. L., & Daly, J. A. (Eds.), *The SAGE handbook of interpersonal communication* (4th ed.). Thousand Oaks, CA: Sage.

Komisaruk, B. R., Beyer-Flores, C., & Whipple, B. (2006). *The science of orgasm*. Baltimore: Johns Hopkins University.

Komisaruk, B. R., & Whipple, B. (2005). Functional MRI of the brain during orgasm in women. *Annual Review of Sex Research, 16*, 62–86. doi:10.1080/10532528.2005.10559829

Kramarae, C. (1989). Feminist theories of communication. In E. Barnouw, G. Gerbner, W. Schramm, T. L. Worth, & L. Gross (Eds.), *International encyclopedia of communications* (Vol. 2, pp. 157–160). New York: Oxford University Press.

Laumann, E. O., Gagnon, H. J., Michael, R. T., & Michaels, S. (1994). *The social organization of sexuality: Sexual practices in the United States*. Chicago: University of Chicago.

Leone, P. (2005). Reducing the risk of transmitting genital herpes: Advances in understanding and therapy. *Current Medical Research and Opinion, 21*, 1577–1582. doi:10.1185/030079905X61901

Lombardo, A. P., & Léger, Y. A. (2007). Thinking about "Think Again" in Canada: Assessing a social marketing HIV/AIDS prevention campaign. *Journal of Health Communication, 12*, 377–397. doi:10.1080/10810730701328875

MacGeorge, E. L., Feng, B., & Burleson, B. R. (2011). Supportive communication. In M. L. Knapp & J. A. Daly (Eds.), *The Sage handbook of interpersonal communication* (4th ed.) (pp. 317–354). Thousand Oaks, CA: Sage.

Mallon, P. W. G., Miller, J., Cooper, D. A., & Carr, A. (2003). Prospective evaluation of the effects of antiretroviral therapy on body composition in HIV-1 infected men starting therapy. *AIDS, 17*, 971–979.

Manning, J. (In press-a). Discourses of sexual health in coming out conversations: Resistance and rejection in personal and healthcare-related relationships. In V. Harvey, & T. H. Housel (Eds.), *Left out: Health care issues facing LGBT people*. Lanham, MD: Lexington.

Manning, J. (In press-b). Shedding light on the dark: Sexuality, computer-mediated communication, and discourses of healthy relational practices. In K. B. Wright, & L. M. Webb (Eds.), *Computer-mediated communication in personal relationships 2.0.*

Manning, J. (2009a). Because the personal is the political: Politics and unpacking the rhetoric of (queer) relationships. In K. German & B. Dreshel, *Queer identities/political realities* (pp. 1-8). Newcastle, UK: Cambridge Scholars.

Manning, J. (2009b). Heterosexuality. In J. O'Brien (Ed.), *Encyclopedia of gender and society* (pp. 413–417). Thousand Oaks, CA: Sage.

Manning, J. (2010). "There is no agony like bearing an untold story inside you": Communication research as interventive practice. *Communication Monographs, 77*, 437–439. doi:10.1080/03637751.2010.523596

Manning, J. (2013). Interpretive theorizing in the seductive world of sexuality and interpersonal communication: Getting guerilla with studies of sexting, purity rings, and intersectional friendships. *International Journal of Communication, 7.*

Manning, J. (2014). A constitutive approach to interpersonal communication studies. *Communication Studies, 65*(3).

Manning, J., & Kunkel, A. (2014). *Researching interpersonal relationships: Qualitative methods, studies, and analysis.* Thousand Oaks, CA: Sage.

Martinez, J. M. (2011). *Communicative sexualities: A communicology of sexual experience.* Lanham, MD: Lexington.

Metts, S. (2004). First sexual involvement in romantic relationships: An empirical investigation of communicative framing, romantic beliefs, and attachment orientation in the passion turning point. In J. H. Harvey, A. Wenzel, & S. Sprecher (Eds.), *Handbook of sexuality in close relationships* (pp. 135–158). Mahwah, NJ: Erlbaum.

Metts, S., & Planalp, S. (2011). Emotion experience and expression: Current trends and future directions in interpersonal relationship research. In M. L. Knapp & J. A. Daly (Eds.), *The Sage handbook of interpersonal communication* (4th ed.) (pp. 283–316). Thousand Oaks, CA: Sage.

Morse, J. M. (2012). *Qualitative health research: Creating a new discipline.* Walnut Creek, CA: Left Coast Press.

Muise, A. (2011). *What are the health benefits of sex? There's an app for that (sort of).* Retrieved from the Science of Relationships website: http://www.scienceofrelationships.com/home/2011/5/26/what-are-the-health-benefits-of-sex-theres-an-app-for-that-s.html

National Campaign to Prevent Teen and Unplanned Pregnancy, & Cosmogirl.com. (2008). *Sex and tech: Results from a survey of teens and young adults.* Retrieved from The National Campaign to Prevent Teen and Unplanned Pregnancy website: http://www.thenationalcampaign.org/sextech/PDF/SexTech_Summary.pdf

Noar, S., Carlyle, K., & Cole, C. (2006). Why communication is crucial: Meta-analysis of the relationship between safer sexual communication and condom use. *Journal of Health Communication, 11,* 365–390. doi:10.1080/10810730600671862

Noar, S., Clark, A., Cole, C., & Lustria, M. L. A. (2006). Review of interactive safer sex websites: Practice and potential. *Health Communication, 20,* 233–241. doi:10.1207/s15327027hc2003_3

Noland, C. M. (2010). *Sex talk: The role of communication in intimate relationships.* Santa Barbara, CA: Praeger.

O'Keefe, J. H., Vogel, R. V., Lavie, C. J., & Cordain, L. (2010). Organic fitness: Physical activity consistent with our hunter-gatherer heritage. *Physician and Sports Medicine, 4,* 1–8.

Palmgreen, P., & Donohew, L. (2010). Impact of SENTAR on prevention campaign policy and practice. *Health Communication, 25*, 609–610. doi:10.1080/10410236.2010.496843

Peterson, J. L. (2009). "You have to be positive": Social support processes of an online support group for men living with HIV. *Communication Studies, 60*, 526–541. doi:10.1080/10510970903260368

Phillips, R. D., & Phillips, S. L. (2006). *Holding hands, holding hearts: Recovering a Biblical view of Christian dating.* Phillipsburg, NJ: P&R.

Roberts, C. (2006). Medicine and the making of a sexual body. In S. Seidman, N. Fischer, & C. Meeks (Eds.), *Handbook of the new sexuality studies* (pp. 81–89). New York: Routledge.

Roloff, M. E. (1996). The catalyst hypothesis: Conditions under which coercive communication leads to physical aggression. In D. D. Cahn, & S. A. Lloyd (Eds.), *Family violence from a communication perspective* (pp. 20–36). Thousand Oaks, CA: Sage.

Rosenbaum, J. E. (2009). Patient teenagers? A comparison of the sexual behavior of virginity pledgers and matched nonpledgers. *Pediatrics, 123*, 110–120. doi:10.1542/peds.2008–0407

Sprecher, S. (2002). Sexual satisfaction in premarital relationships: Associations with satisfaction, love, commitment, and stability. *Journal of Sex Research, 39*, 190–196. doi:10.1080/00224490209552141

Sprecher, S., Christopher, F. S., & Cate, R. (2006). Sexuality in close relationships. In A. L. Vangelisti, & D. Perlman (Eds.), *The Cambridge handbook of personal relationships* (pp. 463–482). New York: Cambridge University.

Sprecher, S., & McKinney, K. (1993). *Sexuality.* Newbury Park, CA: Sage.

Terry, J. (1999). *An American obsession: Science, medicine, and homosexuality in modern society.* Chicago: University of Chicago.

Thompson, T. L., Robinson, J. D., & Brashers, D. E. (2011). Interpersonal communication and health care. In M. L. Knapp & J. A. Daly (Eds.), *The Sage handbook of interpersonal communication* (4th ed.) (pp. 633–678). Thousand Oaks, CA: Sage.

Tiefer, L. (1996). The medicalization of sexuality: Conceptual, normative, and professional issues. *Annual Review of Sex Research, 7*, 252–282.

Tiefer, L. (2004). *Sex is not a natural act & other essays* (2nd ed.). Boulder, CO: Westview.

Vangelisti, A. L. (2011). Interpersonal processes in romantic relationships. In M. L. Knapp & J. A. Daly (Eds.), *The Sage handbook of interpersonal communication* (4th ed.) (pp. 597–632). Thousand Oaks, CA: Sage.

Veiga, L., Teixeira, F., Martins, I., & Meliço-Silvestre, A. (2006). Sexuality and human reproduction: A study of scientific knowledge, behaviors and beliefs of Portuguese future elementary school teachers. *Sex Education: Sexuality, Society, and Learning, 6*, 17–29. doi:10.1080/14681810500508915

Walker, K. L., Hart, J. L., & D'Silva, M. U. (Eds.). (2012). *Communicating about HIV/AIDS: Taboo topics and difficult conversations.* Cresskill, NJ: Hampton.

Weinstock, H., Berman, S., & Cates, W. (2004). Sexually transmitted diseases among American youth: Incidence and prevalence estimates, 2000. *Perspectives on Sexual and Reproductive Health, 36,* 6–10. doi:10.1363/3600604

Wood, J. T. (2008). Critical feminist theories: Giving voice and visibility to women's experiences in interpersonal communication. In L. A. Baxter, & D. O. Braithwaite (Eds.), *Engaging theories in interpersonal communication: Multiple perspectives* (pp. 323–334). Thousand Oaks, CA: Sage.

Yela, C. (2000). Predictors of and factors related to loving and sexual satisfaction for men and women. *European Review of Applied Psychology, 50,* 235–243.

Yep, G. A. (2003). The violence of heteronormativity in communication studies: Notes on injury, healing, and queer world-making. In G. A. Yep, K. E. Lovaas, & J. P. Elia (Eds.), *Queer theory and communication: From disciplining queers to queering the discipline(s)* (pp. 11–59). Binghamton, NY: Harrington Park.

Zimmerman, T. S., Holm, K. E., & Starrels, M. E. (2001). A feminist analysis of self-help bestsellers for improving relationships: A decade review. *Journal of Marital and Family Therapy, 27,* 165–175. doi:10.1111/j.1752–0606.2001.tb01154.x

Chapter 18:

Mexican-American women and health

Emma K. Wertz
Kennesaw State University

INTRODUCTION

Research supports that differences in health status, access to care, and the provision of physical and mental health services are significantly related to race, ethnicity, primary language, geography, and various measures of socioeconomic position, such as educational status, income, wealth, and conditions in childhood. These differences are known as disparities (U.S. Department of Health and Human Services, 2010).

One such health disparity exists in breast cancer. Studies have shown that while breast cancer incidence (morbidity rate) is higher for non-Hispanic White females than for females in other racial and ethnic groups, it is minorities who carry higher mortality rates. In fact, breast cancer is the leading cause of cancer death among Hispanics (Intercultural Cancer Council, 2010).

This disparity could be linked to the to the fact that ethnic and minority women tend to participate in fewer mammography screenings than do their non-Hispanic White counter parts (Calle, Flander, Thun, & Martin, 1993; Frazier, Jiles, & Mayberry, 1996; Smith-Bindman, et al., 2006). This is alarming since breast cancer screenings, which lead to early detection of cancer, have been shown to reduce cancer-related mortality significantly—survival is around 95% if cancer is diagnosed early (American Cancer Society, n.d.a).

This chapter presents a qualitative study into how Mexican-American women define and take care of health, particularly their breast health. The study is important to health communication for many reasons. First, in order to create effective messages, it is imperative that researchers begin to further investigate the cultural beliefs of the sub-groups within the larger Hispanic ethnic category. While the larger Hispanic group shares a common ancestral language, categorizing them together in one ethnic category in health care literature is problematic as each group has their own distinct culture (Torres, 1996).

Second, as the primary health care providers for their families, Mexican-American women have a dramatic impact on the fastest growing minority group in the United States (U.S. Census Bureau, 2000). As a result, it is important to better understand how Mexican-American women define health and take care of themselves.

Finally, previous studies have primarily been conducted in states that border Mexico, with a lack of research outside the southwest. This has drawn criticism from researchers (Schreiber & Homiak, 1981), thus providing an opportunity for this study to give a voice to Mexican-American women in the southeast United States.

Culture, health, and Mexican-Americans

Culture, the values, beliefs, and rules of behavior shared by a group, guides decisions and actions (Leininger, 2001). This means the history and experiences of a cultural group are key to understanding the social and cultural factors of health (Wenger, 1993). For example, Mexican-American culture plays a part in how women react toward the threat of breast cancer, as culture impacts the ways people evaluate and respond to health and illness (Kavanagh & Kennedy, 1992).

Health is the state of wellbeing that is culturally defined or valued (Leininger, 2001) and includes the social and biological activities of individuals contributing to health or changing conditions that are deemed unacceptable (Bauwens & Anderson, 1988). As such, a person's health reflects his or her ability to participate in activities that are culturally meaningful and beneficial according to socially established patterns (Leininger, 2001). When discussing health, the cultural implications of illness must be investigated. The way an individual defines illness, which is often based on cultural assumptions that involve more than symptoms of pain (Sobralske, 1985), is important because it often forms the basis for the perceptions of what is needed and decisions about why, how, for what purpose, and when he or she will seek health care (Fabrega, 1973).

The concept of illness includes considering problems with physical, emotional, spiritual, mental, and psychological matters (Sobralske, 1985). In turn, cultural beliefs, values, family traditions, social structure, and an individual's worldview have an impact on how individuals respond to stress, pain, and illnesses. This means that culture is an integral part of an individual's overall health and health care seeking behavioral processes (Leininger, 2001).

Each culture has unique attributes that set it apart from other cultures (Kavanagh & Kennedy, 1992). Previous research has identified several dominant cultural factors that may influence the health of Mexican-American women. First, family plays an important role in health care from decision-making (Reinert, 1986) to social support (Napoles-Springer, Sanotya, Houston & Perez-Stable, 2005) to caregiving (McCarthy, Ruiz, Gale, Karam & Moore, 2004). In addition, women are usually responsible for maintaining the health of their family (John, Resendiz &Vargas, 1997), and they may use utilize a variety of methods including folk health practitioners (Gonzalez-Swafford & Gutierrez, 1983; Lopez, 2005). Finally, Mexican-American women may be modest or embarrassed about some physical exams or sexual topics (Napoles-Springer et al., 2005; Reinert, 1986) and prefer unhurried interactions with their medical providers, often expecting social interactions as part of the visit (Clark, 2002).

HEARING HOW MEXICAN-AMERICAN WOMEN DEFINE HEALTH: IN THEIR OWN WORDS

So, how do Mexican-American women define and take care of health, particularly their breast health? A qualitative study can best answer this question. Qualitative research is a "systematic investigation that attempts to understand the meanings that things have for individuals from their own perspectives" (Taylor 1994, p.266). Strauss and Corbin (1998) stated it included:

> *any type of research that produces findings not arrived at by statistical procedures or other means of quantification. It can refer to research about persons' lives, lived experiences, behaviors, emotions, and feelings as well as about organizational functioning, social movements, cultural phenomena, and interactions between nations. (pp. 10–11)*

Believing in a world of multiple realities, qualitative researchers operate under the assumption that not everyone interprets and experiences the world in the same way. Qualitative researchers attempt to gain a better understanding of participants' realities by examining their experiences and associated meanings (Strauss & Corbin, 1998). These meanings, created through interactions with others, include anything they come in contact with from simple objects to every-day events (Taylor, 1994). As a result, it is suggested that qualitative methods are used when the purpose of research is to explore attitudes and perspectives of a certain cultural group and to gain a more comprehensive understanding. In the current study, a qualitative method allowed Mexican-American women to voice their thoughts, opinions, and beliefs, in their own words. Focused on understanding the lived experiences of individuals in a specific context, qualitative researchers are unconcerned with statistical generalizations. However, after identifying patterns among participants, some conceptual generalizations about cultural groups might be made. For example, it may be assumed that key concepts could generally apply to similar participants within similar contexts (Taylor, 1994).

Qualitative research moves from specific ideas about a subject or topic to more general ones, which allows for the discovery of shared meanings. Participant responses are seen as fluid, with the constant ability to change. Through the analysis process, those meanings and patterns yield valuable field data that is then applied to a grounded theory approach in which theory often emerges from data (Strauss & Corbin, 1998). Data interpretation, which is heavily reliant upon the researcher's interpretation of the findings, is key to the qualitative research process. As a result, the researcher is considered the research instrument.

Grounded theorists may use a variety of methods, such as interviews, ethnographies, group interviews, or textual analysis as they search for themes and patterns within the data (Strauss & Corbin, 1998). Grounded theory was used for this study because, unlike quantitative research that generally relies on testing theory, this study assists in the building of theory. Strauss and Corbin (1998) posited that as grounded theorists gather and analyze data they "identify, develop, and relate the concepts that are the building blocks of theory" (p. 13).

Interviews. The long interview is considered one of the most effective ways to capture the way participants see the world in their own words. This allows us to see the world of an individual as he or she sees it. As a result, McCracken (1988) discussed the interview as "one of the most powerful methods in the qualitative armory. For certain descriptive and analytic purposes, no instrument of inquiry is more revealing" (p. 9). As such, interviews allow researchers to draw meaning and understanding from interactions with participants as they seek to better understand human behavior and how individuals create meaning.

Interviews are structured to assist researchers in allowing individuals with specific relationships to issues or subjects to express these relationships in their own terms. McCracken (1988) stated:

> *The selection of respondents must be made accordingly. The first principle is that "less is more." It is important to work longer and with great care with a few people than more superficially with many of them...it is important to remember that this group is an opportunity to glimpse the complicated character, organization, and logic of culture. (p. 17)*

Who was interviewed?

Criteria for selection were that women were born in Mexico and moved to the United States, were between the ages of 35 and 50, and were currently living in a large city in the southeast. This age group was selected because the suggested age to begin mammograms is age 40, with many health campaigns targeting this age group (American Cancer Society, 2006).

Original participants were identified through community and informal contacts including Hispanic service organization and restaurants. However, the researcher encountered some difficulty gaining access to the participants. In general, women were apprehensive about the interview procedure, often admitting after the interview that they had originally feared it would involve "right or wrong" answers. When interviews were scheduled with women that were not referred by their close friends, the potential participants often failed to keep their scheduled appointments.

As a result, the researcher relied heavily on the snowball technique (Lindlof & Taylor, 2002), as the preliminary participants were asked for the names of women they thought would be willing to participate in interviews. After women completed the interview, they often appeared to enjoy the process—showing interest in how the data would be used. At this point they were more likely to assist the researcher in finding additional participants. In fact, the women would sometimes phone their friends and schedule the appointments for the researcher during the casual conversations that took place after data collection.

The study's sample included 10 participants. There is no required number of participants when conducting a qualitative study, as qualitative research should be conducted to the point of saturation, or when each interview no longer adds unique information to the collection of data (Glaser & Strauss, 1967; Morgan, 1988; Strauss & Corbin, 1998). Researchers have suggested saturation can occur with as few as five participants or as many as 20—depending on the qualitative inquiry (Lincoln & Guba, 1985). Ten interviews were conducted; however, theoretical saturation was reached at the seventh interview.

The women who participated in the study were dispersed within the targeted age-range; the youngest woman was 35 and the oldest was 50. All of the participants were married and had children living at home. The women had lived in the United States for varying lengths of times, the shortest six months and the longest 35 years. All of the participants, except one, worked outside the home.

What were interviews like?

In order to help the participants feel more comfortable, each interview was conducted in a location familiar to the participant, such as her home. Five interviews were conducted in Spanish and five interviews were conducted in English. An interpreter and translator were used for those interviews that were conducted in Spanish. Freed (1988) suggested interpreters should be similar to the participants, i.e., they should share similar ethnicity, gender, age, and other characteristics that might otherwise interfere with the focus of the interview. Keeping in mind modesty and personal issues, the researcher found interpreters who were female and from Latin America.

Interview topics began with broad questions about how the participants defined health and moved to more specific questions about how they take care of their health and breast health. Participants were allowed to talk freely about their health beliefs and decisions.

How were data analyzed?

Following the tradition of grounded theory, this researcher sought to develop theory. Corbin and Strauss (2008) stated:

> *Developing theory is a complex activity...theory denotes a set of well-developed categories (themes, concepts) that are systematically interrelated through statements of relationship to form a theoretical framework that explains some phenomenon. The cohesiveness of the theory occurs through the use of an over-arching explanatory concept, one that stands above the rest. And that, taken together with the other concepts explains the what, how, when, where, and why of something. (p. 55)*

The researcher in this study described how Mexican-American women maintain their health and breast health in a non-native environment.

As grounded theory dictates, data collection and analysis were conducted simultaneously. All interviews were transcribed and coded within two days of each interview, allowing the researcher to investigate new questions in subsequent interviews that might not have been considered before. The researcher transcribed all interviews that were conducted in English. A transcriptionist transcribed the interviews that were conducted in Spanish. Following interview transcription, three stages of coding: open, axial, and selective (Corbin & Strauss, 2008) were completed; more than 240 hours were spent collecting and analyzing data.

Open coding. All transcripts were coded by the researcher, line-by-line, using an open coding procedure. Strauss and Corbin (1998) described this open coding procedure as the "analytic process through which concepts are identified and their properties and dimensions are discovered in data" (p. 101). In other words, this fluid process allows one to uncover thoughts and ideas, during the process naming concepts that are essentially the building blocks of theory.

During the open coding procedure, codes/concepts were marked in the left column of transcripts, using Microsoft Word. Following each interview, a separate summary list was created for each interview that contained all the concepts for that individual interview. As interviews were conducted, a master list of concepts was also created, with each concept labeled by participant (i.e. P1, P2, P3, etc.). The researcher used consistent codes when possible to mark similar thoughts, ideas, and behaviors. As a result, when the lists were electronically alphabetized, patterns were more easily uncovered.

As the data were broken down, examined piece by piece, and compared for similarities and differences, 295 individual concepts were recorded in the master list. An example of the open-coding process is seen in the interview with P8. She discussed the effect of having a positive attitude on a person's overall health as she stated, "I think if you are not well mentally, you can fall sick." This concept was coded as "believing having positive attitude can overcome physical ailments."

As the researcher created the list of concepts, preliminary categories/themes were marked in a note pad. For example, it was noted that the concept about maintaining a positive attitude might be grouped into a sub-category of "believing positive attitude will promote good health," and a larger category of "the mind and health." These preliminary categories were helpful as the researcher conducted the second stage of the coding process, axial coding.

Axial coding. Following open coding, the researcher conducted the axial coding process as concepts were collapsed and related to broad categories or themes (Corbin & Strauss, 2008). Categories are the "cornerstones" of developing theory as they represent concepts in a broad or abstract manner. Generated through a process of making comparisons that note similarities and differences, categories provide the means by which theory can be integrated (Corbin & Strauss, 1998). The researcher conducted axial coding by printing out the master list of individual codes. These pages were then cut in to individual pieces of paper, each containing one code, that were then placed into piles. Each pile represented behaviors, events, etc. that were related and were then grouped into larger categories. As a result, an outline, or categories and subcategories, emerged. The data were reassembled as the relationships among the categories and subcategories were further uncovered (Strauss & Corbin, 1988). For example, concept such as "defining healthy as being able to take care of her children" and "defining healthy as being able to take care of her home" caused the researcher to note a sub-category of "defining healthy by her ability to take care of her family." Sub-categories were used to create larger categories. For example, "defining health as taking care of the physical body" and "defining health as taking care of the mental self" caused the researcher to note a possible category of "believing health is a combination of the body and mind." Similarly, the sub-categories "feeling health care is her responsibility" and "diagnosing and treating illness" lead the researcher to note a preliminary category of "seeing herself as the first line of defense."

At the completion of axial coding, four categories had emerged: (1) the body and health, (2) the mind and health, (3) the choice to avoid professional medical care, and (4) the belief that the cause of illness should be explained. As noted by Strauss and Corbin (1998), each of the categories, derived from the data, represented the phenomenon, or helped to answer "What's going on here?" (p. 113).

Each of the categories had sub-categories. During the axial coding process, the researcher followed Strauss and Corbin's (1998) suggestion to ask "why? or "how come?" (p. 127). As a result, sub-categories helped the researcher to create and further clarify each category by answering questions such as "when, why, where, how, and with what consequence?" (Strauss & Corbin, 1998, p. 124). These questions also assisted as the researcher identified contextual factors and linked them with process, or what is called the paradigm. For example, while:

> *context doesn't determine experience or set the course of action, it does identify the sets of conditions in which problems and/or situations arise to which persons respond through some form of action/interaction and emotion (process), and in doing so it brings about consequences that in turn might go back to impact upon conditions. (Corbin & Strauss, 2008, p. 88)*

As the researcher analyzed data for context, she continued to ask questions and make comparisons. These comparisons uncovered conditions, actions, interactions, emotions, and consequences (Corbin & Strauss, 2008). Conditions "allow a conceptual way of grouping answers to the questions about why, where, how, and what happens" (Corbin & Strauss, 2008, p. 89). In other words, the researcher attempted to identify circumstances or conditions that lead participants to have a particular response. Responses made by participants to situations, problems, or events were described as actions, interactions, and emotions. Finally, consequences, or the outcomes of actions, interactions, or emotional responses to events were recorded to document what happened as a result of actions, interactions, or emotions. For example, P2 stated:

> *My husband, last year it happened for him to passed out. Two times in one day, one morning. So, they went to the emergency room. And they did all the tests. They did at [local hospital name] hospital. All the tests that they thought it might be, and they didn't discover anything. They didn't know why. They did brain, they did heart, they did diabetic tests, cholesterol tests. And all the things you can imagine. And, it was nothing.... So, I believe, I believe in doctors, yes, I do believe, but I just don't*

believe in the machines.... So, I got my book that I read, for example, when he passed out, we go that book.

In this example, the condition was P2's husband becoming ill, being taken to the emergency room, and failing to receive a diagnosis. The action, interaction, or emotions, or response by the participant, was a failure to trust medical equipment. The resulting consequence was that when they returned home, P2 used personal health texts and treated her husband as she determined was appropriate. Along this line, P2 also noted she often chose to treat herself and her family when they were ill because going to the doctor was often pointless.

Identifying conditions, actions, interactions, emotions, and consequences allowed the researcher to identify processes or "the flow of action/interaction/emotions that occur in response to events, situation, or problems" (Corbin & Strauss, 2008, p. 87), often with the purpose of reaching a goal or dealing with a problem. Using the example above, along with other similar participant data, the researcher determined that when a participant or her family was not feeling well, she preferred to handle the situation on her own as opposed to visiting a doctor who she believed usually failed to provide the reasons for illnesses.

As the outline was further developed, two major themes, grounded in the data, emerged that reflected the dynamics of Mexican-American women and how they maintain their health. These overarching categories included "the belief that health is a combination of the body and mind" and "the belief that health care is a Mexican woman's responsibility." This integration process allowed the researcher to begin the next stage of the coding process, selective coding, when categories were linked around a central or core category and the resulting theoretical formulation was refined (Corbin & Strauss, 2008).

Selective coding. With the goal of building theory, the researcher continued to the next coding stage, selective coding. During this stage, categories were linked around a core category resulting in a "refining and trimming [of] the resulting theoretical construction" (Corbin & Strauss, 2008, p. 263). Corbin and Strauss (2008) stated the "core category represents the main theme or phenomenon of the study, while the basic social process or whatever the process is can be found embedded in that main theme" (p. 266). In other words, concepts alone do not yield theory. Concepts and categories that emerged from the data during open and axial coding must be linked and filled in with detail to construct theory from the data. This resulted in a theoretical or explanatory framework that helped explain the phenomenon investigated in this study. Consistent with grounded theory approach, the process uses a set of carefully defined categories that are interrelated through statements of relationship or patterns to form a framework that explains some relevant phenomenon. As a result, themes are not simply listed but are interrelated into a larger theoretical scheme (Strauss & Corbin, 1988).

The first step in the process involved deciding on a core category. When isolating the overarching theoretical scheme, the researcher followed the suggestions of Corbin and Strauss (2008) and reviewed the scheme for internal consistency and for gaps in logic while filling in poorly developed categories, trimming excess, and validating the scheme. During this process the core category was revised multiple times. For example, the researcher noted "Mexican-American women choose to maintain their own health." However, the category was revised because it failed take into account how the women operate in a non-native environment. "Mexican-American women choose traditional health care practices" was also revised because it failed to encompass the maintenance of health and environment. Following several revisions, the core category, or the phenomenon, for this study was *The Maintenance of Health through Traditional Practices in a Non-native Environment.* The Mexican-American women in this study chose to maintain their health in a culturally traditional manner despite the fact that they now live in a non-native environment. This encompassed the main themes of the research and had the most explanative relevance and the highest potentials for linking the study's categories together, or the ability to theoretically explain what the research is about. In addition, it helped to explain that under these conditions this set of events usually happen. In other words, when Mexican-American women attempt to maintain their health in a non-native environment they choose culturally traditional health practices.

Two main categories were unified around the core category, helping to further explain the phenomenon that was investigated in this study. These categories include: (1) the belief that health is a combination of the body and mind and (2) the belief that health care is a Mexican woman's responsibility. The aim of each participant in this study was to "maintain her health in a traditional manner."

WHAT DOES THIS STUDY TELL US?

As mentioned, interviews revealed a core category, or phenomenon, of *The Maintenance of Health through Traditional Practices in a Non-native Environment.* In other words, the women chose to maintain their health in a culturally traditional manner, or similar to the way they would have in Mexico, despite their new environment. Two thematic constructs emerged from the data that helped to describe how the women define and maintain health, particularly breast health: (1) the belief that health is a combination of the body and mind and (2) the belief that health care is a Mexican woman's responsibility.

THE BELIEF THAT HEALTH IS A COMBINATION OF THE BODY AND MIND

Participants in this study defined health in terms of both the body and mind, believing that in order to be healthy a person should take care of both. Participants often described taking care of both the body and mind as they talked about attempts to maintain their health, discussing how this resulted in a positive health status.

> *P2: I have a body to take care of. I have one body. Then also, that one body is accompanied by a mind, emotions.... You have to be cautious*

> *about how they work.... There is a connection that affects your health. If you are not mentally healthy, then that will be reflected in your emotions. And, then your emotions are going to be reflected in your body, your physical body.*

The body and health

Defining health as an absence of pain. When women referred to the absence of pain in their health definitions, being in good health and feeling no physical pain or painful conditions was often discussed in terms of no suffering from painful conditions such as arthritis or problems with the kidneys or liver. In addition, the women usually discussed having no pain as the ideal situation when they spoke about their own health. For example, P7 said, "Let's say I want to be with no pain.... When I think of me being healthy it is because I don't have pain."

Defining healthy as being active. Being active was an important part of the participants' definition of health. This was evident as the ability to participate in desired activities was often interwoven into their health definitions. Participants usually discussed these activities as the ability to work and take care of their family. In addition, the women commented that being unhealthy was a negative consequence of the choice to be inactive or lazy.

When defining the physical activities that made them feel healthy, the women named work as an activity they were able to participate in because they were healthy. Participants also saw work as something that helped them maintain a healthy lifestyle. Those who did not keep busy with work or other activities were seen as lazy and believed to have negative health because of their inactivity.

> *P3: If I am not healthy, I cannot take care of myself. If I am healthy, I can take care of my family, work, take care of my home. I can't be an active person when I am not healthy.... If you are lazy and always choose to lay around it is not good for your health. Your body needs to be active to be well.*

The mind and health

Believing poor mental health leads to negative physical health. When participants discussed the health of their mind, they usually did so in reference to how their mind affected their physical health or supported the health of the body. This concept was most often discussed in terms of stress and the various ways stress can present itself as a physical ailment. As a result, the women made attempts to take care of their mental health, with some women choosing relaxation techniques such as resting or reading and others choosing more physical activities such as exercising or working.

Women believed having a positive outlook meant they would have good health. They discussed illness as something that could be avoided or overcome by maintaining a positive attitude or as something they had used, in the past, to overcome illness. P2 said, "I keep a good attitude...It's a matter of you having the will to overcome it…I know the sickness, and (think) you're not going to be bigger than me." On the other hand, the women felt those who failed to be mentally positive were more likely to become ill. Chronically-ill friends or family members were described as choosing to be sick.

THE BELIEF THAT HEALTH CARE IS A MEXICAN WOMAN'S RESPONSIBILITY

During the interview process, participants discussed their role as the person in charge of making health decisions about maintaining the health of their families. This often involved the women diagnosing and treating illnesses and determining when to seek professional medical treatment.

The choice to avoid professional medical services

Preferring to self-diagnose and treat illness. Participants preferred to diagnose and treat illness themselves, only turning to professional medical services for conditions they deemed serious or to confirm their self-diagnoses. P9 stated, "We try to know when things are wrong with our bodies instead of having a doctor tell us." If the women would go to the doctor to confirm an illness, they usually used home remedies for treatment.

Similarly, women described choosing not to participate in annual mammograms. Instead, they preferred to conduct manual self-checks for breast lumps. The women believed they were in charge of their individual health care as they reported they were taking care of their breasts by eating properly and manually checking for abnormalities. Participants felt that if something were wrong with their breast they would know about it because they were in touch with their bodies and overall health. If their body was healthy, then their breasts were healthy.

Using home remedies to maintain health and treat illness. Participants reported they frequently participated in the use of home remedies, including herbal cures, to treat illnesses. This allowed the women to control what was prescribed for illnesses and allowed them to use remedies with which they were familiar. While a majority of the home remedies were used for illnesses such as the common cold or stomachache, some women described using them to treat more painful illnesses such as kidney infections or diseases like diabetes and arthritis.

The women in this study felt they face an increased challenge as they attempt to care for their health in the United States. They often discussed the difficulty they had finding natural health supplies they had frequently used in Mexico. When supplies were located, they were usually very expensive, which was an added burden for the women. As a result, they were unable to make certain remedies as they attempted to provide health care for themselves and their family. P9 stated that when she could not find the natural supplies she needed she would have to just "give them [family members] whatever the doctor prescribes."

Avoiding prescription medications. The women often reported consciously avoiding medications, even after receiving prescriptions or buying them and having directions for taking the medications. This was attributed to a fear of possible side effects or addiction. The women stated they did not have these fears with home remedies. When P10 discussed preferring home remedies, she stated, "it stemmed from all of this fear, I guess, of becoming addicted to pills."

Relying on other women for health advice. The women reported they learned to maintain health through the traditional processes of watching other women take care of health and discussing health with other women. Participants reported they primarily learned to make and administer home remedies from older female family members or friends and often described the process of learning home remedies as beginning when they were children. P6 discussed this experience as she said, "When I was a little girl, my mother used to cure us. And, she always used to call me to help. … And, I watched and saw everything. And, I know what she put on it (an herbal rub) and how she cleaned, and I learned a lot."

Referencing printed sources for health information. Participants relied on literature about natural or home remedies and professional medicine as they diagnosed and treated themselves and family members for ailments and illnesses. The women referenced printed material from texts containing both home remedies and scientific medical information. These texts were originally from Mexico and often described illnesses and treatment options, including home remedies, which might be attempted before visiting a medical professional. P2 discussed these texts as she stated, "They have things in them like the way that my mom used to treat us."

Using medical services for serious conditions. The women usually determined how serious an illness was based on how much pain a person experienced. This was associated with the belief that good health meant an absence of pain. In addition, if participants had tried to treat an ailment and it was persistent, this would usually cause them to classify it as a more serious illness. P6 said she would visit a doctor, "if it is something I can't handle…if there is a lot of pain, if something really hurts for a long time. Or, if I maybe have a high fever for a long time that I can't get rid of."

Making changes to health care practices since moving to the United States. The women perceived the U.S. system as reliant on professional medical services with little emphasis on natural medicines. Participants discussed an increase in the use of professional medical services when they first moved to the United States as they attempted to adopt the U.S. approach to health care. The increased use of professional medical services was discussed as a brief period that was followed by a return to a health care regiment that was more similar to their culturally traditional health practices.

The belief that the cause of illnesses should be explained

Believing good health begins with diet. When participants described the diagnosis and treatment of illnesses, they often discussed the food they ate and the importance of a healthy diet. P4 said, "Everything starts with the stomach. If you do not eat well your body will not be well." To promote good health, participants attempted to maintain a diet that avoided fats and fatty meats and cheeses while it promoted vegetables, fruits, and lean proteins. The primary objective of a person's diet was to promote a healthy body and immune system. As a result, illness was discussed as a consequence of improper eating habits, or failing to take care of the stomach.

Believing cancer is caused by injury or genetics. Participants explained cancer as something that was a result of an injury. P2 discussed how she feared she would develop brain cancer because she hit her head during childhood. When she has headaches, she stated she fears she has developed a tumor and is finally suffering the consequence of the childhood head-injury.

The women also discussed breast cancer and its tie to injuries. P4 discussed a woman that died from breast cancer as she stated, "She had hit her breast…She did not know that the tumor was a consequence." If the women had not injured their breast, then they did not worry about breast cancer.

In addition, women also attempted to explain the causes of breast cancer as they discussed that a woman developed breast cancer because she had a history of the disease in her family. Women who did not have a history of cancer in their family felt breast cancer was a risk for other Mexican-American women, and it was not something for which they were at risk. For example, P4 said, "No one in my family has had it (breast cancer), so I don't really worry about it."

Lacking confidence in U.S. professional medical services. Women in this study expected to be told what was wrong with their health or the health of a family member when they visited a physician. Participants felt physicians had failed them when they could not tell them what caused illnesses, even after running multiple, expensive medical tests or sending them to different specialists. P3 expressed frustration as she said, "The doctors do not seem to understand what is wrong with you here, and they send you to many places and want to run so many tests."

This belief contributed to the women choosing to avoid professional medical services. In other words, "Why send a person to the doctor if I will just have to treat them anyway?" The women discussed similar feelings about participating in mammograms as they described having mammograms that returned no abnormal findings. The women often failed to go back for follow-up exams since their first exams did not find anything, choosing to self-manage their breast health through manual screenings.

PULLING IT ALL TOGETHER: SEEING THE BIG PICTURE

It was not a surprise that women in this study defined health in a holistic manner, including both the body and the mind. This belief is consistent with previous research about Mexican-Americans that described a holistic understanding and maintenance of health among Mexican women, including the environment, physical health, and mental wellbeing (Kay, 1977). Discussing good health as something that allowed them to live an active, pain-free life is also a culturally traditional belief and consistent with Abril's (1977) findings that Mexican-Americans perceived good health as having the ability to maintain a high level of physical activity with the absence of pain. This study's participants believed this was important because it meant they could work and take care of their families. This finding supported culturally dominant beliefs since the family and maintaining the family plays an important role in Mexican culture (Molina & Aguirre-Molina, 1994).

Attempting to maintain positive mental health or a sense of wellbeing as a part of their overall health care was also supported by past research as a traditional practice (Kay, 1977). However, two findings from this study related to mental health have not been documented in past research: the concept of using a positive attitude to overcome or avoid illness and the belief that those who were sick or failed to overcome their illness suffered because they did not have a positive attitude.

The data in this study supported previous findings that the responsibility for health care usually falls to women in Mexican and Mexican-American cultural settings (Gonzalez-Swafford & Gutierrez, 1983; John et al., 1997; Lopez, 2005). However, this study did not support past findings that men, the traditional head of the family, are closely consulted by women before health decisions are made (Reinert, 1986). The women in this study did not discuss health decisions with men and believed their health and the health of their family was something for which they were responsible.

Participants also reported they maintained health in a culturally traditional manner as they relied on self diagnoses and treatment of illnesses, relied on other woman for assistance with health concerns, and chose to reserve professional medical services for serious conditions (Abril, 1977; Clark, 1995; Engebretson, 1994; Gonzalez-Swafford & Gutierrez, 1983; John et al., 1997; Kay, 1977; Keegan, 1996; Lopez, 2005). However, while past studies have found that Mexican-Americans often do not seek professional medical treatment because they lack insurance (Trevino, Moyer, Valdez & Stroup-Benham, 1991) or because of language barriers (Stein, Fox & Murata, 1991), this was not the case with participants in this study. While the women saw these barriers as annoying, they did not stop them from seeking professional medical services when they thought they were necessary, usually to confirm their own diagnoses.

Breast health practices were also affected by the avoidance of professional medical services. The women in this study did not participate in mammograms because they preferred to maintain their breast health through the use of self-breast checks. The women failed to support past studies that have suggested Mexican-American women do not have mammograms because of language barriers (Chesney, et al.; 1980, Stein et al., 1991), embarrassment, shame, (McKenna, 1989) modesty discussing sex and their bodies (Reinert, 1986), and expense of the procedure (Garbers, Jessop, Foti, Uribelarrea, & Chiasson, 2003).

The women also discussed beliefs and behaviors that were not noted as culturally traditional in existing literature. For example, prescription drugs were believed to have more negative side effects than benefits. In addition, the women often referred to Mexican printed sources of health information. While these were not considered traditional behaviors, they are in line with culturally dominant practices based on other health beliefs that surfaced during the current study. For example, both of these actions allowed women to participate in the culturally dominant behaviors of diagnosing and treating illnesses without the use of professional medical services.

The temporary changes the women made to their health care behaviors after moving to the United States were often a result of not having access to the supplies they needed as they attempted to maintain their health through traditional methods. In other words, if they could not find the supplies necessary to make home remedies, they felt forced to use professional medical care or prescriptions as a last resort. It was also interesting that these temporary changes included an increase in their use of professional medical services when they first moved to the United States. However, these changes were often dismissed by the women as something they tried for a short period of time because it was the "American way."

The choice to maintain health in a traditional manner often meant the women felt they had to work harder to maintain heath in the United States as opposed to when they lived in Mexico. For example, in addition to having difficulty obtaining natural health supplies the women also had less access to other Mexican women, previously their primary source of health information. As they made additional attempts to maintain health in a traditional manner, they did so because they truly believed in the benefits and felt it was the best way to maintain health, even after trying the dominant culture's approach.

The way the women maintained their breast health was also impacted by their traditional health beliefs. While past studies have suggested Mexican-American women do not have mammograms because of language barriers (Stein et al., 1991), embarrassment, shame, and expense of the procedure (Garbers, et al., 2003), this was not the case with the women in this study. There were no patterns related to a change in breast care depending on whether the women lived in Mexico or the United States. Participants believed in a holistic approach to health care, taking care of both the body and the mind. The women felt they were in touch with the things that were going on in their body and chose to self-diagnose problems with their breasts, being most comfortable with conducting self-breast exams. The women saw no need to have a professional medical test, or mammogram, to maintain their breast health; this was something they could maintain through the traditional practice of self-diagnosis.

These health beliefs were also evident as the women believed that when they diagnose an illness they must know the cause in order to best treat the illness. For example, fighting an illness often meant diagnosing the root cause of the illness, with the women believing most illnesses have a connection to one's diet. This meant the women felt that an ill person had probably eaten an improper diet. Believing health begins with foods that are eaten may be a result of Mexican folk medicine that traditionally has its roots in the belief that illness is an imbalance of the "humors" (blood and bile). Restoring balance is achieved by eating certain foods or herbs (Clark, 1970; Chesney et al.; 1980; LeVine, 1993; Madsen, 1973).

Similarly, an unanticipated finding was that the women also attempted to find a reason for cancer, most often attributing it to an injury. When injury was determined to be the cause of breast cancer, participants believed it was because a woman had hit her breast, causing a tumor. These injuries may have occurred in childhood and manifested themselves in adulthood. This greatly impacted the women's beliefs about the causes of breast cancer.

Women also attributed breast cancer to genetics, believing a woman had breast cancer because there was a history of cancer in her family. This is important as the women in this study discussed cancer as a problem for Mexican women. However, they did not feel personally at risk unless they had a breast injury or a family history of cancer. As a result, the women continued to maintain their breast health by using the traditional practice of self-diagnosis or manual self-checks as opposed to professional medical tests or mammograms.

Belief that diagnoses of illnesses should include determining the cause of the illness often contributed to participants having little or no confidence in U.S. professional medical services. The women felt that when they used professional medical services, they usually failed to receive an adequate diagnosis when the cause of the illness was not determined. Simply stated, they felt that physicians often sent them to another physician or sent them home with a medication, failing to fully explain the illness' cause. As a result, the women discussed that going to the doctor was often pointless. They felt they received no real answers about the cause of the illness and that they could better diagnose and treat ailments, usually using traditional home remedies while avoiding prescription medications.

The lack of confidence in U.S. professional medical services also affected the maintenance of their breast health. Women who had participated in mammograms usually failed to go for follow-up mammograms after the tests were negative. The women went for a mammogram and the physicians did not find anything wrong, resulting in the women believing that mammograms were simply another useless test. They believed professional medical tests often yielded the same "no problems" diagnosis that the women were able to achieve through their own traditional self-diagnoses using manual breast exams.

WHY IS THIS INFORMATION IMPORTANT TO HEALTH COMMUNICATORS?

The findings are important for health communicators in community and public health and health communication. The U.S. health care industry has gone through dramatic changes since 1990, shifting from a more traditional medical treatment model to one that sees the importance of and stresses prevention and wellness (Hetherington, Ekachai & Parkinson, 2001). One of the key objectives in promoting healthy behavior is to engage in regular screening for early disease detection (Champion & Springston, 2004). Unfortunately, screening is not occurring, with minorities most often failing to participate. Studies have shown that while breast cancer incidence (morbidity rate) is higher for non-Hispanic White females than for females in other racial and ethnic groups, it is minorities who carry higher mortality rates. The lower survival rate is due in part to delays in diagnosis and treatment. In fact, in 2003 the annual mammography screen rate for Mexican women was 64% as opposed to 71% in non-Hispanic White women (American Cancer Society, 2006).

The health status of Hispanics has become a national concern for health communicators as they are now the largest minority group in the United States (Smedley, Stith & Nelson, 2002), representing 44.3 million citizens or 14.8 percent of the total population (U.S. Census Bureau, 2007). It is expected that the Hispanic population will reach 53 million by 2020, 80 million by 2040, and nearly 97 million by 2050. To put this into perspective, that means that each year from now until 2050, the Hispanic population is projected to add more people to the United States than the majority, non-Hispanic White group (Day, 1996).

In order to address the higher rate of breast-cancer related mortality among Hispanic women, health communicators must look at the individual ethnic sub-groups that make up the larger Hispanic ethic category, focusing on the possible differences between these groups. As intercultural communication models are formed, health communicators must remember that people pay attention to, ignore, or modify information based upon how it fits with their previously defined attitudes and beliefs (Hill & Dixon, 2006).

These findings are important for public relations in health care settings. As the management of communication between an organization and its publics, public relations must seriously consider cultural identity, which is important as organizations seek to improve their communication with stakeholder publics (Davila, 2001). Strategic public relations management should involve not only segmenting stakeholders into publics, but also creating appropriate messages for those publics once they are identified. Targeted preventative and educational health campaigns provide public relations practitioners and researchers with the opportunity to assist in saving lives and improving health as well-designed public relations messages are essential to effectively inform publics about healthy behaviors and to persuade them to adopt those behaviors. The segmentation of publics often results in intercultural communication as situations arise when an organizational public identifies with a cultural group different from the organization's cultural group. During these times, public relations practitioners can serve as "boundary spanners" (Dozier, Grunig & Grunig, 1995) who can help organizations better understand the perspective of their public, and vice versa. Strategic messages are needed that will both further an organization's goals, such as decreasing health disparities among minority publics, while taking into consideration how a targeted public may react to these messages – possibly based upon cultural beliefs. This means public relations practitioners should be especially interested in the meaning different groups ascribe to health within their larger cultural context.

The following findings are especially useful to health communicators with an objective of increasing participation among Mexican-American women:

- Participants see other women, who are similar to them, as a source of health information.
- Participants maintain their health in order to be healthy so they can work (to provide for their family) and to be able to take care of their family.

- Participants avoid professional medical services because they believe they can achieve similar results using traditional, holistic methods.
- Participants believed cancer is the result of an injury and that they do not have a risk for breast cancer unless they have had a breast injury or have a family history of breast cancer.

As a result, the following suggestions are made for health communicators:

- Mexican-American women spokespersons should be selected for health campaigns.
- Female, Mexican-American community leaders should be involved in the development and implementation of local health campaigns.
- Hispanic churches and local service organization should be used promote health topics—while women mentioned hearing about breast health via mass media outlets, they discussed health and participated in breast health screenings at smaller venues such as when attending presentations at their churches or reading pamphlets or fliers from Hispanic service organizations.
- Health messages should convey that women need to participate in preventative health screenings so they will be healthy and can maintain the ability to work and take care of their family.
- Health messages should convey that preventative health screens with negative results are desired and do not mean one should fail to participate in additional or follow-up screenings. For example, "Medical tests that find nothing aren't useless," and "Just because you have a good mammogram does not mean you do not need to go back."
- Educational materials about the importance of routine preventative screenings should be presented to women when they have a screening. Failure to do so is a missed communication opportunity.
- Messages should support women's efforts to promote health naturally by supporting campaigns with natural ways to maintain health (i.e. foods linked to positive health outcomes or the breast benefits associated with breast feeding).
- Breast health messages should support community (mobile) mammography efforts that Mexican-American women are already accessing.
- Breast health campaigns should use testimonials from Mexican-American women who were the first person in their family to have breast cancer.
- Breast health campaigns should convey that if a woman does not have an injury to her breast she is still at risk for breast cancer.
- Breast health campaigns should convey that breast cancer often has few or no symptoms, making it hard for individuals to detect the disease on their own.
- Breast health campaigns should support the women's self-check efforts with monthly reminder programs.

In conclusion, health communicators must consider that "to communicate effectively [one] must first recognize the distance between what is available and what [is] actually apprehend[ed], and then understand how the resulting differences impede success" (Hill & Dixon, 2006, p. 72). Keeping this in mind when communicating health messages would lead to health programs that would better reach the aforementioned targeted populations, such as the Mexican-American women in this study, as each requires information more closely targeted to their community's pre-defined health beliefs.

REFERENCES

Abril, I. F. (1977). Mexican American folk beliefs: How they affect health care. *American Journal of Maternal Child Nursing, 2*(3), 169–173.

American Cancer Society. (2006). *Cancer facts & figures for Hispanics/Latinos 2006–2008.* (No. 862302).

Bauwens, E., & Anderson, S. (1988). Social and cultural influences on healthcare. In M. Stanhope & J. Lancaster (Eds.), *Community health nursing: Process and practice for promoting health* (2nd ed.). St. Louis, MO: Mosby.

Calle, E., Flander, D., Thun, M., & Martin, L. (1993). Demographic predictors of mammography and pap smear screening in U.S. women. *American Journal of Public Health, 83*(1), 53–60.

Chesney, A. P., Thompson, B. L. Guerara, A., Vela, A., & Schottstaedt, M. F. (1980). Mexican American folk medicine: Implications for the family physician. *The Journal of Family Practice, 11*(4), 567–574.

Clark, L. (1995). Maternal responsibility for health in household. *Health Care for Women International, 16*, 43–55.

Clark, L. (2002). Mexican-origin mothers' experiences using children's health care services. *Western Journal of Nursing Research, 24*(2), 159–179.

Clark, M. (1970). *Health in the Mexican American culture.* Berkley: University of California Press.

Corbin, J., & Strauss. (2008). Basics of qualitative research: Techniques and procedures for developing grounded theory (2nd ed.). Thousand Oaks, CA: Sage.

Davila, A. M. (2001). *Latinos, Inc.: The marketing and making of a people.* Berkeley: University of California Press.

Day, J. C. (1996). *Population projections of the United States by age, sex, race, and Hispanic origin: 1995 to 2050.* Washington, DC: U.S. Bureau of the Census. (P25–1130).

Dozier, D. M., Grunig, L. A., & Grunig, J. E. (1995). *Manager's guide to excellence in public relations and communication management.* Mahwah, N.J.: Lawrence Erlbaum Associates.

Engebretson, J. (1994). Folk healing and biomedicine: Culture clash or complimentary approach? *Journal of Holistic Nursing, 12*(3), 240–250.

Fabrega, H. (1973). Toward a model of illness behavior. *Medical Care, 11*, 470–484.

Freed, A. O. (1988). Interviewing through an interpreter. *Social Work, 33*(4), 315–319.

Garbers, S., Jessop, D., Foti, H., Uribelarrea, M., & Chiasson, M. (2003). Barriers to breast cancer screening in low-income Mexican and Dominican women in New York City. *Journal of urban health: Bulletin of the New York Academy of Medicine, 80*(1), 81–91.

Glaser, B., & Strauss, A. (1967). *The discovery of grounded theory: Strategies for qualitative research.* New York, NY: de Gruyter.

Gonzalez-Swafford, M. J., & Gutierrez, M. G. (1983). Ethno-medical beliefs and practices of Mexican Americans. *Nurse Practitioner, 6*, 29–34.

Hetherington, L., Ekachai, D., & Parkinson, M. (2001). *Public relations in the health care industry.* In R. L. Heath (Ed.), Handbook of public relations (pp. 571–578). Newbury Park, CA: Sage.

Hill, L. B., & Dixon, L. D. (2006). The intercultural communication context: Preparation for international public relations. In M. G. Parkinson & D. Ekachai (Eds.), *International and intercultural public relations: A campaign case approach* (pp. 66–84). Boston, MA: Allyn & Bacon.

Intercultural Cancer Council. *Hispanics/Latinos & Cancer.* Retrieved Feb. 18, 2010, from http://iccnetwork.org/cancerfacts/cfs4.htm

John, R., Resendiz, R., & De Vargas, L. W. (1997). Beyond familism?: Familism as explicit motive for eldercare among Mexican American caregivers. *Journal of Cross-Cultural Gerontology, 12*(2), 145–162.

Kavanagh, K. H., & Kennedy, P. H. (1992). *Promoting cultural diversity: Strategies for health care professionals.* Newbury Park, CA: Sage.

Kay, M. A. (1977). Health and illness in a Mexican American barrio. In E. H. Spicer (Ed.). *Ethnic medicine in the southwest* (pp. 99–166). Tucson: University of Arizona Press.

Keegan, L. (1996). Use of alternative therapies among Mexican Americans in the Texas Rio Grande Valley. *Journal of Holistic Nursing, 14*, 277–294.

Leininger, M. M. (Ed.). (2001). *Culture care diversity and universality: A theory of nursing care.* Boston, MA: Jones & Bartlett Publishers.

LeVine, S. E. (1993). *Dolor y alegria: Women and social change in urban Mexico.* Madison: University of Wisconsin Press.

Lincoln, Y. S., & Guba, E. G. (1985). *Naturalistic inquiry.* Beverly Hills, CA: Sage.

Lindlof, T. R., & Taylor, B. C. (2002). *Qualitative communication research methods* (2nd ed.). Thousand Oaks, CA: Sage.

Lopez, R. (2005). Use of alternative folk medicine by Mexican American women. *Journal of Immigrant Health, 7*(1), 23–31.

Madsen, W. (1973). *The Mexican-Americans of south Texas.* New York: Holt, Rinehart & Winston.

McCarthy, M. C., Ruiz, E., Gale, B. J., Karam, C., & Moore, N. (2004). The meaning of health: Perspectives of Anglo and Latino older women. *Health Care Women International, 25*(10), 950–969.

McCracken, G. D. (1988). *The long interview.* Newbury Park, CA: Sage.

McKenna, M. A. (1989). Transcultural perspectives in the nursing care of the elderly. In J. S. Boyle & M. M. Andrews (Eds.), *Transcultural concepts in nursing care* (pp. 189–220). Glenview, IL: Scott & Foresman.

Molina, C. W., & Aguirre-Molina, M. (1994). *Latino health in the U.S.: A growing challenge.* Washington, D.C.: American Public Health Association.

Morgan, D. (1988). *Focus groups as qualitative research.* Newbury Park, CA: Sage.

Napoles-Springer, A. M., Sanotya, J., Houston, K., Perez-Stable, E. J., & Stewart, A. L. (2005). Patient's perceptions of cultural factors affecting the quality of their medical encounters. *Health Expectations, 8*(1), 4–17.

Reinert, B. R. (1986). The health care beliefs and values of Mexican-Americans. *Home Healthcare Nurse, 4*(5), 25–31.

Schreiber, J. M., & Homiak, J. P. (1981). Mexican Americans. In A. Harwood (Ed.), *Ethnicity and medical care* (pp. 264–336). Cambridge, MA: Harvard University Press.

Smedley, B. D., Stith, A. Y., & Nelson, A. R. (Eds.). (2003). *Unequal treatment: Confronting racial and ethnic disparities in health care.* Washington, D.C.: National Academies Press.

Sobralske, M. C. (1985). Perceptions of health: Navajo Indians. *Topics in Clinical Nursing, 7*(3), 32–39.

Springston, J. K., & Champion, V. L. (2004). Public relations and cultural aesthetics: Designing health brochures. *Public Relations Review, 30*, 483–491.

Stein, J., Fox, S., & Murata, P. (1991). The influence of ethnicity, socioeconomic status, and psychological barriers on use of mammography. *Journal of Health and Social Behavior, 32*(2), 101–113.

Strauss, A., & Corbin, J. (1998). *Basics of qualitative research: Techniques and procedures for developing grounded theory.* Thousand Oaks, CA: Sage.

Taylor, R. E. (1994). Qualitative research. In M. Singletary (Ed.), *Mass communication research: Contemporary methods and applications* (pp. 265–279). NY: Longman.

Torres, S. (Ed.). (1996). *Hispanic voices: Hispanic health educators speak out.* New York: National League for Nursing Press.

Trevino, F. M., Moyer, M. E., Valdez. R. B., & Stroup-Benham, C. A. (1991). Health insurance coverage and utilization of health services by Mexican Americans, mainland Puerto Ricans, and Cuban-Americans. *Journal of the American Medical Association, 265*(2), 233–237.

U.S. Census Bureau. (2000). We the people: Hispanics in the United States, Census 2000 special reports (no. CENSR-18). Washington, DC.

U.S. Census Bureau. (2007). *Minority Population Tops 100 Million.* Retrieved Jan. 5, 2013 from http://www.census.gov/Press-Release/www/releases/archives/population/010048.html

U.S. Department of Health and Human Services. (2013). *Eliminating health disparities: Strengthening data on race, ethnicity, and primary language in the United States.* Retrieved Feb. 18, 2013, from http://purl.access.gpo.gov/GPO/LPS72255

Wenger, A. F. (1993). Cultural meaning of symptoms. *Holistic Nursing Practice, 7*(2), 23–35.

Chapter 19:

Running dialogue: The social and communicative experience of running together

Tessa M. DuBois
University of North Carolina, Greensboro

> *Of all the gifts that running has brought me, the greatest gift by far is the ability to connect with people on a profoundly personal level. There is something magic in the movement of our feet and rhythm of our breathing that breaks down the walls we normally hide behind. All I know is that when I run with someone, we share more than just the road. We share a common experience, which allows us to talk with an ease that only runners know.*
>
> –John Bingham (2007, p. 59)

> *The single adequate form for verbally expressing authentic human life is the open-ended dialogue. Life by its very nature is dialogic. To live means to participate in dialogue.*
>
> –Mikhail Bakhtin (1984, p. 293)

INTRODUCTION

The intense and coordinated physical activity of sports often leads to, and is paralleled by, intensely satisfying communicative experiences between the participants (Coates, 1999). This chapter is based on a qualitative study of communication between long distance runners and focuses specifically on the question of how the embodied experience of running together opens invitational space for free flowing and satisfying dialogue—*health communication*—between two running partners.

Running is analyzed due to the sharing of intimate and private space between two runners. There is something about the synchronic motion of moving forward and the talk that evolves between runners that show potential for blossoming friendships. The chosen route taken by runners is constructed not only during the physical motion of running, but also interactionally constructed by the unfolding of joined discourse that evolves along the route (Allen-Collinson, & Hockey, 2007).

Through studying talk between committed long-distance runners, this chapter explores the more broadly important but under studied question of how communication, coordinated physical activity, and positive health outcomes are interconnected. The parallel between the physical and the communicative is one worth exploring more deeply in the field of health communication.

This chapter connects Victor Turner's (1982) phenomenon of liminality within rituals, with Mihaly Csikszentmihalyi (1990) flow theory, positive communication (Baxter & DeGooyer, 2001), and dialogue theory (Buber, 1958; Bakhtin, 1981; Cissna & Anderson, 1998) to discover how sharing physical activity can open unexpected moments for peak, ecstatic, conversational flow between individuals, with positive results. Narrative data from interviews with 12 runners are excerpted to illustrate the communicative experience of joint physical activity (DuBois, 2013). Ultimately, this chapter echoing Bingham's (2007) position captured in the epigram above, seeks to shed light on the deeper awareness and link between human performance and communication.

SPORT AND COMMUNICATION

Sport and exercise are human activities directed at one's self-fulfillment. They satisfy both psychological and social needs of an individual, which together constitute a spectrum of one's goals and motivations (Kowalkikow, 2009). The term "sport" here however can imply competition, forms of play and leisure, and physical exercise. Physical activity constructs a context in which we, as humans, transform ourselves, extending our potential as we establish new limits to our present being (Rowe, 2008). Although athletic performance is an actual activity, Kassing et al. (2004) state that "communication in, around, and about sport influences both the physical performance of athletes and the social construction of the sporting experience" (p. 374). Communication within sporting communities demonstrates how members enact, (re)produce, consume, and organize the sport. Communication is not only fundamental, but constitutive to the experience of sport. For this reason the "community of sport represents a rich place for communicative exploration and stands as a community that is in fact co-created and sustained communicatively" (Kassing et al., 2004, p. 374).

Why sport?

Arguably, one of the most important health behaviors related to obesity epidemic we face today includes incorporating physical activity into one's lifestyle (American Academy of Pediatrics, 2003; CDC, 2011). Thus, within Health Communication, the study of exercise related talk might begin to show improvements to one's attitude and frequency of exercising. The 2013 study on dialogue during shared runs provide a starting point for Health Communication scholars interested in public health and physical activity by providing a deeper understand to how communication influences one's attitudes and behaviors regarding exercise. Therefore, it is recognized that the context of sport and physical activity is increasingly growing in the field of Communication

Studies and demonstrates an "ideal site for exploring communication" (Kassing et al., 2004, p. 375). Although many scholars today have begun bridging the gap between communication and sport (see Kassing et al., 2004; Meân & Halone, 2010; Krizek, 2008), there's yet very few studies of the actual communicative practices *during* sporting performance (LeCourteur & Feo, 2011). The goal in this chapter is to engage scholarship that sheds light on communication when actually *doing* sport.

MAKING EXERCISE A DAILY RITUAL

The study of embodied performances brings up a focus on *rituals*, since individuals have to know how to do their sporting activity. Communication among team/group members coordinate actions, attitudes, and can integrate members into a particular organizational culture (Lindermann & Cherney, 2008). The integration of sport members relate to Kassing et al. (2004) notion behind sport socialization, which describes sport as a medium by which individuals learn and develop desirable social behaviors, interpersonal relationships, and group cohesion. For example, running together brings a shared understand of interlacing pace and conversation between two runners. Running together adds a level of social benefits to exercise, which may increase people's desire to incorporate physical activity into their daily routine.

Rethinking running as a ritual

French ethnographer Arnold Van Gennep is best known for his work, *The Rites of Passage* (1960) during rituals (e.g. marriage ceremonies, initiation ceremonies). According to van Gennep, rituals act on the body to affect the soul, yet that in order to be effective they must bring together groups of people, who in coming together affirm their individual identity as members of the group and collectively as constituting a group (Turner, 1982). Take for example local running groups who get together weekly to train together. The sport of running brings together a group of people with a similar mentality to running. Thus, rituals unite the body and space (Walla, 2005).

Examining running (as well as any other sport) rituals, there is a shared understanding on the "how-to's" and athletic discourse where individuals learn how to negotiate their body and space in order to perform the activity. These serve as symbolic acts that create sporting performance. When two people come together for a run both become united in synchronized movements, and behaviors, working together to accomplish a certain goal. Running rituals thus serve a form of cultural performance (Rowe, 2008). Take for example the Tarahumara of northwestern Mexico, a group of Native Americans renowned for their long-distance running ability. With widely dispersed settlements, these people developed a tradition of long-distance running for communication, transportation, ceremonial, and competitive purposes (McDougall, 2009). Other running rituals include the Olympics and Boston Marathon, which serve as historical and seasonal public celebrations of international sport.

Community within running rituals

Since rituals unite people together (e.g. sport teams, workout buddies, games/races), they bring the potential to open a spirit of *communitas*, or a sense of community and strong connection among individuals. Interactions are instead characterized by personal honesty, openness, a lack of pretensions or pretentiousness. Thus, communitas designates a feeling of immediate community, and may involve the sharing of special knowledge and understanding (Turner, 1982). Communitas within the running culture may bring social support and enjoyment when exercising as noted by one of the running participants: "There's a journey we both undertake in our preparation for a particular event. There is a sense of camaraderie that comes with belonging to a team who trains together on a daily basis."

Though the communal social and individual psychological impact of the embodied performance, *something* happens; one enters a state of "flow" and emerges with a new sense of meaning or purpose. Flow, identified by the psychologist Csikszentmihalyi (1990), denotes the spontaneous holistic awareness when we act with total involvement in an activity, experiencing a sense of exhilaration, harmony, and bliss. Flow in the running community can be characterized as a "runner's high" or being "in the zone." When we experience flow, we are in control of our present actions, while our daily concerns and stress are minimized, or even put out of mind. It's important to note however that a "runner's high" is a biochemical and psychological sensation within an individual. A "runner's high" also typically occurs more consistently on runs longer than 40 minutes when endorphins are released to the brain and alter one's mood to a more positive emotion and behaviors. This dynamic, in which a physical act profoundly and powerfully impacts one's self-experience, suggests that one's lived-body experience serves as an overarching meaning system between symbolic order and the self (Reischer, 2001). Yet this flow sensation has the potential to open gates to freeing conversation and disclosure. The positive mood and endorphins have the power to open doors for profound, meaningful conversation (Dubois, 2013). Together, communitas and flow bring added motivation to exercising.

Running rites of passage

In all communal and sporting rituals, there comes a processual form of "passage," as noted in van Gennep's work, *The Rites of Passage* (1960). Van Gennep distinguishes three phases in a rite of passage, which can be portrayed to the process of becoming a runner. These phases outlined below are *separation, transition*, and *incorporation.*

Stage 1: Separation. The first phase of separation defines the moment when a person disengages from a social role or status to a new role. The reconstruction of identity begins with separation from some role, relationship, or other key component of the extended self. Separation often occurs literally in time and space, triggered by some external or internal force or event (Turner, 1982). This could be when an individual decides to join a running club due to health concerns. They begin to separate their identity of a non-runner and begin to identify with what it means to be a runner, verse other athletic identities.

Stage 2: Transition. The second phase of transition, also called "limen," meaning "threshold" in Latin, takes place when the ritual subject(s) pass through a period of ambiguity called *liminal space*. Here, liminal space reflects the moment in rituals when individuals stand in the "threshold" between their previous way of structuring their identity, or community, and a new way, which the ritual establishes. During liminal space, the past is shortly suspended or retracted, and the future has not yet begun, thus leaving an instant of "pure potentiality" where individuals are transitioning from one social status to another (Turner, 1982). Reflecting back to the running example, the liminal space of a runner is the "in-between" of a run—the continuous movement towards the end goal, the present challenge for the body and mind, the state of being in the landscape, and the period of transformation to one's (re)creation of self. A runner is aware of the start and finish, yet the in-between of the run serves as the "antistructural" path were normal constraints are lowered for the time being (Rowe, 2008). Liminal space could be the in-between of a marathon race where an individual is transitioning their identity to a marathoner. Liminal space, as a focus to the running study, will soon be explained in further detail.

Stage 3: Incorporation. The final phase, incorporation, includes "symbolic phenomena and actions which represent the return of the subjects to their new, relatively stable, well-defined position in the total society" (Turner, 1982, p. 24). The passage from one status to another is often accompanied by a passage in space, a geographical movement from one place to another, or the crossing of a threshold which separates two distinct areas of pre-ritual and post-ritual. For example, during the award ceremony of the Olympics, athletes pass through a transition to their athletic identity in enhancing their athletic status as an Olympian. After the Olympics are over, these athletes return to their daily routines, yet are changed and enhanced due to their award, accomplishment, and prestige at the Olympics.

UNPACKING LIMINAL SPACE

With each of these phases intact, it is the lived experience of self-transformation during the second rite of passage—liminal space—that breaks down structural expectations and instead, liberates individuals to experience moments flow that may induce dialogue and communitas (Turner, 1982). Here, liminal space during human performance opens room for "conversational flow," in which words flow into one another effortlessly and the conversation takes on a life of its own (Baxter, 2004a). In liminal space, social hierarchies fade, opening new and authentic space to engage with another without expectations or judgment.

Liminal space and communication

From the 2013 study among 12 distance runners, running dyads experienced conversational flow during the liminal space—or, the in-between,—of their run when they experienced the tranquil sensation of flow. While in deep conversation and disclosure, participants lost track of time and mileage, but instead, focused on each other. In these moments, individuals gained a sense of bliss, incitement, and delight that result from a fleeting moment of togetherness. Running together opened new space to enhance physical activity as well as communication. These moments of conversational flow during the run displayed an emerging path for relationship wholeness (Baxter, 2004b).

Participants within the study noticed that during liminal space, their social roles did not interrupt the flow of conversation. For example, one participant noted that as she talked and ran with her younger sister, the younger girl began opening up to where it felt more like they were best friends verse siblings: "I was able to play both the big sister role and friend role—we were on the same level when we run." Another runner, a coach, mentioned he felt inclined and comfortable opening up about his divorce while running with his younger teammates:

> *This is not something you would think of talking to two young girls about. But when you train as hard as we do and struggle and push each other, you form a bond that transcends just about anything. They helped me through some very tough times not really giving me answers or what I needed to do but they listened and shared in my pain just like we do every day as we train together. They literally saved my life through a very difficult time in my life!*

These two examples show how their role of older sister and coach vanished and instead, the social roles and expectations were in balance with their running partners. They experienced a space of spontaneous moments of coming together in conversation, community, and social support. Turner (1982) noted that in the mode of spontaneous communitas, it's important to relate directly to another person as he or she presents their self in the here-and-now, of which is seen in the narrative transcripts above. Individuals who interact with one another in this liminal space become absorbed into a single synchronized, fluid event, or as Turner noted, "one wants to make the Others, We" (p. 48).

RUNNING RELATED TALK

The coming together in both running and conversation was noted by all participants. Although reaching conversational flow is spontaneous and fleeting, the running participants illustrated a patterned process in reaching dialogic moments. The primary theme that emerged from the running study analysis was the concept of (re)entering the liminal space. From here, participants' shared running experiences captured the unfolding of transformative communication (i.e. conversational flow) that left evoking memories on each individual, causing them a desire to relive those moments of running together. This desire to re-enter liminal space from a health perspective can encourage individual to pursue exercise more often because of the social experience it brings. This observation created the cyclic pattern as seen in the model created below:

Entering threshold ◊ Being in space together (conversational flow) ◊ Memory

In the study, running together brought a ritualistic performance that opened unexpected moments for peak, liminal, ecstatic, and conversational flow between runners. Yet running can be substitute for a numerous of other share experiences of play and sport. To better understand the model the following section are divided into the three processes—*entering*, *flow*, and *memory*—to document the experience of human performance and communication.

Phase 1: Entering

Coming together to run is a ritualized activity that unites the body and space in a structural sequence of symbolic acts. Just like coming together in a conversation has a routine process of small talk that gradually unfolds, so typically does a run. For example, two individuals meeting up for a jog have a shared knowledge of the "how-to's" of running, yet when together, each individual learns to negotiate his or her body, pace, and space with his or her communication patterns. This form of unity and synchrony is seen here in this narrative quote:

> *We eased into the first mile at a leisurely pace, as we had done dozens, maybe hundreds of times in the past, and our footfalls fell into rhythm striking the ground in unison like a metronome, tick, tock, tick, tock. (DuBois, 2013, transcript theme I, no. 9)*

In planning a run, there's a start and a finish, yet the space between illustrates liminality. It's a space for the unknown to unfold and in certain moments, the conversational structure of everyday talk to break down, leaving open room for the possibility of dialogue. Thus, together, performance and communication show an ability to create transformation experiences communicatively. But what does this entering of the threshold (i.e. liminality) feel like? Participants noted metaphoric phrases of "walls unfolding;" "boundaries disappearing," "an escape;" and "being in the zone" to symbolically capture this liminal space sensation. These metaphors are detailed below.

Unfolding of walls and boundaries

Coming into liminality is comparable to the beginning of a wall lowering, releasing any structural technique of skillful discussion and instead letting the conversation lead. In the running culture, the saying "hitting the wall" captures the physical and mental breaking point of a runner; an invisible blockade to the path that becomes a barrier in moving forward. Yet the wall here does the opposite. This wall allows one's guard to lower, allowing conversation to freely flow without any societal expectations or judgments to get in the way. As reflected here, "It seems like a small wall is let down while you are running and you can share everything with one another" (DuBois, 2013, transcript theme I, no. 11).

Once a wall is lowered, boundaries disappear creating open space to see where the conversation takes the runners. This entering allows for fluidity between one's body and talk. With the disappearing of walls and boundaries, individuals experienced the sensation of freedom, an escape, and being in and out of "the zone." This sensation captures a spark of flow—a moment in time where daily concerns were limited and instead the runners were experiencing pure bliss in the moment. This reflects a moment that may trigger rational thought and cathartic release through conversation as seen here:

> *There is something about running on the trail from our high school that allows us to talk about literally anything...there's no limitations. We briefly asked each other what our schedules were before we headed back to school, but Taylor immediately transitioned into how her grandma was not doing well. We had an in depth conversation about what has been going on and how it was taking a toll both on Taylor and her family. Running with me was her break and her time to relieve some emotional stress. It is somehow easier to share embarrassing or personal things with her when we are running. (DuBois, 2013, transcript theme I, no. 19)*

Escape, freedom, zoning out/being in the zone

With the disappearing of walls and boundaries, runners experienced the sensation of freedom, an escape, and being in and out of "the zone." Participants' narratives here capture a spark of transcendence and freedom to go beyond the physical discomfort that running brings at times. This flow-like expression is captured by this runner: "The freedom and simplicity of unaided movement and how it heightens the senses making every aspect of life more vibrant. It's life at its purest" (DuBois, 2013, transcript theme I, no. 22).

For the participants, running began to bring clarity, contentment, peace, and satisfaction to the present moment that triggered rational thought and cathartic release between runners. While some participants saw this time as a moment to zone *out* and free their mind of concern or stress, others used this time to experience deep thinking, and instead zoned *in*to particular thoughts. The combining of bodily awareness with communication opened and unfolded a space to create transformative experiences communicatively, as seen in the continuation of the cycle below in theme II—conversational flow.

Phase 2: Flow

Conversational flow captured the moments when runners were so engaged in their conversation that their focus attention on their movement, fatigue, muscular ache, and mileage diminished. Instead, participants gathered a sense of great bliss, incitement, and delight that resulted from a fleeting moment of togetherness. Conversational flow when running together seemed to follow a patterned interaction that began with small talk to better divert one's attention from exercising (e.g. repetitiveness, physical discomfort). Yet by diverting attention of present condition, new space opened for opportunity of greater conversation. This patterned process of conversational flow reflects this linear unfolding:

Diversion ◊ Disclosing ◊ Deep Sharing ◊ Transformative Talk

Diversion. Diversion occurred when runners began engaging in conversation with their partners only to divert their attention from running. The diversion began as small talk, yet with time and mileage, conversation unfolded, as seen here from two runners: "We always talk about our week and what is going on but as the run goes on if you are having difficulties in your life they have a way of coming up;" "The run started out conservatively, and we quickly began chatting about surface level happenings in each of our lives…however, as the run continued, we gradually let our guard down. We began to discuss more serious topics" (DuBois, 2013, transcript theme II, no 14 1). This diversion of physical attention evolved the communicators towards disclosure, as if avoiding and engaging were occurring simultaneously.

Disclosure

Sharing a sporting activity like running or hiking brings a private space for two people to disclose without interruptions or distractions. Disclosure here brought important communicative activity for the development and maintenance of relational closeness. The motion of moving forward and limited face-to-face eye contact may play a part, but it's safe to say that participants noticed themselves being calm when engaging in certain topics with one another they typically would have steered away from if in other settings (e.g. sitting down at lunch). This reflects back to the sense of freedom running brought to participants; freedom in both movement and talk (see transcript theme II, no. 17–19). The privacy of running together created what Goodall and Kellett (2004) called a "spatial container"—a "place" communicatively in which individuals engage in collaborative-collective thinking. Disclosure provided comfort and trust between running partners that continued the communication onward to moments of deep sharing.

Deep Sharing

In running together, partners shared more than a run, but also a space, time, a passion, and commitment to each other in working together to finish. The active form of synchrony between the runners' movements, strides, breaths, and the sharing of time and space created connection and conversation among the participants. It was a synchronized unity, a unique dance-like form of coming together where conversation was likely to create "interactional harmony" (Kim, 2012).

Sharing a run gave the participants the emotions of unity, joy, empathy, and cathartic release, which gave way to deeper connections to their running partner and openness in their conversations. These felt emotions experienced by individuals opened a sense of comfort and willingness to spark meaningful conversation. Yet what is it about being in harmony that opens space for conversation? Baxter, Norwood, and Nebel (2012) drew insights behind this phenomenon in that repetition, as in the repeated movement of running, along with prosody, can create a sense of rhythm that invites the hearer to move along with the speaker and let the conversation flow. One participant in particular observed this occurrence as noted, "After a mile or so, the timing of our dialogue and movement were synchronized and natural, like the strokes of an internal combustion engine" (DuBois, 2013, transcript theme II, no. 20). The synchrony of movement, talk, and listening has the power to create transformative moments.

Transformative Talk

The word "transformative" here means something sparked because of the conversation. Transformative talk from participants reflected Goodall and Kellett's (2004) description of AHA! moments. These profound yet surprising moments brought an awakening to dialogue and opened the possibility for personal and relational change. Certain participants noted particular conversations that came as a surprise to them that they felt comfortable disclosing. They noted that if it were not for running, they would not have openly shared their thoughts and created their bond. These moments were a breakthrough not only for the relationship, but also for individual's trust level in disclosing, as noted by this participant:

> *This level of awareness and peace, these deep, meaningful conversations—none of it would have been possible if we weren't running, and we hadn't experienced this "runner's high." We tried very hard to reach this state of awareness while doing numerous other things (walking, sitting, kayaking, etc.) but only while running were we able to reach this enlightened state of mind, and effectively convey to each other our true feelings, hopes, and desire. Without a doubt, we finished the run feeling stronger, closer, and more loving. (DuBois, 2013, transcript theme II, no. 39)*

These moments were a breakthrough not only for the relationship, but also for individual's trust level in disclosing. These AHA! moments were brief and interrupted ritualized sequence of conversation, yet ended with a transformed person and bond. Because these moments were brief and surprising, the conversation reflected quality over quantity.

Each run came to the end, yet the power of transformative talk allowed one's return back to life as changed individuals. These transformations happened on a shared run and left participants with a desire to re-enter their ritual due to the lasting impressions on one's memory. As one runner wrote, "For those of us who truly embrace it, running is who we are. And that, for me, is enough to get me out there again tomorrow" (DuBois, 2013, transcript theme I, no. 3). Together, running partners created a shared knowledge and a memory of these peak moments. Overall, the conversational flow experienced created memorable moments as seen in the third and final theme below. It was their memory that developed a desire to re-enter the threshold of running together.

Phase 3: Memory

Although dialogic moments appeared in mystic and surprising ways, they left enduring impressions that transcended through time after the run is over. The memorable running moments noted by participants showed how running together created lasting impressions, along with a unique community and support system within their social group, also known as communitas. There was an instant bond, a "click" between two runners who shared a passion of endurance and commitment to running; and this shared knowledge connected two runners together and continued their bond. As one runner wrote:

> *The people that I met over the summer through running and racing are incredible. There are people that I have only seen one or two times but I feel like I have known them forever. It doesn't matter if I never see these people again or only see them once every few months or so, the bond that you create while running is something entirely different than those relationships formed elsewhere... Whether we spent five minutes or five hours with them, they are people that we will always remember. (DuBois, 2013, transcript theme III, no. 1)*

Having this positive experience and social group can enhance one's physical performance by creating enthusiasm and desire to exercise more often. The possibility of reaching the state of flow and transformative talk brings a motivator to physical activity. Thus, physical activity can bring moments of conversation, community, and positive memory. The conversational model presented above illustrates that dialogic moments can spark during times of exercise. Thus showing that during times of muscular exhaustion, beautiful communicative moments can overpower our fatigued physical state.

DIALOGIC MOMENTS DURING PHYSICAL ACTIVITY

The potential for aesthetic beauty exists in everyday communication and lived-experiences. This chapter shows that the beauty of communicative life can be exercised even during physical activity. Thus, aesthetic communication is not a *thing*, rather; it is art in motion that denotes a process of doing or making (Baxter et al., 2012). Given the moments of liminality and flow, it is proposed that shared sporting or physical activities have the possibility of creating an aesthetic activity of coming together in dialogue. Burkitt and Sullivan (2009) demonstrate how embodied experiences allow one to (re)act towards another to create meaning through language. Although research states that capturing emotion through words is difficult, one way people *share* experience is through dialogue with each other.

The study of dialogue

Over the last century, numerous scholars have described and written about dialogue from various perspectives (see Baxter, 2004; Poulos, 2008; Goodall & Kellett, 2004; Anderson & Cissa, 1998). Two original scholars of dialogue in particular are Martin Buber (1958) and Mikhail Bakhtin (1990). Buber's (1958) *I-Thou* relation reflects his concept behind dialogue, in which its basic movement is the turning towards and directing of one's attention to the other. In its application, dialogue is unique in stirring individuals to "get beyond the gray everydayness of relational routines" and be able to live in "peak experiences" (Goodall & Kellett, 2004, p. 161) that lead to a mutual sense of fulfillment in a relationship (Baxter, 2004b).

Experiencing dialogue involves coming together—a moment of "meeting"—in unplanned, yet special moments where each individual has in mind the other and turns to them with the intention of establishing heartfelt connections (Poulos, 2008). Dialogue denotes enjoying in open empathic communication to ideally reach a "transcendent, egoless state of communication" that connects us beyond ourselves generates new feelings, understandings, directions, goals, and so forth between the dialogic partners (Goodall & Kellett, 2004). Thus, dialogue is an experience of togetherness built on openness and empathic engagement of self and other. It is important to note that the relational experience of dialogue, just as the individual's peak experience of flow, is difficult to articulate because it is embodied within a person who interprets it. Yet as an outcome, dialogue yields profound social connections (Goodall & Kellett, 2004).

Unity in physical movement and conversation

The orientation and experience of the running body in the environment has been shown to be crucial to how people understand each other and build relationships through action. To know one's identity to self, body, and others may allow one to connect with others whether it's through shared experiences or dialogic moments (LeCourteur & Feo, 2011, p. 125). Shepherd (2006) comments that when we experience another in communication we come to be in sympathy, or in common feeling with that other. This common feeling is the sense of "sharedness" we often assume in engaging with others. Sharing a run is an act taken upon by an invitation; yet this invitation has the potential to open greater, more profound moments in time and space between self and other. The experience of sharing a time of exercise and sport is a shared presence, a "being-together," and a physical sharing of the human body working in becoming more, together.

CONCLUSION

The findings to this chapter contributed to the understanding of communication, human performance, and health within the ritual of running together. The narratives supported Buber's dialogic notion of *I-Thou* and coming together to express authentic openness with one another to experience a transcendent sense of wholeness (Baxter, 2004b). Experiencing dialogue on a shared run showed open acceptance of the other, and in doing so individuals were able to achieve something greater together that neither of them could accomplish separately. Dialogue existed when boundaries and walls were lowered and partners entered a space of liminality filled with potential of unstructured, communicative flow where everything trembled in balance (Turner, 1982).

The dialogic moments experienced by the participants would not have been achieved if participants were not sharing a run, as some participants explicitly noted. As stated in Bingham's opening quote, something magical in running together breaks down walls and invites and builds conversation. Sharing an intimate space with people around a common bond brought individuals together and brought trust and ease to disclose. The participants showed their act of coming together for a run slowly transitioned to a coming together in dialogue where attention focused solely on the other, instead of time and mileage. This synchronization of movement and talk between the runners became their energy and fuel to finish the run.

This chapter captured the "positive" aspects in health communication showing the beauty it has in transforming people, relationships, and physical activity (Baxter & DeGooyer, 2001). Experiencing dialogue in the midst of one's day can unfold under any circumstances, especially during the liminal space, or "realm of pure possibility" (Turner, 1968, p. 48). Even beyond our physical comfort that physical activity brings, dialogic moments may appear. People desire to come into space with one another to engage in open, freeing, and genuine conversation. For some, running together provides this space. As Bakhtin (1984) sated, "Life by its very nature is dialogic" (p. 293). Dialogue has a transcendent power that is rare and unique in our everyday lives; yet when experienced, we want more. Experiencing true dialogue during running can extend one's attitude toward exercising, and even increase one's duration of physical activity.

The practical goals behind this chapter have the potential to bring greater awareness to the participation of exercise as a means to promote physical and communicative health. Having a partner to run with not only encourages and improves physical health, but also has the power to strengthen one's communicative and interpersonal health. Future research implications include investigating dialogic moments among other forms of exercise where partners experience flow (e.g. gardening, hiking, dancing). This way, we gain understanding of how other forms of coordinated action invite dialogue. This would also add research in regards to relational and health communication. Overall, this study captures a ritualized form of coming together in space, time, and physical movement to show human performance and communication as an aesthetic experience to be shared and re-lived. These fleeting sparks of dialogue brought beauty to communicative life, lasting memory to human life, and opportunity for a healthier life.

REFERENCES

American Academy of Pediatrics. (2003). Prevention of pediatric overweight and obesity. *Pediatrics, 112*, 424–430.

Allen-Collinson, J. & Hockey, J. (2007). Grasping the phenomenology of sporting bodies. *International Review for the Sociology of Sport, 42*(2), 115–131.

Bakhtin, M. M. (1981). *The dialogic imagination: Four essays by M. M. Bakhtin*. M. Holquist, C. Emerson,, & N. Holquist (Eds.), Austin: University of Texas Press.

Bakhtin, M. M., & Emerson, C. (1984). *Problems of Dostoevsky's poetics*. Minneapolis: University of Minnesota Press.

Bakhtin, M. M. (1990). Author and hero in aesthetic activity. In M. Hoquist (Ed.), *Art and Answerability: Early essays by M. M. Bakhtin* (60–102). Austin: University of Texas Press.

Baxter, L. A. (2004a). Dialogues of relating. In R. Anderson, L.A. Baxter, & K. N. Cissna (Eds.), *Dialogue: Theorizing difference in communication studies* (pp. 107–124). Thousand Oaks, CA: Sage.

Baxter, L. A. (2004b). Relationships as dialogues. *Personal Relationships, 11*, 1–22. doi: 10.1111/j.1475-6811.2004.00068.x

Baxter L. A., & DeGooyer, Jr., D. H. (2001), Perceived aesthetic characteristics of interpersonal conversations. *Southern Communication Journal, 67*, 1–18.

Baxter, L., Norwood, K., & Nebel, S. (2012). Aesthetic relating. In T. Socha & M. Pitts (Eds.), *The positive side of interpersonal communication* (19–38). New York: Peter Lang.

Behnke, E. A. (2011). Husserl's phenomenology of embodiment. *Internet Encyclopedia of Philosophy*. Retrieved from: http://www.iep.utm.edu/husspemb/

Bingham, J. (2007). Running dialogue: When you want to get to know someone fast, try going for a slow run together. *Runner's World, 59*.

Buber, M. (1958). *I and thou* (2nd ed., R. G. Smith, Trans). New York, NY: Scribner. (Original work published in 1923).

Burkitt, I., & Sullivan, P. (2009). Embodied ideas and divided selves: Revisiting Laing via Bakhtin. *British Journal of Social Psychology, 48*, 563–577.

Centers for Disease Control. (2011, January). Healthy weight. Retrieved from http://www.cdc .gov/healthyweight/index.htm

Cissna, K. N., & Anderson, R. (1998). Theorizing about dialogic moments: The Buber-Rogers position and postmodern themes. *Communication Theory, 8*(1), 63–104.

Coates, S. (1999). Analyzing the physical: An ethnomethodological study of boxing. *Ethnographic Studies, 4*, 14–26.

Csikszentmihalyi, M. (1990). *Flow: The psychology of optimal experience.* New York: Harper & Row.

DuBois, T. (2013). *Running dialogue: The social and communicative experience of running together* (Master's capstone). The University of North Carolina at Greensboro, Greensboro, NC.

Goodall, H. L., & Kellett, P. M. (2004). Dialectical tensions and dialogic moments as pathways to peak experiences. In R. Anderson, L. Baxter, & K. Cissna (Eds.), *Dialogue: Theorizing difference in communication studies* (159–174). Thousand Oaks, CA: Sage.

Kassings, J. W., Billings, A. C., Brown, R. S., Halone, K. K., Harrison, K., Krizek, B.,…Turman, P.D. (2004). Communication and the community of sport: The process of enacting, (re)producing, consuming, and organizing sport. *Communication Yearbook, 28*, 373–409.

Kowalikowa, J. (2009). Language of sport in the context of communication and culture. *Studies in Physical Culture & Tourism, 16*(1), 63–67.

Krizek, B. (2008). Introduction: Communication and the community of sport. *Western Journal of Communication, 72*(2), 103–106.

Lindemann, K., & Cherney, J. (2008). Communication in and through "murderball": Masculinity and disability in wheelchair rugby. *Western Journal of Communication, 72*(2), 107–125.

LeCourteur, A., & Feo, R. (2011). Real-time communication during play: Analysis of teammates' talk and interaction. *Psychology of Sports and Exercise, 12*, 124–134.

McDougall, C. (2009). *Born to run: A hidden tribe, superathletes, and the greatest race the world has never seen.* New York: Alfred A. Knopf.

Meân, L. J., & Halone, K. K. (2010). Sport, language, and culture: Issues and intersections. *Journal of Language & Social Psychology, 29*(3), 253–260.

Poulos, C. (2008). Accidental dialogue. *Communication Theory, 18*, 117–138.

Rowe, S. (2008). Modern sports: Liminal ritual or liminoid leisure? In G. John (Ed.). *Victor Turner and contemporary cultural performance* (125–148). New York: Berghahn Books.

Turner, V. W. (1982). *From ritual to theatre: The human seriousness of play.* New York City: Performing Arts Journal Publications.

Van Gennep, A. 1960 [1909]. *The rites of passage.* London: Routledge and Kegan.

Walla, N. (2005). Reclaiming the body as home: the bodybased arts as center of the "new village." from *City Repair's 2006 Village Builder.* Retrieved from http://www.bcollective.org/ESSAYS/reclaimbody.pdf

Chapter 20:

When family bullying mandates medical error: Redefining elder abuse

Susan L. Cook
Metropolitan State University of Denver

INTRODUCTION

If the only things certain in this life are death and taxes according to the familiar adage, as aging occurs perhaps the most certain is death. Yet, death may arrive sooner and for "falsely identified reasons" in the current context, confounding whatever certainty is attached to the inevitable final act. In May, 2013, a Center for Disease Control study of death certificates filed in New York City was conducted to determine the accuracy of death causes as listed by the attending physician at time of death. Of all respondents completing the survey tool (n=512), 48.6% of these physicians "had knowingly reported an inaccurate cause of death" (Wexelman, Eden & Rose, 2013, p. 1). The reasons for this false reporting included problems with the guidelines for completing the death certificates as well as missing information about the cause of death. Without an autopsy to determine the actual cause, essentially hospitals and long-term care facilities end up burying their mistakes. If death was premature or untimely based upon wrongly prescribed care or oversights in diagnostics, only when a family member petitions the court for an autopsy can the mistake be examined for the actual cause of the demise. Even then, correcting a faulty death certificate (if desired) may take weeks, if not years.

Though the incidence of death from Alzheimer's disease (Alzheimer's Association, 2013) and dementia has grown exponentially over the last few years, for the compromised elderly a correct cause of death is often ignored. When "Grandpa" dies and he's been a nursing home resident for some time, how many relatives question a reported cause of death such as heart attack (Lee, 2011)? Frontline's segment on this topic explores the incidence of these mistakes and notes the rising instance of autopsies to uncover the truth.

Vulnerable populations for costly medical error include the elderly (Keith, Maio, Dudashi, Templin & Del Canale, 2013) who often rely upon court-appointed guardians to monitor and supervise their healthcare needs. The guardianship appointment process (http://www.guardianship allianceofcolorado.org/) seeks to empower the "most-qualified" relative or acquaintance of the court's ward. However, when the court proceedings are begun by a petitioner (often a relative seeking the position), other relatives are not informed of the petition, thus affording the petitioning individual a clear playing field in the quest for a life-changing decision. One may question whether the court process is appropriate, given what might be the motives of the petitioner, the missing relatives/acquaintances, and often the family dynamics that exist when an aging parent needs assistance.

Guardianship is sought commonly when an individual's competency for self-care or safety issues are questioned. Either behaviors have been noted that put the individual in jeopardy, or observed cognitions presented by the individual appear to lack a reality base that is acceptable by society. If for any reason, an individual is suspected of being "at risk," the county of residence is obligated to become involved in this person's safety, usually through the Adult Protective Services department at the county seat (https://www.co.jefferson.co.us/adultsvc/adultsvc_T204_R1.htm). Adults at risk in Colorado are defined by "mistreatment" as well as "self-neglect" (Section 26-3.1-101, C.R.S). Though the mistreatment of an aging person is often more conflicted in the reporting process, determining if the same person is at risk of self-neglect may be a difficult and contentious process, especially if the person is suffering from cognitive deficits commensurate with aging. The competency hearings connected to the guardianship process (Colorado Statute 15-14-304) are designed to determine if the individual in question understands what appropriate self-care includes and is capable of seeking assistance when needed. The competency process adds another opportunity for communication in determining the assistance needed to protect an aging adult.

Competency hearings include a psychological examination of the targeted individual as the cognitive facilities and behavioral factors are assessed for appropriateness in managing life circumstances, safety, and self-care. Forensic psychiatrists are regularly charged with performing these pre-court hearing assessments, though determining competency for one individual may not equate to competent behaviors for another person. "What judges often don't understand, however, is that 'not all competencies are created equal,'" according to Carla Rodgers, M.D. Thus, defining where a person is on the continuum from "'outspoken to outrageous' becomes a complex undertaking" (Associated Counselors & Therapists). These assessments often rely upon observations as well as simple cognitive tests to create a report on an individual's competency by court standards. Too often observations misinterpret nonverbal behaviors, which even in a normal individual are regarded by communication scholars as ambiguous and vague (see Hall, 1965; Birdwhistle, 2011; Burgoon, 2009; Rapoport, 1990; and Mehrabian, 1980 to name a few).

An additional encumbrance in understanding a person's competency includes auditory issues. An aging person is more likely to have hearing loss as the years accumulate, and failing to acknowledge this loss as well as failing to seek assistive devices is common either for self-esteem or financial concerns. The courts and legal representatives are not obligated to recognize or mandate that the person being examined must have hearing assessments beyond a simple tuning fork test that fails to test comprehension, only hearing of a sound.

Finally, the family dynamics surrounding an elderly person contribute either to the success of the guardianship process or its failure. The Clintonesque adage, "It takes a village," applies to aging citizens as well as minor children. Gaps as noted in the system itself and communication of the initiation of the legal process may not be shored up with good family communication for the benefit of the aging individual, thus opening the door for mishaps in care. Ultimately the aging person (determined to be at risk) may embark on a "slippery slope" of healthcare oversight that ends tragically as these contributing factors combine.

The case discussed here examines the last 18 months of an aging woman's life, noting the initiating, adjusting, and closing phases of care (Schiavo, 2007) that ultimately spelled "DEATH." As well, the predisposing, enabling, and reinforcing factors (Schiavo, 2007; Green & Mercer, 2002) that broke the narrative of care are highlighted in this analysis as these factors frame the health communication gaps and flaws that prompted the individual's demise. Though the patient in this case was determined by the legally filed death certificate to have died of consequences of "Alzheimer's disease," the court-petitioned and granted autopsy determined the primary cause of death to be "fecal impaction in the large bowel," in other words, constipation or "megacolon," a cause of death supported by research as well (Peyrle, Roux, Ferard, Deleau, Kreft-Jals, Hillaire-Buys, Boulenger & Blayac, 2009; Zajecka & Goldstein, 2003; Levin, Barrett & Mendelowitz, 2002; Lim & Mahendran, 2002).

CASE ANALYSIS

The players

The patient and her immediate family members in this case included the eldest daughter and sole guardian of the patient, retired, widowed, and a long time resident of Minnesota; the youngest and only other daughter, working full-time in higher education and resident in Colorado; and brother and sister-in-law, both retired, elderly, and living in the foothills near Denver. Legal staff in this case included the patient's court-appointed representative (Bar admission 1981), the guardian's attorney (Bar admission 1995), the presiding district court judge on this case (three terms on the bench), and the youngest daughter's post-mortem attorney and estate representative. Healthcare providers included the physicians in Ohio and Colorado, hospital staff in Ohio and Colorado, and ancillary care providers including 24/7 sitters, Memory Care coordinator and staffers, geriatric care manager (paraprofessional with journalism degree), and a clinical psychologist who assessed and reported competency concerns.

Initiating phase

The beginning of the end of life for the studied patient began June 8, 2010 (her 89th birthday). The patient was hospitalized in Ohio for four days for a rectal problem. The patient self-admitted, provided history and physical information upon request, and sought treatment to ameliorate the rectal bleeding during morning ablutions. The patient at this time was living with her brother-in-law (aged 87) without additional local family oversight in a small village in northern Ohio. The four days of hospitalization in 2010 prompted cognitive deterioration and ultimate confusion as drugs were administered, tests were given, consults with additional physicians were sought, and no cohesive narrative of the patient's distress was gathered. Discharge notes (Medical Records, June 11, 2010) state that the patient "discusses details of hospitalization but remains bewildered at times and confused . . . needs protected environment such ECF (extended care facility)". At this time and since, no discussion of hospitalism (Pierluissi & Currin, 2007), drug side effects, or other causative factors were considered.

The eldest daughter residing in MN took charge of the patient upon release, ignored the Ohio discharge notes for extended care, and in August, 2010, moved the patient to Denver, CO (the patient's previous home for over 40 years prior to moving to OH in 2007). Upon arriving in Denver, the patient then purchased a house and driving vehicle with the assistance of her eldest daughter. No recognition of the patient's cognitive problems or safety was in evidence as these acquisitions were facilitated. No input from the youngest daughter was permitted or acknowledged. The purchased home was on the far west side of a Denver suburb, bordering a busy highway and the foothills of the Rocky Mountains. Though the bank staff contacted the youngest daughter during the financial negotiations for the house purchase, noting that the patient was unable to manage her funds and did not know what state she was residing in, the eldest daughter with the other local relatives remained in denial about the elderly woman's cognitive capacities and obvious safety concerns. Winter set in, and the patient established her solitary residence with minimal efforts while connecting with old-time friends and relatives in the area.

Between November 2010 and January 2011, the elderly woman was reported (and corroborated by the woman herself) hitch-hiking near her home, phoned police at least six times to report people in her home (no one was found upon investigation), and presented to the local Emergency Room twice with urinary tract infections (common in the elderly and often untreated) (attorney personal communication; Adult Protective Services communication). When the police were phoned in February 2011 by the elderly woman reporting imaginary intruders, the youngest daughter was finally notified by the police when they were at the woman's home. No intruders were found; the police left that evening with the youngest daughter remaining to assist her mother. The mother was at this time appropriately dressed, clean, cognizant, and had cooked dinner as if she were expecting company. Beyond the imagined intruders, nothing appeared amiss, and the elderly woman adamantly insisted she could manage at her home. At this time, she also shared with her youngest daughter the pending competency hearings begun by the eldest daughter, the name and phone numbers for her court-appointed attorney, the court dates for the future, and the fact that she had listed her home for sale because she had "never expected to live here alone" (personal communication, February 6, 2011).

Adjusting phase

This transitional phase focuses on the competency testing, the court proceedings and the ultimate decisions that directed the life (and death) of this elderly woman. On March 23, 2011, a physician examined the patient for physiological and related-cognitive health concerns (spending 30 minutes with the patient and 20 minutes with the patient's attorney (Medical records)). Notable findings at this time included no depression, no constipation or weigh gain, and conflicted findings regarding the hallucinations of intruders and memory concerns. On March 24, 2011, the competency testing was concluded and reported by a clinical psychologist hired by the guardian's attorney (three hours of testing and observation in total). Findings here included "no classical dementia," "depressive disorder seems indicated," "chronic delirium may be present as previously diagnosed in June 2010" [in Ohio], "requires 24 hour care in a facility . . . not capable of driving safely" (Psychological Evaluation, March 28, 2011). The attorneys and the eldest daughter received copies of these reports; the attorney for the patient provided a copy of the report to the youngest daughter who then shared this report with her mother, who was capable at this time of reading and arguing against the findings.

Care provided for the adjusting phase included home sitters 24 /7 (possessing no special credentials or training), regular visits from the youngest daughter, friends visiting weekly, and the patient's attorney providing constant oversight and communication with the youngest daughter. Auditory concerns became obvious with repeated contacts with strangers. During the competency testing, a simple tuning fork hearing test for sound but not comprehension of words was performed and reported as "satisfactory."

Closing phase

This phase began April 2011 and concluded with the death of the patient on December 28, 2011. The court hearing on competency was attended by the patient, the two attorneys, the eldest daughter, and additional relatives. The judge found the patient incompetent, though charming, and stipulated no driving, and 24-hour care in a protected environment (attorney personal communication, April 19, 2011; Court Case 11PR 146, 2011). Throughout the hearing, the patient's attorney noted that the patient failed to demonstrate that she could hear the words that were being said by all participants, though apparently no one believed that an auditory processing problem was a contributing factor to lack of competency. No hearing assessments beyond the tuning fork were performed; no hearing devices were suggested or mandated; no court records mention auditory concerns or deficits.

Following the competency hearing and before the ultimate admission to a protected memory-care facility, the patient remained at home with 24/7 sitters and the freedom to visit and go places with relatives and friends as desired. Medical care was begun to resolve the urinary tract infections and to address behavioral issues related to hallucinatory episodes late in the afternoon and evening. Risperdal, an antipsychotic, was administered daily under the supervision of the 24/7 sitters, though the FDA Safety changes to the Boxed Warning regarding Risperdal states the drug "is not approved for the treatment of elderly patients with dementia-related psychosis" (FDA Safety Information, August 2008).

On April 29, 2011, after choosing her own room, signing the check as a deposit for the room, and measuring the room for furniture selection and placement from her home, the patient was admitted to the memory care unit in an assisted living residence. The eldest daughter and relatives helped the patient move her belongings to the facility the weekend before the admission. On

May 2nd, the youngest daughter visited her mother and noted that the patient was upset, agitated, and hyper. The mother wanted to go out and run errands, so the youngest daughter complied. Upon return from a nearby grocery store, the patient ate dinner with the youngest daughter in attendance. Questions arose from the patient regarding her medicines, but no staff in the facility would divulge what medicines were prescribed. This was the beginning of fracturing the co-constructing of a healthcare narrative. The youngest daughter sought to find out this information for her mother's sake and for her own interest as well in attempting to understand her mother's care and behavior. Prior to admission and the court proceedings, the elderly woman had only been taking a small blood pressure tablet (Lisinopril) for the last three years and had managed her own medicines. Historically, this woman was healthy, requiring only a vitamin tablet daily to remain healthy and sound. While no staff within the facility would share medication information with either the patient or her youngest daughter, as the daughter was leaving the facility she encountered the patient's physician who readily offered that the patient was taking Risperdal "at the request of the eldest daughter" (Personal communication, May 2, 2011).

The following day, May 3, 2011, the youngest daughter received a phone call from the assisted living facility informing her that she was assigned "restricted visitation" by the guardian—which included being observed while visiting her mother and eliminating the option of taking her mother out of the facility for any reason (Facility records, Visitation list, May 5, 2011). From this date until early July 2011, the youngest sibling did not visit her mother. In early July, the guardian contacted the youngest daughter by email, noting that she was now encouraged to visit her mother "before she doesn't recognize you" (Personal communication, July 2, 2011). When queried about visiting restrictions, the guardian denied these and discontinued email communication, fracturing the narrative of health again. Further communication between the sisters was managed through the attorneys.

Medical records, facility records, and conversations with the patient's attorney provided the information for the remainder of this patient's life. From July through October 2011, the patient was ambulatory, self-dressing, managing self-care, and recognizing visitors by name. The patient, a lifelong piano player, read music supplied by her youngest daughter and continued to play the facility's piano occasionally. Upon request from either the facility or the guardian, Risperdal doses increased over this period of time, in spite of the fact that the FDA letter (FDA Safety Information, August 2008) and the report by the Office of the Inspector General (United States) on antipsychotics and the elderly (Levinson, 2011) were circulated by the patient's attorney to all involved parties. Only the initial physician for the patient expressed concern about the Risperdal prescription, and she ultimately resigned from the case in September. No concerns about this prescription are evidenced in the medical records or facility records, and no mention of untoward side effects is recorded. Doses of Risperdal were increased in July and again in August, 2011. In August, an abdominal mass was noted on the patient's chart, describing this mass as "fluctuating in size and hardness" (Medical records, 2011), also noting that the guardian declined further diagnostic procedures.

In September 2011, the initial attending physician upon facility admission requested a complete blood count (CBC) with results reported in the patient's chart, noting nothing out of normal range. Three days following the CBC, the initial physician resigned from the case, and a new physician from Physician Housecalls, LLC was assigned to the patient. The new physician of record requested no new labs, but thyroid medication for weight gain (hypothyroidism) was prescribed by the new physician following his first record in the patient's chart. No weight gain was measured or recorded in any of the patient's records.

In October, 2011, the first required care report and plan were filed with the court with all interested parties receiving copies (including the youngest daughter). The report and plan (Court Case 11PR146, October 17, 2011) were late by four months and vague, noting more information about additional paraprofessionals (geriatric care manager and companions) being hired to ensure quality of life rather than details of care. Specifically missing in this report and plan were any efforts to involve the patient in her own care—prompting a reply to the court by the youngest daughter for lack of "common sense" and oversight in delivered care (Reply to the Court, November 10, 2011). At this time and for the first time, the physician's notes mentioned an auditory loss in the patient, but expressed no concern about further testing or remediation of the loss to aid in appropriate patient care.

By November at Thanksgiving time, 2011, the patient was declining notably. The patient's attorney became concerned and increased contact with the guardian's attorney and the facility coordinator. A wheelchair was needed for mobility, and dressing and personal care assistance was provided by facility staff. At this time, the guardian is noted in facility records as suggesting that the abdominal mass was a "tumor" (Medical records, November, 2011).

On December 12, 2011, the guardian requested hospice admission for the patient upon the strength of the rumor of a "tumor."Hospice admission requires a terminal diagnosis (a disease diagnosis that when running a normal course will end the patient's life within six months) (Hospice Compliance Letter, 2013) certified by a physician. Additional medical notes in the patient's chart note "patient is not losing weight, remains too independent for terminal diagnosis, and not a candidate for hospice admission" (Medical records, December 12, 2011). However, on December 15, 2011, Risperdal was discontinued and the patient's chart noted the following:

> *. . . acute complaint of hard abd [abdomen] a few days ago and facility staff sought consult. . . not being constipated . . but is irregular with her bowel movements . . . few complaints of abd pain . . . not palpable (Medical records).*

When the guardian was consulted by phone about further diagnostics, the daughter noted that the "exact same hardness had been present in August, 2011 . . . patient has not had any surgeries, has lost weight, . . . is becoming more debilitated. . ." (Facility phone conversation with guardian, December 15, 2011). The patient's chart notes however that the patient has dementia and has NOT lost weight at this time. And, the discontinued, conflicted narrative of the patient's healthcare continues . . . .

The remaining days of this patient's life provided a rapid denouement for the healthcare narrative. On December 19th, a portable ultrasound was performed showing "suspicious but unidentifiable mass in LLQ [lower left quadrant], no reports of pain, weight stable, no change in bowel habits" (Ultrasound report, December 19, 2011). Active medications included Colace (stool softener) and Anusol as needed. The plan in the physician's notes stated, ". . . at this time, the dtr [Guardian] has limited goals for treatment, and doesn't want to pursue further testing for CT [CAT scan], Biopsy, etc." The recorded time for the physician's visit include 48 minutes in total with 30 minutes spent in counseling the guardian. On December 20th, the patient was admitted to hospice care with a terminal diagnosis of "abdominal tumor on ultrasound 12/2011 . . . in-state dtr [daughter] NOT to be given any medical info on pt [patient]" (Hospice admission form, December 20, 2011).

As the holidays approached, repeated phone messaging is recorded between the facility coordinator and the guardian related to the need for travel from MN to Denver prior to the New Year planned visit. By Christmas Day, the patient had become nonverbal after telling the youngest daughter who was visiting, "You're going to need help with this" (Personal communication, December 25, 2011). The guardian then filed a visiting schedule with both attorneys on Christmas Day, forcing the youngest daughter to agree to the schedule without input. On December 27th, the guardian restricted care to only comfort medications (morphine by mouth), and the attending physician confirmed these restrictions. The facility coordinator complied. The guardian held medical power of attorney throughout this process, and the language in this document included diagnostics as needed but no resuscitation (Medical POA).

At 8:45 a.m., December 28, 2011, the patient was pronounced dead by the facility staff physician for the attending physician of record. The attending physician eventually signed the death certificate with a cause of death listed as consequences of Alzheimer's disease. The facility record of death notes "Terminal diagnosis: abdominal tumor" (Medical records, December 28, 2011). The coroner released the body by phone on the day of death to the cremation services.

A court-petitioned autopsy (Court Case 11PR146, December 27, 2011) had been granted prior to the patient's demise, having been filed by the youngest daughter when her attempts to gain information and input in the care process had been continually thwarted by the guardian. Complete medical records had also been petitioned and granted by the patient's estate executor. In early January 2012, a forensic coroner, privately hired by the youngest daughter, picked up the body for a complete and detailed autopsy to include the dementia panel and expert review. By March 2012, complete medical records had been requested and procured with difficulty by the private forensic coroner (and ultimately shared with the youngest daughter).

The cause of death was recorded in handwriting on the county-filed death certificate as "Alzheimer's." The Coroner's Report stated the cause of death as "Fecal Impaction within the large bowel (megacolon). . . attributed to unconfirmed Crohn's disease OR Risperdal side effects . . . Of the medications listed in the medical records, risperadone does include constipation as a side effect" (Coroner's report, March 2012). No medical evidence of a diagnosis for Crohn's disease or treatment for this health problem were ever found.

ANALYSIS OF CONTRIBUTORY FACTORS

Predisposing factors

Pre-disposing factors are defined as "factors that exert their effects prior to a behavior occurring, by increasing or decreasing a person or population's motivation to undertake that behavior" (Green & Kreuter, 1999, p. 1; Green & Mercer, 2002). Undeniably, a not-to-be-overlooked factor contributing to this untimely death is the age of the patient, a demographic factor considered to be pre-disposing. The patient was 90 years old at time of death, having reached this age six months prior to the recorded death. Though overtly (and by the patient's own report) healthy for the period prior to 2010, the last 18 months of her life indicate a broken, flawed narrative of healthcare and little competent oversight in assisting this patient with care procurement. The patient's obvious hearing loss to relatives and friends prior to her move back to Denver from Ohio was also a predisposing factor. Not being able to process communication accurately contributed to lack of understanding (confusion) when she phoned the police about intruders. Misunderstandings and miscommunication likely occurred with every interaction about health care and with the 24/7 sitters eventually required by the court. The competency hearings suffered from lack of accurate communication from the assessment of competency through the final hearings as noted by the patient's court-appointed lawyer (personal interview, March 2011). However, a hearing loss is not noted or tested medically until nearly two months prior to the patient's death, somewhat late in the game of care.

The interrupted narrative of healthcare is a major predisposing factor contributing to this patient's death. The patient had a history of lifelong sensitivity to drugs and prescription amounts as her youngest daughter noted upon reflection. Even the blood pressure medicine that the patient took three years prior to June, 2010 was half the normal prescription yet regarded as efficacious for this individual. Family dynamics and the guardian's bullying, know-it-all stance prompted this discontinued narrative, consistently overriding any relative's input and directing the medical professionals to the point of consuming the time spent on medical care in consultation. The guardian was married for 30 years to a medical doctor, and she demonstrated behavior in medical venues (without medical training herself) typical of a doctor's wife who practices medicine by association. Any one of these predisposing factors could have muted the patient's voice and needs in this healthcare narrative to the point of danger. Together these factors precluded appropriate care and guaranteed the early and untimely death of this patient.

Enabling factors

Three distinct enabling factors—the judge's publically-reported predisposition, the financial status of the guardian, and the lack of medical record transfer—exist in this case that make the outcome probable, not just possible. The district court judge on this case was appointed to the bench in July 2001 and completes the current six-year term in January 2017. In this time, survey data supplied by his stakeholders viewed his performance strongly indicating only that he had a "preference for the prosecution" above the average score for this surveyed item (Colorado Judicial Performance,

2010). This preference translates to a preference in this case for the person bringing the petition to court. Thus, the judge appeared to have a preference toward the eldest daughter's petition for guardianship, given the predisposing factor of the patient's age and combined with the patient's hearing loss which impeded her quality participation in the court hearings (no pun, intended).

The guardian's financial status (wealthy and well-off, as well as retired) made it possible for her to hire high-profile probate attorneys to manage all filings, hearings, and legal communication related to the case. The ability to continually provide more funding for the process facilitated the outcome. The quality of care became less of a focus than the quantity of caregivers. Paraprofessionals were hired at rates in excess of $3500 a month for *weekly* visits and reports, paying $875 per visit which lasted only a short time according to the patient and facility providers (personal communication, October 2011). Though the estate of the patient was legally responsible for the fees related to the guardian's services and the patient's care, only the facility and medical costs were covered by the estate with the remainder of the charges covered by the guardian. This funding was reported in the financial reports to the court as well as the care report filed with the court (Court documents, September 17, 2011 & October 14, 2011), perhaps adding to the perception of "care" and "caring" by the guardian and eliminating any questions that might have been asked.

Finally and not unique to this case in the United States by any means, the lack of prompt and complete medical record transfers following this patient from state to state, physician to physician, and facility to facility enabled the probability of this outcome. With a patient that becomes unable (or muted in efforts) of carrying the healthcare narrative forward for continued informed care, adequate backup measures to ensure this continuation and consistency of information fail to exist in the United States. The privacy of medical information remains sacrosanct in America, and HIPPA regulations are staunchly monitored (Leyva, 2013). If family members or knowledgeable patient advocates do not carry this information forward, the narrative becomes broken, incomplete, misinformed, conflicted, and fractured. Though technological solutions to this concern have been offered and tried, ultimately a change in national healthcare information remains currently beyond reach. As long as healthcare providers and facilities can bury their mistakes, the impact of this lack of communication will remain masked, and change in policies is less likely.

Reinforcing factors

Six factors exist upon analysis that reinforced the outcome of this case—the lack of state law about elder abuse reporting, the lack of consistent nursing care, an inadequately trained geriatric care manager, the guardian's distant location in MN, restricted involvement of the youngest daughter, and the guardian's attorney lack of timely communication with the patient's attorney. Each single factor reinforced the probability of the patient's death, but together these six factors sealed the coffin. Colorado (at the time of this case) remained one of three states without a formal elder abuse law that identified types of elder abuse and mandated reporters. By 2013, the legislature in Colorado put forward an elder abuse law (Hoover, 2013), and this law was approved by review committees and signed into law by the Governor on May 16, 2013 (Callender, Crona & Hulbert, 2013).

Could this law have prevented this patient's untimely death? Probably not, but its absence could surely have reinforced the demise.

Consistent and quality nursing care appears to have been lacking in this case. Good nurses are trained to gather input and output (I/O) data daily. The medical records for this patient beyond the hospital records fail to indicate that input and output data were gathered, recorded, or even requested by anyone in the assisting living situation. The constipation that killed this woman took time to accumulate—from its first notice in August to the last days in December. Though medications were provided for stool softening and hemorrhoids, no recorded information exists noting bowel movements or even eating and fluid intake habits. Without this information, transferring care between shifts and across providers becomes a guessing game, and oversight becomes overlooking to the detriment of the patient.

Additionally, hiring a geriatric care manager who has an educational background in journalism and criminal justice further reinforces this case's outcome. The credentials for such paraprofessionals often remain unregulated and consist of certification only from a private organization. These certifications are independently constructed outside standard regulatory concerns for medical professionals (e.g., licensure). The hired care manager owned her own business, cited certification in care management, and conducted business without any legal oversight for standards of care (http://www.compasscaresforseniors.com/story.htm). Even the patient in this case reported that frequently the care manager visited with her personally, received a phone call shortly into the visit, and then disappeared only to return in the next week for another truncated visit (Personal communication, September 12, 2011). No records exist or were filed with the courts regarding this individual's time and charges for care. It can only be surmised that care was insufficient and lacking in time spent.

One incident of poor foot health and an ultimate foot infection from untrimmed toenails supports this inference. The youngest daughter spent time each week chatting with and observing her mother for at least two hours. In that time at one visit, she noted that her mother limped and was wearing slippers only. When she wanted her mother to put on shoes to walk outside in the enclosed garden, the daughter discovered her mother's infected, untrimmed toenails. She sought the nursing staff in the facility to come and witness the problem and requested that they secure care and treatment for the obvious condition. The medical records document this "over-looking" and ultimate need for care that was then authorized by the guardian. An oversight such as this by the care manager should not have occurred if the care manager was adequately educated in noting nonverbal behaviors and then following up on possible causes for problems. Following this incident, all footwear was removed from the patient's room, and the guardian announced that the patient had a doctor's order on file to NOT wear shoes (Personal communication, October 14, 2011). Verifying this order for this patient turned up no such order.

Appointing a sole guardian who does not live locally to the ward coupled with restricting information to a close relative living local to the ward reinforced the outcome of this case in tandem. Had the eldest daughter shared guardianship with her sister or had she permitted the youngest daughter to participate in care, the promptness and quality of care could have been improved. The youngest daughter had 13 years experience working in healthcare at varying positions to include communication specialist in a medical manufacturing company, certification in nursing assistance, and writer of hospital quality assurance reports, prior to receiving a Ph.D. in human communication. This background and the ability to ask questions that elicited quality responses from the patient would have served this situation well. However, the bullying behavior of the eldest daughter, the historic family dysfunctions, and the court's lack of wisdom in appointing a sole distant guardian reinforced the outcome.

Finally, the guardian's attorney practiced information delay when communicating with the patient's court-appointed attorney. Delay and often no response were standard fare for interactions between these two responsible entities. Dysfunctions in this realm mirrored the family dysfunctions that reinforced the errors in this case. When the tumor rumor began in November, communication between the two attorneys eventually over time uncovered the beginning of the abdominal mass in August, but the lost time sealed the fate of the patient. The patient's attorney relied upon the youngest daughter's visits and information to help her serve her client. Given the restricted access of the youngest daughter, this channel for information can only be expected to be less than rich. Minus this channel, the two attorneys could have provided ongoing communication to the benefit of the patient, but the guardian's attorney was indeed responsible to the guardian and her wishes as her fees were paid by this individual. Timely communication is not written into the legal contract between client and attorney. Nor is this timeliness mandated by the courts between attorneys or even with the judge in this case. Indeed, often a "game" of sorts often develops between lawyers as they seek to meet their individual clients' needs, as if a competition exists between the two. In a case such as this involving a compromised ward of the state, this "game" reinforced the patient's demise as miscommunication and no communication framed the rules of the game.

PREVENTIVE RECOMMENDATIONS

Six basic recommendations could have feasibly prevented this untoward outcome even for an aging individual in this context. These recommendations relate to the guardianship process, the prescriptions for elderly confined individuals, daily nursing care mandates, the Medical Power of Attorney monitoring, auditory testing mandates for the hearing-impaired in court proceedings, and laws on elder abuse. Each recommendation could have prevented this outcome; all recommendations together would ensure optimum healthcare for compromised individuals reaching the end of life.

When assigning guardianship in any situation, considering a single individual as a potential guardian provides absolute power for a single entity. When Baron Acton in 1887 wrote in a letter to Bishop Creighton his opinion about power, "Power tends to corrupt, and absolute power corrupts absolutely. . . . " this quote has resonated across the ages as a concern about concentrating power and its negative effects. The power assigned to a single individual as guardian bodes poorly for outcomes, not in all cases, but in this case provides cautionary evidence that should be heeded.

Though medical record transfers remain disparate and disconnected affording any patient a less than cohesive narrative of care, prescribing medicines without laboratory testing that indicates a pharmaceutical need seems less than prudent. Regulatory oversight (and even legal oversight) should include verifying lab tests prior to prescribing medicines especially for institutionalized compromised individuals. Without these lab tests, powerful drugs (such as antipsychotics and thyroid medicines) that are not required fail to contribute to the overall health plan and may influence health negatively, as noted in this case.

In all facilities of care delivery, basic nursing care should include daily monitoring and recording of inputs/outputs as a baseline of care. Few health plans in assisted living mandate this monitoring, and even fewer nurses work in these situations. However, individuals with proper training can ask questions, gather these data, and record this information.

Noninvasive diagnostics for potentially life-threatening conditions should be required by law. As long as the medical power of attorney and the patient's wishes are not violated, performing these diagnostics can help prevent situations as in this analyzed case. Even a manual examination of this patient could have elicited concerns about constipation, thus prompting follow-up and remediation.

Reviewing and requiring auditory testing that include cognitive processing, not just the simple tuning fork test should be considered, especially if hearing loss is suspected and court proceedings are involved. Life changing decisions should be cognitively processed by any individual called to a court hearing. Failing to honor this recommendation permits a miscarriage of justice that is egregious in the 21st century of knowledge management.

Finally, when elder abuse laws exist, every individual working with the elderly population should be trained and aware of legal reporting responsibilities. Training staff on the faces of elder abuse should be required as well. Any individual can (by ignorance) commit elder abuse; knowing what constitutes this form of abuse is remediable and offers preventive insurance. Age should not be a ticket for neglect, exploitation, or direct harm. Aging is inevitable just as death is. The quality of life along this path should be expected and ensured (Alzheimer's Association, 2013; Hospice Compliance, 2011; Lee & Thompson, 2011), especially when "care" is required.

REFERENCES

Alzheimer's Association. (2013). *Alzheimer's disease facts & figures. Alzheimer's & Dementia*, 9 (2).

Associated Counselors and Therapists. *Counseling corner: Evaluation competency.* Retrieved from http://www.beachpsych.com;pages/cc97.html

Birdwhistell, R. L. (2011). *Kinesics and context (conduct and communication).* Philadelphia, PA: University of PA Press.

Burgoon, J.K., Guerrero, L.K., and Floyd, K. (2009). *Nonverbal communication.* Upper Saddle River, NY: Pearson.

Callender, M., Crona, S., & Hulbert, L. (June 3, 2013). *Additional protection for Colorado's elderly.* Retrieved June 10, 2013, from Journal Advocate: http://www.journal-advocate.com/sterling-opinion/ci_23377460/additional-protection-colorados-elderly

Colorado Judicial Performance, 2010. *First Judicial District, District Judge Honorable Stephen M. Munsinger.* Retrieved from www.coloradojudicialperformance.gov/retention.cfm?ret=703.

Food and Drug Agency. (August, 200,). *FDA safety information.* Retrieved June 10, 2013, from Food and Drug Agency Medical Watch: http://www.fda.gov/Safety/MedWatch/SafetyInformation/Safety-RelatedDrugLabelingChanges/ucm123246.htm

Green, L.W., & Kreuter, M.W. (1999). *Health promotion planning: An educational and ecological approach*, 3rd ed. Mountain View, CA: Mayfield.

Green, L.W., & Mercer, S. L. (2002). *Green's model of health education.* New York: The Gale Group, Macmillan.

Hall, E.T. (1965). *The silent language.* New York, NY: Fawcett Premier.

Hospice Compliance. (January, 2011),. *Special report on hospice's eligibility challenge.* Retrieved June 6, 2013, from Hospice Compliance: http://www.hospicecompliance.net/images/pdf/Vol12No1.pdf

Keith, S. W., Maio, V., Dudash, K., Templin, M., & Del Canale, S. (2013). A physician-focused intervention to reduce potentially inappropriate medication prescribing in older people. *Drugs and Aging, 30* (2), 119–127.

Lee, C., & Thompson, A. (December 21, 2011). *Public Broadcasting System.* Retrieved June 5, 2013, from Frontline: Gone without a case: Suspicious elder deaths rarely investigated.: http://www.pbs.org/wgbh/pages/frontline/criminal-justice/post-mortem/gone-without-a-case-suspicious-elder-deaths-rarely-investigated/

Levin, T., Barrett, J., & Mendelowitz, A. (2002). Death From clozapine-induced constipation: Case report and literature review. *Pyschomatics* , *43* (1), 71–73.

Levinson, D. *Medicare atyopical antipsychotic drug claims for elderly nursing home residents.* Office of Inspector General, Department of Health and Human Services.

Leyva, C. (2013, February 3). *HIPPA omnibus rule summary.* Retrieved June 9, 2013, from HIPPA Survival Guide: http://www.hipaasurvivalguide.com/hipaa-omnibus-rule.php

Lim, D., & Mahendran, R. (2002). *Risperidone and megacolon.* Singapore Medical Journal, 43 (10), 530–532.

Mehrabian, A. (1980). *Silent messages: Implicit communication of emotions and attitudes.* Belmont, CA: Wadsworth Publishing.

Pierluissi, E. M., & Currin, S. R. (October, 2007). New take on elder care. *The Hospitalist.*

Rapoport, A. (1990). *The meaning of the build environment: A nonverbal communication approach.* Phoenix, AZ: University of Arizona Press.

Schiavo, R. (2007). *Health communication: From theory to practice.* Somerset, NJ: Jossey-Bass Wiley.

Zajecka, J., & Goldstein, C. (2003). The side-effect profiles of antipsychotic medications. *Primary Psychiatry 10*(8): 78–91.

Chapter 21:

Communicating sex-positive sexuality education: Benefits and strategies of an emerging approach

Jessica A. Nodulman
University of New Mexico

INTRODUCTION

Messages about sexuality are everywhere; at the local shopping mall, Victoria's Secret window displays feature size-zero mannequins dressed in pink leopard-print negligees alongside signs that urge women to "be wild, be a tease, be *that* girl." Top songs from country to hip-hop charts are filled with lyrics about "needing you tonight" and "making your bed rock." Merchandise for children is infused with sexual messages such as baby T-shirts that read, "Does this diaper make my butt look big?" or "Flirt."

Although United States society is inundated with messages about the appeal of sex and sexuality from popular culture, formal sex-education materials in schools more often than not represent sex as shameful, frightening, necessary only for reproduction, and/or romanticized (Greslé-Favier, 2010; Fields, 2008; New York Civil Liberties Union [NYCLU], 2012). Fields's (2008) ethnographic work in middle-school sex education classrooms found that formal sex-education classes often are separated into "girls" and "boys" classes because talking openly about menstruation or erections to both girls and boys is considered too embarrassing. Girls are taught that one in four women will be raped and thus are covertly trained to fear men and men's sexuality. The definition of a clitoris often is not given during sex education, and in one case, the clitoris was deleted from a diagram of female sex organs in a middle-school text book (Fields 2008; Moore & Clarke, 1995). The implicit message here is that female orgasm is not necessary for sex since it does not aid in reproduction. Lastly, sex education often teaches students to wait until marriage for sex because the "best" sex is between a loving, heterosexual, married couple (Epstein, O'Flynn, & Telford, 2003; Fields, 2008; NYCLU, 2012). Pop-culture messages of hypersexuality confront us constantly; formal sex education, however, teaches us that sexuality has dangerous strings attached and is a problematic force in our lives.

In this chapter, I offer a summary of the benefits and communicative techniques used within sex-positive sexuality[1] education—an emerging trend within health communication. Health communication is a complex phenomenon because not only do people seek, process, and share health information(Kreps and Thornton, 1992), they "mingle what they hear and see with their own ideas and experiences" (du Pré, 1996, p. 4). This complexity is only intensified in research on sexuality education because sex and sexuality can be an intensively private at the same time that it is a culturally negotiated issue. Health communication, however, embraces complexities and seeks ways to help scholars theoretically understand those complexities, for practitioners to teach about them, and for the general public to manage them. Improving sexuality education is a complex issue, but it an issue that is best grounded in health communication because this field not only appreciates difficult issues but seeks to apply the results to better our overall health and well-being.

In this study, I examine the sex-positive adolescent sexual health education website, Scarleteen .com in order to outline specific communication strategies used by this organization to advance knowledge on sexual health communication. Perhaps the most important reason for promoting a sex-positive approach to sexuality education and investigating how sex-positive organizations effectively communicate sexuality education is because the majority of citizens in the U.S. physically experience consequences from having poor sexual health. Statistics on unplanned pregnancies, abortions, and sexually transmitted infections (STIs) suggest that people have not learned how to effectively manage their sexual health. Health communication scholars can offer strategies for teaching sexuality education effectively and provide an opportunity to rectify these sobering statistics.

For example, unplanned pregnancies are a common occurrence of risky sexual behavior. At least half of women in the U.S. will experience an unintended pregnancy by the time they are 45, with nearly three in ten teenage girls becoming pregnant at least once before the age of 20. Unplanned pregnancies have serious repercussions, such as missing the opportunity to engage in preconception and prenatal care and a decreased chance that the baby will be breastfed, all of which has been shown to benefit mothers and babies (The National Campaign to Prevent Teen and Unplanned Pregnancy [TNC], 2008, 2010). About one-third of women who experience an unintended pregnancy will have an abortion. Women in their 20s account for more than 50% of all abortions, teenagers account for nearly 20% of abortions, and women 30 and older account for the remaining 25%. Abortions are not inexpensive, are not covered by government funding, and are not easily accessible for many women across the country, especially for minors (Guttmacher Institute [GI], 2011). Not surprising is that 49% of women stated inconsistent condom use as a reason for pregnancy-termination services, because only half of Americans report consistently using a condom during sexual activity (GI, 2011; TNC, 2009). Among unmarried men (between the

Footnote

1. I would like to note that choosing the term *sexuality education* over *sex education* is a conscious decision. As Joan Helmich (2009) states in her excellent commentary on what real sexuality education should entail, "in the words of my friend Gabriel, when he was eight, 'Sex is something you do... sexuality is who you are"— which is why I deliberately talk about sexuality education, not sex education' "(p.7).

ages of 15 and 44) who had sex within the past 12 months, less than half (48%) reported using a condom during the last time they had sex. Furthermore, 78% of unmarried young adults have had sex within the past year; however, 19% use no contraception at all, and 24% use contraception inconsistently. In other words, only about 50% of sexually active young adults consistently use protection (Kaye, Suellentrap, & Sloup, 2009).

Not using a condom leads to serious risks for contracting STIs. There are more than 25 diseases that are spread primarily by sexual activity. One in five Americans has an STI, and it is estimated that 65 million people live with an incurable STI (Centers for Disease Control and Prevention [CDC], 2010; GI, 2009). As with pregnancy statistics, there are race and age disparities among STI rates as well. White Americans acquire STIs through high-risk sexual behaviors, whereas Black Americans are more likely to acquire them through both high- and low-risk behaviors since the black population suffers from a higher STI rate. Although half of STI cases occur among young people 15 to 44 years of age, older adults' rates of STIs are climbing. From 1996 to 2003, cases of chlamydia, genital herpes, gonorrhea, syphilis, and genital warts among people age 45 and older increased 127%. Sharples (2008) explains that a lack of sexual communication by physicians towards their older patients is detrimental to patients' health, and that the rise of STIs among the older generation is due to their lack of sex education. According to the Guttmacher Institute (2009), the three most effective ways to avoid an STI are to abstain from all sexual activity, be in a faithful monogamous relationship, and use condoms correctly and consistently. However, all three of these strategies "rely on the knowledge, behavior and interpersonal skills of adolescents and adults;" therefore, it is imperative that sex education is offered to adolescents and adults so that they are equipped with this knowledge and skill sets (GI, 2009, para. 51).

Discussing sex and sexuality is difficult and at times complicated; therefore, the importance of quality sexuality education cannot be underestimated. However, the two most common approaches to communicating sex education in schools—abstinence-only-until-marriage (AOUM) and comprehensive sex education—are not satisfactory methods. Although proponents of AOUM state that empirical studies prove this policy does in fact work, that argument is simply not supported by the data. Douglas Kirby's 2007 report for the National Center to End Teenage Pregnancy is the most comprehensive empirical study on sex-education programs designed to prevent teenage pregnancy. Kirby found that abstinence-only programs do not have any effect on preventing teen pregnancy. In fact, he found that programs that use a comprehensive approach that encourages abstinence while also giving accurate information about making safe choices are not at odds with the message of abstinence. Instead there is evidence that comprehensive programs delay sexual behavior and increase the use of contraceptives and condoms among the students in these programs.

Though a comprehensive approach to sexuality education has had success (Kirby & Laris, 2009; Kohler, Manhart,& Lafferty, 2008), it is often exclusionary. First, most of the curricula in sexuality-education programs focus on reproductive education—thus these programs implicitly and explicitly teach and enforce a heteronormative curriculum (Epstein et al., 2003; Fields, 2008; NYCLU, 2012). Along with promoting heteronormativity, scholarship has found that sexuality-education programs that are comprehensive may enforce traditional gendered notions or roles (Bay-Cheng & Lewis, 2006; Greslé-Favier, 2010; Hayden, 2001; Fields, 2008; Fine, 2005). In addition, one must only review the grim sexual health statistics within the U.S. to understand that even a comprehensive approach to sexuality education is not serving the sexual health needs of our society. However, a new movement for teaching sexuality education—sex-positive sexuality education—is emerging within the U.S. Sex-positive sexuality education transcends abstinence-only-until-marriage programs and reconceptualizes most comprehensive sexuality-education programs. In the next section of this chapter, I outline this new method and explain why it is an emerging trend that health communication scholars and practitioners should be aware of and consider implementing in sexuality-education programs.

Sex-positive sexuality education

Sex-positive sexuality education offers an alternative to abstinence-only and comprehensive sexuality education. Sex-positive sexuality education is an approach to sexuality education that eliminates ineffective fear appeals and racist and sexist misconceptions about sex and ultimately teaches that sexuality and sex can and should be a positive force in one's life (Corrina, 2009; Fields, 2008; Fine & McClelland, 2006; Helmich, 2009; Kulwicki, 2008). Sex-positive sexuality scholars reframe the representations of sexuality found in formal sex education and within popular culture to help create a healthier culture of sexuality (Corinna, 2009; Fields, 2008; Fine & McClelland, 2006; Kukwicki, 2008; Patton, 1996; Perry, 2008).

To understand a sex-positive approach to sex education, it is important to understand the history of the term *sex-positive.* Sex-positive first was used in the 1970s in conjunction with sex-positive feminism. Sex-positive feminism's origin is associated with sex-industry workers and their supporters who felt women should have the same sexual opportunities as men and have total control over their bodies (Queen, 1997). Perhaps due to broader discourses from conservative Christian organizations as well as politicians, the term *sex-positive* fell out of favor for mainstream usage until the late 1990s and early 2000s when it was re-branded as a type of lifestyle- and sexuality-education philosophy.

> *Carol Queen, a sex educator, author, and feminist activist, defined sex-positive as the: simple yet radical affirmation that we each grow our own passions on a different medium, [and] that instead of having two or three or even half a dozen sexual orientations, we should be thinking in terms of millions. Sex-positive respects each of our unique sexual profiles, even as we acknowledge that some of us have been damaged by a culture that tries to eradicate sexual difference and possibility. (1997, p. xvii)*

In Queen's later collaboration with Comella (2008), they add that sex-positive can be defined as:

> *the cultural philosophy that understands sexuality as a* potentially *positive force in one's life, and it can, of course, be contrasted with sex-*

> *negativity, which sees sex as problematic, disruptive, dangerous. Sex-positivity allows for and in fact celebrates sexual diversity, differing desires and relationships structures, and individual choices based on consent. (p. 278)*

Today, sex-positive sexuality education also is known as *real sex education*, *sexuality education*, *thick desire*, *healthy sexuality*, *feminist sex education*, or even *rights-based, pleasure-positive sex education* (Corinna, 2009; Greslé-Favier, 2010; Helmich, 2009; Fine & McClelland, 2006; Kulwicki, 2008; & Maltz, 2011). Recent scholarship reports the benefits of a sex-positive approach in multiple contexts of sexual health education. According to Welles (2005), "the importance of expanding the dialogue between adults and young women to include sex-positive messages about female sexual desire cannot be overstated" (p.44). Braun-Harvey and de Miranda (2009) explain that a sex-positive environment should be used for clients in treatment for drug/alcohol abuse that have a sex/drug linked behavior. Friedman and Valenti's edited book, *Yes Means Yes!* (2008), calls for sex-positive education as a way to prevent rape. Authors who contributed to this volume believe that since U.S. society traditionally has not valued female sexual pleasure, this leads men to look out only for themselves in regards to obtaining pleasure, by any means possible. They propose that society reevaluate how it constructs female sexual pleasure and consequently change the way we talk, think, portray, value, and have sex. Since they argue that our current culture supports rape, they propose that a sex-positive framework for talking, teaching, and depicting sex could stop ideologies regarding rape within society. Knerr and Philpott (2006) report that 30 international sexual health programs in countries such as South Africa, Australia, Bengal, Delhi, and Cambodia are successfully using a sex-positive approach. Innovative programs, such as "pleasure-focused couples counseling," interactive videogames, education on how to use the Kama Sutra safety, and workshops on eroticizing female condoms, are all approached from a sex-positive framework. Knerr and Philpott state that this kind of approach can go "beyond improving sexual health, to enabling women and men to experience healthier, happier lives" (p. 108). In the US, sex-positive sexuality education workshops for women living in a domestic violence shelter in Georgia also showed success. Tambling, Neustifter, Muska, Reckert, and Rua (2012) report that women attending these workshops indicated feeling appreciative and more engaged in this program compared to traditional sex education programs, and facilitators noticed an increase of condoms taken by participants. Also, even after leaving the shelter, participants would return to attend these workshops.

To date, no research has confirmed the use of sex-positive sexuality education being used in formal classrooms in the U.S. However, as Helmich (2009) states, although "nobody has 'proven' a broader, more comprehensive, positive sexuality education through peer-reviewed research," research has provided tools for what works. In particular she states that a positive framework is important because:

> *We must focus on potential good, not just the potential bad, undesirable or harmful aspects of sexuality. We must focus on personal assets of young people, their strengths, joys, and abilities. Sexuality education should*

> *respect and empower youth. We should celebrate sexuality, life, and even pleasure! And not just pleasure in sex, but more importantly, in relationships. Whether a relationship includes sex or not, we all seek rewarding, mutual intimacy. And we are all sexual. Our young people know this, feel this, and long to understand themselves and others. And in order for sexuality education to be positive, it needs to be taught by trained, comfortable, positive teachers and leaders. (pp. 14–15)*

One of the first aspects that sets sex-positive sexuality education apart from other approaches is its focus on sex as a positive part of a person's life. Consistently, empirical evidence shows that a healthy sex life leads to better physical, mental, and emotional health. While sex-positive sexuality education would not encourage students to have sex for the any of these benefits, it would not lie to them or use ineffective scare techniques. Instead of scaring students about the terrible consequences of sex, it would be honest about both its positive and negative aspects. Sex, in other words, would be presented as something that can be extremely positive if it is treated with respect and occurs when the parties are mutually ready for the responsibilities that come along with being sexually active. Sexual activities that are engaged in consensually should not be subject to sanctions or judgments because sex is conceptualized as normal and something that should not be cloaked in fear or shame. For instance, sex-positive sexuality education believes framing sex in fear and teaching only about risk will not transform human behavior; rather, it only leads people to feel guilty while they still pursue and engage in sex (Banim & Tasker, 1999). Sex-positive sexuality education, then, moves past teaching just about the negatives of sex to building an understanding that when a student is physically, emotionally, and mentally ready, sex can be positive (Corinna, 2009; "Declaration," 1999; Kulwicki, 2008).

Furthermore, sex-positive sexuality education stresses that sex is about more than just reproduction, and that sex is not just a heterosexual act involving penetration from a penis to a vagina (Corinna, 2009; Fields, 2008; Kulwicki, 2008). This philosophy stresses that sexual activities never should be confined to those of a certain sex, age, race, or relationship status, but instead sexual activities should be mutually agreed upon by the interactants (Corinna, 2009). Although sex-positive education appreciates sexual activity and expressing one's sexuality, scholars who support this framework believe that sex is something that students should do when they are ready; therefore, abstinence is an important option to discuss in the classroom, but it cannot be the only message sent. Furthermore, regardless of students' identity positionalities, they do not have to partake in any sexual activity with which they feel uncomfortable. In Fields's (2008) ethnographic work, she found that even in comprehensive sexuality-education classrooms, students of color were taught using a "hidden curriculum" that insinuated that they may need sexuality lessons more so than their white peers. Although there are important sexual health discrepancies among races and/or sexual identities, it never is acceptable for an educator to assume anything about students' sexualities. Sex-positive sexuality education encourages students to fight such stereotypes in their own relationships. For example, even if a couple has dated for three months, and many expect them to become sexually active, sex-positive sexuality education teaches students that the sexual decisions they make are theirs alone.

Sex-positive sexuality education supports the need for advanced communication skills. A sex-positive sexuality education approach could teach such communication skills as perception checking, nonverbal communication, communicating respect for likes and dislikes, and how to build positive climates. These important lifelong communication skills can help students navigate sexuality more efficiently. Sex-positive sexuality education also could acknowledge that people desperately want to have conversations with caring and supportive adults regarding sex (Hilton, 2007). Fields's (2008) work demonstrates that students are desperate for knowledge regarding sex and sexuality but do not know accurate places to find this information. Furthermore, teachers worry about the complexities of teaching sex education (Sandlos, 2010), and remark that they want to teach sex education better but lack skills for doing so. A sex-positive approach trains willing teachers and strategizes with students about how to implement conversations and find resources about sexuality. Also, sex-positive sexuality education strives to teach about the necessity for sexual partners to communicate enthusiastic consent. According to Perry (2008) consent is more than a partner saying "yes" to sexual activity; both partners also need to enjoy themselves as well. If there is any sense of hesitancy or displeasure, the partner would stop because those negative feelings do not support a positive sexual climate.

Perhaps the key element that sex-positive sexuality education teaches is the appreciation of the inherent pleasure of sex and sexuality (Corinna, 2009; Fields, 2008; Kulwicki, 2008). The attention paid by this philosophy to the typically silenced concepts in sex education of female sexual pleasure, desire, and sexualities makes it distinctive (Corinna, 2009; Fields, 2008; Fine & McClelland, 2006; Helmich, 2009; Kulwicki, 2008). Realistically, people already know that sex is pleasurable and thus appreciate when educators are honest with them. Aggleton and Campbell's (2000) study of what young people want in sex education supports this claim; participants stated they wanted to know "non-sexual ways of showing affection, and the pleasurable, emotional and complex aspects of sexuality" (p. 290). Sex-positive sexuality education in schools could promote behaviors like masturbation that even some comprehensive programs do not like to talk about and/or challenge the students to come up with ways that sexual pleasure can be achieved but that are low risk—deep kissing or dancing very close. Adult centers of sex-positive sexuality education also aid women in this respect because these centers focus on helping women achieve sexual pleasure. Overall, a sex-positive approach to sexuality education embraces feminine sexual pleasure and equips both women and men with knowledge, respect, and an understanding of the female body and communication skills and autonomy to be sexually healthy.

Important to note is that sex-positive sexuality education is *not* pornography education for students in schools (Kulwicki, 2008). Pornography is defined here as graphic videos that demonstrate coital positions and/or sexual techniques. Research shows that the largest viewers of porn are adolescent males. If porn is where these young men are learning about sex, they will not be equipped to handle real relationships and will have poor expectations for sexual behavior. However, sex-positive sexuality education for adults may incorporate the use of sex-positive pornography as it is an encouraged practice by sex therapists for adults who are struggling with sexual problems.

Although there is an emerging understanding of what sex-positive sexuality education is and an appreciation of the benefits of using this approach, currently research does not investigate how educators communicate this approach. Many scholars have supported a sex-positive approach to sexuality education, but I have found no research that confirms any formal school based sexuality-education programs that currently are enacting this approach, which is most likely due to the constraints of school boards, state mandates, and fear of losing governmental funds or grants. The study of sexual health communication as a scholarly area needs to fill this gap in the research and offer actual communicative strategies for people of all ages to use to talk about sex. It is vital to our population's health and well-being that communication experts arm educators with sexual communication strategies because traditional formal sex-education messages typically teach that sex should be something that should not happen between young adults and should not be discussed among older adults. Therefore, I examine an organization outside of the school setting that has implemented this approach and present the strategies they use to communicate it. Understanding how sex-positive sexuality education should be taught is essential because a new method for teaching about sexuality provides hope for revolutionizing and correcting confusion about sexuality education.

I contribute theoretically, then, to our understanding of health communication and sexual health communication strategies. The study of health communication provides the foundation for this study. As Hemingway (2006) explains, sex education "invites multidisciplinary and interdisciplinary debates along with pragmatic partnerships" from areas of study such as biology, sociology, political science, and psychology (p. 6). But even though the study of sex education is multi- and inter-disciplinary, it is impractical unless it can be communicated effectively to learners. And since sex education is fundamentally an endeavor to explain, maintain, or improve learners' sexual health and well-being, sex education ultimately is a health issue. Thus, health communication is the best area of scholarship to ground this study. Clearly, the communication field is essential to understanding how sexual health is discussed by educators and the general public alike.

Bochner (2009) wrote that modern medicine "needs a new storyline;" one that would give medicine more heart but also "a different plot structure; fresh metaphors; distinctive characters; modified scenes, a new moral to the story" (p. 160). I propose that sexuality education needs a new story line as well. There are many benefits to changing the way we communicate about sexuality education in this nation. One only has to look at our STI, pregnancy, abortion, sexual assault, and intimate partner violence rates to understand the need to change how we communicate about sex and sexuality. A shift to a sex-positive approach may be the critical factor in creating a new, healthier, approach to sexual health for our nation.

Method

In order to understand this revolutionary approach to communicating about sexuality, I completed a case study to investigate how a culture of sex-positive sexuality education is communicated on Scarleteen.com (referred to as Scarleteen). Scarleteen exemplifies a web based sex-positive sexuality-education organization that is geared towards adolescents and young adults. Scarleteen, the highest-ranked website for sex education and sexuality, provides "comprehensive, inclusive and sex-positive advice, help and accurate information about teen and young adult sexuality" (Alexa, 2011, para. 1). Founded in 1999 to meet the need for online sex and sexuality information targeted specifically for young adults, this site remains a model organization for successful sex-positive sexuality communication. This site is valuable because the site creator and director, Heather Corinna, is a leading voice in the revolution to re-conceptualize sexuality education to include a sex-positive approach. This website provides insight into how best to communicate the difficult but necessary conversations about sex and sexuality with teens, offers an example of how sex-positive communication can be transmitted completely through computer-mediated communication (CMC) channels, and offers the opportunity to investigate the sustainability of a grassroots organization. Despite having a budget lower than the median-annual household income in the U.S. and not using *any* federal, state or local funding but instead depending on public support, Scarleteen manages not only to stay operational but to be a relevant leader in the field of sexuality education ("Help Lift Sex," 2011, para. 6).

Data on Scarleteen consisted of a selection of texts from the Scarleteen website. Since Scarleteen is such a large data set, I limited my analysis to 10 articles chosen at random from four sections of the site: (1) "Skin Deep: Anatomy, Body, General Health, and Body Image;" (2) "SexYOUality: Just What It Says—Sex and Sexuality Basics and Not-So-Basics;" (3) "Take Two: Relationships and Relationship Issues;" and (4) "Pink Slips: Issues Specific or Pertaining to Female-Bodied or Identified People." I also examined 15 discussion threads from the "Message Boards: The Busy, Fully Moderated Discussion Community at Scarleteen" ("The Scarleteen Tour," n.d., para. 2). These units of analysis provide an opportunity to investigate how Scarleteen communicates sex-positive sexuality education in a variety of contexts and on a variety of topics. Scarleteen is a free, public website, and I did not need to sign-in or register to view and/or access any of the data. On July 20, 2011, I downloaded the articles and posts from the message boards section of the site for a total of 40 articles and 15 message posts. I used a thematic analysis to investigate the strategies used to communicate sex-positive sexuality education on Scarleteen.

RESULTS

Successful health communication education initiatives must use effective communication strategies. A strategy is "the overall approach a program takes" to disseminate its message (National Cancer Institute, n.d., p. 251). Communicative strategies are thus the "guiding principles" within a health program (p. 41). Strategies are often based on an organization's knowledge of their audience's wants and needs. Based on my research of Scarleteen, I found that successful sex-positive sexuality education/communication occurs when interactants use a person-centered approach that includes self-disclosure and humor while disseminating information that is clear. In the following section, I offer examples of each of these sex-positive communication strategies.

Person-Centered Approach

First, a person-centered approach was demonstrated on Scarleteen. Person-centered messages are valuable during interactions because they acknowledge and legitimize feelings and are commonly listener centered, emotion focused, and nonevaluative (MacGeorge, Feng, Wilkum, & Doherty, 2012). Site founder and writer, Heather Corinna, volunteers, and even fellow members on the Scarleteen message boards work hard to legitimize and value each other. In a response to a Scarleteen user who was dealing with his mother's homophobic jokes toward him, Corinna writes on the message board, "I'm really sorry your mom has been making these sorts of comments. In particular, mean jokes about your sex life just aren't okay—that's sexual shaming, which is a type of abuse, most definitely…To boot, yelling isn't nice to hear at any time, and I'm sorry she's making you hear a lot of it" ("My Mom," 2011, p. 1). In other posts, Corinna gives person-centered messages such as, "In the meantime, big hugs your way, gal," "I'm so sorry that you're feeling that way, Dee. You're right, it is incredibly hurtful and painful," and "I had no idea you did finally wind up asking your Mom for help (yay!) and that DID make a big difference (double-yay!)." "That's fantastic" is another response offered to users' struggles with homophobic family members ("Homophobic Family & Friends," 2011, pp. 1–20).

In addition, within my sample from the site, every message that a user posted seeking help and assistance was answered in a timely fashion. At times, multiple Scarleteen volunteers would reply to the same question. In addition, the Scarleteen volunteers extensively check back with the users. For example, on July 13, 2011, at 6:26 a.m., a user posted a question to the message boards seeking advice on gender identity and dating relationships. By 7:26 a.m., Corinna wrote back with some advice and also asked more probing questions. Throughout the morning, Corinna and the user exchanged 11more posts culminating in Corinna's concluding post in the thread at 12:40 p.m. ("Gender and Relationships," 2011). This example demonstrates the high level of person-centered communication Scarleteen provides on the message boards. By posting messages back and forth until there is some sort of resolution on the topic, Scarleteen engages in an extremely high level of personalized communication with users that is completely free of charge and available at all times.

Self-Disclosure

Next, the communicative strategy of self-disclosure was used often on Scarleteen. I observed many different examples of self-disclosure on Scarleteen. From a communication perspective, self-disclosure is defined as revealing private information about yourself to others (Wheeless, 1978). Self-disclosure can be especially useful in educational contexts as it helps facilitate learning (Downs, Javidi, & Nussbaum, 1988). A recent study by Mazer, Murphy, and Simonds (2007) investigated teachers who posted high levels of disclosure visible to their students on the social media site Facebook. They found that students were receptive to this disclosure, and students felt self-disclosure positively impacted their anticipated motivation, affective learning, and classroom climate. These research studies highlight the importance of self-disclosure in an educational setting and through the use of computer-mediated communication in particular.

Messages of self-disclosure are prominent throughout Scarleteen. Self-disclosure serves two functions on the site. It lends insight to inexperienced users on common topics and offers a new perspective on taboo or marginalized issues with which users might be unfamiliar. First, the authors of the articles at times use very personal information to inform users about topics to which they may not yet have been exposed. For example, in an article on condom use, Corinna is able to challenge men's common excuse for not wanting to use a condom during sex—they say it changes the sensation—by using her own personal experience. Corinna (2010a) explains:

> *as someone who has had a barrier over a much more sensitive part than a penis (the clitoris) and has also used hormonal medication can tell you…a latex barrier, when used properly doesn't change sensations more than most methods do for women. (p. 6)*

Furthermore, Corinna also offers personal examples to add support to her argument that there is an average genital size. She tells users, "I wear a smaller-average [*sic*] diaphragm size (I'm a 65 these days), and given the clitorises I have seen up close and personal and via photos, I'd say my clit is right in the middle" (Corinna, 2010b, p. 4). Similarly, in response to message board questions from a user including "Why do most lesbians have short hair and have numerous piercings and seem to be really…kind of creepy?," Corinna responds by explaining "That's a hard question to answer, because to be honest, I've never found lesbians as a whole group to be any more or less creepy than anyone else." She continues using personal references by explaining she has a "couple piercings in my own face, and I'd have short hair myself if I didn't look like such a dope with it and/or could be sure I could afford regular haircuts to keep it looking decent. ϑ" ("Homophobic Family & Friends," 2011, p. 5).

At times, too, self-disclosure fulfills another function for Scarleteen. It serves to explain topics with which users may not yet have come into contact. By including first-person accounts of topics such as asexuality, homosexuality, abortion, diseases, or disability, Scarleteen authors serve to de-stigmatize certain topics. To explain issues of gender, performance, and expressions of masculinity, Heather Corinna shared a story from her youth in the message boards ("Gender and Relationships," 2011):

> *When I was growing up, my Dad carried a bag that people always interpreted as a purse. Like him, I never quite got what makes a bag a bag and a purse a purse: isn't a purse a bag? But despite that, and people giving him crap about this purse/bag he LOVED (it was a thing of serious art, I remember) around masculinity, my father never took the bait, in large part because unlike some people who thought differently, he didn't see how what kind of bag her carried had anything to do with his masculinity. (p. 5)*

Overall, then, one of the ways that Scarleteen provides credible information to its users is by sharing instances of self-disclosure. Since this site is targeted toward adolescents, personal examples allow the older or more experienced authors of the site to share experiences they have already had with inexperienced young users. As prior research (Downs, et al., 1988; Mazer et al., 2007) suggests, the self-disclosure from educators on Scarleteen appears to help the authors convey information and potentially increase user motivation, learning, and creation of a positive climate to discuss sexuality.

Humor

A third communicative strategy Scarleteen implemented was humor. Humor positively functions to help people relate to each other, relieve uncertainty, and create a more open and relaxed environment (Meyer, 2012). Correspondingly, effective communication is also practiced on Scarleteen through the use of humor. Humor was used in articles and in interactions with users. In an article about women's genital sizes, Corinna employs a humorous metaphor of a "Vagzilla" to describe why women should be happy and proud to have a large vagina instead of ashamed or worried if their vagina does not fit a cultural standard of being "tight." Corinna makes use of humorous figurative and descriptive language throughout the entire article; however, one of the best examples of her humorous creative writing is her explanation of Vagizilla:

> *I am wholeheartedly enjoying this image of Vagzilla, much like a very large sea creature of some kind, pulling its pink, fleshy feet (which totally make a noise, it's like "scholp, schlop") across the earth. It waves its VERY HUMONGOUS labia around like big, flappy, sea-anemone hands, and it makes a huge whooshing sound, like wind through trees in a storm when it does. (Corinna, 2010b, p. 4)*

The Vagzilla is a humorous metaphor used in this article to encourage women to understand large genitals as a positive experience rather than as something about which to be ashamed.

In addition to having complete articles peppered with humor, light-hearted jokes or references were also used in articles and message board postings. For example, in an article on vaginismus, or painful penetration, Corinna (2011) organized the article to read like an FBI case file. The title of the article is, "The FBI File: Vaginismus," and throughout the article, headings such as "Wanted For," "Known Accomplices," and "Weapons" are used to explain this difficult and painful condition (p. 1). The use of humor in regards to a serious topic can help relieve tension about a serious topic and help readers feel at ease. Since humor is helpful in developing a trusting relationship, releasing tension, and facilitating open mindedness it is unsurprising that Scarleteen utilized humor as a sexual communication strategy (Dziegielewski, Jacinto, Laudadio, & Legg-Rodriguez, 2003).

Clarity

The last strategy for communicating sex-positive sexuality education was clarity. Scarleteen offered outstanding examples of clarity. Clarity has been studied in the communication discipline in regards to teacher clarity. Teacher clarity can be defined as an instructor's ability to engender a specific meaning of course content to his/her students through the use of verbal and nonverbal messages. Research has shown that clarity is important in the instructional process and that students are less apprehensive towards teachers who are clear and use immediate behaviors (such as being person centered). Issues of teacher clarity are appropriate for Scarleteen since it essentially serves a teaching or instructional function for teens (Chesebro & McCroskey, 2001).

Scarleteen's use of clarity is most noticeably depicted within the length of articles on the site. Within my data sample, it was common for articles to be 2,000 words or more. Even though the article topics varied greatly, the length of the articles was consistently extensive. The detail of the articles serves a strategic purpose: Because the authors of the articles do not have to limit their word count, they are able to write clear, nuanced articles that cover many of the components within the cores values of Scarleteen's construction of sex-positive sexuality education. They provide enough detail to probably address any issue a teen might be wondering about and thus serve to lessen users' apprehension towards issues because they are well defined and explained.

Scarleteen also employs clear communicative strategies by explaining unfamiliar terms to users of the website. As in one example, within the message-board topic, "Gender and Relationships," Corinna uses the word *genderqueer*; however, she does not assume that users understand this term. She writes, "To make sure I'm clear, someone who was assigned male sex, but who identifies as a woman or as a genderqueer and wears clothing they feel is reflective of them which someone identifies as 'women's clothing,' isn't 'dressing up as a woman.' They're dressing as themselves. Do you understand what I'm saying?" ("Gender and Relationships," 2011, p. 4).

Another resource that Scarleteen offers its users to aid clarity is pictures or diagrams. Clarity helps reduce apprehension, so the use of pictures and diagrams to help explain issues visually may help users conceptualize information differently or more effectively and thus lessen their concerns about it (Chesebro & McCroskey, 2001). One particularly interesting and useful graphic that was made to lessen apprehension was a chart Corinna designed to give a visual representation of the size of different parts of the female anatomy like the labia minor, clitoris, and vagina. Unfortunately, there is a cultural myth that a woman is more desirable if she has small genitals, so women can be apprehensive about having larger labia or vaginas. Corinna recognizes this concern, and her chart helps to lessen this apprehension. This chart is a resource for users because it provides a way to understand complex information in a user-friendly manner. Instead of just listing the numerical sizes, Corinna used a bar graph, different colors, and even a comparison of size to her pug dog to explain how the size of female anatomy varies (Corinna, 2010b).

Through the use of detailed articles, explanations of terms, and diagrams and graphs, Scarleteen clearly expresses its approach to sex-positive sexuality education within the articles and message posts on the site. Similar to Chesebro and McCroskey's (2001) findings in regard to teacher clarity, Scarleteen's use of clear information to educate users also may serve to lessen user apprehension toward the material. By receiving information that is well defined, extensive, and includes visual learning, the user may be more equipped to understand topics about sexuality. And when a topic makes sense, it may appear to be less scary, confusing, or troubling, and thus the receiver will feel more confident about it and less apprehensive.

DISCUSSION

In this chapter, I outlined the benefits to implementing a sex-positive approach to teaching sexuality education and offered concrete examples of how to communicate this approach based on my research on Scarleteen.com. For health communication scholars and practitioners, there is great significance in understanding and implementing this emerging approach to sex education. Health communication scholars and practitioners must always stay abreast of new trends within sexual health. A sex-positive approach to education is predicated upon factors that health communication experts appreciate the importance of such as, inclusivity and the importance of communication.

The results from this study indicate that sex-positive sexuality education is often communicated by being person centered, using self-disclosure and humor, and being clear. These specific communication strategies can help health communication scholars and practitioners alike. Most apparently, these communication strategies can be implemented by those teaching formal sex education programs; however, health communication experts can also start to disseminate these strategies in various formal and informal sexual communication contexts as well such as, patient-provider, family, and religious contexts.

In patient and provider interactions, providers need to stop ignoring sexual communication with their patients. As Sobecki, Curlin, Rasinski, and Lindau's (2012) research showed, only 40% of OB-GYNs asked their patients about sexual problems and only 28% routinely confirmed patient sexual orientation. Providers need to start having conversations about sex with their patients and use these communicative strategies. Second, within family communication, parents should remember to not just talk to their children about sex in clear terms but also remember to use person-centered techniques and appropriate humor during their interactions. Children who are struggling with discussing sex with their parents should remember the importance of clarity despite being hesitant to communicate. Finally, practitioners within diverse areas of communication such as religious communication should also promote these successful sexual communication strategies. For example, many young people and adults turn to members of their church to guide them through turbulent times; therefore, church officials should discuss sex and sexuality with clarity and comfort in order to benefit their parishioners.

The mission of sex-positive sexuality education is lofty. For centuries, shame, guilt, silence, and fear have been intertwined with sex and sexuality education. In order to help construct a healthier sexual culture within the United States where people feel comfortable talking about issues regarding sex and sexuality and value sex for the positive benefits it can bring to life, sexuality education needs to be overhauled. This study is an important first step in explaining a new approach and offering communicative strategies for how to re-envision and ultimately potentially revolutionize sexuality education into an agentic and positive experience.

REFERENCES

Aggleton, P., & Campbell, C. (2000). Working with young people—Towards an agenda for sexual health. *Sexual and Relationship Therapy*, *15*(3), 283–296.

Alexa. (2011). Site information for Scarleteen.com. Retrieved March 27, 2011, from http://www.alexa.com/search?q=scarleteen.com&r=home_home&p=bigtop

Banim, M., Guy, A., & Tasker, P. (1999). Trapped in risky behaviour: Empowerment, disabled people and sexual health. *Health, Risk & Society*, *1*(2), 209–221.

Bay-Cheng, L. Y., & Lewis, A. E. (2006). Our "ideal girl": Prescriptions of female adolescent sexuality in a feminist mentorship program. *Affilia*, *21*(1), 71–82.

Bochner, A. P. (2009). Vulnerable medicine. *Journal of Applied Communication Research*, *37*(2), 159–166.

Braun-Harvey, D., & de Miranda, J. (2009). Sexual health: A new ally in addiction treatment improvement. *Alcoholism & Drug Abuse Weekly*, 5–6.

Centers for Disease Control and Prevention. (2010). Sexually transmitted disease surveillance 2009. Retrieved from http://www.cdc.gov/std/stats/

Chesebro, J. L., & McCroskey, J. C. (2001). The relationship of teacher clarity and immediacy with student state receiver apprehension, affect, and cognitive learning. *Communication Education*, *50*(1), 59–68.

Corinna , H. (2009). What is feminist sex education? Retrieved from www.scarleteen.com/article/politics/what_is_feminist_sex_education

Corinna, H. (2010a). Love the glove: 10 reasons to use condoms you might not have heard yet. Retrieved from http://www.scarleteen.com/article/body/love_the_glove_10_reasons_to_use_condoms_you_might_not_have_heard_yet

Corinna, H. (2010b). Vagzilla! (or, all genitals great and small). Retrieved from http://www.scarleteen.com/article/body/vagzilla_or_all_genitals_great_and_small

Corinna, H. (2011). The FBI files: Vaginismus. Retrieved from http://www.scarleteen.com/article/body/the_fbi_files_vaginismus

Declaration. (1999). Sexual rights: An IPPF declaration. International Planned Parenthood Federation. Retrieved March 25, 2011, from http://www.ippf.org/NR/rdonlyres/9E4D697C-1C7D-4EF6-AA2A-6D4D0A13A108/0/SexualRightsIPPFdeclaration.pdf

Downs, V. C., Javidi, M., & Nussbaum, J. F. (1988). An analysis of teachers' verbal communication within the college classroom: Use of humor, self-disclosure, and narratives. *Communication Education*, *37*, 127–141.

Du Pre, A. (2000). *Communicating about health: Current issues and perspectives.* Mountain View, CA: Mayfield.

Dziegielewski, S. F., Jacinto, G. A., Laudadio, A., & Legg-Rodriguez, L. (2003). Humor: An essential communication tool in therapy. *International Journal of Mental Health, 32*(3), 74–90.

Epstein, D., O'Flynn, S., & Telford, D. (2003). *Silenced sexualities in schools and universities.* Stoke on Trent, UK: Trentham Books.

Fields, J. (2008). *Risky lessons: Sex education and social inequality.* New Brunswick, NJ: Rutgers University Press.

Fine, M. (2005). X. Desire: The morning (and 15 years) after. *Feminism & Psychology, 15,* 54–60.

Fine, M., & McClelland, S. L. (2006). Sexuality education and desire: Still missing after all these years. *Harvard Educational Review, 76*(3), 297–338.

Friedman, J., & Valenti, J. (Eds.). (2008). *Yes mean yes! Visions of female sexual power and a world without rape.* Berkeley, CA: Seal Press.

Gender and relationships. (2011). [Message board post]. Retrieved from http://www.scarleteen.com/cgi-bin/forum/ultimatebb.cgi?/category/5.html

Greslé-Favier, C. (2010). The legacy of abstinence-only discourse and the place of pleasure in U.S. discourse on teenage sexuality. *Sex Education, 10*(4), 413–422.

Guttmacher Institute. (2009). In brief: Fact sheet. Facts on sexually transmitted infections in the United States. Retrieved March 19, 2011 from http://www.guttmacher.org/pubs/FIB_STI_US.html

Guttmacher Institute. (2011). In brief: Fact sheet. Facts on induced abortion in the United States. Retrieved March 19, 2011 from http://www.guttmacher.org/pubs/fb_induced_abortion.html

Hayden, S. (2001). Teenage bodies, teenage selves: Tracing the implications of bio-power in contemporary sexuality education texts. *Women's Studies in Communication, 24*(1), 30–61.

Helmich, J. (2009). What is comprehensive sexuality education? Going waaaaay beyond abstinence and condoms. *American Journal of Sexuality Education, 4,* 10–15.

Help lift sex ed to a higher plane: Support Scarleteen! (2011). Retrieved from http://www.scarleteen.com/help_lift_sex_ed_to_a_higher_plane_support_scarleteen

Hemingway, J. (2006). Reframing sex education. *Sex Education, 6*(4), 313–315.

Hilton, G. L. S. (2007). Listening to the boys again: An exploration of what boys want to learn in sex education classes and how they want to be taught. *Sex Education, 7*(2), 161–174.

Homophobic family & friends. (2011). [Message board post]. Retrieved from http://www.scarleteen.com/forum/ultimatebb.php?/ubb/get_topic/f/9/t/001198.html#000001

Kaye, K., Suellentrop, K., & Sloup, C. (2009). The fog zone: How misperceptions, magical thinking, and ambivalence put young adults at risk for unplanned pregnancy. Washington, DC: The National Campaign to Prevent Teen and Unplanned Pregnancy.

Kirby, D. (2007). Emerging answers 2007: Research findings on programs to reduce teen pregnancy and sexually transmitted diseases.Washington, DC: National Campaign to Prevent Teen and Unplanned Pregnancy.

Kirby, D., & Laris, B. A. (2009). Effective curriculum-based sex and STD/HIV education programs for adolescents. *Child Development Perspectives*, *31*(1), 21–29.

Kneer, W., & Philpott, A. (2006). Putting the sexy back into safer sex: The pleasure project. *IDS Bulletin*, *37*(5), 105–109.

Kohler, P. K., Manhart, L. E., & Lafferty, W. E. (2008). Abstinence-only and comprehensive sex education and the initiation of sexual activity and teen pregnancy. *Journal of Adolescent Health*, *42*(4), 344–351.

Kreps, G. L., & Thornton, B. C. (1992). *Health communication: Theory & practice.* Prospect Heights, IL: Waveland Press.

Kulwicki , C. (2008). Real sex education. In J. Friedman & J. Valenti (Eds.), *Yes means yes! Visions of female sexual power and a world without rape* (pp. 305–312). Berkeley, CA: Seal Press.

MacGeorge, E., Feng, B., Wilkum, K., & Doherty, E. (2012). In T. J. Socha & M. J. Pitts (Eds.), *The positive side of interpersonal communication* (pp. 161–177). New York, NY: Peter Lang.

Maltz, W. (2011). Promoting healthy sexuality. Retrieved from http://www.healthysex.com/

Mazer, J. P., Murphy, R. E., & Simonds, C. J. (2007). I'll see you on "Facebook:" The effects of computer-mediated teacher self-disclosure on student motivation, affective learning, and classroom climate. *Communication Education*, *56*(1), 1–17.

Meyer, J. C. (2012). Humor as a personal relationship enhancer: Positivity for the long term. In T. J. Socha, & M. J. Pitts (Eds.), *The positive side of interpersonal communication* (pp. 161–177). New York, NY: Peter Lang.

Moore, L. J., & Clarke, A. E. (1995). Clitoral conventions and transgressions: Graphic representations in anatomy texts, c1900–1991. *Feminist Studies*, *21*(2), 255–301.

My mom. (2011). [Message board post]. Retrieved from http://www.scarleteen.com/cgi-bin/forum/ultimatebb.cgi?/category/5.html

The National Campaign to Prevent Teen and Unplanned Pregnancy. (2008). Fast facts: The consequences of unplanned pregnancy. Retrieved from http://www.thenationalcampaign.org/resources/pdf/fast-facts-consequences-of-unplanned-pregnancy.pdf

The National Campaign to Prevent Teen and Unplanned Pregnancy. (2009). Fast facts: Men in the United States: Unplanned pregnancy, sexual activity, and contraceptive use (data as of 2002). Retrieved from http://www.thenationalcampaign.org/resources/pdf/fast-facts-consequences-of-unplanned-pregnancy.pdf

The National Campaign to Prevent Teen and Unplanned Pregnancy. (2010). Why it matters: Linking teen pregnancy prevention to other critical social issues. Retrieved from http://www.thenationalcampaign.org/why-it-matters/pdf/WIM_Full%20Set.pdf

National Cancer Institute. (n.d.). Making health communication programs work. U.S. Department of Health and Human Services.

New York Civil Liberties Union. (2012). Birds, bees, and bias: How absent sex ed standards fail New York's students. Retrieved from http://www.nyclu.org/files/publications/NYCLU_SexEd_report.pdf

Patton, C. (1996). *Fatal advice: How safe-sex education went wrong.* Durham, NC: Duke University Press.

Perry, B. (2008). Hooking up with healthy sexuality: The lessons boys learn (and don't learn) about sexuality, and why a sex-positive rape prevention paradigm can benefit everyone involved. In J. Friedman & J. Valenti (Eds.), *Yes means yes! Visions of female sexual power and a world without rape* (pp.193–208). Berkeley, CA: Seal Press.

Queen, C. (1997). *Real live nude girls: Chronicles of a sex-positive culture.* Pittsburgh, PA: Cleis Press.

Queen, C., & Comella, L. L. (2008). The necessary revolution: Sex-positive feminism in the post-Barnard era. *The Communication Review, 11*(3), 274–291.

Sandlos, K. (2010). On the aesthetic difficulties of research on sex education: Toward a methodology of affect. *Sex Education, 10*(3), 299–308.

Scarleteen.com. (2011, 2012). Retrieved from www.scarleteen.com

Sharples, T. (2008, July 2). More midlife (and older) STDs. *Time.* Retrieved from http://www.time.com/time/health/article/0,8599,1819633,00.html

Sobecki, J. N., Curlin, F. A., Rasinski, K. A., & Lindau, S. T. (2012). What we don't talk about when we don't talk about sex: Results of a national survey of U.S. obstetrician/gynecologists. *Journal of Sexual Medicine, 9,* 1285–1294.

Tambling, R. B., Neustifter, R., Muska, C., Reckert, A., Rua, S. (2012). Pleasure-Centered Education Program: A comprehensive approach to pleasure-oriented sexuality education in domestic violence shelters. *International Journal of Sexual Health, 24,* 267–289.

Welles, C. E. (2005). Breaking the silence surrounding female adolescent sexual desire. *Women & Therapy, 28*(2), 31–45.

Wheeless, C. R. (1978). A follow-up study on the relationships among trust, disclosure, and interpersonal solidarity. *Human Communication Research, 4*, 143–157.

Index

A

B

C

D

E

F

G

H

I

J

K

L

M

N

O

P

Q

R

S

T

U

V

W

Y

www.ingramcontent.com/pod-product-compliance
Lightning Source LLC
LaVergne TN
LVHW080015210926
848481LV00011B/3028